CITY BOYS

City Boys

Cagney, Bogart, Garfield

ROBERT SKLAR

PRINCETON UNIVERSITY PRESS

Copyright © 1992 by Princeton University Press
Published by Princeton University Press,
41 William Street, Princeton, New Jersey 08540
In the United Kingdom: Princeton University Press, Oxford

Library of Congress Cataloging-in-Publication Data

Sklar, Robert.
City boys : Cagney, Bogart, Garfield / Robert Sklar.
   p. cm.
Includes bibliographical references and index.
ISBN 0-691-04795-2
1. Men in motion pictures. 2. City and town life in motion
pictures. 3. Cagney, James, 1899–1986—Criticism and
interpretation. 4. Bogart, Humphrey, 1899–1957—Criticism
and interpretation. 5. Garfield, John—Criticism and
interpretation. I. Title.
PN1995.9.M46S56 1992
791.43'028'092273—dc20   91-31723

This book has been composed in Linotron Trump Medieval

Princeton University Press books are printed on
acid-free paper, and meet the guidelines for permanence
and durability of the Committee on Production Guidelines
for Book Longevity of the Council
on Library Resources

Printed in the United States of America

10 9 8 7 6 5 4 3 2 1

For Adrienne

Contents

Contents

Illustrations

1. Boys playing cat stick, 1898. Photograph by Byron, the Byron Collection, Museum of the City of New York.
2. Children's party, ca. 1900. Photograph by Byron, the Byron Collection, Museum of the City of New York.
3. *The Doorway to Hell* (1930). International Museum of Photography, George Eastman House.
4. *The Public Enemy* (1931). International Museum of Photography, George Eastman House.
5. *Taxi!* (1932). International Museum of Photography, George Eastman House.
6. *Hard to Handle* (1933). International Museum of Photography, George Eastman House.
7. *Footlight Parade* (1933). The Museum of Modern Art/Film Stills Archive.
8. *A Midsummer Night's Dream* (1935). International Museum of Photography, George Eastman House.
9. *The Petrified Forest* (1936). International Museum of Photography, George Eastman House.
10. *Black Legion* (1937). International Museum of Photography, George Eastman House.
11. *The Return of Dr. X* (1939). International Museum of Photography, George Eastman House.
12. *The Roaring Twenties* (1939). The Museum of Modern Art/Film Stills Archive.
13. *Four Daughters* (1938). The Museum of Modern Art/Film Stills Archive.
14. *They Made Me a Criminal* (1939). International Museum of Photography, George Eastman House.
15. John Garfield publicity photograph, 1941. The Museum of Modern Art/Film Stills Archive.
16. John Garfield publicity portrait. The Museum of Modern Art/Film Stills Archive.
17. *Angels with Dirty Faces* (1938). International Museum of Photography, George Eastman House.
18. *The Strawberry Blonde* (1941). International Museum of Photography, George Eastman House.
19. The Cagney family. International Museum of Photography, George Eastman House.

Preface

Our most popular and most scholarly instincts conspire, no doubt unwittingly, to overlook film performance.

In the popular realm, stardom and celebrity enact their own myths, of which luck and effortlessness seem to play a necessary part. Because motion picture stars have achieved levels of wealth and fame inaccessible to most of us, the construction of their popular images places them in a separate world, beyond the bounds of our own mundane concerns to do a job, manage a career, strive for satisfaction and accomplishment in work. As part of the complex trade-offs in their promotion and consumption, the vast popular discourse on film performers emphasizes their lives, their loves, their toys, and their tragedies—everything about them except how they go about their professional work as performers.

Cinema scholarship has tended to suppress film performance for other reasons, but no less thoroughly. Besides the obvious impediment—everyone who goes to the movies has no difficulty forming opinions about acting, without scholarly assistance—there are also more serious theoretical issues. Film studies has grown into a major academic discipline through emphasis on narration and the spectator, the making and consuming of narrative texts. Questions of performance point strongly in other scholarly directions: toward intertextuality (no one performance is fully understandable without reference to a performer's other films and roles) and toward stardom as a metatext (with spectators following star performances and careers as much as, or more than, individual film narratives).

Works such as James Naremore's *Acting in the Cinema* and Richard Dyer's *Heavenly Bodies: Film Stars and Society* have slowly begun to establish a place for performance in cinema scholarship. A concern with performance widens the scope of film studies: toward biography, the developing of craft and the managing of careers; toward the production process, and the roles of such others as producers, writers, directors, and cinematographers in the shaping of performances; and toward the formation of discourses on performance through publicity, criticism, and reception. Inevitably, a focus on performance leads to broader social and cultural considerations—

toward the performance of self (paraphrasing Erving Goffman) and the construction of identities not only on film but in everyday life.

This book is a study of film performance in its cultural, social, and political dimensions, through combined professional biographies of James Cagney, Humphrey Bogart, and John Garfield. These three performers—two whose legends have grown over time, one who has been unfortunately neglected—are brought together in the framework of the twentieth-century American mass media phenomenon of the City Boy. This figure was not merely a gangster or a tough guy, but was rooted in the language and mannerisms of urban male street life. He was a fictional construction—drawn from, but not necessarily similar to, young urban men in American society.

The City Boy was a product of performance, genre, and ideology, transmuted into popular entertainment. He did not so much mirror social life, if contemporary observers are to be believed, as create a model for life itself to imitate. Arising from the teeming ethnic polyglot of the modern industrial city—especially New York—he began playing a central cultural role with the more or less simultaneous occurrence, in the late 1920s, of talking pictures and the Great Depression. His rise to prominence alongside the cowboy as a major figure in the representation of American manhood seemed to suggest important changes in concepts of male behavior—of individualism in relation to social constraint, of sexuality, romance, and family life. One could find aspects of this new type in a number of movie performers of the 1930s and 1940s, Hollywood's classic era, but the ones I have chosen to focus on, both because of their diversity and because of their similarity (and, to be sure, personal preference), are Cagney, Bogart, and Garfield.

The book examines their careers through four interrelated and fundamentally inseparable themes: First, the structures and determinants of the Hollywood film industry, the practices and conditions of moviemaking as they affect performers' careers. Second, the capacity of actors through style and presence to construct screen characters, and their struggles during the production process for the power to control performance. Third, the screen image or persona that arises around a performer through cumulative roles, and related publicity and critical discourses. Fourth, though not least important, is the performer as a public figure. In the professional lives of Cagney, Bogart, and Garfield, American society and politics moved from the era of Coolidge to the age of Eisenhower—through the Great Depression, World War II, and the bitter McCarthy years. The Hollywood film industry went from the advent of talking pictures, through its Golden Age in the 1930s and 1940s, to a crisis engendered by the anti-Communist blacklist, the breakup of monopoly structures, and competition from television. During these years all three men became involved (not to say enmeshed) in national political causes; these involvements, in turn, reshaped in basic ways their screen personas, their performances, and the circumstances of their filmmaking careers.

One could debate whether, nearing the end of the twentieth century, the City Boy survives as a performance type in American mass media. The answer, of course, is yes, just as the cowboy survives. It is likely that both are indispensable to American cultural self-definition. Yet both figures are intimately tied to history, and it is only through examining their specific historical status in institutions, representations, and the lives of performers that we can understand their changing significance. This book is intended as a contribution to such a project.

I

City Boys Go National

1

A Society of Ragamuffins

The opening scene of the 1981 movie *Ragtime*: It is early in the twentieth century, sometime before World War I. A black musician plays a piano in a nickelodeon motion picture theater. On the theater's screen, newsreel images flicker. An intertitle appears: "New York City Reports Hottest Summer in 30 Years." This is followed by images of children jumping up and down under the cooling spray of an overhead sprinkler on a city street.

Ragtime marked the return to the motion picture screen—after an absence of two decades—of performer James Cagney, who was born in New York City on the eve of the twentieth century and bred in those city streets. It was his sixty-third and final appearance in a theatrical film. Watching the eighty-two-year-old Cagney's performance as New York City police commissioner, one can also imagine that among those children captured on an early strip of celluloid, playing in the street as New York simmered, might have been a red-haired Irish lad, Ma Cagney's boy Jimmy. From the newsreel footage through the contemporary performance stretch fourscore years of historical transformation within a single lifetime. The film paid homage not only to the actor but also to the cultural type he, among others, had made a central figure of American mass culture and mythology. *Ragtime* marked the last hurrah of the city boy.

As Milos Forman's film begins with a glimpse of kids at play on city streets, so E. L. Doctorow's novel on which the film was based closes with a related image—though considerably more suburban, more organized, and certainly more commodified. Tateh, the Jewish socialist turned movie director, watches kids at play on a California lawn and, Doctorow writes, "suddenly had an idea for a film. A bunch of children who were pals, white black, fat thin, rich poor, all kinds, mischievous little urchins who would have funny adventures in their own neighborhood, a society of ragamuffins, like all of us, a gang getting into trouble and getting out again. Actually not one

movie but several were made of this vision."[1] Perhaps also a substantial part of the motion picture industry was built upon it, not to
mention a fair portion of twentieth-century American ideology and
consciousness.

It was a vision that looked back to an imagined past as much as
or more than to a possible future. One can choose which relation,
"white black" or "rich poor," is the more fantasized. City life in the
period of Cagney's childhood, of Doctorow's novel and Forman's
film, can be characterized more by its "vivid and moving social contrasts" (in the words of novelist Theodore Dreiser) than by Tateh's
idealized vision of social unity.[2] British photographer Joseph Byron
recorded these contrasts in turn-of-the-century New York, often in
the lives of children. One such picture (Figure 1) shows half a dozen
boys of the lower orders playing "cat stick" (an early version of stick-
ball) on a dirt surface alongside a high wooden wall. They all wear
caps, shirts, and knickers. Two have on shoes and socks, the others
are barefoot. One boy, cap askew, looks at the camera with something white protruding from his mouth—impossible to tell whether
tongue, gum, or cigarette. On the wall, well above the boys' eye
level, is a chalked line score by innings.

Another photograph (Figure 2) shows a children's party from the
same era. Some eighteen children are sitting around a large dining
room table, with three adults standing at the far end. An enormous
sideboard nearly covers one wall, with crystal glassware on every
visible surface; another cabinet appears to hold chinoiserie and other
objets d'art. The girls are wearing frilly white dresses, the boys are in
dark suits with ties or waistcoats. The table is laden with cakes, a
sign that the party is about to commence.

These photographs demarcate two worlds, two of many worlds in
the same city, that coexist but do not touch. Yet as Dreiser collected
his prose sketches of pre–World War I New York not far into the
1920s, he was already somewhat sentimentally lamenting a loss of
the city's zest and tang from a diminution of those contrasts. He
placed the blame for the change on organized spectacles and mass
diversions, like football games and automobile exhibitions. Motion
pictures might have been mentioned in this connection, too. Like
Doctorow's Tateh, filmmakers could concoct visions of social felic-
ity that bridged the barriers of class and ethnicity that the photographer and the novelist had observed.

Where else but on the silver screen could rich and poor share
funny adventures—forging a bond, as Doctorow put it, as an imagi-
nary society of ragamuffins, as we might all wish ourselves to be?
Where else but in the movies would an Irish Catholic kid, James

Cagney, born in 1899 on the Lower East Side to the wife of a bar-keeper, and a Protestant Anglo-Saxon kid, Humphrey Bogart, born at the end of that same year on the Upper West Side to a doctor's wife (the mother was also a noted illustrator), be found together wearing cowboy outfits—with the barkeeper's son wearing the white hat and the doctor's son the black? This happened at a ranch belonging to the Warner Bros. motion picture company, in the making of a 1939 west-ern called *The Oklahoma Kid*. To be sure, they had appeared to-gether before, in a 1938 crime movie, *Angels with Dirty Faces*, ad-hering somewhat more predictably to their offscreen social origins: the barkeeper's son played a sympathetic but doomed criminal, and the doctor's son, a crooked lawyer for the mob.

It is difficult to imagine young James Francis Cagney, Jr., of East 79th and East 96th Streets in any other but a happenstance encoun-ter with young Humphrey DeForest Bogart of West 104th Street, whose childhood environments resembled, respectively, those of the "cat stick" players and the young partygoers. Yet social change was bringing them closer. Dreiser noted among the transformations in New York's East Side during the early twentieth century a vast in-crease in what he called civic betterment and social service ven-tures, particularly in education. The East Side Cagneys were benefi-ciaries: James Cagney graduated from Stuyvesant High School, and World War I gave him a chance to attend Columbia University for a year as part of the Student Army Training Corps. That was one more year of higher education than the privileged Bogart attained; his schooling ended when he left Phillips Academy in Andover, Massa-chusetts, before completing a year there, to enlist in the navy during the war.

School and war can be great levelers, but the linchpin of the con-fluence of two disparate lives—the reason, of course, why anyone would write and read about them—was popular entertainment. In their early twenties, both Cagney and Bogart began their careers, more or less by chance, as performers in Broadway legitimate thea-ter. There was little in the background of either man to suggest a bent in that direction—though each seemed for some time to play characters with backgrounds closely resembling his own.

It is not easy to know how much to make of this convergence between life and art. The leap from performance in everyday life, as Erving Goffman defined it, to performance within the codes of com-mercial entertainment is infinitely complex—involving elements of skill, discipline, perseverance, and whatever soupçon of creativity that can be nurtured into a distinctive performance persona. When James Cagney received the American Film Institute Life Achievement Award in 1974, he ended his acceptance speech by recalling the names of his childhood companions who, he said, "were all part of a stimulating early environment which produced that unmistakable touch of the gutter without which this evening might never have happened at all."[3]

Humphrey Bogart, on the other hand, had to jettison entirely a performance persona linked to his youthful background and make a radical and wholly unexpected shift in style, appearance, and demeanor—in the role of killer Duke Mantee in Robert E. Sherwood's 1935 play *The Petrified Forest*—in order to rescue his career from near-oblivion. The successful screen persona he slowly forged thereafter owed more to the heritage of the cat stick players than to the bourgeois milieu of the partygoers from which he stemmed. Though he had never experienced "the gutter" in the same way that Cagney had, Bogart nevertheless became no less legendary as another version of the city boy.

By the mid-1920s, when Cagney and Bogart were getting established in their haphazard careers, civic betterment had been extended to the arts: there were social service ventures to find kids with talent and encourage them, train them, and move them forward toward professional lives. One famous program was run by educator Angelo Patri at P.S. 45 in the East Bronx. A difficult teenage Jewish boy named Jacob Julius Garfinkle—later Jules, then John, Garfield—enrolled there in 1926 after a childhood on the Lower East Side and in Brooklyn's Brownsville and the Bronx. Art proved to be a leveler. It brought Garfield, born in 1913, the son of a clothes-presser, a half-generation younger than Cagney and Bogart, into their orbit as successor, competitor, and fellow city boy.

As these young men developed their professional performance skills in live drama during the mid- to late 1920s, the commercial popular culture of the period began to formulate character types into which each of the city boy trio would eventually be fitted—and from which each would periodically rebel. The Jazz Age, it seems, also had its vivid contrasts. During the 1920s there developed (perhaps in reaction against the extreme forms of social conformity demanded during World War I) an emphasis, stronger than ever, on unbridgeable difference between social groups. Its ugly side was legislative restriction on immigration, based on ethnicity or national origin; its positive quality, a new recognition of the vitality of cultural variety.

Still, these signs of what we would now call multiculturalism, both desired and externally enforced, existed side by side with an increased emphasis (as novelist Dreiser noted) on the organized and mass character of 1920s cultural life. While there were many cultures—separated on the basis of race, class, ethnicity, and (though not then so openly) gender and sexual preference—there was but a single emerging mass culture. Its characteristics of absorption, mediation, and transformation of social phenomena had become far more ingrained than in the commercial culture of the pre–World War I era; in the 1930s and later they would become more greatly developed still.

By the mid-1920s the commercial arts had begun to incorporate the increasingly sensational aspects of contemporary social deviance and conflict into their productions. The Philip Dunning–George Abbott stage production *Broadway*, opening in September 1926, was the first prominent work to employ the fresh argot of the underworld and display a yeasty variety of urban types (Cagney, who had experience as a dancer as well as an actor, was understudy to Lee Tracy in the major role of Roy the Hoofer). In movies, Josef von Sternberg's 1927 silent classic *Underworld* decisively shifted the locus from Dunning and Abbott's world of entertainment—backstage at the nightclub, where varied classes and ethnic groups mingled their desires—to the world of the criminal, the gang leader, or, in the derogatory locution that became the preferred term, the gangster.

Interest in gangs (criminal and noncriminal), their leaders and members, was not entirely a phenomenon of commercial exploitation. It stemmed more broadly from the era's awareness that cultural conflict produces social consequences, and found expression in academic scholarship and popular writing as well. The famous series on urban sociology sponsored by the University of Chicago dealt frequently with gangs, though focusing on adolescent rather than criminal groups. In *The Gold Coast and the Slum* (1929), sociologist Harvey Warren Zorbaugh saw gangs as a response to cultural conflicts arising when American-born children of immigrants are "precipitated into American cultural life": "The boys' gang is an adjustment that results from the failure of the family and community to meet the boy's problems," Zorbaugh wrote. "For gangland is but the result of the boy's creation of a social world in which he can live and find satisfaction for his wishes."[4]

In his popular history *The Gangs of New York* (1928), journalist Herbert Asbury took a different tack. He defined gangs as large organized bodies of a thousand men or more. Often controlled by crooked politicians, they were a feature of New York slum life for more than a century. But as he saw it, reform was making them obsolescent: "There are now no gangs in New York, and no gangsters in the sense that the word has come into common use."[5] What continued to exist he regarded as small-time mobs of perhaps half a dozen criminals.

Even as these books were being published, however, the impact of Prohibition—more specifically, the widespread public demand for illegal alcoholic beverages and the willingness of criminal gangs to supply them—overran their scholarly and journalistic viewpoints. The Chicago beer wars and the exploits of "Scarface" Al Capone captured the nation's attention at all levels. Eventually they would find their memorable cultural representation in the early Depression gangster films.

In the commercial popular arts, of course, there are few new subjects beyond the footlights, under the klieg lights; few innovations that do not have a precedent. Distinctive urban street types in the movies, for example, go back at least as far as Elmer Booth's vivid performance as the Snapper Kid in D. W. Griffith's two-reel 1912 film *The Musketeers of Pig Alley* (which also filmed its performers among actual New York Lower East Side street life in several brief scenes). But in decisive moments of emergence or transformation, a handful of predecessors or even incipient generic patterns are less significant than the actual conjunction of events and their modes of representation in the popular arts.

At the end of the 1920s the Hollywood movie industry made room for a new entry among its well-entrenched, but ever-malleable, genres and conventions. *Underworld*—the film's title in France, *Les Nuits de Chicago*, made unmistakably clear the desire to exploit recent notoriety—and a few other movies had begun to develop the codes of the gangster genre. According to the exceedingly rough but not unhelpful index to film subjects in *The American Film Institute Catalog of Feature Films, 1921–1930*, only a dozen films about gangsters were produced in the first half of the 1920s. An upsurge began in 1928, and in 1930 alone twenty-five gangster movies were released, fully one third of the entire output of the decade.

In 1929 the gangster for the first time surpassed the cowboy as a subject for Hollywood moviemakers. This may be one of the overlooked watersheds of American cultural history. In commercial popular culture, this ranks with—and perhaps completes—the historian Frederick Jackson Turner's declaration at the end of the previous century that the time of the frontier had passed. The concept of frontiers remains perhaps the strongest and most enduring of American national metaphors, but by the end of the 1920s a rapidly urbanizing society had begun to assert its distinctive qualities fully, perhaps predominantly, into imaginative life.

If the cowboy came to represent the quintessence of the frontier—

as opposed, say, to the ranch boss, the farmer, the lawman, or, most surely, the native American—so the gangster came to represent the city even more than such other urban figures as the corporate businessman, the socialite, or the cop and private eye. The gangster, however, never exhausted the motion picture vocations of the city boy type.

There are important differences between the cowboy and the city boy in American mythology and its underlying ideology. Both embody a traditional dilemma for the American male—independence and isolation, on the one hand, attachment and responsibility on the other. The cowboy, however, was and remains fixed in the past, a permanent character, a figure of constancy. However vivid a potential role model, he is a man whom time and change must ultimately defeat.

For the movie audiences of the 1930s, however, the city boy was a contemporary, one recognizable both in daily headlines and in daily life. He was a part of their volatile present and their unknown future. In the city boy, rigidity is contrasted with resilience, and he becomes a focal point of the forces of change in American social life. Unlike the cowboy, he demonstrates the necessity and possibility of a malleable character. This figure may have something to tell us about the fate of rebels in American culture and society, about the value of individual moral codes within larger social constraints, about adaptability and social usefulness, and about survival. These are, as it turns out, issues central to the lives and careers of the city boy performers James Cagney, Humphrey Bogart, and John Garfield.

The city boys of the movies, it should be remembered, were not merely reflections of social actuality. They were, instead, social constructs: the product of genre and convention, of the creative instincts and commercial calculations of producers, writers, and directors, among others, and, in the end, of performers. Perhaps above all, they were products of ideology, or, more precisely, of ideologies in contention. The Hollywood dream machine was no monolith: the struggle over interpretation, of large issues as well as small, went on at every level, from decisions made in executive suites down to daily choices on the set, how actors dressed, their facial expressions, how they spoke a line.

The formation and definition of the city boy came not only from dominant practices—both in ideology and commercial exploitation—but also from oppositional culture. Dissident viewpoints, including those held by the performers themselves, often contested, supplemented, and reoriented how the figure looked, spoke, and behaved on-screen, and what he signified. The role of left-wing politics in the on- and offscreen careers of the movies' city boys is as central to this narrative as it is to the history of Hollywood filmmaking in its classic era, from the advent of sound through the 1950s. Cagney, Bogart, and Garfield were themselves members of the liberal and leftist communities in the movie capital, and their careers were deeply affected by their political affiliations. Their professional lives are worth retelling not only for their well-remembered triumphs but also for the forgotten, suppressed, or elided record of their struggles.

2

**Roughneck Sissy and
Charming Boy**

About ten minutes or so into *The Public Enemy*, a 1931 Warner Bros. motion picture, after a title card indicating that the year is 1915, two men enter the frame from the right side, their backs to us, walking with a certain insolent ease toward an unmarked door in a dirty alley, while from somewhere honky-tonk piano music faintly can be heard. The man on the right crosses to the left and pauses on the threshold, then swings around so we can see his face, scanning the alley with a scrutiny that balances bravado and wariness. Seeing that it's safe, he pulls his shoulders back into a loose-limbed stance, spits into the alley to mark it as his territory, pushes up the back of his cap so the bill will fall low over his forehead, and passes through the door—and into history.

The man who scans and spits is James Cagney, playing the Irish hoodlum Tom Powers, who meets his inevitable end as a corpse trussed like a mummy and left at his mother's doorstep. Of the more than sixty motion picture roles Cagney played in his career, perhaps no other has remained so vividly in the public consciousness. This one performance seemed to personify, for audiences in 1931 and for decades after, the urban disorder spawned in American society by Prohibition and briefly romanticized in the chaotic and rebellious early years of the Great Depression.

There were other memorable performances in the rich and varied gangster cycle of that period, particularly by Edward G. Robinson in *Little Caesar* (1930) and Paul Muni in *Scarface* (1932). These two distinguished actors, however, soon moved on to other types, making their greatest impact on contemporary audiences as Pasteur and Zola and Dr. Ehrlich in Warner Bros.' "biopic" cycle of the later 1930s.

Cagney's portrayal of Tom Powers was not a one-shot. It marked,

instead, the beginning of one of the most remarkable sustained periods of character creativity by an actor in the history of movies. In
the collaborative working methods of American moviemaking during the studio era, and certainly not without struggle, Cagney established a new cultural type on the American screen and in the
world's imagination. It was the urban tough guy—small, wiry,
savvy, and street-smart, a figure out of the immigrant ghettos and
ethnic neighborhoods of Chicago and New York, a quintessential
twentieth-century American city denizen, with no exact parallel in
the literary traditions and theatrical conventions from which bits
and pieces were drawn.

Cagney was joined in shaping and transforming this urban character not by Robinson and Muni, with whom he shared its beginning,
but by two actors who succeeded and in some sense superseded him,
Humphrey Bogart and John Garfield. Cagney, Bogart, and Garfield,
more than any others, in the middle decades of the twentieth century, in the era of the Great Depression, World War II, the cold war,
and the Hollywood blacklist, in the classic years of the studio system from the arrival of sound to the advent of television, were the
city boys of American movies.

■ ■ ■ ■

Less than two years and only three more movies after *The Public
Enemy*, Lincoln Kirstein, a young Harvard intellectual, presciently
noted the emergence of the new urban type in the movies—and credited James Cagney as the movie performer who embodied the figure.
(Kirstein became better known in the dance world than as a film
critic; in 1933 he invited Russian choreographer George Balanchine
to the United States, and they established the School of American
Ballet and, eventually, the New York City Ballet.)

In the spring of 1932 Kirstein published a brief appreciation of the
actor, "James Cagney and the American Hero," in a literary journal
called *Hound & Horn*. "He is the first definitely metropolitan figure
to become national," Kirstein wrote. The type of the American pioneer, as he saw it, had been transmogrified into "a short, red-headed
Irishman, quick to wrath, humorous, articulate in anger, representing not a minority in action, but the action of the American majority:—the semi-literate lower middle class. . . . When Cagney gets
down off a truck, or deals a hand at cards, or slaps his girl, or even
when he affords himself and her the mockery of sweetness, he is, for
the time being, the American hero, whom ordinary men and boys
recognize as themselves."[1]

The critical word here is "majority." For Kirstein in the early 1930s the movies were not an art but a rich field of types created for the mass of moviegoers, which the socially perceptive could also enjoy. Later audiences (and intellectuals) would discover Bogart and Garfield as fresh incarnations of this American hero. In the late twentieth century two of these three performers have gained iconic status among the movie types who pervade our era's cultural nostalgia. Yet it remains to ask to what extent they retain their social force as figures of "majority" self-recognition, as a type of the American hero speaking to or for the times.

Cagney created his own type, Kirstein's essay averred, which could at once be put "in its proper niche in the Hall of Fame of our folk legends." In the eyes of the astute observer in 1932 there were no obvious predecessors or comparisons to the Irish street kid from New York who made it big playing an Irish street kid from Chicago. In popular entertainment nearly everything is like some other thing, but Cagney seemed genuinely *sui generis*. The streets of Yorkville glimmered in his electric body—his quick gait, his rapid-fire slangy talk, his sharp movements, even the Yiddish that he gleefully spoke in the 1932 movie *Taxi!* You could tell he was the real thing the minute you saw any other actor try to take on, as a role, what Cagney *was* almost by birthright.

Still, even so original a figure as Cagney may prove that there are no exceptions to the show business rule that nothing and no one is wholly original. For the James Cagney whom Kirstein saw on the screen in 1932—the short, redheaded Irishman, quick to wrath, humorous, articulate in anger—leaps from the pages of Maxwell Anderson's 1925 play *Outside Looking In*, in the character of Little Red, which Cagney happened to play in his debut as a legitimate stage actor.

Outside Looking In was one of the benchmark plays of what was called the "new realism" in the American drama by a coauthor of the previous year's famous World War I play *What Price Glory*. Anderson adapted his play from a 1924 memoir by the writer Jim Tully, *Beggars of Life*, which told of Tully's youthful adventures riding the rails with hoboes. Tully was redheaded and Irish, and the character Little Red was based on the author. Anderson also took from the book a teenage prostitute Tully had written about, considerably softened her situation, and concocted out of her and Little Red a romantic couple on the run from the law.

With the self-deprecating tone that he frequently took in his autobiography, Cagney wrote that he got the part because he was one of the few redheaded actors around town. In whatever manner Cagney became Little Red, what is important is that the character was a distinctive figure in Anderson's play before Cagney brought him to life on the stage, and that in Little Red can be seen the embryo of the movie type Cagney was to become. What marks the figure in Anderson's conception is his doubleness—living the hobo experience but also apart from it, observing it, foreshadowing the future writer that the memoirist Jim Tully would become.

A central event in the play is a "kangaroo court" where Little Red is put on trial by the other hoboes, charged with being "a sissy and sleeping in bed and eating in restaurants." The "judge" tells Little Red, "You're accused of being a member of the middle-class and I'm damned if I ain't beginning to believe it." Little Red exclaims, "The Middle Class! Jesus!" with guilty fervor.[2] Though he explodes in violent wrath after his "conviction," the play clearly lets its audience know that Little Red will escape the hobo life, as its original audience was already likely to have been aware that Jim Tully went on to become the hoboes' retrospective chronicler.

A hint of the doubleness in the part and in the performance comes through in the *New York Times* critic's remark that Cagney "is sullen as Little Red and imaginative." He was a roughneck and a sissy, a gutsy rescuer (of the girl) and a callow dupe, a violent, gentle boy, a figure not of contradiction but of structural opposites. (Tully's memoir was made into a 1928 Paramount movie, *Beggars of Life*, featuring Wallace Beery as a hobo leader and Louise Brooks as the girl. Little Red is called simply "The Boy" in the credits and played by Richard Arlen with little if any of the stage character's complexity. The director, William A. Wellman, later directed *The Public Enemy*.)

When *Outside Looking In* closed, Cagney had a chance to play the roughneck sissy role of the decade—the lead, Roy Lane, a song-and-dance man in a gangster's nightclub, in the play *Broadway* (Cagney had begun his stage career as a dancer on Broadway and in vaudeville). This production, wrote its coauthor and director, George Abbott, not immodestly, "was destined to be one of the biggest successes in the history of the New York theatre, both artistically and financially."[3] Cagney may have had a shot at the part at a stage of development before Abbott became involved, but the showman brought Lee Tracy in with him; Cagney signed on as Tracy's understudy with a chance to play the lead in the London company.

By the time that cast was put together, however, the show was a New York triumph and Tracy had put his mark on the role. There were "artistic differences" between the producers and Cagney (as the actor recalled it, because they wanted him to mimic Tracy too slavishly) and Tracy replaced him on the London tour. (Five years later, when movie star Cagney walked out in a dispute with Warner

Bros. on a picture called *Blessed Event*, the studio put Lee Tracy in his part; did they mean to open up old wounds?)

There were several years of barely getting by before another director recognized in Cagney the qualities of his stage persona as Little Red. He went back to the vaudeville work that he had done before the Anderson play; took a small but memorable role in the 1927 *Women Go On Forever*; and played two seasons in a review produced by the Grand Street Neighborhood Theatre, *The Grand Street Follies* of 1928 and 1929, in which he sang and danced and, in 1928, did the choreography with Michael Fokine.

In the fall of 1929 he was picked for another roughneck sissy role, by the playwright-director George Kelly. Author of *The Show Off* (1924) and the Pulitzer Prize–winning play *Craig's Wife* (1925), Kelly is rated by some theater historians second only to Eugene O'Neill among 1920s American playwrights (another distinction is as uncle of Grace, the future movie star and princess). The playwright was directing his own *Maggie the Magnificent*. Cagney's character, Elwood, was described by Kelly as a "tough-looking little blonde," but not tough enough to escape domination by his mother, his wife, and finally by his sister Maggie, of the title.[4] Joan Blondell won raves as Elwood's floozie wife Etta, and Cagney was also noticed for his performance in a role much like Little Red, a recklessly adventurous boy, weakly dependent on women.

Here was a figure strikingly different from the main masculine types in popular entertainment. The cowboy of the movies and the pulps generally kept his distance from women, even when he was not overtly antagonistic toward them. Then there were the charming and clever young heroes of genteel middle-class background (juveniles or romantic leads, in stage lingo) who wooed and wed and held their women in romantic thrall. The roughneck sissy neither escaped from women nor conquered them. His most important relation to women was not as lover but as son. Cagney was not the only actor portraying this type of character; another, Edward Woods, made his movie debut playing a very similar figure in the 1930 First National film *Mother's Cry*. It is not insignificant that Warner Bros. picked these two roughneck sissy types when they were casting for the young gangsters of *The Public Enemy*.

The emergence of cultural types in popular media marks a response, a mediation, a mode of participation in wider cultural discourses. In 1920s American culture one of the dominant themes was voiced in the behaviorist psychology of John B. Watson. Among Watson's most influential publications was the 1928 book *Psychological Care of Infant and Child*, which castigated American mothers for coddling their children. These overindulged youngsters, claimed

Watson, were being molded toward lifelong dependence. Especially for males, too much mother love was turning them into mama's boys. This theme was taken up and expanded by Philip Wylie into his notorious attack on American "momism" in a 1942 book, *Generation of Vipers*. Between Watson's book and Wylie's were the peak years when the urban tough guy held sway in American popular entertainment. The formation of the city boy as a cultural type was fully interwoven with the broader social discourse about overprotective mothers and overdependent sons.

This configuration appears yet again in Cagney's next, and last, stage role—in Marie Baumer's *Penny Arcade*, which had a brief Broadway run beginning in March 1930. Teamed again with Joan Blondell, the actor played a small-time hood who is the "weakling son" of a matriarch on the Coney Island midway. This time he won the lion's share of the reviewers' raves, and the play turned into a vehicle carrying both Cagney and Blondell to Hollywood. They repeated their roles in *Sinner's Holiday*, the 1930 Warner Bros. movie adapted from *Penny Arcade*. The Cagney whom moviegoers saw in his first film was playing a role almost identical to those he had played on Broadway since *Outside Looking In*.

In his film debut, Cagney moves with a swayback swagger, his hands and elbows high at his chest. He speaks rapidly in a high-pitched, sometimes frightened voice, appearing somewhat self-conscious about delivering lines in what Broadway reviewers called gashouse lingo, in which the words "these," "them," and "those" come out "dese," "dem," and "dose." These appear as little more than stylized gestures, however, alongside the behavior required of him performing as a son with his mother (played by Lucille LaVerne).

The script attempts to explain the character's weakling state by reference to his father's drinking: it suggests that booze killed the old man and somehow weakened the son even before he was born. So the mother protects and babies him. In return, he lies to her, and relies on her. The director, John Adolfi, heightened emphasis on the mother-son scenes by shooting the two together in tight two-shot close-ups. Cagney sits in LaVerne's lap and she puts her arms around him. In a final farewell scene, when the son is about to be taken away for committing a murder, mother and son hug again, and he kisses her on the mouth. Spectators who had come to the movie expecting roughneck realism found themselves witnessing an oedipal romance/nightmare.

This powerful strain of dependence underlies the character type James Cagney brought to his career in the movies. The extraordinary late twentieth century project of psychoanalytic and feminist theorists to reconceptualize gender can provide important insights toward understanding this fictional character structure. So far, however, its application to cinema has focused on female characters and on men or male performers who seem to challenge stereotypes, rather than men within the framework of "masculine" norms; and the historiographic issues of gender definition within specific societies and past cultural formations has barely been touched.

Dependence is a concern for every human being, and (as Dorothy Dinnerstein in *The Mermaid and the Minotaur* has suggested) particularly so for men in the development of their masculine self-image. Yet concepts of cultural character in the United States invariably stress that Americans prize independence above all other personal traits and virtues. The notion of dependence continues to conjure up images of mama's boys in the shrill tones of Watson and Wylie. Other societies, such as Japan, have constructed concepts of character in which dependence is regarded as necessary and valuable in family and social relations. In *The Anatomy of Dependence*, Japanese psychiatrist Takeo Doi has drawn a connection between dependence and rebellion, alienation, and the loss of authority in periods of social crisis—periods similar to the one the United States entered in the early 1930s. The trait of dependence shown by Cagney's characters on Broadway and in *Sinner's Holiday*, rather than a sign of aberrant behavior, was a central aspect in the shaping of the city boy as a cultural type.

■ ■ ■ ■

Throughout the 1920s Humphrey Bogart pursued a moderately successful career on Broadway that seemed in almost every way the antithesis of Cagney's—not least in the ease with which, without theatrical training, he managed to be steadily employed in commercial plays for nearly a decade. With his silver-spoon background as the son of a prosperous New York physician, even his desultory record as a private school boy at Trinity and Andover or his brief stint in the U.S. Navy in the last months of World War I could not do much to tarnish his genteel pedigree, or the family connections that got him started in the theater. The theatrical producer William A. Brady was a neighbor of the Bogarts on West 104th Street. Brady's wife, Grace George, and their daughter, Alice Brady, both stage performers, helped the young Bogart get apprentice work in Brady theaters and productions. Once he got his feet wet in drama, he moved fairly effortlessly into a character type that seemed to suit him in temperament and appearance, a type that probably had as many parallels to his own private experience as did the roughneck softie to Cagney's.

This type—as already briefly noted—was known in the theater world as the juvenile, or romantic lead. In early twentieth century American culture, however, the figure was no mere theatrical convention: he was more like a fundamental principle of the social order, one of the cornerstones of the ideological edifice holding American society together. In literature he was the genteel romantic hero, whose fictional character traits were brilliantly devised to manage the contradictions in middle-class American values. F. Scott Fitzgerald tried to model his life on this fictive prototype; the writer also perpetuated the figure in his popular fiction, and unveiled its pathos in such classic works as *The Great Gatsby* and *Tender Is the Night*.

"Though poor of purse he was rich in charm." A reviewer wrote those words to describe Bogart's final Broadway role, before the actor's own excursion to Hollywood: it presents the cultural type in a nutshell. On one hand, the figure represented middle-class yearning for upward mobility; on the other, it stood for that class's concern for male domination, as well as its desire to constrain the lawless freedom of the rich. All of these complex wishes could be united in the clever young man who harnesses his imagination, wit, and will to the goal of winning the heart and hand of a rich young woman.

There are innumerable variations of wealth, age, and marital status in this basic pattern: Bogart played many of them while he learned to act, while making a living at acting, in nearly a dozen productions between 1922 and 1930. For decades people have laughed at the legend of the man who would become *Casablanca*'s Rick playing a toothsome juvenile in white ducks rushing on stage, racquet in hand, calling out, "Tennis, anyone?" This jejune image, however, masks the fact that his plays and performances stood at the heart of American popular entertainment in the 1920s.

Cradle Snatchers, a play that came midway in Bogart's development as a stage actor, ran for over a year from 1925 through 1926, and closed just short of the Broadway benchmark of five hundred performances. William Fox acquired movie rights and a young Howard Hawks (who would figure importantly in Bogart's life two decades down the road) directed the silent film adaptation in 1927. (The same story served as the basis for a 1929 Fox early sound musical, *Why Leave Home?*) Three other Broadway plays in which Bogart appeared were made into movies by different companies. When audiences erupted in "gales of hysterical laughter" at a play like *Cradle*

Snatchers, as reviewers reported, they were laughing with Bogart and his stage cohorts, not, as late twentieth century spectators might do, at them.

To be sure, Bogart had a rough beginning. His performance as a "rich and dissolute youth" in *Swifty* (1922) was roundly ridiculed by several reviewers. By 1924, however, when he appeared in *Nerves*, one of those who had hooted at him two years earlier took it back. "Mr. Bogart is really capital," wrote Alexander Woollcott (a reigning wit of the Algonquin Round Table) in the *New York Herald-Tribune*. "He is a young actor whose appearance here two seasons ago in a terrible play called *Shifty* [sic] was recorded by your correspondent in words so disparaging that it is surprising to find him still acting. Those words are hereby eaten." Woollcott remembered Bogart if not the play's correct name; under either title, it seems that Bogart as an actor had made a swift shift.

In ability, that is, not in typecasting. Playwright Barry Connors described the character Bogart played in his next production, *Hell's Bells* (1924), as "a regular fellow of 27, well educated, ambitious, self-reliant and industrious."[5] Only the age of his characters changed.

Cradle Snatchers was notable as a genteel comic effort to explore changing sexual attitudes toward the double standard and women's "emancipation." The play concerns three wives who are vexed by their husbands' assignations with flappers. The wives persuade three college boys that they are available for romance. The various machinations explode into farce when the husbands bring their paramours to a secret house in Glen Cove, Long Island, only to find their spouses and the "campus romeos" already there. Bogart's role called for him to masquerade as a "Spanish sheik," a parody of the European lovers who were entrancing female moviegoers at the time.

Bogart presumably could have gone on playing romantic leads so long as Broadway had theaters. In 1930, however, while he was in yet another genteel comedy embarking on yet another lengthy run, he made a one-reel movie short for the Vitaphone Corporation. The film, *Broadway's Like That*, was primarily a movie tryout for Ruth Etting, the vaudeville and radio singing star. It failed to open a movie career for Etting (her motion picture fame would come a quarter-century later, when Doris Day played her in an MGM biopic, *Love Me or Leave Me*, with James Cagney as her racketeer lover and promoter); but it did arouse Bogart's interest in the medium.

Perhaps not every Broadway actor was just then heading west, but a goodly share of them were giving the new talking pictures the benefit of their pear-shaped vowels. Just as the Bradys had given him his start in the theater, Bogart had a leg up in the movie business through a brother-in-law who was a story editor in Fox's New York office. In short order he was on his way to Hollywood with a Fox contract, and by the summer of 1930 he was working in his first feature movie as—surprise!—the juvenile romantic lead.

The film was called *A Devil with Women*, but the title character was not played by Bogart. The lead actor was Victor McLaglen, the burly, battered-looking British actor. McLaglen, like Cagney with Little Red, owed his character type to the playwright Maxwell Anderson: he had become a star playing the roistering marine Captain Flagg in Fox's 1926 movie version of Anderson and Lawrence Stallings' hit play *What Price Glory* (Cagney would also, a bit too late, take on this role). Capitalizing on this successful performer and character type, the Fox studio made virtually a subgenre out of his wanderer-adventurer exploits. By the time McLaglen found himself paired with Bogart, the formula may have become a little threadbare. *A Devil with Women* was just another skirt-chasing caper through some comical Central American revolution or another (like the one the marines were then fighting in Nicaragua against a "bandit" named Sandino).

Holding his own against McLaglen turned out to be a formidable task for Bogart; in his Broadway vehicles he was usually the most manly thing around. Alongside McLaglen's soldier-of-fortune he looked considerably more like the rich little twerp who was merely implicit in his genteel boy Broadway roles. The script called for Bogart to win the girl while McLaglen, loser on the romantic battlefront, jocularly goes off to quash some other banana republic insurrection. Bogart's performance, however, seems only to signal how incongruous was the entire project of the film. To match McLaglen's constant ear-to-ear grin, Bogart plays a coltish fool, tossing his head, slapping his knees, and laughing with his mouth open so wide you can almost see his tonsils. He looks like an actor who is uncomfortable not only with his part, but also with his body. He employs a few stock gestures that he repeats again and again: arms awkwardly held in front of his body; then pushing back his jacket; then fists at the belt; then into the pockets; then back to the belt, arms akimbo. Smiles, arch delivery of lines, more smiles. *Variety*, in panning the picture, had the wit to suggest that the fault lay not so much with Bogart as with the "silly" action given him to play.

It is unlikely that there was much in Bogart's first movie role inherently any sillier than what he had performed successfully on Broadway in hits like *Cradle Snatchers*. The question is, did it appear silly because it was on celluloid, or because the times were changing? Not everyone, to be sure, saw a problem. The *New York Times* film reviewer found "young Mr. Bogart . . . good looking and intelligent," his performance "ingratiating." *A Devil with Women* appeared only a year after the 1929 stock market crash, and silliness was not yet out of vogue. Bogart's Broadway type—the romantic juvenile, the genteel hero—would survive for a time in the Great Depression era and even thrive in such musical comedy personalities as the young Dick Powell. Still, it would be harder to be a silly young man, in life or as represented in popular entertainment, in the Great Depression era than in the Roaring Twenties. The producers of entertainment came to recognize the obsolescence of cultural types more quickly, in general, than the reviewers. Their money was at stake.

▪ ▪ ▪ ▪

As Cagney and Bogart made their separate ways toward Hollywood in the early months of 1930, the American motion picture industry stood on the cusp of a major transformation. Its changes at the end of the 1920s were of an unusual dual character: on one hand internal and institutional, they were also external and national. First came the transition to sound production—necessitating (in addition to the aesthetic and technological challenges the talkies posed) a heavy financial burden of investment in new production equipment and the wiring of theaters. Then came the stock market crash, which depressed stock values as well as ticket prices, admissions, and revenues. A majority of the principal Hollywood production companies suffered severe losses, and several went into receivership during the worst Depression years.

Given these difficulties, apparent and impending, a Broadway actor might have found early 1930 not the most propitious time to risk exposing himself to the hazy sunshine of the other coast. On the contrary: Hollywood had the welcome mat out for Broadway veterans. They had already shown that they could act and talk at the same time, a feat not every silent screen performer had mastered; perhaps more important, they were willing to work for salaries well below the prime Hollywood pay rates of the free-spending 1920s. Whether or not they could perform in talkies with greater skill than silent movie actors, the bottom line with the Broadway imports looked good to Hollywood producers: their talk was cheap.

For comparison, take the situation of silent screen star Richard Barthelmess. (Dedicated fans of Hollywood movies may recall him best from Howard Hawks's 1939 *Only Angels Have Wings*, in which he played a cowardly pilot who redeems himself.) Barthelmess made his mark in the D. W. Griffith classics *Broken Blossoms* (1919) and *Way Down East* (1920), playing opposite Lillian Gish. In the early 1920s he became a model of a boy hero in the movies: his homespun, bucolic style appealed to a moviegoing population that yearned for an imagined simpler America.

In 1926 First National secured Barthelmess's services by offering him a contract paying more than $7500 per week, and also gave him the right of approval over his stories, directors, and fellow actors. A new contract in 1928 increased his salary; on September 27, 1929 (his agent had brilliant timing), he signed yet another contract, not to take effect until 1931, that effectively doubled his rate by promising him the same amount of money for half the work. In two days of work Barthelmess could make more money than the vast majority of moviegoers earned in a year.

What made him appear so valuable to his employers? In the era of the Hollywood studio system (from the 1920s to the 1950s) stars sold pictures. Monopolizing production and distribution, the big movie companies also controlled exhibition by owning the top first-run theaters in major cities (in 1948 the U.S. Supreme Court declared this system in violation of antitrust laws, and the studios were ordered to give up ownership of theaters). Promotion and press coverage created a demand that filtered down to thousands of smaller theaters throughout the country. Rationalizing their production system, the movie studios sold "blocks" of pictures to these independent exhibitors and chains even before the films were made. The promise of pictures with popular stars was the fuel that made the system operate. Even stars like Barthelmess who earned colossal sums were probably worth more to their employers than what they were paid.

This mode of operation was not fundamentally altered by the onset of the Great Depression, but it did receive a severe jolt. Warner Bros. took over First National only five weeks after Barthelmess signed his 1929 contract; by 1931 (a year when the company reported a loss of nearly $8 million) Warners was obligated to pay the star $187,000 per picture for the next two years. Cutting costs to the bone by using unknown names from Broadway, the studio could bring in one of its early 1930s first-run productions—salaries, sets, costumes, film stock, overhead, depreciation, the works—for only a few thousand dollars more. Barthelmess found himself making far too much money for his own good: his fabulous deal from the 1920s was, in the Depression years, the ruin of his career. He was one of several silent stars who faded from the talkies because his salary, not his voice, was too high.

Studio heads discovered they could pay Broadway actors one tenth of what Barthelmess was making, and it would be more money than they had ever seen in their lives. Joan Blondell came out to Hollywood at $250 a week, Cagney at $500, Bogart at a reported $750. The entire sum of cast salaries on *Sinner's Holiday*, for ten actors, was $5100 a week. Maybe making a picture like that, without stars, was taking a risk in terms of the normal promotion and sales system; but then again one or two of those unknowns might emerge as stars, as Cagney and Blondell were soon to do.

The Warner brother who was vice-president in charge of production, Jack L. Warner, would take the opportunity of that fortuitous change in status to remind his actors that a contract was a contract: if he had to honor Barthelmess's deal and pay him over $7000 a week, then his fledgling stars would have to honor the deals they signed as unknowns at under $700. (Warner may have been among the tightest-fisted of Hollywood moguls, but throughout the industry a virtual crusade was waged during the 1930s to keep salaries from soaring back to 1920s levels. In 1938, after several years of renewed movie industry prosperity, the Treasury Department reported that only the three most highly paid actors were earning incomes of between $400,000 and $500,000 per year, comparable to the salaries Barthelmess and others had attained by 1926.)

Cagney and Bogart were part of a flood of Legit Names (as *Variety* called them) pouring into the movie capital in 1930. The weekly trade paper reported that former Broadway thespians were in double digits at nearly every major studio. A list prepared by Warner Bros. counted twenty names at that studio without mentioning either Cagney or Joan Blondell, though Bogart was included on Fox's list of twenty-one.

The standard option clause in Hollywood contracts made it easy for studios to buy up actors by the bushel, pick out the ripe ones, and throw the rest back. Most contracts bound the actor for up to seven years, but gave the studio the option of dropping the performer after every six-month period. A studio such as Warner Bros. could, without difficulty, employ all twenty of those former stage players for half a year for less than it was paying one of its former silent screen stars. Imagine the value of the investment if one, two, or three of them became stars in their own right.

Bette Davis started at Warners in 1932 at $400 a week and was thrown into five pictures in her first six months. Errol Flynn, an Aussie who didn't know any better, signed in 1934 at $150 a week.

Olivia de Havilland, still a teenager, signed a contract in 1935 that began with thirteen-week options. There was hell to pay with all three of them when they discovered how they had been exploited, and their tempestuous battles with the studio made headlines. There were no headlines for the majority of fledgling movie actors whose options after six months or a year were not, as the saying went, picked up.

One such figure from that tide of Broadway players who went west in 1930 was—Humphrey Bogart. How could such an inglorious dismissal have come about? Bogart's second assignment at Fox in *Up the River* had been considerably more important than the first: it was a "comedy-drama" of prison life directed by the studio's premier director, John Ford. This time the actor's assignment as a romantic lead was matched not against an older warhorse like McLaglen, but a newcomer who was almost his exact contemporary, Spencer Tracy. Tracy was making his own motion picture debut, playing a convict, after starring on Broadway in John Wexley's 1930 death row drama *The Last Mile*. *Up the River* achieved considerable success; Bogart amply shared in the reviewers' praise. Variously described as "charming" and "likeable," he was said to possess "oodles of promise" and "personality plus." Reviewers hoped they would see much more of him. To top it all off, he was compared favorably by several writers to John Boles.

John who? Like Richard Barthelmess, this was an actor whose reputation has not survived the years; but he was a name to contend with in 1930. Boles was a domestic version of Rudolph Valentino, one of those all-purpose "Spanish sheik" types (as Bogart's comic character in *Cradle Snatchers* was called), bred on American soil. By 1930 he was a household name from starring in such recent costume dramas and early sound musicals as *The Desert Song* (1929), *Captain of the Guard* (1930), and *Song of the West* (1930). Boles's career had struck a hidden iceberg, however, and was about to sink fast. Universal studio's official historian offers the opinion that Boles's performance in his final major role for that company, as the philandering husband in the 1932 *Back Street*, was "an embarrassment."[6] Little did the kindly reviewers who compared Bogart to Boles realize that such praise was like a first-class ticket on the *Titanic*.

What was important, however, was not the decline of the individual, but of the type. The growing economic crisis was causing audiences to look less favorably on the old-fashioned romantic lead—whether he was costumed in burnooses or ruffles, like Boles, or played the nice young bourgeois boy next door, like Bogart. Even Valentino might have had difficulty navigating the swift current of cultural change. Boles could not, and neither could Bogart. Despite the sheaf of favorable reviews, Fox never again gave Bogart as big a role as his assignment in *Up the River*. He played in three more films at Fox and in a loan-out to Universal before his contract was dropped at the end of May 1931.

Still, a viewing of *Up the River* suggests that there were difficulties with the individual as well as with the type—no matter what the contemporary reviewers had to say. Bogart had not gotten over the physical awkwardness he displayed in *A Devil with Women*, nor advanced beyond the stock gestures of unbuttoning his jacket and shifting his hands from his pockets to his hips. Worse, the actor was left in the lurch more than once by John Ford's quick and casual style of filmmaking.

Whatever Ford's considerable directorial skills as a creator of visual images, he was no doubt more highly valued by studio accountants as a swift and cost-efficient worker. *Up the River*, a film that runs ninety-two minutes, was shot in less than three weeks. The total exposed footage, incredibly, was less than one-third the amount that Raoul Walsh, for example, used on another Fox feature shot a few months later. Ford quite simply set up the camera for medium or medium-long shots, showing the actors from head to toe, and let it roll for long uninterrupted takes. Unless an actor muffed a line, he would call out "Print it" and move on to the next scene.

Bogart was thoroughly caught off guard by Ford's methods. In one lengthy scene, in which he had some of his most important lines and the possibility of making a strong impression in a verbal duel with another actor, Bogart stands with his back to the camera throughout the entire shot. Elsewhere he plays scenes where only his back or a diminished side profile can be seen. He might as well have been auditioning for a part as the Invisible Man. Did Ford care? Obviously not. The more difficult question is why Bogart would accede to this form of actor's suicide, or let himself be maneuvered into it—and in a short time out of a job.

Like a number of other films made in 1930—a year of economic and cultural change in American society, of technical and personnel change in the movie industry—*Up the River* seems to point simultaneously toward past and future. Spencer Tracy and his sidekick Warren Hymer, playing incorrigible but comic lawbreakers, suggest the future: the 1930s genres of crime and comedy, and their not-infrequent mixture. Bogart and Claire Luce (the actress, not the playwright Clare Boothe who married *Time* founder Henry Luce), playing callow young lovers who find each other during their incongruous imprisonments, recall the genteel past. Their character types aside, the contrast between Tracy and Bogart was telling: Tracy, at thirty years of age, looked like a man; Bogart, the same age, appeared but a boy. In the crisis of the Great Depression, movie audiences lost tolerance for the sentimental problems of Bogart's juvenile type; their concerns were epitomized by the title of a 1933 Warner Bros. film, *Wild Boys of the Road*.

■ ■ ■ ■

Already in 1930, Warner Bros. was setting its sights decisively on the future. Darryl F. Zanuck, the executive in charge of day-to-day production under Jack L. Warner, was still in his twenties, younger than Tracy and Bogart (and Cagney). He was moving the studio toward the style of fast-paced, action-oriented drama, based on contemporary events, that made Warner Bros. films seem synonymous with everyday life in the Great Depression era. One issue still to be determined in the middle of 1930, however, was what male types would predominate in these contemporary action films. This question was at the forefront when casting began for Cagney's second picture, *The Doorway to Hell*.

Now almost completely forgotten, *The Doorway to Hell* in fact initiated the famous Warners cycle of gangster dramas, and in its own time stirred up quite a fuss. (It preceded *Little Caesar* by a few weeks, *The Public Enemy* by a few months; all three films were nominated for Academy Awards in the scriptwriting category for 1930–1931.) The controversy over *The Doorway to Hell* centered on the characterization of its gangster leader, named Louie Ricarno, who was loosely based on Al Capone. When the studio cast the role, it drew up a description of this character: "About thirty-five, good looking, always neatly dressed. Little of anything of the fiction type of gangster about him. The type of man whom women love and men admire."[7] The "fiction type of gangster" was an obvious reference to W. R. Burnett's sensational 1929 novel *Little Caesar*, whose protagonist, Rico Bandello, was a brutal, comic lout whom Edward G. Robinson was soon to immortalize ("Mother of Mercy, is this the end of Rico?") on film at the Warner Bros. subsidiary, First National. Despite what was going on at First National (where Hal Wallis ran production), Zanuck was not yet prepared to abandon the 1920s-style gentleman gangster, at least not for the starring role.

Feeling its way in the midst of those rapidly changing times, the studio wanted to play it both ways: exploiting the public's fascination with gangland violence, but sugarcoating it with a hero any middle-class mother could love. The answer was Lew Ayres, still in his early twenties, who had just scored a major hit in Universal's antiwar drama, adapted from Erich Maria Remarque's World War I novel, *All Quiet on the Western Front*. Warners sent one of its contract players, Douglas Fairbanks, Jr., to do a picture at Universal, in exchange for Ayres's services in *The Doorway to Hell*. The clean-cut, idealistic, boyish Lew Ayres was thrust into the man-sized role modeled on Scarface Al.

Louie Ricarno's sidekick in the film was named Steve Mileaway. The casting notes described him as "in a minor way the man about town, but with certain characteristics that mark him for the gangster and gigolo." Cagney was signed for this part almost as soon as he had finished *Sinner's Holiday*. He was not on a term contract, having come out to Hollywood only to do the *Penny Arcade* adaptation (return ticket to New York guaranteed); *The Doorway to Hell* gave him three more weeks at $500 a week.

At the Strand, Warner Bros.' flagship theater in Times Square, the studio's first gangster picture was a smash. It was held over for a three-week run. In the press, advertisements featured Ayres as the "Baby-Faced Killer." Elsewhere on the entertainment pages, however, reviewers were delivering a different verdict on the casting strategy. One said that supporting actors Cagney and Robert Elliott (as a police detective) "take the picture away from the featured name" by "the power they put into their respective duties." Another speculated as to why the studio would cast "nice little Lewis Ayres" as a gangster czar, and suggested that "it would have helped *The Doorway to Hell* considerably had he swapped roles with James Cagney, one of the finest realistic actors that the talkies have produced." We might need to discount this praise a bit, on the suspicion that one of Cagney's pals among the New York reviewers was trying to give his career a boost. Still, when the picture opened soon after in Los Angeles, reviewers there also liked Cagney. The studio's casting choice even became the subject of an advisor's communication to the movie czar Will H. Hays: putting "a young man of fine features" in the role of a ruthless gangster, worried Dr. Carleton Simon, could create too much sympathy for the criminal type. Ayres would not have been convincing in the role, however, "were it not for the true to type supporting characters."[8] Virtually all of the reviewers of the film commented on the incongruity of a juvenile lead in a gangster role; and in every one of these responses, the disparity was highlighted by comparison to what was seen as a "realistic," "true-to-type" supporting performance by James Cagney. What exactly did Cagney do to merit this praise?

One thing he did *not* do was shy away from the camera, à la Bogart. Nearly every time he appears on the screen, in fact, Cagney creates so much business as to call almost exclusive attention to himself. In one early sequence, in which he is calling on gangsters to come to a conclave, he faces the camera, pulls a cigar from another gangster's pocket, ostentatiously sniffs it, then returns it; with another gangster, in side view, he busily adjusts his jacket, sticks out his chin, straightens his tie, then supplies the topper by pulling down the other man's suspenders. At the meeting itself, where Ayres holds center screen, Cagney—off to one side—keeps drawing the spectator's interest by shifting his eyes and raising his eyebrows.

These little gestures would not add up to much if they did not, cumulatively, provide some much-needed energy to an overly literary and oddly genteel script. The gangster hero wants nothing more than to retire to Florida, where he can play golf and write his memoirs; Cagney's role is assigned most of the film's earthiness and comedy. As written, the character of Mileaway is intended to be somewhat weak: he cannot hold the gangster coalition together after Louie Ricarno retires, and at the end, grilled by the police, Mileaway confesses to a murder Louie committed to prevent the gangster boss from learning about his affair with Louie's wife. Mileaway is another roughneck sissy, and Cagney gave the familiar type a flair and conviction that Ayres could not match.

At the end of production on *The Doorway to Hell*—well before the film's release prompted the debate on gangster characterizations—Warner Bros. offered Cagney a long-term contract. It differed in subtle ways from the standard: the complete term was five years instead of the customary seven, and the option periods were a full year rather than the normal six months. The starting salary of $400 a week, however, represented a 20 percent cut from his one-picture weekly earnings. After one year this would go up to $550, in the third year to $750, and to $1000 and $1250 in the fourth and fifth years, respectively.

For Hollywood, these were modest numbers: but $16,000 guaranteed for the next twelve months could not have looked too shabby, considering the worsening national economic situation. What Warner Bros. executives did not anticipate, when they more or less accidentally made James Cagney into a star in *The Public Enemy*, was that the redheaded roughneck softie (whose quickness to wrath on the screen Lincoln Kirstein would soon celebrate) would express his anger even more swiftly and articulately, offscreen, at them.

3

The Private Enemy

Jack L. Warner could never fathom the depths of his stars' ingratitude. "We took you up from oblivion," he would say, "and brought you up to where you are now"—unaware that his words merely fueled a rage that money could assuage, but not contain.[1] Anger was one of the conditions of stardom in the studio era, because few stars could ever entirely ignore their fundamental helplessness, and the arbitrary nature of their success. However much they might see themselves in retrospect as Destiny's darlings, they knew that careers were made, or lost, as much by whim or chance as by their own capacities for self-determination. James Cagney had ample opportunity to contemplate his dependency, and stoke his anger, both before and after he almost did not get the leading role in *The Public Enemy*.

Cagney was not the original choice to play Tom Powers. It is quite possible that he would not even have survived at Warner Bros. until the film was made if his option period had not run for a full year instead of the standard six months. During his first half-year as a contract player, July to December 1930, he had worked in only one picture—and that had come at the beginning, in the summer. He played a minor part as a train brakeman in William A. Wellman's railroading drama *Other Men's Women* (1931). Then he was laid off for three months, under a contract provision that limited the studio's obligation to pay him to forty weeks in a year. When he returned in late November, the studio still found nothing for him to do through the year's end.

As 1930 came to a close, the future of the urban tough guy appeared a good deal brighter than James Cagney's future movie career. Big-city audiences were responding enthusiastically to movies like *The Doorway to Hell* that dramatized and stylized the high-speed tempo and nervous energy, the elegance and squalor, the noise and violence, of metropolitan life. When that picture opened strongly in Los Angeles after its successful holdover run in New York, Warner

Bros. rushed to prepare a sequel. Early in December the studio purchased another story drawn from Chicago's notorious 1920s beer
wars: an unwieldy unpublished novel, "Beer and Blood," by two
young coauthors, Kubec Glasmon and John Bright. They also signed
Glasmon and Bright to help craft a script out of it. For the lead role
of Tom Powers they picked a young actor, Edward Woods, a handsome juvenile in the Lewis Ayres mold.

Here the legend takes over. A standard story is recounted by
Henry Cohen in his edition of the film's screenplay: director William A. Wellman, "typically for those days, was still finishing another job when shooting began on *The Public Enemy*, and not for
several days did he catch up with the rushes. By then Bright and
Glasmon were after him to reverse the Cagney and Woods assignments. Wellman saw and agreed."[2] It is anecdotes like these that
keeps the media business alive, to be sure, but besides being preposterous on the face of it (directors did not "typically" show up late for
their assignments and let some assistant do important takes), it is
also not true. Eddie Woods never got to utter any of Tom Powers's
lines in front of a camera.

Two weeks before shooting started on the film, production records make clear, Woods was shifted to the role of Tom's sidekick,
Matt Doyle, and replaced as Tom by James Cagney. Never mind all
the claims to genius for recommending this change (for the record,
claimants include coauthor Bright, director Wellman, and producer
Zanuck, who at least had the power to accomplish it). As is usually
the case, forces larger than individual percipience were working to
provide Cagney with his unexpected opportunity for stardom (and
Woods his ticket to immortality as an also-ran).

These forces were converging in the movie industry's troubled
politics of self-regulation. Motion picture codes and an industry
watchdog structure were in place well before 1934 (when, under
pressure from religious groups' organized boycotts, the producers'
association set up a Production Code Administration with strong
coercive powers). In 1931, however, code administrators—concerned
with state and local censorship, and persistent lobbying for federal
regulation of movies—could only attempt to persuade producers to
reject what many saw as an increasing tendency to exploit sex and
violence. Colonel Jason S. Joy monitored production for the Hays
Office in 1931, and had been put on guard by public criticism of excessive violence in *The Doorway to Hell*. This led him to be concerned about Warners' "Beer and Blood" script in preparation. He
called on Zanuck to justify the project, and received a lengthy defense from the producer on January 6, 1931.

Zanuck argued for the film on sociological and educational grounds. One of its themes, he wrote Joy, would be the necessity of improving the environment "and living conditions in the lower regions" in order to stop crime and gang warfare.[3] This approach had surfaced briefly in *The Doorway to Hell*, in an incongruous scene in which gang leader Louis Ricarno visits his old neighborhood and inveighs against the conditions that caused a brother and sister to die from tainted milk; Louie's wife adds sardonically, "Life's cheap in a neighborhood like this." What was needed to make this perspective more effective, as responses to *The Doorway to Hell* had already made clear, was an actor who looked as if he could have been a slum kid.

Two days after Zanuck responded to Joy, production started at Warner Bros. on *The Millionaire* (1931), a vehicle for the venerable British actor George Arliss. Cagney suddenly found himself thrown into a small part, his first work in months. His entire role consists of a brief but intense scene lasting no more than two minutes. He plays an insurance salesman visiting Arliss, the retired millionaire. "Not hardly what you'd call a gentleman, sir," the butler introduces him, "not a bit like you and me." He talks a blue streak, in an ungrammatical streetwise lingo, warning the wealthy man to take up some activity.

Cagney's scene was scheduled for shooting January 13–14, 1931. On January 15, a cryptic memo from the casting department notified all concerned that Edward Woods would play the role of Matt in *The Public Enemy*, due to begin production at the end of January. While it is traditional in Hollywood to accept the legend and ignore the facts, these are the options: imagine Darryl F. Zanuck watching nonexistent rushes of Edward Woods playing Tom Powers (with Bright and Wellman twisting his arm to change cast assignments in mid-production)—or picture the producer observing the rushes of James Cagney in a little test role, a fast-talking salesman who looked the part of an Irish mug for which juveniles like Ayres and Woods were too dangerously handsome.

■ ■ ■ ■

Cagney's initial claim to the role of Tom Powers was that he lacked conventional good looks. Moralists in and out of the motion picture industry would not have to worry that a comely boy like Lew Ayres or Edward Woods would make a gangster look appealing, and so glorify crime. Their physiognomic theories, however, were too narrow and perhaps outdated in their notions of appeal. When *The Public Enemy* opened, reviewers (who in those days went to movies with the masses instead of in private screening rooms) discovered that spectators took to the gangsters anyway.

As Andre Sennwald wrote in the *New York Times*, "The audiences yesterday laughed frequently and with gusto as the swaggering Matt and Tom went through their paces, and this rather took the edge off the brutal picture the producers appeared to be trying to serve up." The Times Square movie crowd responded not to the anomalous doubleness of a clever boy playing a ruthless killer, but to the intrinsic doubleness of a figure familiar in the neighboring Broadway legitimate theaters, the roughneck sissy. In this most full and complex portrait yet, the type could evoke feelings of joy and fear and pity, and rise from a sociological case to a tragic hero.

How much of this triumph was Cagney's, how much already established in the scripted role that Edward Woods might have played? The sociological bent of the "Beer and Blood" project gave Tom Powers, from the start, depths that few of the earlier movie gangsters had: a social history, a biography, a family. Unlike Louie Ricarno or Little Caesar, he has a living mother: he is a son and younger brother. Although, of all of these Warners gangsters, Tom's behavior was the most cold-blooded and vicious, he was the least monstrous among them, because basic aspects of his life were familiar and normal and likeable.

The final script for *The Public Enemy* was delivered three days after the casting change was made. Shooting started a week later, in the assembly-line schedule common in that era. It is unlikely that there was sufficient time to tailor the character conception to Cagney's screen persona—if anyone even had a clear idea what Cagney's screen persona was. The roughneck softie was strongly evident in the screenplay by veteran scenario writer Harvey Thew; the writer already knew the type, since he had adapted *Penny Arcade* to the screen as *Sinner's Holiday*.

Thew's Tom Powers is not only a younger brother, he is his mother's perpetual baby—and his babyness is linked to the violence that helps him rise to gangster power. The film's women quickly recognize this aspect of his character. The blonde Gwen, played by Jean Harlow, expresses her interest in him by calling him a "spoiled boy" and her "bashful boy." Jane, the girlfriend of absent gang leader Paddy Ryan, seduces a drunken Tom while putting him to bed, telling him he is a "fine boy" and a "good boy."

Tom rushes into several of his most brutal or impulsive acts, significantly, after these scenes of vulnerability and passivity with women: he dashes from his tryst with Gwen to shoot the horse that killed his gangster friend Nails Nathan; waking up to discover that he has spent the night with Jane, he defies Paddy Ryan's orders and storms angrily from the hideout into a hail of machine-gun fire that kills Matt, though Tom survives. Earlier, Nails goads Tom into killing Putty Nose, the gang leader of his youth, by telling him that Putty Nose "thinks you're soft." Like Little Red in Anderson's *Outside Looking In*, Tom Powers flies into a rage whenever anyone penetrates his tough-guy facade.

Tom's last speaking lines come when his mother and older brother visit him in the hospital—after he has been wounded during his murderous attack on a rival gang to avenge Matt's death. (As he collapses in a gutter after the shoot-out, he gasps, "I ain't so tough"—one of the few lines in the movie added to the script during production.) Lying in his hospital bed, weak and bandaged, he whispers to his mother, "You must like Mike better than me." She exclaims, "No, no Tom! You're my baby!" The gruesome final image of the dead Tom, left at his mother's doorstep, has often been described as a corpse trussed like a mummy; but in fact he is swaddled in a blanket like an infant in a nightmare fulfillment of his dependence.

The written script provides a strong foundation for Tom Powers's character, but Cagney does not merely inhabit or present this figure: in the precise dictionary sense, he creates it. With his body he causes it to exist in a photographed image on a movie screen—he brings it into being. His short, quick movements, his clipped diction, his mobile eyes and mouth, are counterpointed with, at other moments, an almost sultry languor. These are the dual characteristics of the roughneck and the softie: combined, they shape a figure whose tension is barely under control—a bundle of suppressed rage, waiting to strike.

In a scene in which Tom picks up his first girlfriend, Kitty (Mae Clarke), at the "black and tan cafe," screenwriter Thew had written in a stage direction for the actor: as Tom signals the black headwaiter to remove the comatose escorts of Kitty and Mamie (Joan Blondell), he hits the black man "playfully on the arm."[4] At some point early in production Cagney and director Wellman quite obviously had seized upon this brief notation and decided to build it into a gestural signature. It became the sign of Tom's contradictory personality, at once brutal and lovable. This gesture, which soon came to be called a short-arm jab, becomes Tom's principal means of expressing affection, pleasure, or gratitude. Usually double-pumping with his right arm, Cagney uses it at least a dozen times in the film—with Paddy Ryan, with the headwaiter and with Kitty in the "black and tan cafe," with Gwen and with Jane, and several times with Matt.

The person he most often playfully punches, however, is his mother. (She also jabs him once in return.) This marks it as a harmless boy's gesture, fusing his roughneck and his softie sides—his veneer of cynical superiority and, lying just below the surface, his dependence. Yet at the same time it contains the suppressed violence that continually erupts: when he slaps Jane, strikes a bartender, punches Putty Nose. The one person he does not use it with, significantly, is the only character to whom Tom can never feel superior—his older brother. Twice he tries to strike Mike in anger; twice he fails. Both times he gets slugged to the floor instead.

A legend has grown up over the years around Cagney's performance in *The Public Enemy*, but this ominous playfulness, so central to the character of Tom Powers that Cagney created, forms no part of it. Instead, the legend concerns only one notorious moment: the famous scene in which Cagney pushes a scalloped half-grapefruit into Mae Clarke's face. It is perhaps ironic that the grapefruit episode did not grow out of the character, or from Cagney's performance, but was adapted from an incident in Chicago gangland lore that Glasmon and Bright used in their novel. It has dominated, and therefore skewed, many recent interpretations of the movie. These regard the grapefruit assault as a major escalation in the war of men against women, opening the way for an atmosphere of misogyny in the early days of talking pictures that has grown more entrenched in American movies with the passing decades.

Clearly, the symbolic import of this scene has grown retrospectively. Reviewers in 1931 did not even mention it, caught up as they were in the film's general atmosphere of violence—including even more physically punishing attacks on women, as when Tom slaps Jane or pushes his mother. It misses the point, however, to think of Tom Powers solely as a misogynist, as one who hates women.

Tom does not hate women: he is drawn to women and dependent on them, and if he hates anything, it is the vulnerability and passivity—his softie side—that his dependence forces him to acknowledge. The men and boys in the Great Depression audience who responded to Cagney's performance, and the women, too, were drawn not merely to the violence, but to the actor's portrayal of the complex personality that lay behind it. Cagney's playfulness and humor partially redeemed his gangster character, made Tom Powers vivid, likeable, and pathetic in his own violent end.

■ ■ ■ ■

In the same month, April 1932, that Lincoln Kirstein's essay appeared, hailing James Cagney as the new American hero, the actor staged a heroic—or foolish—revolt against his employer, the Warner Bros. motion picture company. The anarchy and tendency toward destruction that Kirstein celebrated in Cagney's screen persona seemed truly to be traits of the man behind the image.

In the midst of one of the most desperate and uncertain periods in the nation's history—while the Bonus Army marched on Washington and was routed by federal troops; when dairy farmers poured milk into the road to protest the two cents a quart they were getting for milk; in a year when Warner Bros. was to report a net loss of over $14 million—Cagney refused to work until his salary of $1400 a week was raised. His walkout (in effect, a one-man strike) lasted six months, and the conflict was resolved only after the movie industry stepped in to arbitrate the dispute. Cagney achieved his goal: his salary was more than doubled. But a stormy actor-studio relationship had turned into an embittered one.

The conflict between Cagney and Warners seems grotesque by any standard outside the movie industry itself; but one of its ironic consequences was to propel Cagney into the wider world of social struggle. The very excess of means that Cagney came to command in the midst of national crisis compelled him, as it did others in the movie field—out of guilt or altruism or a need to be involved in the issues of their times—to use his outsize income in support of social causes. Within a short time, in a forgotten (and also biographically suppressed) episode of his career, Cagney became the first major movie industry figure to gain national headlines for a reported involvement in Communist activities. There is a connection, therefore, between the bizarre financial squabble of 1932 and the later political crises that would come to dominate Hollywood, involving Cagney along with Bogart, Garfield, and many others.

In 1932, however, the single issue was money. The struggle actually had begun a year earlier, a few weeks after *The Public Enemy*'s release confirmed the studio's expectation that Cagney would be a sensation. By that point the actor had already completed work in two more films following *The Public Enemy*. Zanuck had worked fast after grasping, midway through production on the gangster film, that he had, more or less accidentally, uncovered a potential gold mine: he assigned Cagney almost as a special project to writers Glasmon and Bright, the original creators of Tom Powers.

At that moment the writers were working on a script for Edward G. Robinson as a follow-up to *Little Caesar*. The Jewish actor who had won fame as an Italian gangster would, in *Smart Money* (1931), change his ethnic stripes and play a Greek barber turned big-city gambler. Zanuck ordered a small part in the picture to be built up with five or six more scenes so it could serve as a suitable follow-up for Cagney, too. "Little Caesar and The Public Enemy . . . Together!"—the eventual promotional angle had already become obvious. They even wrote in a scene of Robinson and Cagney eating grapefruit for breakfast. Such a reference to a previous film was a frequent practice in 1930s studio movies. It rewarded regular movie-goers with a kind of intertextual prize, while promoting the studio's general product line. Robinson was paid $35,000 for his four weeks' work on *Smart Money*; Cagney got $1600.

Glasmon and Bright then set to work concocting an original story expressly for Cagney, even before *The Public Enemy*'s release. Again they turned to their Chicago roots and built a tale of con artists, based on the so-called "Larceny Lane" section of a fashionable hotel lobby, where confidence men and prostitutes mingled. In *Blonde Crazy* (1931), Cagney starts out as a bellhop, advances to con man, then makes a redeeming sacrifice before being carted off to jail. It was his first major role as other than a gangster: he speaks in a deeper voice, without accents or fractured grammar. When the film finished production, he was sent home on July 7, 1931, for the full twelve-week layoff on his second contract year. That's when the trouble started.

It all has an indistinct air (unlike the all-too-specific grievances of later struggles). Cagney headed back east for his three-month vacation; almost as soon as he arrived, Warners called him back to work. The problem was, there was no work for him to do; Glasmon and Bright were working on a new script for the performer, adapted from an unproduced play about the New York taxi industry, but it was far from ready. If they had decided belatedly that it was folly to allow their newest box office sensation to lie fallow for the next three months, there was little they could do about it (no other project was mentioned). The studio's action has the appearance of a pure gesture of power—the "divine right" of movie companies to control their stars' lives.

Cagney refused to return. Following standard procedure when temperamental talent balked at orders, the studio suspended him, removing him from the payroll. Here was another problem: he already *was* off the payroll, and expected to continue so for another couple of months. All through August 1931, Warner Bros. officially held back nonexistent sums, and Glasmon and Bright worked feverishly on their uncompleted script. In early September Cagney was restored "in the good graces of the company," and began production on *Taxi!* (1932) while the studio put the final touches on a new five-year contract paying him $1400 a week.[5]

Taxi! was to become a symptomatic text for progressives who had hopes that the economic crisis might impel Hollywood—or give more opportunity for progressives working in the movie industry—to portray working people acting in a united and militant way. The film provided sufficient promise of what they were looking for, but its failure to go further only deepened their disappointment in mainstream commercial filmmaking. The first part depicts the struggles of independent taxi drivers against Consolidated, a monopolistic taxi combine. It draws a sympathetic portrait of the taxi drivers, and hints at their capacity for collective action. Soon, however, the focus shifts to crime drama, abandoning further treatment of economic structures in favor of the traditional emphasis on evil individuals as the cause of social inequities. Cagney's role displayed similar contradictions: his screen figure shows a new maturity as a taxi driver who falls in love and marries (Loretta Young plays the wife), but his quick temper and violence toward women still link him temperamentally to Tom Powers.

Cagney's screen persona was developing through his own performance style and the successive characters created by writers Glasmon and Bright. Who directed their scripts did not seem to matter much; for the record, they were studio hands Alfred E. Green on *Smart Money* and Roy Del Ruth on *Blonde Crazy* and *Taxi!* The next project, however, changed the power mix considerably. The writers were handed an original story by Howard Hawks, who had also persuaded the studio to let him direct it.

Hawks was the most successful independent director in Hollywood history. He went from studio to studio—over a nearly fifty-year career he worked at every one of the eight major companies—blatantly flouting budget restrictions, ignoring production schedules, and undermining studio rules. Others who defied the studio moguls in even minor ways found themselves blackballed from the industry, but Hawks managed to thrive through rebellion and disdain. It is one of Hollywood's greatest mysteries.

Among Hawks's subversive practices—here, for once, subversion is the proper word—was to reconceive the screen personas of a studio's stars. *The Crowd Roars* (1932) offers a different Cagney than had been seen previously. Playing a race car driver, the actor gives what might be called his first adult performance—he is more subdued and intense, and he does without the incessant smiling and hand movements that had been a dominant part of his gestural repertoire.

Reaction to *The Crowd Roars* was contradictory. Newspaper reviewers panned the film, and many expressed their dislike for the change in Cagney's screen persona by judging his performance as weak, or below par. But, if for no other reason than its thrilling auto racing sequences, the film did well at the box office; perhaps the public liked better a Cagney who did not throw punches at women. For Warner Bros., however, the negative press response to Cagney required remedial action. Hawks could not be disciplined, since he was not on the payroll, but Glasmon and Bright remained to take the heat. *The Crowd Roars* was their last Cagney picture, and both left the studio before the end of 1932.

Care of Cagney was transferred to writers Robert Lord and Wilson Mizner, whose scripts were breezier, more satirical, and more topical than Glasmon and Bright's work. Their first effort for him, *Winner Take All* (1932), was about a battered prizefighter who temporarily becomes a darling of Park Avenue society. That was finished in March 1932, and Cagney was given a three-week layoff. Round number two of his personal fight was about to begin.

■ ■ ■ ■

The layoff began on April 1, 1932. Cagney left by train for New York. When he arrived, there was a notice waiting for him from the studio, ordering him to report back. This was a deliberate provocation: You are a yo-yo, we hold the string. Warner Bros. was geared up for a confrontation. They expected the actor to refuse to report, and he obliged them. Both Zanuck and Harry Warner fired off notes to Jack L. with gleeful suggestions on how to make the actor suffer.

Once again, it was a dispute over weekly salary figures that, for many in the motion picture audience, would have amounted to a year's pay. Unlike the 1931 disagreement, which seemed merely tactical, this one went on all through the spring and summer of 1932. As was customary in the movie industry, Warner Bros. blackballed the actor, informing other studios of their conflict and warning them not to employ him. Cagney gave interviews saying that he might give up his movie career and study to become a doctor.

For Warner Bros., what was at stake was its power over actors; the viability of contracts was not a principle it could claim, since contracts were enforced so inconsistently. For Cagney, the issue (however untoward it might appear in such a time of crisis) was a more equitable share of his value to the studio. Ultimately, as it turned out, what the studio most wanted was to have Cagney making pictures that might help their balance sheet in a money-losing time; after six months the problem was to find a way to save face. This was provided by the Academy of Motion Picture Arts and Sciences, which was then functioning as the industry's company union. It called an arbitration hearing. In one evening, meeting with the Academy's committee and separately, Cagney and Warner hammered out a new agreement.

Cagney would be paid $3000 a week, more than double the previous figure. Some $1250 of this, however, would be held back—placed in a trust account as a hedge against future walkouts or production disruptions by the actor. In this manner, the studio could announce that Cagney's salary had been raised only $350 a week, rather than $1600. Other agreements may or may not have been reached that evening; these putative deals would become bones of contention in a later, even further escalation of their struggles.

The picture Cagney had refused back in April, *Blessed Event* (1932), was already in the theaters, with Lee Tracy (whom Cagney had understudied in George Abbott's *Broadway*) in the lead role. He went back to work on a new production, with a script by Lord and Mizner, directed by Mervyn LeRoy, called *Hard to Handle* (1933). His character was referred to by the nickname "Lefty"; he was a con artist with the habit of running away from the scene of conflicts he had created. This film has the curious distinction of being his only performance from the early 1930s that Cagney does not mention in his autobiography. For Warner Bros., *Hard to Handle* clearly was a biopic about its own most difficult star.

"Lefty" is a thought-provoking nickname. During his half-year without movie work Cagney, known as an avid reader, had read one of the most important books of the early Depression years, *The Autobiography of Lincoln Steffens* (1931), in which the famed journalist and reformer uttered his much-quoted line about the Soviet Union: "I have been over into the future, and it works."[6] Then in his mid-seventies, Steffens lived in Carmel, in northern California, and enjoyed mingling with the progressive community in Hollywood.

While *Hard to Handle* was in production, Steffens visited Los Angeles and met Cagney at a lunch. Cagney and his wife became friends with Steffens and his wife, Ella Winter, an activist and author of a book based on her recent travels in the Soviet Union, *Red Virtue: Human Relations in the New Russia*, published in 1933. Through this connection, Cagney's political involvements developed. He moved from a highly publicized struggle with Warner Bros. to a low-profile commitment to struggles larger than his own; low-profile, that is, until it hit the front pages of the nation's newspapers.

■ ■ ■ ■

When *Picture Snatcher*, the Cagney film that followed *Hard to Handle*, was released in May 1933, one New York reviewer described its notable features—barroom brawls, the "nervous atmosphere" of a tabloid newspaper city room, scenes of desperate gangsterism—as instances of "the modern temper." Many of his readers would have recognized this phrase not as an empty cliché but as a catchword for the cultural spirit of the times; it derived from Joseph Wood Krutch's 1929 book *The Modern Temper* (in which, as Alfred Kazin wrote, "a whole postwar generation found its primer").[7]

Krutch's book was about the sense of loss felt by the disillusioned young intellectuals of the 1920s: loss of the certainties that had sustained their parents' generation, of the faith and the values that World War I had exalted and consumed. He saw his own generation of pessimists and skeptics losing the emotional vigor and energy that those discarded myths had sustained. Power was passing from intellectuals, Krutch wrote, to a new type of man: one who lacked myth and poetry, was devoid of transcendental cravings—perhaps even of soul—but who possessed "a cunning adaptation to the conditions of physical life." This was a new barbarian, "too absorbed in living to feel the need for thought." These new men were besieging the old civilization not, as in the past, as savage hordes from without, but from "within the confines of our own cities."[8]

To the scribes of the entertainment pages, James Cagney's screen persona *was* this new man: the modern barbarian emerging from the city streets to take on the physical world without illusion. When *Picture Snatcher* opened in Great Britain, the London *Times* wrote of Cagney's character: "He is a man of action, and he never thinks." The observation was not merely an echo of Krutch's book, or of the earlier New York reviews, but demonstrated how omnipresent these ideas were.

As Cagney films began to roll off the Warner assembly line after the Academy settlement—five were released in 1933, four in 1934—reviewers were compelled to hunt for fresh synonyms to describe this man of action. Cagney was vigorous, vital, and alert, they wrote. He was pugnacious, belligerent, hard-boiled. He was exuberant; he had gusto and swagger. He carried the aura of urban excitement. As the public relations con artist of *Hard to Handle*, as the ex-convict newspaper photographer of *Picture Snatcher*, as the small-time crook turned movie star of *Lady Killer* (1933), as the heir chaser of *Jimmy the Gent* (1934), he was the dynamo of energy, the maestro of cunning, unburdened by faded illusions, surviving and succeeding in the modern world.

With *He Was Her Man* (1934), among the last and most unusual of this period's films, the London *Times* reviewer made what may seem, in retrospect, an inevitable comparison to the literary paragon of the modern temper—Ernest Hemingway. "The gruff and unornamental manner of Mr. Hemingway's and other American novels," the reviewer wrote, "together with the unbridled romanticism which so often lurks beneath it, could hardly be more clearly or completely displayed than in this film." Cagney, said the writer, "is as necessary to the film as Mr. Hemingway's prose style is to his novels, and an admirable substitute for it." *He Was Her Man* was not an entirely accurate index of Cagney's performance style: the actor usually relied more often on the gift of gab than in this film, or in comparison with Hemingway's laconic heroes. The correlation of performance style and prose style, however, was shrewd, and remains provocative. Both styles (Cagney's and Hemingway's) were based on physicality—the act without the thought. For a number of 1930s commentators, Cagney, like Hemingway's heroes, became an exemplar of modern man.

The problem for the performer in being elevated to this role, however, was that the discourse was not always capable of distinguishing style from actuality. The *New York Times* alluded to this in a rave article about the actor in July 1934: "He was, and continues to be, so brilliantly right in his interpretation of a particular type of the American male, a type that has been spawned in large numbers out of the slum districts of New York and Chicago, that it is a natural thing to suspect that he is not acting at all."[9]

Within the Warner Bros. organization a minor dispute arose over whether to exploit this propensity to imagine Cagney's performance style as a natural emanation of his own character. While the West Coast studio, in charge of production publicity, fostered an image of an offscreen Cagney who was quiet, bookish, a homebody, the New York office, promoting pictures when they were released, seized on the "slumdom to stardom" theme. With *Lady Killer*, to be sure, the West Coast gave New York plenty to work with. Cagney's character plays a New York sharpie (with a job as usher at the company's showcase Times Square theater, the Strand) who goes to Hollywood and becomes a star. Warner East Coast publicists built a campaign around the film as Cagney biography: "Here's your ticket to see the story of Jimmie's own sensational screen career written in living drama!" In Burbank, the executives who had to work on a daily basis with the actor found this "exceptionally bad."[10]

Cagney had reason to feel ambivalent about his reputation as exemplar of the new barbarians. When Franklin D. Roosevelt became President and launched his New Deal program in March 1933, the emotional vigor and energy of intellectual life, however much it had slackened in earlier years, surely quickened. Revitalizing myths and illusions proved easier to find than Joseph Wood Krutch had anticipated. Cagney himself aspired to participate in these intellectual movements, through his friendship with Lincoln Steffens. "An earnest fellow," was how Steffens described Cagney in a letter to his wife, "eager to do better and better" as an actor.[11]

The most popular of Cagney's films in this period—the musical *Footlight Parade* (1933)—was, in fact, the most New Dealish, and the one in which he played his least barbarian role. Cagney's character is Chester Kent, artistic director of a company producing "prologues": stage entertainments performed in conjunction with movie screenings. (Fanchon and Marco, the most famous prologue producers of the era, served as a model for the movie's fictitious company.) The story line concerns Kent's efforts to persuade a skeptical owner of a movie theater chain that the prologues had box office value, despite the higher costs of live entertainment. Cagney is the dynamic leader and idea man who steps in at the last moment to sing and dance in the climactic production number, "Shanghai Lil," staged by Busby Berkeley. This ends in a famous overhead shot of dancers, carrying color cards, forming first the American flag, then Roosevelt's face, and finally the Blue Eagle emblem of the New Deal's National Recovery Administration.

Footlight Parade was the third of Warner Bros.' Busby Berkeley musicals of 1933. In box office draw it ranked behind its predecessors, *42nd Street* and *Golddiggers of 1933*. Still, the picture earned around $1.5 million in rental income (the studio's share of box office receipts), and produced a net profit of over $1 million—twice the picture's negative costs. It was by far the most financially successful of all of Cagney's early 1930s films, and it made a big dent in Warner Bros.' deficit, which ran over $6 million in 1933.

Moreover, the picture appealed to filmgoers without the benefit of good reviews: critics were lukewarm, if not hostile. They panned the musical's book, and said of "the ruthless Mr. Cagney" only that his performance displayed his versatility as a song-and-dance man.

The Busby Berkeley dance numbers, wrote Richard Watts, Jr., in the *New York Herald-Tribune,* provided a clue "to all of the fantastic combination of spendthrift imagination and naive lack of sensibility which apparently is Hollywood." Naive lack of sensibility—well, that charge might sting—but spendthrift, as far as Warner Bros. was concerned, never.

Reviewers, it seems, preferred Cagney the barbarian slum dweller to Cagney the cosmopolitan showman. *Footlight Parade's* popularity, however, suggested that public taste was at odds with critical opinion. When *He Was Her Man* was released in 1934, *Variety* shrewdly observed that critics would like it and the public would not. It was right on both counts: it did less business than any other picture Cagney made at Warners after he became a star. Reviewers themselves sometimes questioned whether the ruthless Mr. Cagney would appeal to audiences in the hinterlands, beyond his devoted following of urban ethnics who swarmed to the Strand in Times Square. They also wondered if repeated scenes of violence against women were limiting his box office potential.

Cagney's audience was in fact primarily urban. His other, more characteristic productions were barely earning one fourth in rentals of what *Footlight Parade* brought in. Because they were made so cheaply, with negative costs (including the share of studio overhead and depreciation that each picture had to carry) below $250,000, they made money. Still, the popularity of Cagney's song-and-dance performance gave Warner Bros. pause. During 1933 his screen persona became a subject of discussion at the studio. Up through *Hard to Handle,* his stories and characters had been created by the successive writing teams of Glasmon-Bright and Mizner-Lord. After that, various writers were the sources of original stories and scripts. Studio management, rather than any of its creative personnel, regarded itself as the "author" of Cagney's character.

This is clear from the recorded notes of a story conference Darryl Zanuck held with the writers of *Lady Killer* in the spring of 1933. The executive pointedly reminded the writers about the studio's requirements for Cagney's character. He instructed them to develop Cagney's part "more in accord with the kind of character Cagney plays best on the screen as, whenever Cagney departs from this type of characterization, audiences do not like him." (This could have referred only to *The Crowd Roars.*) "He has got to be tough, fresh, hard-boiled, bragging—he knows everything, everybody is wrong but him—everything is easy to him—he can do everything and yet it is a likeable trait in his personality."[12]

This sounds simple, but it was not. Five months later, when all of *Footlight Parade* was completed except the "Shanghai Lil" number, after Zanuck had departed and been replaced as associate executive by Hal Wallis, frantic rewriting and reconstructing of the *Lady Killer* script were still going on. The production start loomed. When offered the directing assignment, Roy Del Ruth (who had directed Cagney in *Blonde Crazy, Taxi!,* and *Winner Take All*) tried to beg off. He told Wallis that the script was "nothing but a hodge podge of loosely constructed routines that are similar in appearances and treatment to nearly every gangster picture that Cagney [has] appeared in."[13] Del Ruth nevertheless took it on, and turned the picture into a fairly funny hodgepodge, a gangster-Hollywood-comedy-drama. But when it was released, box office returns fell back down to pre–*Footlight Parade* levels.

This production inaugurated a new crisis in Cagney's relationship with his employer—the issue this time was not money but screen persona and performance. Management appeared to be floundering in its role as "author." Despite some executives' concern about the melding of actor and fictional character in the publicity for *Lady Killer,* his next picture, *Jimmy the Gent,* marked the first and only time Cagney's given name was used in a film title. The script called for him to revert to the street accents and bad grammar of his earlier slum boy–barbarian roles. He may have been making a silent protest against this project when he appeared on the set with the sides of his head shaved, Prussian-style, also for the first and only time in his career.

Jimmy the Gent also marked, more significantly, the beginning of Cagney's efforts to claim for himself the role of "author" of his screen persona and performances. He began to alter, on the set, the studio's version of his character that Zanuck had articulated for *Lady Killer.* Wallis, who closely monitored the daily rushes and made extensive comments by memo to producers and directors, complained to director Michael Curtiz that Cagney was "trying [too] hard to characterize" his role. "I visualize James Cagney in this picture as a fast talking, smart alecky, smart cracking mug," the executive wrote. To Wallis, Cagney was not playing the part sufficiently "in the typical Cagney manner."[14] The actor indeed had begun to rebel against playing the mug.

Fortuitously, Cagney was aided by the policies of the newly empowered self-regulating arm of the producers' association, the Production Code Administration. This body began its work of reviewing scripts and finished pictures in 1934, in an effort to stem public demands for greater state censorship of screen sex and violence. One of its first targets was the newest Cagney picture, *He Was Her Man*. This modest gangster film, paradoxically, gave Cagney one of his best parts of the period, as an ex-gangster who nobly sacrifices himself to save the heroine (the original story was by Robert Lord). But the PCA demanded changes in the ending before it would allow the picture to be released, and later banned the film entirely. Box office returns plunged to even lower levels. Wallis faced a dilemma: he wanted Cagney to play the rowdy and vulgar mug, but the actor, the moviegoing public, and now the industry's watchdog seemed aligned against him.

Warner Bros.' management found a nimble solution: put the rowdy and vulgar mug in a military uniform. Perhaps as a sign of their close ties to the Roosevelt administration, the Warners had launched a series of films promoting military preparedness. One, about naval training, had the working title "Join the Navy." Segments were shot aboard the battleship USS *Arizona* (one of the vessels sunk on December 7, 1941, in the Japanese attack on Pearl Harbor, with heavy loss of life). It was released as *Here Comes the Navy* (1934), with Cagney playing a cynical working-class tough who becomes a navy man.

Reviewers marveled that "bad boy," "sassy," "tuffy" Cagney could make his way through a film without punching a lady. Even the strictest movie moralist, wrote one, could find this effort "clean as a snowdrift." An even greater marvel, from the studio's perspective, was what happened in movie theaters: on a budget no less modest than those for Cagney's earlier projects (negative costs under $250,000), the picture earned over $800,000 in rentals, more than double what the actor's recent films had been bringing in. To top it off, *Here Comes the Navy* was nominated for an Academy Award as Best Picture (the movie industry must have wanted to display its patriotism, because Warner's military musical *Flirtation Walk* also won a Best Picture nomination that year).

The sour note in this success story came from Cagney; his performance is suffused with an egregious self-mocking manner. His next assignment can be understood only as punishment for insubordination. It was tantamount to a B picture (the Warner B unit had not yet been formally established), with a breakneck twenty-day shooting schedule and a minuscule $155,000 budget. Worst of all, Cagney's character in *The St. Louis Kid* (1934) is a truck driver who is assigned to end a strike of milk farmers.

There was trouble from the start. Wallis complained about Cagney's performance as soon as he saw the first rushes. He wrote to director Ray Enright: "When [Cagney] first read the script, he objected to playing another tough character and I can see that he is doing his best to soften him up and make him as much of a gentleman as possible and still keep him a truck driver. . . . There is naturally an objection to slugging dames and all that stuff today but, at the same time, we don't want to lose Cagney's real characterization which is a semi-tough character."[15]

In his next missive Wallis told the director that the boss, Jack L. Warner, had endorsed his criticisms: "I want you to call me on the phone when you get this and let me know if you are directing the picture or if Cagney is directing it."[16] Cagney had shifted the field of battle, and the weapons. The struggle was now out in the open on the sound stage, and the issue was how much power he could have to determine "Cagney's real characterization."

■ ■ ■ ■

Three days after *The St. Louis Kid* finished shooting, the actual Cagney (not his characterization) became front-page news. "Film Actor Named in Coast Red Plot," ran the headline in the *New York Times* of August 18, 1934. Police in Sacramento, California, had raided what they described as the city's "Communist headquarters" and seized documents that led to the indictment of seventeen persons on charges of criminal syndicalism. The most sensational disclosure in the press accounts was a letter from Ella Winter to Caroline Decker, secretary of the Cannery and Industrial Workers Union, concerning James Cagney's financial support.

"I have Cagney's money again," the letter was quoted as saying. "I could send some for the strikers—but I want to send it for gas and oil for the pickets, for food relief, not for defense at present." Elsewhere she wrote, "Cagney is fine this time and is going to bring other stars up to talk with Stef about communism." Other letters mentioned Cagney's role in the Screen Actors Guild, "the employees' rebellion against the producers," and gave Cagney's address in Beverly Hills if Miss Decker wanted to write him for typewriter ribbons.[17] The following day reports surfaced that the names of Lupe Velez, Delores del Rio, and Ramon Navarro were found in the alleged Communist files. This seemed to suggest that someone had been searching for names of Hispanic performers who might be approached to lend support to a Hispanic workers' cause; the additional revelation took some of the onus off Cagney as the sole movie personality implicated, and lent a certain air of fantasy to the whole connection between film actors and a "Red plot."

Cagney denied having given money to support communism, and Steffens told the press that Cagney's contributions had gone to relieve misery in a San Joaquin Valley cotton strike. This was not yet the era of McCarthyism: it appeared to be no more than a two-day wonder in the papers, although headlines flared again when the trial of the seventeen began in January 1935. Still, Warner Bros. had to be concerned about the popularity of its star. There was less to fear from public reaction, in those Great Depression days of radical ferment, than from a hostile campaign by the right-wing press. Fortunately for the studio, the most fearsome figure of the right-wing press had just come knocking at its door.

Publishing magnate William Randolph Hearst, the figure in question, also operated a motion picture production company, Cosmopolitan Pictures. It had been associated for a dozen years with Metro-Goldwyn-Mayer, where its principal function was to produce starring vehicles for the publisher's paramour, comedienne Marion Davies. In mid-summer 1934 Hearst and Metro had a falling-out, and Cosmopolitan shifted its base to Warner Bros. Soon the private bungalow of Miss Davies would be placed on a truck and hauled across town from Culver City to Burbank. Some months were to pass, however, before Davies would go before the Warner Bros. cameras. In the meantime, William Randolph Hearst was assigned a substitute star: James Cagney. The "Lefty" of *Hard to Handle* was about to change his moniker to "Righty."

Without reading the trade press—or the Hearst press—one would not have known that William Randolph Hearst had financed two Cagney pictures. The name Cosmopolitan does not appear anywhere on their title credits. The most important clues were the rave reviews that appeared in Hearst's chain of newspapers. The first Cosmopolitan production, *Devil Dogs of the Air* (1935), was virtually a remake of *Here Comes the Navy*, with Cagney now playing a U.S. Marine Corps pilot (along with his chum and rival from the navy picture, Pat O'Brien). The non-Hearst press greeted the picture as the derivative, formulaic work it was, but it turned out to be another box office success.

After completing this project, Cagney put in an appearance in Warners' expensive film version of Max Reinhardt's production of *A Midsummer Night's Dream* (1935). His role was as one of Shakespeare's performing mechanics, Bottom the Weaver, whom the impish Puck transforms by replacing his head with an ass's. One has to wonder what Warner executives thought this would do for Cagney's screen characterization, and if any among them derived satisfaction from seeing their troublesome star wearing an ass's head.

For their battles resumed on the second Cosmopolitan picture, *G Men* (1935). The plan, with the story and screenplay by Seton I. Miller, was to construct a new, doubled Cagney characterization—he could be both Tom Powers and the dynamic leader of *Footlight Parade*, a barbarian and a New Dealer at the same time. The spectator could respond to the Cagney she or he liked best: a slum kid who dedicates himself to serving the state, or the old familiar rough and vulgar mug beneath a new bureaucratic veneer.

This was having the cake and eating it, too. Though the PCA had placed a ban on gangster pictures, how could you show the FBI smashing criminals without plenty of gangland violence and clattering machine guns? Cagney plays a lawyer who was put through school by a benevolent mobster. When he sees a boyhood pal, now an FBI agent, shot down, he joins the FBI and vows to bring the killers to justice. This gives his character a chance to be integrated into sensational scenes drawn directly from the daily headlines (the Kansas City Massacre; the raid on Little Bohemia, Wisconsin) out of which the FBI was already constructing a legend of its triumphs over Depression-era gangsters like John Dillinger, "Baby Face" Nelson, and "Pretty Boy" Floyd.

G Men was a clever idea; the only roadblock was the star. Cagney resisted delivering the performance the studio was looking for. Wallis's memos to director William Keighley might have been carbon copies of those he sent to Enright on *The St. Louis Kid*. Cagney's scenes had no "guts," no "sock." The actor was playing the role too soft. "I can't seem to get you to let the fellow be a mug from the East side," the executive wrote. "We can have him a little more of the old Cagney character, with a little tougher accent and not being so perfect in his English." Wallis ordered a new scene added to the opening sequence, to have Cagney punch out a crooked ward heeler; this would toughen up his character a little, make clear that he was once a "gutter rat" despite his LL.B., Ph.D., and Phi Beta Kappa key.[18]

The tough little mug working for the good guys achieved the double appeal the studio was aiming for. At the Strand in Times Square—the temple for Cagney's metropolitan fans—the picture ran from 8:00 A.M. to 4:00 A.M. But its appeal reached far beyond the urban faithful. Made on the standard quarter-million-dollar budget for Cagney films ($260,000 was the exact figure), *G Men* was the first since *Footlight Parade* to earn more than $1 million in rentals.

A threshold had been crossed in the actor's popular appeal. A modest, sentimental ethnic comedy, *The Irish in Us* (1935), made on a $240,000 budget, immediately topped *G Men* and was to earn over $1.3 million in domestic and foreign rentals, bringing in an astounding million-dollar profit. Reviewers could not recount the plot, they noted bemusedly, because audience laughter drowned out the dialogue.

In the film, Cagney, O'Brien, and Frank McHugh play Irish brothers on Manhattan's Lower East Side. Mary Gordon is their lovable Ma, and the seventeen-year-old Olivia de Havilland, shortly after her screen debut as Hermia in *A Midsummer Night's Dream*, was cast as the boys' romantic interest. The Cagney-O'Brien-McHugh trio (along with the redoubtable Warners supporting player, Allen Jenkins) supplied most of the laughs, but the fresh and charming de Havilland also made a substantial contribution to the picture's success. Her future after this film had no more room for low-budget surprises: she went into the studio's new cycle of million-dollar costume epics like *Captain Blood* (1935) and *Charge of the Light Brigade* (1936) with Errol Flynn, not Cagney, as her co-star.

The felicitous but singular pairing of Cagney and de Havilland emphasized by its triumph the absence of strong female counterparts in Cagney's previous work. The crux of the problem was that the studio's conception of the barbarian mug left little room for romance; it wanted women characters not so much to love him as to tame him. But Warner Bros. also lacked female leads who could hold their own with the actor. For some reason, the partnership with Joan Blondell that had begun on Broadway and in *Sinner's Holiday* was never exploited by the studio, although they appeared effectively together in *Blonde Crazy*, *The Crowd Roars*, *Footlight Parade*, and *He Was Her Man*. Bette Davis, whose screen characterization was as much a problem as Cagney's, didn't click with him in *Jimmy the Gent*.

When Warners borrowed female leads from other companies it often chose patrician types like Virginia Bruce (*Winner Take All*) and Gloria Stuart (*Here Comes the Navy*) who could put the street tough in his place. By 1935, except for the de Havilland picture, the studio seemed to have settled on supporting player Margaret Lindsay as Cagney's female partner. In *Devil Dogs of the Air*, *G Men*, and *Frisco Kid* (1935), she functioned more effectively as governess than as girlfriend.

In mid-decade, however, there were more serious concerns with Cagney's screen career than Warner Bros.' failure to come up with adequate female pairings. The left-wing monthly *New Theatre*, in a perceptive but troubled appreciation of the actor, identified the issue as a transformation of his movie roles. The article began by repeating the (by now familiar) theme of Cagney's special rapport with city men, but gave this notion a more pointed ideological perspective:

"Cagney is the perfect portrait of the American urban man and boy, whose life is so insecure and dangerous that the only buckler they can forge for themselves up to the present has been in the anarchic, ruthless, funny and tender violence which is apparent (as their reflection) in his every gesture;—his walk, his nervous fists, his abrupt silences and his steady mounting rage." The dilemma it posed was that this remarkable screen persona was faced with increasingly inappropriate story material with which to work.

A few months earlier the same journal had urged readers to boycott Hearst-produced films, including *Devil Dogs of the Air* and *G Men*. It had also referred to *Frisco Kid* (1935), Cagney's first period piece, set in gold rush days, as a "strike-breaking" film. The article on Cagney ended by imagining his situation as "quite intolerable" as he "finds himself forced into testimonials against the best possibilities of that class from which he springs and whose heroic representative he could be."

Taxi! was compared with the Clifford Odets play about a taxi strike that was the sensation of 1935 in New York's radical cultural circles: "*Waiting For Lefty* would have made the real picture that all of Cagney's well-wishers have been expecting since *The Public Enemy*."[19] "Forrest Clark," the author of this article, counted as one of Cagney's earliest well-wishers; it was the *nom de plume* of the man who in 1932 had written "James Cagney and the American Hero," Lincoln Kirstein.

Lefty Cagney would not arrive. *Frisco Kid* indeed was Cagney's most reactionary picture: after many scenes of brutal violence, it climaxes when the respectable classes rise up with an outburst of vigilante retribution, smashing saloons and gambling dens on the Barbary Coast and executing the movie's bad guys. *New Theatre* had good cause to interpret the film as a reaction to San Francisco's 1934 general strike—and as representing a conservative urge to adopt means beyond the law to preserve the existing social order. Cagney plays one of the brutal, violent upstarts; he is saved from the gallows only by the intervention of a genteel woman (the aforementioned Margaret Lindsay). She pleads before the vigilante committee's hanging judges that his capitalist instincts have been perverted by bad company, and would flourish in the right environment. The picture could be read as yet another Warner Bros. parable of Cagney's career.

Within the studio's executive suites, the forces of law and order were equally wary of Cagney himself. In September 1934—hardly a month after the press headlined his name in connection with the Sacramento "Red plot"—Cagney's attorneys wrote Jack L. Warner asserting their understanding that, as part of the Academy arbitration two years earlier, Warner and the actor had made a private, verbal agreement limiting Cagney to no more than four pictures a year. "We are apparently about to have another battle with Cagney," wrote a Warner lawyer to the contract department head, "and it is my suggestion that the battle be pushed to a head before the end of Cagney's present term and while we have the trust fund available."[20]

Ah yes, the trust fund: a day had arrived when Warners executives would find its existence justified. In late March 1935, rushing to complete *G Men*, the studio planned both day and evening shooting sessions on the scheduled final day. Cagney worked from 10:00 A.M. to 5:40 P.M.; told to report back for more work at 7:00 P.M., he left the lot and did not return. The last scenes were postponed and completed the following day.

This was just the sort of insubordination the trust fund had been set up to penalize. The assistant director and the unit manager gave notarized depositions describing Cagney's refusal to return for the evening work session. A detailed breakdown of the extra day's costs was compiled—from Cagney's star salary to the lowliest grip's two-dollar-a-day wage. The direct cost came to $1820.12 (of which the director's and three star salaries made up fully two thirds); with overhead and depreciation added, the grand total reached $2420.76. This amount was to be deducted from the portion of Cagney's salary sequestered in the trust account; later, the figure was reduced to $1754.09 with the elimination of Cagney's day rate ($666.67) from the penalty charge. Even with this concession, as the Warner contract man told the lawyer, "I can assure you that it is not J.L.'s intention or desire to let Cagney get away with anything."[21]

The assurance was hollow. A month after Cagney's disobedience, the actor held a long conference with the boss—a rare event, since Jack L. Warner avoided face-to-face meetings with his stars, fearing they would get the better of him in such private sessions. In this case, his apprehension was merited. Warner told his contract man to cancel the trust fund charges. "Every time I turn around," the Warner lawyer railed, "I feel made more foolish with respect to any deal concerning Cagney. We are directed to do something, assume a definite stand and then feel the ground cut from under us."[22] Warner did not even have the satisfaction of gratitude from Cagney for his leniency. The matter of the purported verbal agreement was still hanging fire. Cagney's attitude was growing increasingly insubordinate. What could studio executives have been thinking when they placed the actor in the hands of Mr. Insubordination himself, director Howard Hawks, for *Ceiling Zero* (1935)?

The picture featured Cagney and Pat O'Brien doing their by now familiar buddy number as commercial airline pilots. On the set, in the usual Hawks manner, the atmosphere was free and easy. One day Hal Wallis sent the production supervisor a memo saying, "O'Brien is doing a little too much barking."[23] This note gave director and cast some ideas for script revision. In the finished picture, Cagney tells O'Brien, "I've got little cocker spaniel barks just the way you do," and yaps like a dog. In his death scene, Cagney's last words to O'Brien are: "Stop barking."

Shortly after the film was completed, Cagney's lawyer (a new one—it was not always easy to find attorneys in Los Angeles willing to take on a movie company) wrote Warner that his client would perform no further services until the alleged verbal agreement was incorporated into his contract. The studio ordered Cagney to report on a new picture, *Over the Wall*; he refused, and was suspended. The actor thereupon sued the studio in Los Angeles County Superior Court, seeking to cancel his contract.

Moviemaking is a litigious business, and suits by stars against their studios were not entirely rare. Old Warner Bros. hands remember the 1936 court case in England between Bette Davis and the studio (she lost), and also Olivia de Havilland's successful 1944 litigation. De Havilland's suit established the important principle that motion picture companies could not—through the suspension clause of standard contracts—hold an employee under contract for more than seven calendar years; it violated the law against involuntary servitude. Cagney's suit has disappeared from history. He assisted in the obfuscation, with brief and misleading references both in his autobiography and "authorized biography."

Cagney did say in *Cagney by Cagney* that the inequity he felt was that the studio was paying him "only a very small percentage of the income deriving from my work."[24] Indeed, it is likely that more money was his prime motivation, even though it was never mentioned in the suit (his salary was clearly spelled out in a contract running through October 1937). The complaint was pressed on the grounds that Jack L. Warner had, at the time of the Academy arbitration in September 1932, "falsely and fraudulently and with intent to deceive" promised Cagney that he would appear in no more than four pictures a year.[25] More appearances, the complaint argued, would destroy the plaintiff's popularity with the public.

The case came to trial on March 3, 1936. Both sides submitted depositions and affidavits alleging what promises were or were not made inside the hearing room, or outside, at the Academy back in 1932. Suddenly, a week into the trial, the plaintiff dropped a bombshell. Cagney's attorneys offered evidence that Warner Bros. had been advertising *Ceiling Zero* on billboards and on a theater marquee with Pat O'Brien's name above Cagney's, thus violating the plaintiff's contract clause guaranteeing him top male billing.

This broke the back of the Warner Bros. defense. Sitting without a jury, Judge Charles L. Bogue declared that the defendant had breached the contract by "improper billing that was not casual or inadvertent."[26] The question of whether a verbal promise had or had not been made back in 1932 got lost in the shuffle (the judge's decision implied that Warner had falsely and fraudulently made his promise, but that Cagney had waived his right to complain by continuing to work after discovering it). No matter: on April 2, 1936, Cagney's Warner Bros. contract was canceled, annulled, and terminated.

Significantly, the judge also issued an injunction preventing Warner Bros. from interfering with Cagney's employment at any other motion picture studio. Warners immediately announced its intention to appeal the decision to the California State Supreme Court, however, and it remained to be seen whether any of Warner Bros.' nominal competitors would dare touch Cagney while his contract dispute was still before the courts. The plaintiff nevertheless walked out of the courtroom to all appearances a free man, ready to take his destiny as a motion picture actor—and the valuable legacy of his unique screen persona, the representative of urban American men and boys—into his own hands.

II

City Boys as Hollywood Types

4

Baby Face

During the first half-decade of the 1930s—the years of James Cagney's rise to iconic status as the movies' resourceful working-class hero—Humphrey Bogart's career could just as vividly have become an emblem. He might have represented (had anyone else besides his closest friends been aware of them) the failures and disappointments far more commonly experienced during the Great Depression. He had flopped in Hollywood. He was stumbling as a stage actor. In a turbulent, hard-boiled, cynical era, he was trying to hang on as an overage juvenile, when audiences were barely tolerating the theatrical type in its proper youth.

Rose Hobart, a performer who played opposite Bogart in a Depression-defying 1932 Broadway confection, *I Loved You Wednesday*, remembered the actor at least as a person who confounded one's expectations. Instead of being nice when he was nobody and nasty when he was successful, he was a good guy when things were going well; in the early 1930s, therefore, he was "an absolute son of a bitch."[1]

Still, he possessed the will to face up to adversity, and overcome it. He took that step decisively in the fall of 1934, when he was invited to try out for a part in an upcoming Broadway play by Robert E. Sherwood, *The Petrified Forest*. It is not clear what part he went in to read for, but he emerged as Duke Mantee—the scarcely human, monosyllabic, ruthless killer of the play.

Movie and stage performer Blanche Sweet, also in the original cast, remembered that from the very first rehearsal Bogart had formed an interpretation of his character. He did not vary it, she said, by a single verbal inflection or facial expression throughout the entire six months of performances. Theater critics responded with skeptical admiration for an actor whom they had lately been calumniating for muffing his lines in indifferent comedies. That tired juvenile Humphrey Bogart, they wrote, "of all people," was scoring a success as one of the most violent men ever portrayed on the Broadway stage.

Within a year the role would (though not without further tribulations) return him to Hollywood, this time to stay. It would forever transform his public persona—except for moments when (to the delight of both the initiated and the unwitting) he would revert, with ironic high comedy, to the performance style of the juvenile romantic. How this opportunity came to him to change his stage image radically (and, even more importantly, how he was able to seize it) has never been satisfactorily explained. There are suggestive bits of evidence, however, that others had noticed his capacity for menace well before he was picked for Duke Mantee; and indeed that Bogart himself had begun to develop a darker side to his performance persona sometime earlier as well.

■ ■ ■ ■

There was, to begin with, his final film at Fox. *A Holy Terror* (1931) was a western in the improbable but not uncommon subgenre featuring a playboy-on-the-plains. At least he was not the playboy; but he did have a bigger part than in any other picture since *Up the River*. His role was as the playboy's antagonist, a surly ranch foreman.

Working against type did not improve Bogart's performance: he still looked uncomfortable and physically awkward, and did not know any better what to do with his hands, shifting them as before from belt to pockets, pockets to belt. What was remarkable, however, was how much older he appeared than when he had started a year earlier. Maybe it was merely a change of makeup: now he was a glowering, shadow-jawed adult, not the callow grinning boy of *A Devil with Women*. It was not a complete transformation; the *New York Daily News* reviewer called him "a bad man of the politer type." Still, the bland Dr. Jekyll becomes considerably more interesting when we realize that an evil Mr. Hyde lurks beneath the surface.

The problem for Bogart was getting an opportunity to display either of these personalities, the familiar old or the potential new. After Fox decided not to renew his option, he did not find steady work over the next three and one-half years. Though he appeared in six plays and four movies during this period, the Broadway notices grew increasingly snappish about his performances, and movie reviewers paid him no notice at all.

He returned to Hollywood in December 1931 to play the romantic lead opposite Dorothy MacKaill in a risqué but turgid comedy-drama, *Love Affair* (1932), produced by Columbia Pictures. He's a flying instructor, she's a playgirl; it's quite obvious that they sleep together out of wedlock. This quite perturbed the Hays Office, which, at the time, could do nothing about it. The moralists had the consolation that the picture played only one day in New York, as half of a double bill at Loews 83rd Street theater.

A few months later there was another movie opportunity as a non-contract player at Warner Bros. Director Mervyn LeRoy used him for small parts in two pictures; it appears that LeRoy thought he was getting Dr. Jekyll, then saw the potential of Mr. Hyde. The first role (originally intended for J. Carroll Naish) was as a New York party-goer in *Big City Blues* (1932). Bogart smiles and delivers desultory one-liners—this may be as close to a document of his Broadway stage persona as we can get. In the second film, *Three on a Match* (also 1932), however, he plays a gangster's henchman. He assumes a grating voice, a stern look, and an air of barely suppressed violence, accentuated by a new gesture of curling his upper lip and baring his teeth.

This was a small revelation; but nothing came of it. He went back to Broadway to appear in *I Loved You Wednesday*; Rose Hobart found his spirits as low as his prospects. There was, however, one more film in this most depressed interlude of his career. It was *Call It Murder* (1934), an independently produced adaptation of a Theatre Guild play, shot in New York in a rarely used silent era studio. A sign of the production's marginal status and meager resources was that they gave Bogart star billing, with his name before the title.

His role as Garboni, a "foreign" gangster, was in fact one of the lesser parts. Nevertheless, it gave him further opportunity to try out his new, harsher screen persona. Working alongside Theatre Guild actors (primarily playing his scenes with the actress Sidney Fox), he speaks in a style distinctively less theatrical than that of the others—more "down-to-earth" than anything he had done on-screen before. It was his voice that showed the promise of menace in this film, rather than his physical appearance and movement; he still had the callow look of a juvenile.

Bogart's performance in *Call It Murder* helps to sort out the legends surrounding his casting as Duke Mantee. It lends credence to the version that recounts how Arthur Hopkins, the Broadway director, soon after receiving Sherwood's new script in mid-1934, was attending one of Bogart's desultory stage vehicles. It was a mystery melodrama called *Invitation to Murder*. He heard the voice of an actor working hard to change himself from sweet to mean; he knew at once who would play Sherwood's killer.

This tale is more plausible than the competing version, which proposes that Sherwood, knowing of Bogart's desperate straits, put him forward for the part of Boze Hertzlinger, an ex–football player. In his biography of the playwright, John Mason Brown writes of Bogart, "He had the build. He bulged with strength. He was all male."[2] Brown must have been thinking of some other guy. Bogart was shorter and no less frail than the actor who was to play the effete intellectual, Leslie Howard. Put a football in Bogart's hands and the work might have turned into a drawing room comedy. Put a gun in an actor's hand, however, and his physique does not matter. In Bogart's voice Arthur Hopkins could hear the man with a gun.

What remained for the transition from Dr. Jekyll to Mr. Hyde to be complete was for the physical presence to match the voice. Bogart let his beard grow out into a stubble and wore his hair longer on top, shorter on the sides; these, however, were only cosmetic aspects of the character. More fundamentally, he (as Blanche Sweet remembered), or director Hopkins, or perhaps most plausibly the two together, had the transformative intuition that, as far as Mantee's character, less could be more. There had been enough of brawling, wisecracking gangsters. Mantee was a new breed (as Gramps says in the play, "gangsters is foreigners and he's an American")—a killer, plain and simple.

Bogart toned down his performance, speaking slowly, instead of rushing his words as he had in *Call It Murder*. He was seated through much of the play, moving little; when he did move, it was in an almost pathological way, his head lolling, arms swaying, fingers curled like claws. Now there was no uncertainty about where to put his hands. He made his awkwardness work for him. His Duke Mantee became a complete Mr. Hyde, a less-than-human shell in which a man was held. The tragedy for Dr. Jekyll became a triumph for Humphrey Bogart. Like the good doctor, however, he might soon wish for an elixir that could restore him from the monster he had become.

■ ■ ■ ■

Inevitably, Bogart saw *The Petrified Forest* as his ticket back to Hollywood. Warner Bros. purchased the movie rights to Sherwood's play for a hefty six-figure sum, and signed Leslie Howard at a substantial high five figures to repeat his starring Broadway role. Bogart asked Howard to support him for the movie part of Duke Mantee. As early as August 1935, with the film scheduled to begin shooting in mid-October, the casting department had penciled in Bogart as the third lead, behind Howard and Bette Davis, who would play Gabriele, a young artistic soul stranded in the great American desert.

Then studio politics intervened. The problem concerned what was perceived as the waning career of Edward G. Robinson. Jack L. Warner had become exasperated with the star. As Warner saw it, Robinson had far too generous a contract and was a malcontent (not unlike Cagney) who was refusing the gangster roles that had made him famous. Robinson had one more picture on the fat contract he had signed after *Little Caesar*, and after that Warner intended to let him go. Warner decided that Robinson's farewell performance should be as Duke Mantee: it was a big-budget picture that could absorb Robinson's $80,000 salary, and a presold product that Robinson's dimming box office prospects could not harm. Bogart's name was erased, Robinson's replaced it.

Here the legends once again take over. The standard version is that Leslie Howard told Jack Warner, in effect: Make this picture without Humphrey Bogart, and you make this picture without me. Would that friendships were always so steadfast! The archival record reveals only that on September 9, 1935, Howard in London sent a cable to Burbank stating: "Bogart asked me to approve him. Tell Mr. Warner Yes."[3]

What can be read into the gaps of this concise note—what else occurred that was never committed to paper—is anyone's guess. What is clear, however, is that the cable did not deter Warner Bros., even *after* it was received, from trying to persuade Robinson to appear in *The Petrified Forest*. The sticking point, it turned out, was Robinson himself. He refused to waive his contract provision giving him star billing over all other male performers. He would concede only to sharing co-star status with Leslie Howard, but nothing less. Warners had committed itself to Howard as the top-billed male star in *The Petrified Forest*. Since Robinson had recently been turning down gangster roles, his intransigence signaled that Duke Mantee was a part he did not want.

Finally, on October 7, with a week to go before the cameras rolled, Bogart signed a one-picture contract for *The Petrified Forest* at $750 per week, the same sum he had earned three years earlier in *Big City Blues* and *Three on a Match*. He was back in pictures, and how others were managing their careers had greater impact on his fortunes than how he was managing his own. Robinson's tactics, perhaps more than anyone else's, had gotten him through the door at Warner Bros.; now Cagney's behavior, fortuitously, seemed to be giving him a chance to stay.

It was on November 29, 1935, the day before *The Petrified Forest* finished shooting, that Cagney's lawyers informed the studio of its imputed breach of contract. Warner executives fully expected the struggle that quickly ensued—if not the court case and its surprise outcome. Robinson wanted nothing to do with gangster parts; Cagney was due for a suspension, at the very least. In the crime pictures that still formed a staple of the studio's production, who was there to supply the menace?

Here was a new figure, this man who did so well as Duke Mantee, and he came cheap. On December 10, 1935, Warner Bros. added Bogart to its collection of contract players. He signed for four half-year terms and five annual terms, starting at $550 a week and rising to $1750 in the seventh and final year—which would, should the contract run its course, be 1942. The year 1935 marked a turning point for Bogart, carrying him from the depths of despair to Broadway success and a Hollywood contract; his ascent was not, however, any more than Cagney's triumph in *The Public Enemy*, solely personal. The tone and themes of Sherwood's *The Petrified Forest* seemed to express important changes in American culture during the mid-1930s. New viewpoints on social violence and disorder made the public receptive to the phenomenon that Bogart discovered he could provide. They help explain why a sentimental and somewhat facile play and movie became so memorable to their spectators: the work spoke the Big Thoughts of the era.

The Petrified Forest gathered its representative types in a dingy gas station/eatery in the Arizona desert. There was the disillusioned intellectual (Leslie Howard's poet); the barbaric killer (Bogart as Duke Mantee); the dreamy artist; the former football player; the plutocratic couple with their black chauffeur; the cackling old pioneer; the superpatriot. In Krutch's *The Modern Temper* of 1929 the traditional intellectual was on the wane and a new metropolitan barbarian on the rise; in Sherwood's 1935 play both types were equally as obsolete as the desert's fossilized remains.

The difference between these two harbingers of their respective zeitgeists lay in their attitude toward the barbarian. *The Petrified Forest* responded to the transformed cultural climate following the inauguration of Roosevelt's New Deal. The administration's campaign against lawlessness had put pressure on popular media to end what was seen as a glamorization of the gangster. Successfully promoting itself as a national crime-fighting force, the FBI offered models of law-and-order heroes to replace the violent antisocial figures of the gangster genre. Cagney's *G Men* was in production at the same time that *The Petrified Forest* ran on Broadway.

Gangsters were the "last great apostle[s] of rugged individualism," as the intellectual in *The Petrified Forest* calls Duke Mantee. The immigrant mobsters apotheosized in the early Depression years in films like *Little Caesar* and *The Public Enemy* had represented perverse avatars of the success ethic. But by mid-decade many such figures were dead or, like Al Capone, in prison, and rugged individualism had fallen from grace like Herbert Hoover in the New Deal's emphasis on social collectivity and state activism.

The criminals made famous by the FBI's "Ten Most Wanted" list were isolated troublemakers rather than capitalist entrepreneurs who manufactured beer and ran businesses like the Prohibition gangsters. They were Midwestern bank robbers with old-stock American names: John Dillinger, Clyde Barrow and Bonnie Parker, "Baby Face" Nelson and "Pretty Boy" Floyd. Unlike Tom Powers in *The Public Enemy*, for whom "the state" was no more than a friendly neighborhood cop, these lawbreakers faced mass federal firepower as the government reasserted its authority to suppress social disorder. Though later eras might regard them differently, the popular arts of the mid-1930s faced strong pressures against portraying them as heroes. A character like Duke Mantee could not excite young male moviegoers, as had Tom Powers, to admiration and perhaps emulation, at least in voice and gesture. One could stand in awe of Mantee, be frightened by him, even feel sorry for him—but Bogart's compact, repressed, aberrant interpretation made it unlikely one would ever wish to *be* him.

■ ■ ■ ■

As malefactors of indeterminate ethnicity supplanted immigrant gangsters, Bogart found steady work in Warner Bros. crime dramas. An actor could make quite a nice career out of playing such figures: witness Barton MacLane. But who remembers him? With Cagney headed for the courts, however, and Robinson presumably at the end of his string at the studio, an ambitious actor could hope for more varied roles. Warners at least had plenty for Bogart to do: during 1936 he appeared in eight films, double the number Cagney was claiming as his maximum. It was not uncommon for Bogart to go from one production to another without a break, and on occasion he worked on more than one picture in a day.

Bogart's ascension, however, continued to be blocked by Robinson; though putatively going, the older actor was not exactly gone. This set a pattern for Bogart's position at Warner Bros. for years to come. One actor or another would cast a shadow over him: get better assignments, more sympathetic roles, greater attention and deference. After the maneuvering around *The Petrified Forest* almost cost Bogart his chance for a comeback, the pattern was confirmed with *Bullets or Ballots* (1936). The film was supposed to be Robinson's final assignment at Warner Bros., and turned out instead to be a surprise hit that earned the actor a contract renewal.

Robinson plays an undercover cop who infiltrates the rackets and dies a hero after exposing the bankers and businessmen who control the mob (the reputation of bankers and businessmen had presumably fallen so low in 1936 that no reviewer accused the studio of socialistic propaganda). The role gave Robinson a chance to display his manic, anarchic gusto on the law's side (as Cagney had done in *G Men*). Audiences loved it. Bogart's role in the picture was as a mobster lieutenant and rival to the aforementioned Barton Mac-Lane. His character was one-dimensionally evil, yet Bogart brought the type to life with some loutish comedy that made reviewers take note, even if they could not quite define what he had done: one wrote of his "baneful and somehow abnormal intensity."

Nevertheless, the focus of Bogart's work at Warners became less performance than endurance—and exploitation. From February 1936, when he started on his first picture as a contract player (*Two against the World*, a B-unit remake of the 1931 newspaper melodrama *Five-Star Final*) he worked through June almost without a break. He began to revert to old habits: on *China Clipper*, his assignment after *Bullets or Ballots*, in a minor role as a commercial airline pilot, he smiles and shifts his hands from pockets to belt in awkward juvenile style, as if he had forgotten the transformation he had carefully achieved. There were reasons for this atavism: with a week's work remaining on *China Clipper*, another production—*Isle of Fury* (1936), a B-unit melodrama based on a Somerset Maugham South Seas novel—lost its lead actor. The casting department immediately suggested Bogart as a replacement. Bogart complained, but he allowed himself to be ferried over to Santa Catalina Island, where location shooting had already begun, and cast and crew awaited a leading man.

In "Humphrey and Bogie," an essay on Bogart in her book of memoirs, *Lulu in Hollywood*, actress Louise Brooks displayed remarkable recall about the actor's performance in this inconsequential film. "He was Humphrey again," she wrote, meaning the journeyman Broadway juvenile, "reciting his memorized lines, striking attitudes while he waited for the other actors to get done with theirs."[4] Bogart certainly looked distracted and incongruous in pith helmet and pasted-on mustache, but Brooks perhaps was not aware that the actor hardly had time even to memorize his lines.

Why did Bogart put up with these indignities? Brooks speaks of his lethargy, his loneliness, his fundamental inertia, as keys to his character as man and actor. Now he was working regularly for the first time, despite the Depression; he might have taken pride in the fact that Warner Bros. was willing to give him so much to do. There were also complex personal aspects to his heavy schedule: his wife, Mary Philips, was a stage performer whose career required her to be in New York, and she returned there (this was Bogart's second marriage; there had been a brief union with actress Helen Menken in the 1920s).

Perhaps a compensation for this marital separation would come from progress in his own career. An opportunity seemed almost immediately to beckon. Warner Bros. was launching a second wave of "social problem" films reminiscent of the early 1930s. One project was *Black Legion* (1937), based on recent headlines: in the late spring of 1936 a native fascist organization preying on Jews, Catholics, and Communists had been exposed in Michigan—a version of the Ku Klux Klan in the industrial heartland. Warner Bros. responded as in Darryl Zanuck's days, producing a treatment and script within weeks of the revelations. The fictional story centered on an ordinary factory worker, embittered when his chances for advancement appear to be thwarted by "aliens"; he joins the Black Legion and leads himself and his family to tragedy and ruin.

Now that Edward G. Robinson was fully restored to star status at the studio, a role such as this would normally be his as by right. (He already had performed memorably as a working man in such pictures as *Two Seconds* of 1931.) But there was a potential problem: Robert Lord, the picture's supervisor and author of the original treatment, raised it in a memo to Hal Wallis. Although Robinson would undoubtedly be outstanding as the worker, Lord wrote, "the great trouble would be that he is decidedly not American looking. While he does not look particularly Jewish, he is distinctly a foreign type. I am afraid that, because of the peculiar nature of this story, Robinson, active in an organization to combat foreigners, might be ludicrous and ruin the whole picture. My opinion is that we must have a distinctly American looking actor to play this part."[5]

Bogart was certifiably American: he got the role. To compensate for the lack of "big names in the picture," Wallis proposed to Warner that the Hearst organization be persuaded to make it a Cosmopolitan production. With Hearst's backing, Wallis said, "we can definitely put Bogart over [that is, build him toward stardom], and it

should help make the picture a smash."[6] But as preparations continued (Hearst chose not to get involved), the studio kept Bogart busy.
He played a small role as a family man in *The Great O'Malley* (1937),
perhaps to get accustomed to the change in screen image contemplated for *Black Legion*. That picture finished shooting on a Saturday
in mid-August 1936. After resting on the Sabbath, Bogart started on
Monday in *Black Legion*. As with *Isle of Fury*, everyone else had
been ready and waiting for him, while he was finishing another picture. If this was to be his big chance, an idle Sunday was hardly time
to prepare himself.

Directed by studio hand Archie Mayo, with whom Bogart had
worked on *The Petrified Forest*, *Black Legion* skillfully establishes
the factory workers' everyday lives. Bogart's character, Frank Taylor,
runs a drill press on a plant floor filled with machines. The workers
lounge and pass the time on their break; at home, in the evening,
Frank dries dishes and listens to a radio adventure serial with his
son. He is an average guy with yearnings for worldly goods and a
latent capacity for resentment: this latter trait is activated when a
promotion to foreman that Frank is expecting goes instead to a
bright "foreigner," Dombrosky. Frank reacts in a "sorehead" manner, and the Black Legion swiftly recruits him. The group threatens
Dombrosky and forces him to leave town; Frank secures the foreman job.

Bogart handles the changes in Frank's behavior with tact and
subtlety—through simple answers and daunting rituals, a plain, callow, moderately ambitious man becomes careless, prideful, and increasingly violent. He gets fired from the foreman job and, after
striking his wife, drives her and his son to leave him. Enmeshed by
the Black Legion, he finds himself persecuting and, by accident,
murdering his best friend. Frank is arrested and put on trial with
the others. In a court of judgment, he rediscovers his family feelings
and confesses his crime, implicating the other Black Legion members and putting an end to their threat. He is sentenced to life imprisonment, and *Black Legion* ends bleakly with a final shot in the
courtroom tracking in to a close-up of his wife's face as he is led
away.

Critical reaction compared the film to the early Depression
shocker *I Am a Fugitive from a Chain Gang* (1932) for headline-
oriented social significance. Bogart's performance drew detailed
scrutiny: he was generously praised for maintaining coherence and
audience sympathy through a rapidly changing characterization. Reviewers freely predicted that this triumph would launch him toward
stardom. "The production is almost certain to make a top-flight
character star out of Humphrey Bogart," wrote *The Hollywood Re-*

porter, Bogart's staunchest and steadiest advocate among the press. "No more B-pix for Bogart!" exclaimed the *New York Post*. A consistent booster of former Broadway stage actors, Robert Garland in the *New York American* nominated Bogart for the part of Rhett Butler in *Gone with the Wind*. Reviewers for the first time linked Bogart's name to the studio's top male stars: they counted him a success in a role demanding the skills of Robinson or Paul Muni (unaware, perhaps, that one of those actors had been denied the part because of ethnic background). Only one negative note was sounded among the critics—Howard Barnes in the *New York Herald-Tribune* praised the actor with the caveat that "one might have wished the nervous energy of Jimmy Cagney in the part." A redheaded Irishman, however, might also have been excluded by reason of ethnicity.

It was hardly a plus, being an old-stock American, if that qualified you to play killers and fascists. As if to compensate, the studio gave an Irish name to his next role, as Joe "Red" Kennedy, a doomed convict, in the prison drama *San Quentin* (1937). "If the Warner Brothers are mad at Mr. Bogart," a Brooklyn paper commented, "they are certainly using the right method of easing him off the screen." Mad at Bogart? After this picture they renewed his option for the second time. It was a case rather of mismanagement (or nonmanagement) of a performer's career. The relentless demands of the studio's production commitments—it released fifty-six films in 1936 and sixty-six in 1937, half of them B pictures—made the careful planning of performers' assignments an unaffordable luxury.

The most egregious Warner Bros. failure during the 1930s in developing a performer's career—certainly the most publicized—concerned Bette Davis. Early in the decade, the studio placed her in one mediocre film after another. Then she was loaned out to RKO and gave a stunning performance as the waitress in *Of Human Bondage* (1934). Because of its allegedly immoral tone (the Hays Office almost succeeded in halting the production) the picture was ignored for Academy Awards in a year when moralism counted more strongly than in most. She was compensated in 1935 with the actress Oscar for her role in a Warner Bros. picture, *Dangerous*. This did nothing to abate her unhappiness with the studio; perhaps emboldened by Cagney's successful court action, she fled to England in 1936 and signed to make a picture there.

Jack Warner and a crew of lawyers steamed after her. They gained from a British court an injunction preventing her from working in that country, so long as the brothers Warner held a valid contract for her exclusive services. Having claimed this victory, however, Warner was anxious to reclaim the good will of his leading female star. The studio offered her a strong character part in *Marked*

Woman (1937), based on an original script by two new contract writers from New York, Robert Rossen and Abem Finkel.

Drawing on headline events, as had *Black Legion*, the film's narrative was constructed from the recent exposé of a New York City prostitution ring run by Italian gangster "Lucky" Luciano. Davis would play the lead as one of the prostitutes, sanitized by code requirements into nightclub "hostesses." The leading male role was a crusading district attorney, modeled after New York City's ambitious young prosecutor (later governor and two-time presidential candidate) Thomas E. Dewey. The assignment went to Bogart.

This was a more important part than the ubiquitous law-enforcement roles for which the studio usually hired lawyerly looking freelance actors. Warner Bros. emphasized its significance (more than attempting to give Bogart a boost) when it placed his name on the same card as the film title. It read: Bette Davis/ in/ *Marked Woman*/ with Humphrey Bogart. Davis had not yet been positioned as a star of women's melodramas, as she was later to be. The problem of how to promote the film to women may have prompted putting the Davis and Bogart names together. A movie about bad girls who suffer violence and a bitter end was not exactly dripping with MGM glamour; this at least may have suggested a screen relationship to those moviegoers looking for mitigating romance.

The Rossen-Finkel script did in fact introduce a subtle undertone of possible romance into the story. It softened the film's harsh edges by making the district attorney something less than a wooden knight: it gave him feelings toward the Davis character, lessening the condemnation of the women and making the ending even more poignant. Bogart's task was to work with Davis in insinuating into their relationship—ostensibly between an upright law enforcer and a fallen woman whom he needs as his chief witness against a racketeer—some hint of mutual attraction.

After a year of unremitting labor in nine pictures at Warner Bros., this was, astonishingly, the first real possibility of a romantic scene for the former Broadway romantic lead (his character had been married in three films, but those relationships did not involve romance). The handsome Jekyll had indeed become a menacing Hyde: as if to prove it, Bogart had a difficult time carrying off the assignment. In some scenes, he reverts to the earnest boyishness of his juvenile days. In the climactic moment, he hardly holds up his end at all.

With the trial over—the racketeer convicted and sentenced—Davis and Bogart encounter each other on the courthouse steps, amid the encroaching fog. He asks, "Where will you go?" She answers, "Places." In cross-cut close-ups, her eyes are bright and searching, her expression guarded but expectant. "What will you do?" he asks. "I'll get along," she replies, "I always have." A moment has passed. Davis and the other hostesses fade away in the fog. In the background are heard voices of the press, surrounding the district attorney, speaking of him as the next governor. Whatever attraction the lawman felt for the Davis character had to be suppressed, inevitably, by his political ambition. The problem is that neither Bogart's voice nor his facial expression conveys any of the possible complexities of his character's inner feelings.

More vexing than this, to his employers at least, was Bogart's sartorial sloppiness. Hal Wallis dashed off several memos to director Lloyd Bacon about the actor's appearance. Once he complained about Bogart's rather noticeable five-o'clock shadow. Later he admonished Bacon about Bogart's dress: "His collar is spread open and his tie isn't tied nicely into a knot and he wears those barber-pole bright ties and those plaids."[7] Indeed his shirt collar was out and his tie askew in the climactic close-ups with Davis, if anyone had cared to notice.

Behind the scenes of his desultory romantic performance in *Marked Woman*, Bogart was involved in a passionate real-life romantic drama. Now officially separated from Mary Philips, he began a tumultuous affair with actress Mayo Methot, who was also performing in the film as one of Davis's pals and sister hostesses. She would soon become his third wife. However this affected him, he was unable to give an adequate impersonation of the neat and prim Thomas E. Dewey, let alone perform the more subtle aspects of his role. The moment for "putting Bogart over" had passed. After *Marked Woman*, studio executives became convinced that he could not carry an A-picture male lead. For the foreseeable future, in any films of importance he would again be placed in the shadow of another male star.

This became clear when he began working on *Kid Galahad* (1937), a week after *Marked Woman* finished shooting. Davis accompanied Bogart from one production to the other, but the star of the new picture, and Davis's love interest, was Edward G. Robinson. Bogart's role was as a gangster, even though he was clearly of "American" stock, while Robinson's character was of Italian ethnic background. In this mostly lighthearted pastiche, directed by Michael Curtiz, Bogart's job was once again to supply the menace.

■ ■ ■ ■

During the *Kid Galahad* production, Warner Bros. received its first request from another studio for a loan of Bogart's performing services. With nearly all the major players under long-term contract, it was common practice for the movie companies to use their chattel as assets and as bargaining chips—they could be loaned out for profit or in a barter deal. Though there were many varieties of exchange, the standard practice was to charge on a so-called four-plus-three basis: the borrower would pay a guaranteed minimum of four weeks of the performer's actual salary, plus 75 percent of that figure (three weeks' pay) to the lender. This additional sum was not paid to the actor, but retained by the lending studio as interest, or overhead, or a service fee. There were pretty pennies to be made in such arrangements. They reduced the contract holder's obligation, while adding to its treasury.

The request for Bogart, however, created a dilemma for Warner Bros. Simply put, the studio did not want to lend him as cheaply as it was paying him. He was coming to the end of his second option period (the third twenty-six-week unit of his seven-year contract) and he was making only $650 a week, an egregiously low figure for someone who had played several important male lead roles. He had earned more than this—$750 a week—as "outside talent" on *The Petrified Forest*. The equivalent freelancer in 1937 could surely command $1000 to $1250 a week. It would not look good—it would be certain to rebound badly—if other studios were to know the secret of Bogart's puny wage. Moreover, knowing that Bogart was worth more than he was being paid, the studio saw a chance to make a usurious profit on the deal.

Bogart was offered to the prospective borrower, independent producer Samuel Goldwyn, not at the standard four-plus-three, but for a flat $2000 per week, minimum five weeks. Of the $10,000 total fee, therefore, Bogart would get around $3500 (his salary was due to go up to $700 at the impending option renewal), Warner Bros. $6500—more like 185 percent profit instead of the usual 75 percent. In addition, Warner Bros. asked for first male billing and no less than second billing for the actor whom, in *Kid Galahad*, they were relegating to third position. Third position was what was agreed upon, and the deal was made.

Goldwyn, however, soon came to smell a fish. This probably occurred when Bogart was loaned out a second time in 1937 to another independent producer, Walter Wanger. The Wanger deal called for an exchange of several players, all at actual salaries, with no vigorish attached—Henry Fonda at $2500 a week from Wanger to Warners for *Jezebel*, the Burbank studio's effort at an antebellum Southern melodrama that might preempt *Gone with the Wind*; Joan Blondell at $2250 and Bogart at $700 to Wanger for his picture. Following the

Goldwyn precedent, a Warner executive proposed that Bogart be paid at $1400 a week, but this blatant move was quickly squelched, perhaps because the studio did not want to jeopardize the Fonda loan.

Goldwyn probably learned of Bogart's true numbers through the Wanger deal. When the opportunity came, he raised a stink. In December 1937, Warner, having borrowed director William Wyler from Goldwyn for *Jezebel*, needed to extend the director's time. Okay, said Goldwyn, only if we readjust the previous Bogart loan to standard four-plus-three. With extra time—Wyler, who directed the Goldwyn picture that Bogart appeared in, was a notoriously slow worker—the total cost of Bogart's loan had come to $15,640; adjusted to four-plus-three, Warner refunded Goldwyn $8024.

Putting a brave (and false) face on it, a Warner contract executive wrote his Goldwyn counterpart in his covering letter with the check, "I would like to establish at this point that the price for Mr. Bogart for outside studios at the time was $10,000 for five weeks' work, and we established this rate in two or three studios in addition to your own."[8] Warner Bros. never ceased to try and buy Bogart cheap and sell him dear throughout their nearly twenty-year relationship with him.

All these details of haggling over money are necessary for understanding Bogart's situation at Warner Bros. in the framework of the Hollywood studio system. More important, certainly, was the role for which Goldwyn wanted the actor: the part of "Baby Face" Martin in the screen adaptation of Sidney Kingsley's powerful play *Dead End*. This production had followed *The Petrified Forest* to Broadway by a season, and together the two dramas of social significance signaled the two sides of a watershed in 1930s American culture.

Sherwood's play looked backward and represented the first phase of Roosevelt's New Deal administration—rejecting the intellectual pessimism of the 1920s, but still seeing the bleak landscape of America; looking to Europe for models, and positing the state primarily as a unit of force. Kingsley's play looked forward into the second phase of the New Deal and 1930s culture—focusing on the practical consequences of economic injustice, the deleterious effects of environment, particularly on the young, and especially the brave possibilities of amelioration through reconstruction. The passive hero of *The Petrified Forest* was a writer, the activist hero of *Dead End* an architect.

The strongest link between the two works was that, in their movie versions, the same performer played the killer. Goldwyn's choice of Bogart for "Baby Face" Martin put the definitive stamp on the actor's screen persona of the 1930s. Goldwyn made far fewer films than the major studios; thus he gave most of them more "prestige" buildups, and more sustained promotions, than Warner Bros. could do for the steady stream of program pictures in which Bogart played. The average moviegoer would have recognized "Baby Face" Martin—particularly with the character's obvious echo of the actual "Baby Face" Nelson—more readily than even Duke Mantee. Though both were killers, there were crucial differences between them. Mantee in *The Petrified Forest* was both a force of nature and a social freak: an animal-like barbarian who, as the intellectual pointedly proclaimed, was the rapacious extreme of an outmoded free-enterprise individualism. He was plotting his way forward even as his end was foredoomed. "Baby Face" Martin in *Dead End* (1937) is a man moving backward—moody, nostalgic, and confused, returning to the haunts of his youth in search of the place where he had lost his way. "The famous 'Baby Face' Martin used to live on this block," says the film's architect hero (played by Joel McCrea). "He wasn't such a bad kid either—at first. He was smart and brave and decent—at first." Duke Mantee was a symptom of general social breakdown; *Dead End* defines "Baby Face" Martin as someone deformed by slum conditions which could and should be changed.

Through this perspective, *Dead End* oddly renders Bogart's character almost as pathetic as he is menacing. Particularly harrowing is his reunion with his slatternly mother, who violently rejects him with a slap in the face. "You no good tramp," she screams. "You dog—you dirty yellow dog you. Don't call me Mom. You ain't no son of mine." Encountering his childhood girlfriend, he finds her a prostitute coughing with TB. Faced with such rejections and recognitions, "Baby Face" becomes in Bogart's interpretation a morose, hesitant figure, pulling at his earlobe, running a thumb across his lower lip, animated by sudden bursts of angry violence. In a climactic incident, he stabs the architect and dumps him in the river. Only slightly hurt, the hero stalks and slays the killer, collecting the reward that will enable him to begin rebuilding the city in the model of his dream of social justice.

"Audiences must be wondering by this time," mused a writer in the *Brooklyn Daily Eagle*, "whether Mr. Bogart is an actor or really a mobster." His mobster had become a monster. Like Mr. Hyde, he seemed to have drunk the potion once too often, or mixed the brew too strong. The nickname "Baby Face" was only a cruel joke to accentuate the hideous visage. Other romantic leads of Anglo-Saxon appearance—Henry Fonda and Joel McCrea are two examples—had matured into versatile character actors of star quality. At Warner Bros. the situation seemed all the more propitious for Bogart, because the principal competing male stars—Robinson, Muni, Errol Flynn, the absent Cagney—by appearance or accent were too distinctively "different" to play contemporary "American" heroes. The problem, some thought, lay in Bogart himself: specifically, in his perceived shortcomings as an actor.

Irving Rapper, who moved from Broadway to Burbank in the mid-1930s as a dialogue director before making his directorial debut with *Now, Voyager* in 1942, worked with Bogart as dialogue director on *Two against the World, The Great O'Malley,* and *Kid Galahad* in this first phase of the actor's Warner Bros. career. In *Two against the World,* a scene calls for Bogart's character, a sensationalistic radio producer—after realizing that his "yellow journalism" tactics have caused several deaths—to walk into a bar and almost tearfully admit to the bartender his responsibility. Rapper worked with Bogart to deliver the lines "very dramatically and choking up," as he recalled. "I tried to get this quality out of his voice," Rapper said; Bogart could not do it. As Rapper remembered it, the performer told him, "Irving, I can't cry. I'm not an actor."[9] This story may be apocryphal, but it also may point to a general view held at Warner Bros. about the actor's capabilities.

There was a touch of irony, then, in Bogart's second 1937 loan-out, directly after *Dead End,* for a role as a motion picture studio executive. Bogart was reunited with Leslie Howard in Walter Wanger's *Stand-In* (1937), directed by Tay Garnett, one of Hollywood's more interesting fables about itself. Howard plays a prim Eastern banker who saves an independent studio from crooked financiers in a fantasy of capital leading labor in the services of movie art. Bogart is an angry, alcoholic producer whose image is softened by his habit of carrying a Scottish terrier around in his arms. At one point (while the terrier is on a leash) he picks up a tennis racquet, swings a backhand, and inspects the strings—somebody's idea of a bit of business (and not the last time it would occur) recalling his "Tennis, anyone?" days as a Broadway juvenile.

When Warner Bros. informed him that his next assignment was as a wrestler's manager in *Swing Your Lady* (1938), Bogart, through his agent, refused the role. This rebellion seems to have been a financial ploy. Warners was certainly amenable to an adjustment. They offered an immediate $300 per week bonus on his current contract while negotiations proceeded on a new one. In December 1937 the second contract was signed, starting him at $1100 per week (still below the going rate for actors of his status) and reaching $2000 in the sixth and seventh years.

By the time the contract was agreed upon, *Swing Your Lady* was almost in the theaters. The picture belonged to the Hix Pix genre of the famous *Variety* headline (STIX NIX HIX PIX)—a lame comedy about wrestling matches in the Ozarks and the love life of a lady blacksmith, interrupted by frequent renditions of country tunes. Bogart got first billing on this one, which the studio considered sophisticated enough (or was sufficiently desperate at that moment for product) to give a Times Square opening at the Strand. An uncredited brief appearance as a reporter was made by a new $200 per week contract player, Ronald Reagan.

Arranging for Bogart's new contract was among the last official acts of Maxwell Arnow, who was leaving his position as head of the Warner Bros. casting department. Arnow was succeeded in December 1937 by Steve Trilling—and if there was another studio executive more antipathetic to Bogart than Trilling, the surviving records do not reveal him. It was probably not Trilling who assigned Bogart to *Men Are Such Fools* (1938), a "woman's genre" picture directed by musical specialist Busby Berkeley, but it was Trilling who recommended that Bogart be billed *sixth* behind a collection of newcomers and nobodies. Ultimately Trilling's superiors placed Bogart third in the cast list—behind Wayne Morris, whom the studio was promoting as a romantic lead, and Priscilla Lane, one of several new ingenues on the lot. They were, to be sure, the leading players in this Faith Baldwin soap opera about career-versus-marriage. Bogart's task was to play the Older Man who almost steals the heroine from the hero.

As if this were not comedown enough, a further humiliation was contemplated for the man who, not long before, appeared on the verge of star status. While *Men Are Such Fools* was in production, Trilling tried to work out a "crossplot" for Bogart—studio jargon for casting an actor in two pictures shooting at the same time. This bit of efficiency was usually reserved for noncontract, typecast supporting players (such as the men who played police detectives in gangster films) whose roles were sufficiently minor that they could be fitted into two simultaneous shooting schedules. The scheme proved unfeasible, and perhaps Bogart was not aware of it. He could not have been unaware of management's new indifference to him, however, when he was assigned once again to the B unit for the first time since before *Black Legion*.

His demotion was to *Crime School* (1938), the primary purpose of which was to exploit the young actors who had played the dockside gang in *Dead End*—first known as the Dead End Kids, in Burbank they were renamed the Bowery Boys. Vincent Sherman, the script's coauthor and the film's dialogue director, recalled his instructions from the story department: Take the first half of *The Mayor of Hell* (a 1933 Cagney vehicle set in a reform school), knit it together with the second half of *San Quentin* (Bogart's recent prison film), and produce a brand-new hybrid.

Hackneyed and derivative as this may sound, the film rode the Bowery Boys' ingratiating antics (as well as its commitment to the theme of ameliorative environmentalism articulated by *Dead End*) to surprising popular success. Enthusiastic trade reviews prompted the studio to upgrade the picture from the B ranks and give it a full-fledged first-run opening in New York. "The same Strand audiences that used to tear down the theater doors in the days of the early Cagneys were out in full force yesterday, rain or no rain," the *Journal-American* reported when the picture opened, "and practically drowned out the dialogue on the screen with their approving hoots and applause." Bogart's role in *Crime School* was the same as Cagney's in *The Mayor of Hell* (as well as Pat O'Brien's in *San Quentin*). Nobody was breaking down the Strand's doors, however, to get a look at him—to learn his gestures and mimic his voice, as they had Cagney's. "Bogart's work is getting fairly well standardized," wrote Archer Winston in the *New York Post*. "Either he's a tough mug outside the law or an understanding (and tough) law enforcer. He's always good, though it is difficult to keep on being excited about it."

Just about everyone had ceased to be excited about Bogart's work—including perhaps the actor himself. Looking back on the past three years from the perspective of 1938, he could at least have the satisfaction of knowing he had come a considerable way since the opening curtain of Robert E. Sherwood's play. He was making over $40,000 a year—modest by star standards, but pretty wonderful for a journeyman actor. He was working steadily in pictures—though with too many tiresome roles in too many mediocre films. Somewhere the chance for stardom had slipped away from him. The cause of this missed opportunity was not entirely clear. What was apparent was that his hard-won transformation—from Jekyll to Hyde, from loverboy to killer—had been insufficient; or, more likely, incomplete. Though the callow youth had become a hardened gunman, he remained Baby Face in either incarnation: unformed, insubstantial, immature.

5

The Studio Labyrinth

To say that life was hard for Hollywood movie performers in the studio era would be ludicrous. They were among the most highly paid salaried employees in the world. Though they often worked from early morning until late at night, and on weekends, there were frequent times when they were paid and did no work at all. Even if the glamorous movieland life depicted in the fan magazines was substantially a publicity concoction, most performers lived far more comfortably than, for example, the studio secretaries or set builders around whom they worked, not to speak of the vast majority of moviegoers during the Great Depression.

To say that their work involved struggle, however, would be more accurate. Being well paid, able to afford servants or join a country club, and so on went hand in hand with an ability to manage and maintain a career—one that could wane, as many did, as well as rise, and that periodically encountered the hurdle of "option" renewal, when a studio could cancel a contract that had many years to go. No one could be guaranteed that the studio would manage careers wisely, or even responsibly or attentively. There were just too many stories to develop, too many pictures to cast, too many productions to watch over, too much product to move into theaters—and not enough good parts to go around. It was easier to pigeonhole or type-cast performers, to slot them into familiar genre categories, to use them as often as possible in repetitive roles. We of later generations might find among the studio era's genre productions unanticipated complexities or aesthetic marvels—a gem of cinematography or performance—but for many of their creative workers they were treadmills of mediocrity and indifference. It was in getting off the treadmill that the tactics of struggle came most compellingly into play. The city boys, as we know, eventually won their wars, though along the way lost many a battle.

■ ■ ■ ■

James Cagney could have served as the shining beacon of performer as fighter if he had not in later years so thoroughly obfuscated his struggle as to efface it from memory. He said it was merely about money, not about freedom, independence, or performers' rights, and perhaps this was true, if we see money as a lever with which to obtain those other things. Meanwhile, there is plenty of evidence to indicate that performance and screen persona were never far from his field of concerns.

Among court cases of the 1930s pitting actors against studios, Cagney's legal victory over Warner Bros. in 1936 was clearly the most important. Yet its outcome proved surprisingly inconclusive. The case set no precedent and established no principle, because it was decided basically on a quirk: a breach of the actor's billing clause that was not even part of the original complaint. Though it might have hurt Warner Bros. by depriving the studio of one of its most popular performers, the company still managed to make money off of Cagney. In 1936 it rereleased several of the actor's earlier films—for that era, an unprecedented recycling of "old product," realizing additional profit at no extra production cost (or payments to the actor). Meanwhile, the company expected, not without warrant, that it would overturn Cagney's victory on appeal.

The appeal process proved an effective barrier to Cagney's exercising his legal award of freedom. It worked as well as a blacklist; other companies' lawyers could argue that hiring Cagney might subject them to liability because his contract was still under court review. Only Sam Goldwyn, a producer who held himself aloof from the studio system, was willing to say publicly that he had a project for Cagney—if the actor won on appeal.

The trade press reported that Cagney was negotiating with British Gaumont to appear in an English film as an "American gangster hiding in the British army," but nothing came of it. Eventually the actor found an independent producer, Edward L. Alperson, willing to face the expected wrath of Warner Bros. Alperson's small company, Grand National Films, Inc., agreed to finance a film, paying Cagney $100,000 (one third of the budget) plus a percentage of profits. Great Guy went before the camera in November 1936 and was rushed into New York's Criterion Theatre for a New Year's Eve opening.

The film held its own among Times Square revelers. It broke all house records, playing to over 220,000 spectators in a seven-week run. Away from Cagney's Gotham fanatics, however, Grand National had difficulty finding theaters to book the picture. No evidence can be found to suggest that Warner Bros. or other studios made a direct effort to curtail the picture's success; but exhibitors, who depended on the major companies for nearly all of their product, were likely to be as wary as producers had been of aligning themselves with Cagney's defiance. Nevertheless, *Great Guy* managed to earn gross receipts of slightly more than $1 million.

With *Great Guy*, Cagney had his first opportunity to shape his own screen image, free from studio control. Once again, however, freedom proved an ambiguous legacy. Since his popular appeal had been built on his Warner Bros. screen persona, how free was he to challenge fans' expectations with a radical change of type? For the moment, economic survival as an independent was his primary goal: prudence dictated limits to innovation. His character in *Great Guy* represents only a small shift away from the mugs they made him play in Burbank. He is on the law's side, as a crusading inspector of weights and measures—but he's also an ex-boxer, with a barely suppressed violent side that causes him occasional chagrin and brings chastisement from his girlfriend. At the end, he corrals the villain after a furniture-smashing free-for-all. The most noticeable change from his Warner Bros. performance style is a moderation of the brash, high-speed delivery of lines that Hal Wallis favored. He speaks in a slower, more subdued way, without the ungrammatical, slangy street accents that had characterized most of his roles since *The Public Enemy*. These alterations were sufficiently subtle, however, to escape reviewers' notice; they saw *Great Guy* as just another typical Cagney picture, and wondered if he could break the performance mold that had survived his split from the studio.

Something to Sing About, produced in July 1937, was Cagney's answer to this criticism. Beneath its musical comedy veneer is one of the most cynical and angry films made in that era in the genre of Hollywood movies about Hollywood. The picture had the bad timing to appear shortly after David O. Selznick's production *A Star Is Born* (1937), the Fredric March–Janet Gaynor version of a tragic Hollywood love story (remade in 1954 and 1976). Beneath *its* veneer of pathos the Selznick film took an uncritical, self-congratulatory attitude toward Hollywood, which was, not surprisingly, the preferred perspective. Reviewers ignored Cagney's critique, in favor of his picture's musical aspects. They regarded his performance as his reincarnation as a "romantic juvenile."

Something to Sing About does in fact present a Cagney hardly seen before on the screen, as part of the film's theme that the Hollywood system shapes screen personas that contradict and betray performers' actual selves. He portrays a New York singer–dancer–band leader who accepts a Hollywood offer, then endures a complete transformation in the studio's hands—his appearance by a makeup man, his dress by a wardrobe man, his speech by a dialogue director. A venal studio boss lies to him, cheats him out of vacation time, and forces him (for publicity purposes) to keep his marriage secret, precipitating a rift with his wife. The film's Hollywood is a place of duplicity and false appearances. The actor's Japanese valet is capable of perfect English but customarily speaks in an Oriental singsong. An American starlet is given an Eastern European name to aid her appeal. Cagney's hoofer gladly leaves the movie world and makes it safely back onstage in New York.

In late 1937 the question of Cagney's changing screen persona was suddenly overshadowed by the renewal of his legal battle. The California Supreme Court had taken under consideration Warner Bros.' appeal. Rumors were rife that its decision would be for reversal. Studio executives now had to consider what the consequences would be if the court handed back to them a defeated, recalcitrant actor. They decided that a preemptive compromise was preferable to a public triumph. Talks were initiated with Cagney in December 1937, and an agreement was reached with astonishing speed—actually it was a series of agreements, signed between January 3 and 13, 1938. The centerpiece was a new Cagney contract, to commence April 25, 1938, and run for seventy-eight weeks, paying him $4500 weekly for the first year and $5000 thereafter. It specified that he would make five pictures during the one and one-half years, more than satisfying Cagney's previous complaint about appearing in too many pictures. As a sweetener, there was a special contract solely for Cagney's first project upon his return. He would play in the movie version of Bella and Samuel Spivack's hit Broadway comedy about Hollywood, *Boy Meets Girl*. (His role as a wacky screenwriter would largely efface from memory the bitter figure he had portrayed in *Something to Sing About*.) His salary for this one-picture deal was $150,000—an unprecedented figure for Warner Bros. since the stock market crash.

Among other legal documents was an agreement by both sides to seek a state supreme court reversal of the 1936 superior court decision: the reversal was duly ordered by the court. There was also a formal cancellation of the punitive indemnity clause of Cagney's 1932 contract, which had held back part of his salary in a trust fund. One by one the old thorns were extracted, and actor and studio proclaimed their relationship healed.

Amidst the exchanges of papers and signatures tidying up past disputes, one minor document held significance for the future. This was an agreement with Grand National Films. The independent production company—having sustained Cagney throughout his two-year experiment with freedom—now relinquished the contract it had recently signed to develop for the actor a project called *Angels with Dirty Faces*.

■ ■ ■ ■

Warner Bros. had changed in the more than two years that Cagney had been away. Though still perhaps the most tightfisted of the major studios, it had begun to loosen the purse strings. The movie industry had generally recovered from the worst years of the Great Depression. Its business practices, as well as entertainment values, were adapting to the cultural transformations in American society set in motion by the Roosevelt administration's response to the economic crisis.

Considering the central importance of radicalism in the arts and intellectual life during the Great Depression, it is also true that the New Deal fostered a conservatory, if not conservative, cultural agenda in which radicals were often significant participants. Around the administration's efforts to recast popular understanding of national historical origins and development, there grew up a lively discourse about the American past and its heroes in historical fiction, plays, biographies, even epic poems. The movie industry's contribution to this tendency was a movement beginning in mid-decade to expand the genre of costume dramas based on historical novels and popular classics. Besides being enormously popular, these films served to appease the social groups who had been in the forefront of efforts to strengthen movie censorship to counter what they conceived as excessive sex and violence in Depression social dramas. Studios discovered that spending more on "production values"—lavish costumes and sets, or the new three-color Technicolor process—could make more money. Cagney signed his new agreement just as Warner Bros. completed production on its first $2 million picture, *The Adventures of Robin Hood* (1938), starring Errol Flynn.

Flynn's films were the most obvious signs of the studio's transformation. The young Australian had been typed originally as one of those suave aristocrats who lounge about in English country house mysteries—until someone discovered he would make the perfect swashbuckling hero for the emerging cycles of historical pictures and literary adaptations. He had made the first of these, *Captain Blood*, when Cagney was still around finishing *Ceiling Zero*. It was followed by such others as *The Charge of the Light Brigade* and *The Prince and the Pauper* (1937) before *Robin Hood*.

Paul Muni's changes were even more striking. In the first half of the 1930s he had specialized in playing victims of injustice in contemporary social problem films, ranging from the 1932 Depression classic *I Am a Fugitive from a Chain Gang* to 1935's *Black Fury* (about coal miners) and *Bordertown* (about the tribulations of a Mexican-American lawyer). Moving with the times, however, he suddenly switched to portraying nineteenth-century historical figures: he won the actor Oscar for his role as the title character in *The Story of Louis Pasteur* (1936) and was nominated again the following year for *The Life of Emile Zola* (which gained Warner Bros. its first Academy Award for Best Picture).

Bette Davis was another performer whose screen persona the studio had undertaken to transform. Preparing her for the star status it had not previously acknowledged, Warner Bros. moved her away from the streetwise ladies of *Marked Woman* and *Kid Galahad* with the lead role in a melodrama of the antebellum South, *Jezebel* (1938), for which she won an actress Oscar.

With all these ventures into new styles and subjects, Warner Bros. remained committed to the contemporary social dramas that it had made almost uniquely its own genre—and that secured it an enduring reputation as *the* socially conscious studio of the Depression era. The diversion of talent like Muni and Davis to other genres, however, had made reconciliation with Cagney that much more important. He could bring his comic, anarchic energy to roles that neither Robinson nor Bogart, the remaining specialists in crime and social drama, could handle.

None of these men was precisely in the bloom of youth. Robinson was already in his forties, Cagney and Bogart just a year or so away (Cagney had begun to take five years off his age). Though the studio had brought in a number of romantic juveniles (among them Jeffrey Lynn, Wayne Morris, and Ronald Reagan), they were definitely too corn-fed and all-American to play urban figures. Between the Bowery Boys on the teenage side, and Cagney and Bogart on the brink of forty, a gap existed for another, younger city boy. Early in 1938 the studio found him in New York's Group Theatre: he was known as Jules Garfield, he was just past his twenty-fifth birthday, and when Warner Bros. signed him, Jack Warner rechristened him "John."

■ ■ ■ ■

Born Jacob Garfinkle on Rivington Street on New York's Lower East Side, Garfield came of age in a different era from Warner Bros.' older city boys. The formative public event of Cagney's and Bogart's adolescence had been World War I: it gave the Irish kid from Yorkville the chance to attend Columbia University, and the rich kid from Riverside Drive and Andover a crack at navy life. For Garfield, growing up in the boroughs of Brooklyn, Queens, and, principally, the Bronx, to which Lower East Side Jewish families aspired after the war, the crucial events were the stock market crash and the onset of the Great Depression. As a rebellious kid turned apprentice actor, he was drawn into the New York theater world's ideological ferment in the early 1930s. The Group Theatre was his Andover and Columbia. While not yet twenty years old, he began playing small roles on Broadway, for the Theatre Union, and for the Group. In Clifford Odets's *Awake and Sing*, directed by Harold Clurman for the Group in 1935, he drew raves for a strong performance as a kitchen sink idealist—an ideological juvenile, a 1930s proletarian version of the romantic boy.

In *Having Wonderful Time*, a Catskills comedy directed by Marc Connolly on Broadway in early 1937, Garfield demonstrated that he could step up in social class and play the bourgeois juvenile roles that had been Bogart's stage stock-in-trade. It was probably this performance, rather than the small parts he continued to play in Group productions, that attracted Hollywood's attention—even though many of the Group's leading figures (including Odets and Clurman) had begun doing motion picture work.

Then came the traumatic incident whose impact Garfield apparently never got over. In a new play, *Golden Boy*, Odets had written the lead role of Joe Bonaparte (a young man torn between old world and new, undecided between a career as a violinist or as a prizefighter) expressly for Garfield. Clurman, however, would not let him play the part: he considered Garfield too callow an actor, and gave it to the more experienced Luther Adler. Out of loyalty, Garfield took a minor role in the production; but he did not disguise the fact that he felt crushed. When a Warner Bros. offer came, he did not hesitate.

It was only for a small part in *Four Daughters* (1938), based on a short story by the popular writer Fannie Hurst. Garfield's performance turned out to be the most striking debut of the decade for a Warner Bros. player. None of the studio's leading stars had carried off their first opportunity as notably as Garfield did in the role of the cynical, wounded, self-pitying lost soul Mickey Borden. Into a household of sentimental, musical young women—presided over by a genial musician father in a bucolic suburban setting, with variously suitable swains hovering about—comes the electrifying dark presence of Garfield's doomed orchestrator, thick black hair curling over his forehead, his eyes half-lidded by the weight of despair. He was the sort of man whose untapped genius needed only the right woman to kindle his self-esteem, and audience reaction suggested that many young women imagined themselves as candidates.

Director Michael Curtiz, who had been in charge of Errol Flynn's costume epics, had probably been assigned to the picture because Flynn was originally scheduled as its star and romantic lead. As an antidote to the sweet, bland unreality of the main narrative line, Curtiz gave Garfield's minor role a major emphasis. He let the camera linger on Garfield's vulnerable, defended, belligerent face, wreathed in cigarette smoke: it was probably these privileged, lengthy close-ups (extraordinary for a noncontract, low-billed newcomer) that led some of the New York reviewers to see Garfield as a stronger presence on the screen than on the stage.

Four Daughters was an entirely serendipitous triumph. This film full of nobodies was nominated for an Oscar for Best Picture of 1938; Curtiz received a nomination as director; and Garfield, no longer a nobody after its release, was nominated in the supporting actor category for his first screen role. By that time, of course, the studio had picked up the option for a five-year contract that it had carefully written into the one-picture deal. Like Bogart before him, Garfield had already been sent off to the B unit, to learn the facts of Burbank life.

■ ■ ■ ■

Nineteen thirty-eight was a triple-crown year for Michael Curtiz. The journeyman director (born Mihaly Kertesz in Budapest), who had taken on nearly fifty directorial assignments for Warner Bros. since emigrating from Europe in 1926, suddenly found himself the toast of Hollywood. *The Adventures of Robin Hood* as well as *Four Daughters* was nominated for the Best Picture Oscar; in the director category, he received two *separate* nominations—one for *Four Daughters* and the other for the picture he made next, *Angels with Dirty Faces*. Curtiz's hot hand carried over to the actors with whom he worked: besides Garfield's nomination as supporting actor, James Cagney gained his first actor nomination for his performance in *Angels with Dirty Faces*, and won the New York Film Critics' actor award.

On the face of it, Curtiz was an unexpected choice to direct *Angels with Dirty Faces*. In his dozen years with Warners he had worked with every genre known to humankind—except a gangster film. His one previous encounter with Cagney had been not entirely propitious, on *Jimmy the Gent*. In choosing a director, however, Hal Wallis wanted someone who could handle Cagney with authority.

Cagney's first picture back with the studio, *Boy Meets Girl*, had been given to Lloyd Bacon, the house director who presumably knew the actor best: he had directed seven of Cagney's fifteen films between the 1932 walkout and the 1936 court case. Bacon was no Hawks, but Cagney and co-star Pat O'Brien behaved as if they were back on the set of *Ceiling Zero*—O'Brien barked his lines and Cagney speeded through his lines and movements. Since it was a comedy, their send-up performances did not compromise the movie, but they did exasperate the associate executive producer. "I'm afraid we are going to lose a lot of laughs unless we watch these boys carefully," Wallis memoed Bacon. "They are dashing their stuff off at such a pace and running their words together so that you don't know what they are talking about, and as a result you don't get the funny dialogue."[1] For unexplained reasons Wallis never succeeded in getting retakes on the scenes he regarded as most offensive.

He expected Curtiz to keep a tighter rein on *Angels with Dirty Faces*. There were other reasons besides the contentious star. The original story that Warner Bros. had purchased from Grand National was a throwback to the urban gangster dramas of the early 1930s. Its author, Rowland Brown, had also written the original story on *The Doorway to Hell* back in 1930. There were echoes of that film (as well as of Hawks's 1932 *Scarface*) in the first treatment, and the alarm bells went off at the PCA office. As the script gained shape, however, it took on more of the coloration of its own time—particularly the pervasive view that environment determined destiny. When the Bowery Boys were added, *Angels with Dirty Faces* became the Warner Bros. riposte to Goldwyn's *Dead End*.

It was as if Warner Bros. was saying: We'll show you the proper way to make an urban crime picture. First, cast James Cagney instead of Humphrey Bogart as the lead criminal. That gives the menace figure a violent comic energy, not morose lethargy. Then change the good guy from an architect to a priest. This retains the notion that a slum environment can sway kids toward crime, but eliminates possibly socialistic ideas about remaking the environment for the better. The priest can emphasize that faith and morality can survive in any environment: changing *people* is more important. Compare the titles—*Angels with Dirty Faces* is ultimately concerned, not with city streets, but with the grace of God.

The triumph of theology over sociology, however, was icing on the cake; the studio's principal ambition was to revitalize the crime genre with which Cagney had been so memorably associated before the break. Cagney plays Rocky Sullivan, O'Brien is Jerry Connolly— youthful pals whose paths diverge when Rocky is caught pilfering from a boxcar and Jerry gets away. Rocky's way leads (through a swift montage of headlines and prison documents) to reform school, the state pen, and gangland. By virtue of being able to run a little faster, Jerry grows up to be a priest.

Their relationship resumes when Rocky returns to the old neighborhood after getting out of jail. He enters the church where Jerry is conducting the choir, and joins in the singing. It ends in the famous death row sequence: Jerry pleads with the fearless Rocky to go out "yellow" rather than defiant, to prevent the neighborhood toughs (the Bowery Boys) from admiring him and following his path. Rocky refuses, but as the two men walk together toward the death chamber, the shift of light from the priest to the condemned man indicates that God's grace has been transmitted, and received. "I don't want to die, oh no please," Rocky cries, unseen, while on the screen Jerry casts his glance toward heaven.

The subtle variations of character that marked Cagney's award-winning performance concealed the behind-the-scenes struggle that went into its making. Simply put: Cagney and Hal Wallis resumed their dispute about how tough a mug Cagney was to be. A good part of the force in Cagney's characterization comes from his playing against the narrative. He created a genial, lightly comic figure—deft rather than brutally violent—in whom one could recognize the former choirboy whom "they" made into a criminal. This performance made plausible Rocky's capacity for redemption and transfiguration. From Wallis's viewpoint, however, what was missing was the barely suppressed barbaric anger that propelled Tom Powers in *The Public Enemy*. After viewing the daily rushes, the executive conferred with Curtiz and ordered retakes on two crucial scenes to get more menace into them. Both involved Cagney playing opposite Humphrey Bogart.

Bogart's role was as Frazier, a crooked lawyer fronting for the mob. He betrays a promise to give Rocky a share of the loot when the latter is released from prison. Rocky confronts the lawyer first in a nightclub office, later at his apartment. Wallis in fact wanted to change Bogart's performance as much as, if not more than, Cagney's. Frazier's reaction of fear on seeing Rocky was to have been the sign of his betrayal. Seeing this, Rocky would get angry and (as Wallis anticipated) precipitate a rising cycle of tension and menace that climactically erupts with Rocky shooting Frazier—one of the murders for which he gets the chair. Wallis described in detail the performance, cutting, and lighting styles he wanted in the retakes. He made sure that they were done. Still, he did not get precisely what he asked for. In Cagney's performance there is an exaggeration—a kind of inauthenticity—that undercuts his menace in the more violent scenes. In a long sequence at the nightclub that begins with Rocky killing the lawyer and another mobster and ends with the police capturing him after a shoot-out, Cagney fires his gun in a wild, jabbing manner, implying impulsiveness more than accuracy. Otherwise he moves through these scenes in a deliberate way—except when he delivers some rapid-fire lines to O'Brien when the priest appears.

Despite the retakes and Wallis's insistent desire to get more "guts" into the picture, ultimately Rocky Sullivan is Cagney's creation (abetted no doubt by Curtiz), and a decisive triumph for his own conception of his screen persona at Warner Bros. Rocky was a bad man by force of circumstances only, who could recognize goodness and act on it, even if it doomed him. It was a characterization whose pathos would infuse the late-1930s revival of the gangster genre.

■ ■ ■ ■

Humphrey Bogart's role in *Angels with Dirty Faces*, though it got him third billing behind Cagney and O'Brien, was not that much of a plum. Since he was only in four scenes, the casting department once again tried to work out a "crossplot" for him so that he could appear simultaneously in a B production.

This plan was unsuccessful, but it hardly diminished Bogart's work schedule. After having appeared in only five pictures during 1937 (three at Warner Bros., two on loan-outs), in 1938 the studio put him in eight films—almost without let-up. He finished on *Crime School* on March 2, for example, and reported to *The Amazing Dr. Clitterhouse* (1938), already in production, the next day. On Saturday, March 12, he worked on *Clitterhouse*, the next day did retakes on *Crime School*, and Monday morning was back to the other picture again. Talk about the importance of "actor's preparation"! At this point, however, Bogart did not have to do much that he had not done a hundred times already.

The circumstances of his casting on *Racket Busters* (1938) make clear Bogart's situation at Warner Bros. Like *Marked Woman*, this was to be based on one of Thomas E. Dewey's crusading investigations—into the role of crime rackets in New York City's trucking industry. (Also like *Marked Woman*, the original script was cowritten by Robert Rossen.) There was a Dewey role and a rackets boss role (as in *Marked Woman*), but the best part—equal to Bette Davis's character in the other film—was as an independent-minded truck driver. This figure, Denny, gets compromised by the rackets, but in the end agrees to testify in court and gets the racket boss convicted.

Originally Hal Wallis thought of Cagney to play Denny. Later, when *The Amazing Dr. Clitterhouse* was finishing up, he proposed Bogart to the film's associate producer. "I think he could do it very well," Wallis wrote, "particularly because of the change of character in the middle of the picture where he slides over to the other side. Don't forget that Bogart played a similar part in *Black Legion* and did it very well, and also played a straight part in *Marked Woman*."[2] Ultimately the role of Denny went to a surprise choice, George Brent, a contract player best known as a romantic lead opposite Bette Davis in the string of pictures that led her to take ship for England. Bogart instead got the crooked part as the racket boss, wearing a black shirt with a white tie.

The pattern now was set. When scriptwriters wanted to identify a ruthless "supergangster" they simply indicated on their cast of characters: "Humphrey Bogart type."[3] This happened, for example, on a B-unit production, *King of the Underworld* (1938), and Bogart naturally got the role. As B pictures went, this one was unusual. The female lead was Kay Francis, the studio's highest-paid star. At the height of her popularity with women moviegoers in 1935, she had signed an unusual contract, giving her three years guaranteed at $5250 per week, with options covering four more years. In that three-year period, however, her popularity and value had waned precipitously. When option time finally came due in 1938, the studio (with no intention of renewing) ungraciously played out her string with B-picture assignments.

Those involved in the film (the third of Francis's four final B pictures, and a remake of the 1935 *Dr. Socrates*) seemed to regard their responsibilities with an ironic disdain. The result, surprisingly, was a sardonic treatment of the usual clichés. Bogart, for one, demonstrated a comic side to his gangster persona that had hardly been visible before (notable only in *Bullets or Ballots*). In any chronicle of Bogart's "emergence," this unlikely work rates a place for reigniting the capacity for humor in his portrayal of mobster killers.

Finally, in late 1938, the casting department achieved its elusive goal: it got Bogart into two pictures shooting simultaneously. One was *The Oklahoma Kid* (1939), a western comedy-drama (and his second picture with Cagney) in which Bogart's villainous character, deprived of any mark of purity, wore not only the expected black hat and the customary black shirt, but also a black tie. The other was *Dark Victory* (1939), the famous Bette Davis film about a Long Island socialite who dies of a brain tumor.

In the Davis film, Bogart plays Michael O'Leary, a horse trainer. He has one major scene with the star, in which he confesses his love for her, only to learn of her impending death. Her key words to him—"Are you afraid to burn, Michael?"—refer not only to a cigarette lighter's flame, but to transgression and damnation. Louise Brooks describes him in this film as "stricken with grotesque, amateur embarrassment."[4] This seems an exaggeration, especially since his character—separated by class barriers from his employer—cannot speak his love for her other than with tentative awkwardness.

Bogart does drift in and out of his Irish accent. This was not exactly repertory theater, however. Here is an example of how bleak working conditions could be for motion picture performers whose situation seemed for whatever reason ripe for—the word is not mere knee-jerk rhetoric—exploitation. There is no other record of a motion picture player of Bogart's prominence being forced to shift from role to role on a daily basis.

■ ■ ■ ■

Neither Warner Bros. nor John Garfield immediately turned the actor's screen persona into a carbon copy of his Mickey Borden character in *Four Daughters*. That was attempted only after the film's surprise success made him into an instant star. The studio's initial intention was to turn Garfield into a carbon copy of *James Cagney's* screen persona. The vehicle was *Blackwell's Island* (1939), the B picture to which Garfield was assigned immediately after *Four Daughters*. Like *Marked Woman* and *Racket Busters*, it was based on events from New York City's seemingly endless supply of crime and corruption—in this instance, a 1934 clean-up of a prison that had been under the control, with official collusion, of mobster inmates. Garfield plays a crusading reporter who gets himself sentenced to the prison to abet the reforms from inside.

Anyone who thought the sardonic, sleepy-eyed Mickey Borden was the authentic John Garfield (only Warner Bros. employees could have thought this, for the time being, since *Four Daughters* had not yet been released) would have been surprised at his quite passable

Cagney imitation: he talks crisply, wisecracks, grins, and dashes about in the familiar Cagney manner.

What motive could possibly lie behind so obvious a cloning of the Cagney screen persona? It seems to represent not so much a desire to copy Cagney's physical presence on-screen (though that was its outward manifestation) as to retain and transmit his particular social symbolism from the early 1930s: the uncanny rapport with the young, rootless, working-class city boys about which Lincoln Kirstein had written. Even as Warner Bros. diversified into genres such as biographical pictures, westerns, and women's films, it wished to maintain—as a central aspect of its identity as a manufacturer of entertainment—its special relation with the New York crowds, not only for sentimental or cultural reasons, but for the important revenues produced at the Strand and other New York theaters. Since Cagney was growing older and was reluctant to play the mug, Garfield (with youth on his side and the city streets in his blood) was an obvious heir to the Cagney tradition.

Four Daughters hit the theaters, however, while *Blackwell's Island* was in postproduction, and Garfield's impact as Mickey Borden put the Cagney succession in a different perspective. To represent New York's young men, Garfield no longer needed to be Cagney. He could now be himself—or rather, his new screen self—and stand for the boys and men of the later 1930s as Cagney had for the earlier. More victim than rebel, more social case than social phenomenon, more a pouter than a fighter, the Garfield screen persona was reactive, a product of environment and chance. The serendipitous bonus, on the evidence of *Four Daughters*, was an appeal that Cagney had never commanded: young women were as likely to knock down the Strand's doors as young men.

The immediate result of the success of *Four Daughters* was the shelving of *Blackwell's Island*; later, scenes were added and a new ending was shot to build it up for A-picture exploitation. It was released as Garfield's third picture, since so blatant a Cagney imitation would not serve as an encore to Garfield's *Four Daughters* triumph.

The vehicle chosen instead was *They Made Me a Criminal* (1939). Though it was a remake of a 1934 Douglas Fairbanks, Jr., film (*The Life of Jimmy Dolan*), the substitution of Garfield—as well as the addition of the Bowery Boys, and the introduction of the victim theme—made it seem new in 1939. Garfield plays a prizefighter who is framed for a murder he did not commit. He goes on the lam and ends up at a ranch in the Arizona desert, where, improbably, the Bowery Boys have been shipped by a friendly East Side priest.

As a follow-up to *Four Daughters*, *They Made Me a Criminal* was an inspired choice. Garfield's notices were, quite simply, remarkable. "His playing shows insight, study, sincerity and restraint," *Variety* wrote. "Given a few more such complimentary parts, he can scarcely miss becoming a major star. Fact that he is such a distinct personality and fine actor make [sic] him a screen natural." The *New York Daily Mirror* reviewer compared his acting to that of Muni and his smile to that of Clark Gable. In the *New Yorker*, John Mosher read into Garfield's performance the same social significance once found in Cagney: "I thought there was some discretion and common sense in his toughness. There is nothing noisy, stagy, or showy about him. One can find hundreds such along Sixth Avenue, spelling out the signs in front of the employment agencies." There were also hundreds such crowding into the Strand.

These reviews were unusually precise in their description of Garfield's screen persona: he does not work so hard to create a character as in *Four Daughters*, nor ape another's mannerisms as in *Blackwell's Island*. It is a quiet but subtly powerful performance. He works through restraint to build a self-assured character, one who can make mercurial swings to laughter or anger, and gradually reveal a vulnerability that has no trace of self-pity.

It was indeed the kind of performance that could bear comparison with Cagney's style of the early 1930s—not by emulation, but by making it new. It was more rounded than the Mickey Borden role, therefore more available for young men and boys to identify with; in tune with the later 1930s mood, it was less violent and anarchic than the early Cagney, with an irony and cynicism capable of tempering by social circumstance. Garfield did not get along with director Busby Berkeley ("I believe this picture has made John Garfield almost a Bolshevik," the unit manager wrote, with reference to his rebelliousness as an employee rather than his political ideology);[5] nevertheless, he produced a deeper characterization than that of Mickey Borden, one worth remembering in the months to come.

This was the screen persona the studio obviously had in mind when it assigned Garfield to play the young Porforio Diaz, the Mexican general who later ruled as dictator for decades, in the big-budget biopic *Juarez* (1939). In Mexico there was apparently some trepidation about a novice New York actor playing one of that country's powerful and controversial figures, though none at Warner Bros., where Hal Wallis was highly pleased with Garfield's characterization. Garfield does bring some much-needed energy and verve to a solemn, ambivalent picture. Paul Muni plays Juarez as a combination of Abraham Lincoln and a cigar-store Indian, and Brian Ahearn steals the sympathy as a good-hearted, thickheaded, doomed Maximilian. With his mustache and Vandyke beard, and his unmistakable New York accent, Garfield seemed to most reviewers, however, badly out of place. "His tongue is the tongue of Jules," wrote one, and the *New York Daily News* claimed he was made up to look like Leon Trotsky.

Juarez was merely an interlude, however, while Julius and Philip Epstein were preparing their not-quite-sequel to *Four Daughters*—it was finally called *Daughters Courageous* (1939). It began shooting within a few days of *Juarez*'s completion, and in the interim Garfield signed a new, seven-year contract starting at $1500 a week—nearly double what he was then earning. With Michael Curtiz again directing, all the nobodies from the earlier film were together again: only this time Garfield's name headed the list.

Since Mickey Borden had died at the end of *Four Daughters*, a general reincarnation was necessary. The four motherless sisters of Westchester County became sisters abandoned by their father in Carmel-by-the-Sea. Garfield was reborn as Gabriel Lopez, an American-born son of a Portuguese fisherman, caught between two worlds. He charms the same girl in the same pouting, despondent manner, then goes off to wander the globe so she can marry her respectable beau. (Though Cagney's screen persona lacked Garfield's sex appeal, he was more likely to end up paired at the end of a film.)

More comic, more farfetched, and in some ways more tedious than its predecessor, *Daughters Courageous* elicited different responses from female and male reviewers. "John Garfield remains the most electric personality we can remember," Jane Chapin wrote in *The Journal of Commerce*. "The boy has an intensity that is . . . hypnotic to an audience." An Indianapolis reviewer wrote, "I found myself wishing he were back on the screen right after he left it. I kept wondering where he was." Dick Pitts of a North Carolina paper, meanwhile, spoke for a number of other men who reviewed the film: "What I'd like to know is when they are going to take Garfield's voice out of the East Side and let him portray something other than a cynic who's so tough he inhales cigarette smoke." Garfield's undeniable sexual appeal was beginning to divide the genders like the furor over Rudolph Valentino in the 1920s.

Would Garfield have wanted to become his generation's sex symbol? If so, he made the mistake of signing with the wrong movie company. Warner Bros. possessed neither the experience nor the managerial skills to engineer such an image for one of its own. Tough guys and worldly women were the personas they could build, supported by contract writers who could create their characters and directors who could animate them. The die was cast for Garfield when the Epstein brothers and Curtiz—the writers and director who had abetted his surprise emergence as a sexy screen presence—were assigned to do an actual sequel to *Four Daughters*, called *Four Wives* (1939). Because his character had died in the earlier film, Garfield was not included.

Garfield's screen persona was placed instead in the hands of writer Robert Rossen. Another product of fecund Rivington Street on the Lower East Side, Rossen (previously cowriter of *Marked Woman* and *Racket Busters*) had also collaborated on the antilynching film *They Won't Forget* (1937). In Hollywood he had joined the Communist party. His Garfield vehicle, *Dust Be My Destiny* (1939), was his first solo screen credit and his most overtly ideological screenplay thus far.

Garfield's character goes from false imprisonment, to an abusive county work farm, to a trial for a murder he did not commit. With Lewis Seiler (promoted from the B unit) directing, Garfield delivers a lengthy defense of American society's "nobodies," while facing the camera, in a single take. The studio played up a love interest (with Priscilla Lane of *Four Daughters* and *Daughters Courageous*) as a means of preserving Garfield's sex appeal, but the sentimentality only compromised the film's bleakness, without any mitigation of it. The *Daily Worker* proclaimed Garfield "excellent"—possibly it was promoting Rossen's screenplay by valorizing the performance of the left-leaning but non-Communist actor. The bourgeois press grumbled about wasting Garfield's abilities in roles as Fate's whipping boy.

Another assignment only exacerbated matters—*Castle on the Hudson* (1940), a remake of the studio's 1933 penitentiary drama, *20,000 Years in Sing Sing*, which had starred Spencer Tracy and Bette Davis. In version two, Garfield does his Cagney imitation for half the picture and finally masters Tracy's gestures in the later reels. When the film was released in March 1940 the chorus of criticism from the New York reviewers began to take on the tone of an organized cabal. "It's about time either he or his producers knocked it off," wrote William Bochnel in the *World-Telegram*, in words almost identical to those of several others, "because his playing is becoming monotonous and in no way reflects the fine acting talent he possesses."

Warner Bros. executives may have read these reviews; someone at the studio at least collected them. What impact they had is open to speculation: probably little. But Garfield did not need to wait six months for the reviews to come in on *Castle on the Hudson* to know that something had gone drastically askew with his career. Praise for his performance in *Daughters Courageous* had poured in, and two films already in the can would erode—or at least considerably alter—the powerful screen presence he had so swiftly attained. When he was assigned to another crime film within a few days of completing the Sing Sing picture, he opted for struggle. He refused to report, was suspended, reinstated, laid off, then suspended again for turning down another assignment. All together he did not work for nearly four months, from late August to late December 1939.

The film that brought him back to work was clearly intended to be a conciliatory gesture on the studio's part—an effort to break the monotony and give his acting talent greater room to express itself. The Epstein brothers wrote the script; Henry Blanke (producer on *Four Daughters* and *Daughters Courageous*) supervised; and, though Curtiz was not available, the directing job was given to one of Garfield's old friends from his theater days, Vincent Sherman. The vehicle was Maxwell Anderson's 1927 play, *Saturday's Children*. Bogart had played in its Broadway run, and it had already been the source for two movie versions.

Saturday's Children (1940) did not turn out to be a happy experience. There was difficulty casting the female lead, for the part of Garfield's wife. The original choice, Jane Bryan, retired from the movies; Olivia de Havilland preferred to go on suspension rather than take it; and a third actress was dropped after a week's shooting. Anne Shirley was finally brought in from outside to take the role. The front office was critical of Sherman for working too slowly, and the director's explanation was that Garfield "was playing a different characterization than he had ever done before, and that he was having difficulty in getting Garfield into it."[6]

The part of Rags Rosson was indeed a departure for Garfield: the character was a diffident young office worker and aspiring inventor who yearns for overseas adventure, but is trapped into marriage, parenthood, and a dispiriting, impoverished domestic life. Garfield, in spectacles, speaks his lines in a slow, soft voice that is decidedly a departure from the brash, loud style he had played before. It was not a part calculated to make any hearts throb. The film was a modest success and some reviewers found Garfield's change in style a "welcome relief," while others saw only more of Mickey Borden.

Within a fortnight of finishing *Saturday's Children*, Garfield was again suspended. He took the opportunity to return to New York and play on Broadway in *Heavenly Express*, with such other Hollywood exiles as Aline McMahon and Harry Carey, Sr. The play lasted only three weeks. By the end of May 1940, he was back in Burbank, doing time in the B unit for his show of independence. Pat O'Brien was with him, playing out the string—in the inimitable Warner Bros.

way—on a contract whose final option the studio had decided not to take up; the female lead was Frances Farmer, returned to Hollywood following her Group Theatre stint (when she had appeared with Garfield in *Golden Boy*) and finding occasional B-picture work with Warners. The film was *Flowing Gold* (1940), an oil-field drama. Garfield again was a man on the run from an unjust accusation.

One B picture followed another. *East of the River* (1940) was one of the projects that, in an earlier script version, Garfield had refused (and the cause of one of his fall 1939 suspensions). Wallis had relegated it to the B unit, and when it came his way again, Garfield had seen reason not to reject it. Early in the production, however, Garfield took off half an hour to confer with Harry M. Warner, the New York–based company president, who on periodic visits to the West Coast occasionally put in a word with his brother Jack on "artistic" matters. What was said has not been saved for posterity, but Garfield returned to the set and was "apparently unable to remember his lines," as the assistant director wrote in his report on the day's work: he required sixteen takes on one shot, fourteen on the next.[7] Whether the cause was distress or rebellion, Garfield's agitation was not unwarranted. To all the world it looked like he was getting the Kay Frances–Pat O'Brien treatment: when you don't want them anymore, send them to B-picture purgatory until you're able to cast them loose for good.

It is unlikely that the studio had any intention of letting Garfield go before his contract's full term had run. Why, then, squander their investment in him by letting his talent go to waste (as reviewers more and more bluntly proclaimed)? In later years many of Garfield's 1930s colleagues were to compare his early movie career with the James Dean phenomenon of the 1950s. Though it may seem farfetched to those who venerate Dean and remember Garfield hardly at all, the idea provides some useful perspective. Garfield (at this stage of his career) and Dean both adopted the screen persona of a petulant boy. The most obvious difference between them lies in the quantity of their screen work. Dean's legend is based on the three films he made before his early death—*East of Eden* (1955), *Rebel without a Cause* (1955), and *Giant* (1956). In approximately the same time period as Dean's full screen career, Garfield had already played in ten films. Had Garfield, by some circumstance, only been seen in *Four Daughters*, *They Made Me a Criminal*, and *Daughters Courageous*, his place in movie mythology might be as secure as Dean's.

Fortunately for Garfield, he lived beyond his twenty-fifth year and just three motion pictures; but history and longevity combined to drain from him the aura that still surrounds Dean. If Dean's petulant boy crystalized the 1950s concern with troubled affluent adolescents, Garfield's petulant boy—in 1940, with Europe already at war—seemed increasingly anachronistic, whether as sex symbol or pathetic victim of social forces. By mid-1940 his screen persona had reached a dead end.

▪ ▪ ▪

Central to Garfield's problems was that the studio (which liked best his screen persona as a junior James Cagney) already had the authentic Cagney to play "Cagney" roles. Several times in 1939 and 1940 both men were candidates for the same part. Only once (in *Dust Be My Destiny*, for which Cagney was considered too old) did Garfield get the part.

Around 1939 Steve Trilling's casting department began drawing up charts listing possible performers for cast consideration. Each substantial part in a picture would have three to more than a dozen names suggested for it. As an example, for the star role of Frank Ross, reporter, in *Each Dawn I Die* (1939), the chart listed Cagney first, Garfield second, and (an unlikely addition to that duo) James Stewart third. Humphrey Bogart headed the list of five names for the second male lead as "'Hood' Stacey, Underworld Big Shot." Had this casting held up, it would have been the third consecutive Cagney film in which he had played together with Bogart. (After *Angels with Dirty Faces* had come the western *The Oklahoma Kid*, not quite so distinguished a work as their first collaboration; *Variety* gave the film one of its infrequent negative reviews of a major studio A picture, and the *New York Herald-Tribune* saw it as an example of Hollywood reviving the western genre to retain a market in fascist countries.)

One day before *Each Dawn I Die* was scheduled to begin shooting, the third Cagney-Bogart collaboration was suddenly deferred. On the eve of production Warner Bros. signed on George Raft, the former Paramount star, to play "Hood" Stacey. A few weeks later it made a long-term deal with Raft, and the one-time associate of New York gangster Owney Madden drove a hard bargain. In his first year he was to make only one picture at $50,000, with the right to make three outside films. Another contract, agreed upon several months later, established him at three films per year at $55,000 each, rising to $75,000 in four annual options.

Few people in or out of the movie industry considered Raft much of an actor. He had, however, an undeniable screen presence—an aura of authority—that made him a stronger partner for Cagney than Bogart had proven to be in *Angels with Dirty Faces* or *The Oklahoma Kid*. Stacey was to be a bad man who acts nobly, rather than a bad man who acts in character; Bogart had never played such a role.

Raft's arrival was a double blow to Bogart. He lost the Stacey part (he had been in the picture's preliminary budget as late as forty-eight hours before shooting began) and he faced a future in which Raft had considerably higher priority for any tough-guy roles the studio offered. There was no consolation for him: he went without assignment for five months, using up unpaid vacation time he had accumulated during three years of nearly nonstop labor.

For Cagney, *Each Dawn I Die* was a curious film, offering a twist on the Cagney screen persona that satisfied Hal Wallis, though not many others. The actor plays a crusading investigative reporter who is framed by a crooked district attorney and sent to a brutal prison where prisoners are sadistically mistreated. Protesting his innocence and the injustice done to him, he becomes embittered, enraged, wrathful, and perhaps unbalanced, with alternating bursts of violence and tears. There are obvious parallels to *I Am a Fugitive from a Chain Gang*, but the 1939 film lacks the historical and social specificity of the earlier work. Cagney appears almost despondent in a role that dramatized the character's degradation without demonstrating his humanity. Wallis, however, got the grit and guts he was looking for in Cagney's performance style. It marked the first time since the actor's return to the studio that the executive did not complain about Cagney's softness and order retakes. Perhaps there was something about seeing the rebellious performer in prison stripes that appealed to the associate executive producer.

It was an experience Cagney was determined not to repeat. In July 1939, culminating negotiations that had been going on for months (and that had begun with a rare face-to-face conference between the actor and Jack L. Warner), Cagney signed a new contract that again broke new ground for Warner Bros. in the sound era. It covered eleven films to be made over four years, at a salary of $150,000 per picture—plus 10 percent of gross earnings over $1.5 million on each film. In addition, Cagney was to have story approval, and the right to terminate the contract at any time he wished (in standard contracts, right of termination belonged solely to the studio). Of all the contract concessions, the most "severe" (from the studio's viewpoint) was giving in to the actor's demand for a share of the profits. In a warning letter from Burbank to the New York office, the contract department head had written, "It is difficult to suppress information relating to motion picture deals, and should the provisions of paragraph 33 [the percentage clause] happen to fall into the hands of the *Variety* or any trade paper, upon which they would, of course, capitalize, we may find some rather belligerent artists on our hands, such as Flynn, Muni, Davis, etc."[8] There is no record—certainly not in their own contracts—that these artists heard a word about it.

Cagney had supplied, at least for himself, a provisional answer to the question, How much is a star worth? For now, it was no less than 10 percent of the gross. If his pictures earned less than $1.5 million, his percentage would go up. Warner Bros. had no fear that that would happen. In fact, the six films Cagney made under the new contract each earned more than the base figure—several considerably more— and the actor was paid nearly $1 million in additional income.

Two pictures remained to be made on the extant contract before the new one took effect. Cagney immediately went into production on *The Roaring Twenties* (1939). In many ways this was a remarkable film for the era. The original story was written by Mark Hellinger, a former Broadway columnist who had become a Warner Bros. producer. Its premise was that a cultural abyss had opened—in less than a decade—between the Prohibition era and the later 1930s, dominated by the New Deal, the rise of fascism, and the imminence of war. The atmosphere of the recent past seemed distant, yet the names and events had not faded from memory. Hellinger based his story on actual people and places from New York in the nightclub era, particularly Texas Guinan and Larry Fay, and their famous nightspot, the El Fey Club. The contrasting moods—of documentation and reverie—poise the film between condemnation of a lawless and violent era (necessitated by the Production Code) and nostalgia for an apparently simpler time, when the mugs were city boys, not foreign dictators.

Warner Bros. made a surprise choice in signing Raoul Walsh to direct the film. This venerable former actor and longtime director, whose credits went back before World War I, had lately been biding his time directing musicals and comedies at Paramount. The chance to do *The Roaring Twenties* at Warner Bros. offered his career a reprieve, and he made the most of it.

Though Walsh had a reputation as an "action" director, in his hands *The Roaring Twenties* became a film less about action than about character. This offered a reprieve to Cagney, too. Though his character is a "bad" man here, as opposed to a "good" man in *Each Dawn I Die*, his respective performances are almost antithetical. He creates a subdued, gentle, almost sweet characterization of a man who was a bootlegger and even a killer. Wallis again dashed off memos to the director, imploring that Cagney be made tougher. The screen evidence suggests that he did not succeed.

Another beneficiary of Walsh's direction was, surprisingly, Humphrey Bogart. The actor had returned from his lengthy holiday to the most ignominious role of his entire career, as a vampire (a mad doctor, escaped from the grave, with a brush haircut marked by a long white streak up the middle) in a B picture, *The Return of Dr. X* (1939). From this he went directly into *The Roaring Twenties*. One might have thought Bogart's part was a natural for Raft, who had actually worked at the El Fey Club as a dancer in the 1920s. Though Raft was playing crooks and convicts, however, he was not exactly playing heavies; and in any case, since he was limited to only one picture on his current contract, a more starring role had been selected for him.

Thus the third, and last, collaboration between Cagney and Bogart came to pass. Bogart would be a bad guy in *The Roaring Twenties*: his part was like a dozen other bad guys he had played before, yet this performance was a little different. If Walsh's attention to character subtleties was incongruous (at least by reputation), nevertheless it worked for Bogart as well as for Cagney. Bogart seems more alive, more energetic, in performance than he had been in a long time. He delivers his lines more tersely; he takes his hands out of his pockets and finds bits of business to do with them, like the old Cagney trick of brushing off another man's lapel; he tries out some of the facial tics, like baring his upper teeth, that were to become his signature mannerisms. It may not have amounted to a lot, but it led a *New York Herald-Tribune* writer to call Bogart's performance "the best thing of its kind I have ever seen."

Despite this performance and its acclaim, Bogart's work life at Warner Bros. continued to be frustrating. The major studios (not just independents like Goldwyn and Wanger) began to ask for Bogart loan-outs; Warner Bros.' answer invariably was no. The actor was in demand for appearances on radio drama programs; since he had no rights in his contract to do such work, Jack Warner permitted him to accept only on the condition that he give half his fee—which usually approximated his weekly salary—to the Los Angeles Community Chest.

These loan-out and radio requests suggest that Bogart was gaining some recognition in the entertainment community. To Warner Bros. management, however, he remained a utility man and stock role player. In the Raft vehicle *Invisible Stripes* (1939) he plays another bad guy with none of the Walsh-influenced verve. (The film, however, does play an interesting game with its status as fiction. Raft's character goes to a movie—a Warner Bros. movie, naturally, the

1939 *You Can't Get Away with Murder*. In the theater vestibule he looks at a promotional still picture, in which the actor Humphrey Bogart is visible. At that moment Bogart, playing a character in *Invisible Stripes*, walks out of the theater.)

There was a further demotion. The part of the bandit leader John Murrell in a Civil War western, *Virginia City* (1940)—Michael Curtiz directing, Errol Flynn the star—was considered a natural for John Carradine, but he was unavailable, still finishing *Gone with the Wind* (1939). A similar type, Victor Jory, was the second choice. Somehow, Bogart ended up with the role. He wears a pencil moustache, long sideburns, and a string tie, and speaks with a phony Hispanic accent. "Audiences would like to see more of Bogart than the script provides," said *Variety*, not mentioning whether they wanted more of the accent.

While Bogart was undergoing the usual travails, Cagney finished his old contract with *The Fighting 69th* (1940). This film concerns the 69th New York regiment and Father Frances P. Duffy (the figure honored by a monument at 49th and Broadway) in World War I. Cagney plays a loudmouthed, unlikeable recruit whose sudden cowardice in combat causes the deaths of many of his comrades, but whose moral conversion at Father Duffy's hands leads him to a heroic sacrifice. The film broke the Strand's attendance record set by Cagney in *G Men* five years earlier. It drew contradictory reactions, however, to its representation of the military experience. Some American commentators feared it might be a spur to militarism; in Britain, on the other hand, its surprisingly realistic scenes of battle were read as calls for pacifism and avoidance of the European war. The Americans were closer to the mark than the British: the film takes its place among other Warner Bros. pictures of the period, such as *Sergeant York* (1941) and *They Died with Their Boots On* (1942), in fostering an attitude of preparedness for war. Like those other works, *The Fighting 69th* vividly portrayed the steps whereby civilians turn themselves into soldiers.

The new Cagney contract had set up what amounted to a Cagney unit on the Warner lot: the actor's brother William would function as associate producer on all his films, and would do the negotiating over studio projects requiring the actor's approval (James usually returned to his farm on Martha's Vineyard between pictures). In retrospect, this setup seemed designed to give William production experience that would be valuable for future independent endeavors. During the last months of 1939, all had agreed that the inaugural film would be based on Aben Kandel's 1936 novel about (where else?) New York's Lower East Side, *City for Conquest*. Early in 1940, however, script delays on that picture forced them to find a substitute. William had already rejected a project, *Torrid Zone*, on behalf of his brother, calling the script "a typical Cagney vehicle and that is just the reason he would refuse to do it."[9] Cagney had been too long off the screen, however, and when the studio insisted on submitting it formally to the actor, he accepted it.

Bill Cagney had it right: *Torrid Zone* was a throwback to the early 1930s Cagney programmers. Concocted of comedy, violence, and sexual innuendos, its main innovation was that it was set in a banana republic. Another difference is that Cagney had put on some weight over the years—a pot belly shows in some undershirt shots. A third was the actor's resistance to playing the mug. The syndrome by now was all too familiar: an objectionable script, Cagney's revolt, Hal Wallis's distress. Director William Keighley began receiving memos that were carbon copies of memos the executive had sent him as far back as *G Men* and as recently as *Each Dawn I Die*: Make Cagney stop playing a gentleman, make him tougher. Neither as a movie nor as an experience was *Torrid Zone* a promising way to start Cagney's new deal.

City for Conquest (1941) was something different. When it began shooting in late May 1940, the picture carried nearly a year of preparation: it was the project intended to showcase Cagney's new status as the studio's highest-paid, profit-participation star. He was only disappointed in that his desire to have Michael Curtiz as director was not fulfilled; Anatole Litvak got the assignment. *City for Conquest* is *The Roaring Twenties* updated to the Depression years: it is a documentation and reverie not so much on history as on the composite Warner Bros. portrait of those years. It moves, as the script says, from Essex Street (on the Lower East Side) to the Essex House (on Central Park South)—from the studio's fictional immigrant ghetto to its equally fictional luxury penthouses. Cagney is an aspiring welterweight who loses the championship, and his eyesight, in a crooked fight. There is his girlfriend (Ann Sheridan), an aspiring dancer who betrays him, and his brother (Arthur Kennedy), an aspiring boy composer, for whom he sacrifices all.

It is a film filled with all the usual clichés, and yet its touching power derives in part from their familiarity. It draws even more on the poignancy of Cagney's somber, quiet, almost self-effacing performance. He had at last achieved the understated screen persona that he and Hal Wallis had been battling over. *City for Conquest* is an unabashedly sentimental film, but it carries the gravity of its summation of the films that spoke for an era. It bears the density of the studio's recognition that a watershed movement had arrived—that an epoch, the interwar years, was ending. *The Roaring Twenties* had been another such marker (*High Sierra*, in preproduction while *City for Conquest* was shooting, would be a third).

Speaking of poignancy, *City for Conquest* was yet another of Bogart's near misses. Until a few days before production began, he was set for the relatively small role of Googi, a gangster. Suddenly, however, as with *Each Dawn I Die*, the studio put another actor in the part. It was not a star figure like Raft, but a stage actor with no previous Hollywood experience. One of the company's New York executives had spotted the actor playing a gangster in Group Theatre's *Golden Boy* (in which Garfield had also appeared). "His characterization of Fuseli was the most unusual, ruthless, and dynamic thing I have ever seen," the executive wrote Hal Wallis.[10] His name was Elia Kazan, and his only previous movie appearance (almost certainly unknown to Warner Bros.) had been in a little production by a New York left filmmaking group, *Pie in the Sky* (1935). Kazan came out to Burbank and brought his dynamism to Googi in *City for Conquest*.

Once you've seen Kazan as Googi, it's difficult to imagine Bogart in the role. Whether it was the parts he got to play, or those that were taken from him at the last minute, nothing for which Warner Bros. considered Bogart seemed tailored to him; they were roles meant for other actors, from John Carradine to Bela Lugosi. Slowly, however, there were signs of change. The studio may have been giving more attention to finding appropriate parts, or he was working harder to make his screen persona more distinctive; perhaps these went hand in hand. The first evidence came in an unlikely vehicle, *It All Came True* (1940). This was a mixed-genre concoction (gangster comedy with music) based on a Louis Bromfield novel. As Grasselli, a crooked nightclub owner, Bogart kills a man and hides out in a Broadway boardinghouse inhabited by over-the-hill entertainers. He ends up transforming the place into a night spot and turning himself in to the police. The director was Lewis Seiler, a recent graduate from the B unit, among whose distinctions seems to have been an ability (also seen earlier in *King of the Underworld*) to draw out, or condone, Bogart's comic side.

Since *King of the Underworld* escaped most peoples' attention, Bogart's performance as a menace with a sense of humor was headline news in the entertainment pages. "Bogart Steals Comedy Honors," the *Boston Post* topped its review; in New York the accolades read, "Humphrey Bogart Excels" in the *World-Telegram*, and "Humphrey Bogart Tops" in the *Brooklyn Daily Eagle*. He had never before been praised in quite such big type. Novelist Bromfield, who was becoming a close friend of the actor, wrote a personal letter to Wallis after the production ended (but before the reviews were in) hailing Bogart's performance and adding, "I doubt that his talents as a comedian, which are very great, have been enough appreciated."[11]

Without the reviews as further proof, Bromfield's letter may have been read as special pleading; it was not enough to prevent Bogart from getting another stock gangster assignment, opposite Edward G. Robinson in *Brother Orchid* (1940). This was the first recorded occasion on which Bogart made a serious complaint: he spoke to Steve Trilling, who reported to Wallis that the actor was "very disgruntled."[12] Justly so—Bogart's role was a throwback to the one-dimensional heavies of *Kid Galahad* days. When the *It All Came True* reviews arrived, however, Bogart found himself with Raoul Walsh again in *They Drive by Night* (1940).

He had a relatively secondary part in this important but uneven film—half social-realist drama about truckers, half woman's genre melodrama about a neurotic rich wife who murders her husband and makes a play for another man. Bogart plays George Raft's younger brother, a trucker who loses an arm after falling asleep at the wheel and driving off the road. He's a domestic man—a husband on-screen for the first time since *Black Legion*. Under Walsh's direction, he creates a humane, multidimensional portrait. "Bogart is excellent as the hard-working driver and Raft's brother," *Variety* wrote. "He can easily graduate from gangster and heavy assignments."

While working with Walsh on *They Drive by Night*, Bogart heard the rumors (along with the trade press, the Hollywood columnists, and every concerned movie fan from coast to coast) that Paul Muni was refusing Warner Bros.' offer of the starring role in Walsh's next picture, an adaptation of the W. R. Burnett novel *High Sierra*. Muni had, at this point, a contract signed in 1937 paying him $112,500 per picture, as well as "absolute right" of story approval, and the right to terminate the contract if the studio failed to produce a project worthy of his interest.[13] In two years only two scripts had met Muni's standards: *Juarez* and *We Are Not Alone* (1939), in which he plays an Austrian doctor accused of murdering his wife. It is likely that Muni will be remembered best for two remarkable 1932 performances—as the unjustly imprisoned engineer of *I Am a Fugitive from a Chain Gang* and the neurotic Italian gangster of the Howard Hawks–Howard Hughes film *Scarface*. By the latter half of the 1930s he preferred playing nineteenth-century heroes like Zola, Pasteur, and Juarez. The doomed bank robber Roy Earle of *High Sierra* was not at all to his taste; when he definitively refused it, his contract was voided by mutual agreement.

The role was decidedly to another actor's taste. Following up on his new boldness—first demonstrated in protesting his *Brother Or-chid* part—Bogart on May 4, 1940, sent Wallis a telegram: "Dear Hal: You told me once to let you know when I found a part I wanted. A few weeks ago I left a note for you concerning *High Sierra*. I never received an answer so I'm bringing it up again as I understand there is some doubt about Muni doing it. Regards. Humphrey Bogart."[14] Despite later claims by George Raft that he, too, refused the part, there is no evidence in the studio's production records (once Muni's refusal was definite) that it was offered to anyone other than Bogart. Others might object to playing a convict, a killer, a man who dies at the end—yet all of these had been aspects of Bogart's stock character as it took form after *The Petrified Forest*, and few of his roles had the added breadth or density that Roy Earle promised. It had become a standard line in reviews of his films that the studio should give him something of greater consequence to do. On the evidence of *The Roaring Twenties*, *It All Came True*, and *They Drive by Night*, all in the past year, Warner Bros. executives seem to have agreed that he had earned it.

6

Pushcarts and Patriotism

High Sierra (1941), with Humphrey Bogart in the Roy Earle role, began shooting on August 5, 1940. Less than two weeks later, in the midst of the biggest break of his career, Bogart's name flashed across the country in front-page headlines. He was named in testimony before a Los Angeles grand jury—along with nearly twenty other Hollywood personalities, including James Cagney—by one John L. Leech as a sympathizer, contributor, and possibly a member of the Communist party.

Nothing Bogart had done as a stage or motion picture actor through mid-1940 had given him as much national prominence as this allegation. Though far more famous names were invoked in the assertions of Hollywood support for Communist activities (besides Cagney, they included actor Fredric March and director Fritz Lang), when the House Un-American Activities Committee held hearings to give the accused an opportunity to rebut the charges, the first witness called was Humphrey DeForest Bogart. This was all the more unusual in that Bogart's name had never been mentioned in testimony directly before the committee.

The episode began in July 1940 when Congressman Martin Dies of Texas, the committee chairman, sitting alone in an executive session in Beaumont, Texas, heard testimony on Communist party activities in California from the same John L. Leech, who identified himself as a former member of the party's state committee. In a broader context, it had commenced with the surprise announcement, a year earlier, of a nonaggression agreement between the Soviet Union and Nazi Germany. This brought to an end the Popular Front era of American radical politics.

During the heyday of its Popular Front strategy in the mid-1930s, the Communist party had forged coalitions with liberals to pursue shared goals; in Hollywood, with a considerable number of Jews in important positions (as well as a strong contingent of émigrés from nazism), the most extensive collaboration had occurred in antifascist organizations. The Nazi-Soviet pact destroyed not only that unity, but also a certain immunity the Communist party had gained from right-wing attacks because of its participation in the American political mainstream. Now that Communists were allied with fascists instead of liberals, their past activities suddenly became vulnerable to retrospective scrutiny and condemnation. Martin Dies was setting this inquiry in motion by calling Leech to testify.

Leech's revelations covered many aspects of the party's work in California, including its efforts to recruit racial minorities and its activities during a contentious San Francisco dock strike; however, Dies and his staff seemed particularly interested in the party's Hollywood connections. All together, perhaps half of Leech's estimated forty or so Hollywood contributors to the party were discussed by name during four days of testimony in Beaumont. Asked to offer an explanation for their involvement, Leech suggested that they supported the party because they feared nazism and anti-Semitism.

None of the committee's or Leech's Hollywood names reached the press until the witness was called to repeat his allegations before a Los Angeles County grand jury nearly a month later. What was Congressman Dies's role in this? Only the calendar provides a clue. Details of Leech's grand jury testimony were "made public"—someone gave transcripts to the press—on Wednesday, August 14, 1940, and appeared in morning papers on the 15th. On Friday the 16th, in Los Angeles, Dies took testimony from Bogart, the actor's business manager, and Leech.

Could there be some connection among Dies's presence in Los Angeles (with his staff), Leech's testimony before the grand jury, and its leak to the press? Perhaps the only unexpected aspect was that Leech would leave out some names from his Beaumont account and add others not named there: the new names included those of March, Bogart, director Gregory La Cava, and writer Clifford Odets. This surprise precipitated an unknown chain of events that, with lightning speed, led Congressman Dies, his secretary, and his investigator to congregate for an executive hearing within twenty-four hours of the press revelations, and pulled Humphrey Bogart off the *High Sierra* set to deny the charges. The chairman's haste indicated that he feared for the continuing effectiveness of his operation if he allowed reckless charges to stand against prominent persons whose employers were politically well connected.

Bogart's testimony was brief. He answered "No" to all questions of involvement with the Communist party and Popular Front organizations. Asked to give his own views on "un-American activities" in Hollywood, he replied that, in his opinion, "subversive activities" were going on in Hollywood but not, principally, by Hollywood people. "I think Hollywood people are dupes for the most part," he said. He recalled the many requests for contributions he had received in the mid-1930s—the first surge of Popular Front activities—"but somehow God in Heaven guided me along the correct path," and he had refused. Dies then gave Bogart the requested absolution. "While we've had investigators working in Los Angeles and California for a considerable period of time," the chairman said, "there has never been any suggestion or charge or accusation or inference that involved your name." When Bogart left, Dies went on the record and told the press the same thing.

Then it was time to grill Leech as to why the witness had put the chairman in the position of granting clearances to people of whom the committee had never taken cognizance. Leech began his self-defense confidently, boldly asserting that he knew Bogart to be a Communist party member. On this occasion, however, Dies did not absorb such revelations complacently. He took the stance of an aggressive defense attorney representing Bogart (as well as Cagney and several other performers). He asked hard, probing questions of his ex-Communist witness, forcing admissions that his accusations were based on vague recollections, hearsay, and bold leaps of inference. In fact, Leech had no evidence against Bogart—or Cagney—at all. Though no single word or phrase connotes the chairman's disbelief, the overall impression that rises from cold pages of published transcripts is of Dies palpably distancing himself from a witness exposed as unreliable.[1]

The Federal Bureau of Investigation did, however, take an interest in Leech's charges. It opened a file on Bogart, noting in a memo the accusations and the actor's denials. The memo also noted additional information: "In October 1936 it was confidentially reported that Bogart had made a contribution to the Seattle Post-Intelligencer newspaper guild strike and also to the Salinas lettuce workers strike."[2] The FBI took no position on the veracity either of Leech or of its unnamed informants.

Though Dies had questioned the witness on Cagney's behalf at the Los Angeles hearings, Cagney's situation remained considerably different from Bogart's. In the Beaumont hearings, the committee's investigator had prompted Leech's recollection of the actor with the remark, "Much has been said about his connection with the Communist Party."[3] This gave the witness leeway to expatiate on Cagney's 1934 political activities and to link him further with the Communist party. When news of Leech's grand jury accusations reached him, Cagney was back East on Martha's Vineyard. Arrangements were made for him to travel by airplane and meet with Dies in San Francisco (whence the committee entourage had moved) on Tuesday, August 20.

Given the circumstances, Cagney was not in a position to appear either naive or belligerent. He denied being a member of the Communist party, or knowingly contributing to it; but he spoke frankly about his support for radical causes that inadvertently, perhaps, had associated him with Communists. He mentioned contributions to the Salinas lettuce strike (there was some confusion over how many strikes, and which, he gave money to), the Scottsboro defense, the Tom Mooney Defense Committee, and toward the purchase of an ambulance for Loyalist Spain.

At this point the chairman interrupted his investigator's questions to ask the actor if he also gave to such organizations as the Boy Scouts and the Community Chest. When Cagney answered affirmatively, Dies offered this interrogatory observation: "In other words you have been a liberal contributor to causes that you thought were worthy and appealed to your humanitarian impulses?" These hardly sound like the words of a witch-hunter; one might almost think they had been written for him, perhaps on a typewriter in Burbank.

Chairman Dies was quite willing to let Cagney off the hook with an admonition to be careful about where he gave his money. He even went so far as to ask the actor if anyone was trying to injure his reputation. "You have made no enemies that you know of?" Dies asked.

The Catholic church, he might have answered. Church officials had vetoed the suggestion that he play the title role in *Knute Rockne—All American* (1940), a biopic about the legendary University of Notre Dame football coach, because of his public support for the Spanish Republic. But Cagney chose not to speak of politics. Though he trivialized the question, his answer was nevertheless revealing. He told of being annoyed in public by people who wanted to challenge him because of the hoodlum roles he played. In nightclubs they came up and pushed him in the face: "They have an active dislike for me because of the kind of parts I play. That, of course, is an unreasonable attitude, I would say."[4]

Shortly after, Dies met the press and publicly absolved Bogart and Cagney (along with Fredric March, who had testified in Los Angeles, and writer Philip Dunne, who appeared before the committee in San Francisco) of charges that they were sympathetic to communism. Others named by Leech were later to seek Dies's absolution in New York, but it appears that Dies had managed to hear and clear the four most prominent liberals named by his (as it was becoming obvious) none-too-trustworthy witness.

▪▪▪▪

On the morning in August 1940 when "Hollywood Stars Accused as Reds" made the *New York Times* front page, the paper's main headline, covering five columns in three tiers, proclaimed: "British Seek Parachute Invaders Reported Sent as Suicide Squads; R.A.F. Bombs Big Plants in Italy." Five months later, when *High Sierra* opened in New York, it was accompanied by a short film on the London Blitz, *Christmas under Fire*, and a personal appearance by its narrator, war correspondent Quentin Reynolds. The Battle of Britain did not preoccupy every American's mind in the fall and winter of 1940–1941, but it was in the field of vision nonetheless, a signal that, once again, life was taking a decisive turn.

Warner Bros. had already found a way to lighten the impact of the European crisis on its familiar genre productions—or at least to incorporate within them the feeling that old forms were being overtaken by world events. It inscribed in some of its most successful genre pictures an elegiac mood: by creating an aura of obsolescence, it managed paradoxically to give the forms renewed dramatic force. This had worked in *The Roaring Twenties* by setting the film in the recent, but distanced, past; in *City for Conquest* by showing the transformation from past to present.

High Sierra was in the same mode, but it took greater risks: it brought the past into the present, making the elegiac tone more poignant by building it into the protagonists' consciousness. The central risk was that the sense of an ending would be overlooked by reviewers and spectators, who might then see the film (as indeed some did) only as another gangster picture, inappropriate for the times; or even worse, mistake the note of elegy for a favorable attitude toward gangsters. It was up to Bogart as Roy Earle to carry the major burden of interpretation. The studio had not given him a role with so much responsibility since *Black Legion*; but it also put him in the hands of a production team that seemed ideally assembled to bring out his strengths. Perhaps the composition of that group had even been a decisive factor in Bogart's assignment.

As associate producer on *It All Came True*, Mark Hellinger supervised one of Bogart's most distinctive performances; earlier, he had written the original story that set the nostalgic tone for *The Roaring Twenties*. He was associate producer on *High Sierra*, working with director Raoul Walsh, who had demonstrated an ability (in *The Roaring Twenties* and *They Drive by Night*) to draw from Bogart previously untapped resources of subtlety and energy. No less important than Bogart's previous affinities with Hellinger and Walsh was the fact that Roy Earle was a fully developed character, not merely a type. The figure had been created in W. R. Burnett's novel, and Burnett had been hired to work on the screenplay with John Huston. Earle possessed a personal history and an interior life, carried over intact, though necessarily truncated, from one medium to the other. It was a part Bogart could inhabit rather than invent from scratch. In more than two dozen pictures since *The Petrified Forest*, the opportunity to play a character conceived elsewhere than in a screenplay had occurred less than a handful of times—principally in *Dead End* and *It All Came True*.

What was missing from the propitious ingredients that went into *High Sierra* was confidence from the front office. Hal Wallis objected to the casting department's pro forma recommendation that Bogart be billed first on the picture. He proposed to Jack Warner that Ida Lupino, the female lead, be placed ahead. "Lupino has had a great deal of publicity on the strength of *They Drive by Night*," Wallis wrote in a memo to Warner, "whereas Bogart has been playing the leads in a lot of 'B' pictures, and this fact might mitigate again [*sic*] the success of *High Sierra*."[5] Lupino got first billing, but nobody was fooled. It was Bogart's picture.

High Sierra opens with Roy Earle gaining a pardon after eight years in a Midwestern state prison—a further instance of the prominence prison narratives and scenes had assumed in the city boy pictures of this period. The pardon, we soon learn, was arranged through bribes paid by a gangland boss, who wants Earle for a major robbery. Headlines announcing Earle's release call him the "famous Indiana Bank Robber," a reference contemporary audiences would certainly have associated with the legendary Indiana bank robber John Dillinger, whose name is later invoked in the movie's dialogue. The film clearly links Earle with Dillinger, while it also takes pains to put a certain distance between the fictional character and the historical person. In the movie, Earle goes to jail in 1932. Dillinger was in prison from 1924 to 1933, and then began his famous escapades that led to his death at the FBI's hands in 1934. It is a small point, but in Hollywood's discursive practices an important one, that the fictional Roy Earle is not a participant in the national crime scare and murderous shoot-outs of the early New Deal years (dramatized in *G Men*). He is in a sense their sole survivor and, in 1940, an atavism from another time.

Still, we are meant to see in Earle some of Dillinger's legendary stature, specifically because of their shared social origins. Earle is an Indiana farm boy whose life of crime is an exile from the natural world he was born to. Leaving the prison, he heads for a nearby park and looks around wonderingly, remarking, "Grass is still green, trees are still growin'." On his way west to take up his gangland duties he stops off at the old family farm, where the current landholder fears banks more than archcriminals. Later, at his High Sierra hideaway, Earle mutters in his sleep, "Sure I'll go back to the farm . . . sweet Indiana farm . . . but you're holding me back . . . don't hold me back . . . farm's the best . . . yes, that's the best . . . you can't take that away . . . you can't." Earle's sense of displacement goes far beyond his eight lost years of freedom, to his unrecoverable innocent youth. Bogart's sad, thoughtful, yearning looks are directed toward what his character's inner eye alone can see.

Some commentators on the film (in 1941 and later) have objected to the extensive narrative attention devoted to Earle's relationship to the callow teenager Velma (Joan Leslie), yet his feelings for her are central to the pathos of his own self-conception. This ward of grandparents driven off *their* Indiana farm, spared adulthood by the handicap of her deformed foot, is indeed the alter ego, the double, of Earle's fantasized youth. By arranging the surgery to heal her deformity, helping to cure the defect that contained her in innocent isolation, he unwittingly destroys the fantasized future he imagined with her. Leaving the cocoon where he had found her, she "falls" into the world he inhabits, and her casual betrayal of his dreams forces his bitter reacknowledgment of his own expulsion from an imagined Eden into the world of necessity, time, and death.

Bound by necessity, Earle is compelled to lead a robbery of a Palm Springs–style resort hotel in the California desert; bound by time, Earle is acutely aware how swiftly it is running out for him. "'Member what Johnny Dillinger said about guys like you and him?" Doc Banton (Henry Hull) remarks to Earle. "He said you were just rushin' toward death. Yes, that's it—rushin' toward death." After these lines there is a quick wipe to a shot of the dog Pard, the film's sign for mortality, the carrier of bad luck—whom Earle adopts, tries unsuccessfully to shake, and then embraces as his fate. The robbery goes poorly, the gangland boss dies, Earle shoots the venal ex-cop Kranmer (Barton MacLane): death closes in as he drives back into the high mountains in a final, futile gesture of escape.

The film's dominant tone of anachronism and symbolism was heightened during production beyond what was in the screenplay. Added in the shooting was a scene in which the fleeing Earle hears about himself on the car radio after the announcer says, "Turning from the European news, ladies and gentlemen. . . ." Also added was the radio reporter who speaks poetic prose into his microphone as Earle is cornered in the mountains. "The tall pine trees clustered around like a silent jury," he embellishes the scene, "and up above a defiant gangster from a simple farm on the flats of Indiana about to be killed on the site of the highest mountain peak in the United States." These radio voices function as a chorus exhorting both world events and nature to stand in judgment on the atavistic, doomed Roy Earle.

Contemporary reviewers also delivered their verdicts: perhaps surprisingly, in light of *High Sierra*'s later rise to classic stature, these tended to be negative. *Variety* panned the film; so did a majority of the New York papers, including the *Journal-American*, *Post*, *Sun*, *World-Telegram*, and *PM*. In *PM* Cecilia Ager concluded her review, "Everybody and everything is easy to understand, except the curious path along which the audience sympathy is directed." The critical consensus did not appreciate what it viewed as the film's sentimental treatment of characters whom the *Sun*'s Eileen Creelman called, "dull-witted" and "unlikable," "rats without charm."

It was their way of saying that the times were out of joint not only for the fictional Roy Earle but for the movie that doomed him to that fate. Creelman in the *Sun* harked back to the beginning of the gangster cycle and *Little Caesar* (also adapted from a W. R. Burnett novel) and unfavorably compared Roy Earle to that film's "sympathetic" criminal Rico. How memory misserved. Edward G. Robinson's Rico was a good deal more dim-witted and violent than Roy Earle, but the rebellious spirit of the early Depression years turned him (like Cagney's Tom Powers in *The Public Enemy*) into an antisocial hero. The world of 1941 had lost its sympathy for devils.

Some, however, had not lost sympathy for actors. Bogart's performance was almost unanimously praised—in some quarters, lavishly. His admirers noted the doubleness of his characterization. "He is at once savage and sentimental," wrote Howard Barnes in the *New York Herald-Tribune*, "fatalistic and filled with half-formulated aspirations. This is one of the finest performances of a fine actor." John Mosher in the *New Yorker* devoted a lengthy paragraph to describing "Bogart's icy and literal and unextravagant performance," and made the first comparison between Bogart and Cagney, in print, anywhere, that implied that the two men could be discussed on the same level as actors: "Adept and quick as he is in the use of violence when it is needed, there's a suggestion of coolness in his movements and behavior which is quite different from the pent-up tension and agonized neuroses of a Cagney."

These comments are as perceptive as they are generous. Icy. Lit-

eral. Unextravagant. The terms get to the heart of Bogart's performance as Roy Earle just as surely half a century after the film was
made as they did the week of *High Sierra*'s release. After years of
playing the interchangeable Jack Bucks and Frank Wilsons and
Chuck Martins of Warner Bros.' easily forgettable gangster films, Bogart had developed the characterization to a point where he could
almost appear to *be* the figure on the screen, rather than project him.
This involved, almost certainly with Raoul Walsh's encouragement
(since it first became evident in *The Roaring Twenties*), paring down
the mannerisms, moving through the part in a restrained and quiet
way: literal and unextravagant, as Mosher wrote. The menace (the
iciness) remains, without the psychopathology of Duke Mantee or
"Baby Face" Martin, or the jaw-clenching and teeth-baring of the
Jacks and Franks and Chucks.

That, however, is only half the story. The other half involves the
doubleness that Howard Barnes noted: Bogart's capacity simultaneously to project opposing aspects of his character, savagery and sentimentality, fatalism and aspiration. To have become simply less os-
tentatious would have turned him merely into a second-string
"Humphrey Bogart–type"—a Barton MacLane or one of the other
guys in the gangster/convict chorus. It was not only playing a bad
guy, it was playing a bad guy who was also something else, like Grasselli in *It All Came True*—a little comic, a little sentimental, a little
self-reflective. From another perspective, what was happening was
that Bogart was finally learning to relax the discipline and will that
had turned an overage genteel boy of Broadway into Duke Mantee.

Bogart the killer had proven himself, and also carried himself as
far as he could go. Actors with only one dimension do not often become stars. Actors who create surprise, embody contradiction,
impel the spectator to hold two conflicting ideas in the head at the
same time, stand a better chance. To accomplish this, Bogart did not
have to construct a new screen persona. Instead he had to readmit
into his screen style the genteel comic traits of his stage-acting days.
Bogart's Roy Earle had the attributes both of a killer and of a romantic lead: this was one aspect of *High Sierra* that had the potential to
make viewers uneasy, and contributed to the negative reviews. It
also had the potential to boost Bogart out of character parts and into
star roles.

There is one subtle but striking moment in the movie that appears
neither in Burnett's novel nor in the Huston-Burnett screenplay. Roy
Earle enters the Tropico Hotel to case the joint for the planned robbery. He is dressed in a suit and tie when everyone else is wearing
sports clothes; to make himself look less conspicuously out of place,

he picks up a stray tennis racquet and carries it with him through the hotel. The tennis racquet was someone's idea of an inside joke (as in *Stand-In*)—a reminder of Bogart's youthful stage persona as the country-club type. It placed a kind of historical seal on Bogart's new screen persona: a man both icy and sentimental, who might be holding a tennis racquet one moment, a gun the next.

■ ■ ■ ■

Some people—like reviewers Barnes and Mosher—caught the signal. Some others, among them studio executives Warner and Wallis, apparently did not. Though it has become customary in writings about Bogart to describe *High Sierra* as the film that made him a star, that was hardly the case on the Warner lot in the following year. In some ways, the period after the Dies Committee ruckus and *High Sierra* was one of the most frustrating in Bogart's career.

The day after shooting closed on *High Sierra*, Bogart sent a telegram to Wallis, saying, "Dear Hal: Thanks very much for *High Sierra*. Hope we did as well as you hoped we would. Kindest regards."[6] Someone apparently was advising the actor to step up his personal diplomacy. There is no surviving response from the executive, though actions spoke as loudly as words: within a week Bogart was back on the treadmill, assigned to a remake of *Kid Galahad* called *The Wagons Roll at Night* (1941). The setting was changed from a boxing to a circus milieu, and Bogart was given the more important Edward G. Robinson role from the original film, but it played—or he played it—more like his own conventional bad-guy part in *Kid Galahad*. "Mr. Bogart is badly hampered in a ridiculously fustian villain role," wrote Bosley Crowther in the *New York Times*. Among the dictionary definitions for "fustian" are worthless, cheap, claptrap.

Notwithstanding this initial setback (and reassured when the studio took up the third option on his six-year contract, raising his salary to $1650 per week for its fourth year), Bogart maintained his diplomatic initiative: he was angling for a gangster part, but it was one with a difference, like Duke Mantee or "Baby Face" Martin—a figure created for the stage, by Irwin Shaw in his Group Theatre play *The Gentle People*. The studio's preferred associate producer for prestige literary adaptations, Henry Blanke, was developing the project, eventually released as *Out of the Fog* (1941); Bogart had not worked in a Blanke production since *The Petrified Forest*, and the producer had proposed Raft, Cagney, or Garfield for the gangster role.

Politicking for the assignment became unexpectedly heavy. When

Anatole Litvak was selected as the film's director, he came out in favor of Raft. Jack Warner—the man with the only vote that counted—was leaning toward Bogart. (The actor had sent him a telegram saying, "Dear Jack. It seems to me that I am the logical person on the lot to play 'Gentle People.' I would be greatly disappointed if I didn't get it. I would like very much to talk to you about it.")[7] Blanke threw his weight behind Garfield: the producer ordered tests of Garfield in the role. He carried his case personally to Warner, but the studio head remained adamant on Bogart for the gangster, Garfield for the romantic lead.

Then Blanke found an unexpected ally. Ida Lupino, assigned as the female lead, made it clear that she did not want to work with Bogart. That decided matters: Garfield got the gangster part. Lupino's reasons have never been revealed.

Out of the Fog—where the competitive struggle happens to be most baldly documented—makes clear that Warner Bros. was blessed with a surplus of performers and cursed by a dearth of important parts. Even the boss could not get the man he wanted into the part. Jack Warner wrote an exasperated memo about it to Hal Wallis. "Naturally we want to do as well as we humanly can with these people [i.e., performers]," he concluded, "but there is only so much you can do."[8]

Losing *Out of the Fog*, Bogart was assigned to *Manpower* (1941), along with George Raft and Marlene Dietrich. Raft—again, for unexplained reasons—played the Lupino game; apparently he had sufficient clout with studio executives to get Bogart removed (even though the picture's budget was raised by over $100,000 in salary and overhead when Edward G. Robinson took over the part).

Bogart was livid. He shot off a lengthy telegram to Wallis, saying, in part,

> I understand he [George Raft] has refused to make the picture if I am in it. . . . I tried to get George to tell me this morning what he was angry about and what I was supposed to have said but he wouldn't tell me. I feel very much hurt by this because it's the second time I have been kept out of a good picture and a good part by an actor's refusing to work with me. . . . I could see no way to protect myself against these insinuations and accusations and I think it's up to the company to protect me inasmuch as we are all concerned in the business of making good motion pictures.[9]

Bogart was not the only actor with whom Raft could not get along (small consolation for him). During production Raft verbally abused

Robinson and started a fistfight. It was not a staged encounter; though the studio leaked photos of the brawl to the press and used it to promote the picture, the two men punched in earnest.

Though not fighting, Bogart was also not working. When the studio removed him from *Manpower*, casting head Steve Trilling assigned him to a Civil War western, *Bad Men of Missouri* (1941). Bogart sent the script back by messenger with a note: "Dear Steve, Are you kidding—this is certainly rubbing it in—since Lupino and Raft are casting pictures maybe I can. Regards, Bogie."[10] He refused to report for work on the film, and was suspended without pay for more than five weeks while Dennis Morgan took over the role.

Here was an actor, on the verge of star status after *High Sierra*, unable to land a satisfactory part in his own studio. The incongruity was apparent to others in the industry: while he was suspended, MGM and Columbia tried to get Warners to loan out his services—in vain. Almost half a year had passed since he last appeared before a camera. Only the vagaries of George Raft's self-concept as an actor gave Bogart an opening to work again.

The project was not that auspicious; Raft had a penchant for turning parts down. Wallis's idea was to tell Raft to report, but not let him know what he was to report for. The picture was writer John Huston's first film as a director. It was a remake not merely of one but of two previous Warner Bros. films made from the same literary source; though it was not a B-unit project (not with the upscale Blanke as associate producer), its budget of under $400,000 was skimpy. Other than the lead part—for which Raft was slated—no well-known names were in the cast, and nearly all the talent came from outside the studio.

Raft, not surprisingly, said no. Looking down to the end of the bench, as in a B-unit football movie, coaches Warner and Wallis saw nobody left to throw into the game but Humphrey Bogart. The picture was *The Maltese Falcon* (1941).

For once, circumstances could hardly have broken better. Bogart's character, Sam Spade, is on the screen during almost the entire film—unusual even for star vehicles. Hardly any performer in the cast had any connection to his earlier career: there were few who might regard him disdainfully for his B-picture past, none making more money than he was on the picture. (The one cast member who had formerly outranked him—ex–Warners contract player Barton MacLane, now a freelancer—ironically took the role of Sam Spade's antagonist, Lieutenant of Detectives Dundy.) His main co-workers, Mary Astor, Peter Lorre, and Sydney Greenstreet, were distinctly different from the familiar 1930s Warner Bros. character types, and superbly complementary to him in their unique styles. Above all, the part of Sam Spade—as if written expressly for him—fit perfectly the new screen persona Bogart had been developing: a fusion of comedy and menace.

It was too good to be true; someone had to bring things back to their usual status of contention and adversity. Hal Wallis, as usual, provided the occasion. Huston was shooting the film in sequence with the script, and the executive's complaints began the moment he saw the first several days' rushes. He disliked the tempo that the director and his leading actor had adopted. "I think my criticism is principally with Bogart, who has adopted a leisurely suave form of delivery," Wallis memoed producer Blanke after watching the second day's work. "I don't think we can stand this all through a picture, as it is going to have a tendency to drag down the scene and slow them up too much. Bogart must have his usual brisk, staccato manner and delivery, and if he doesn't have it, I'm afraid we are going to be in trouble."[11] Wallis specifically mentioned the early scene in which Sam Spade answers the telephone in the middle of the night and responds laconically to news that his partner has been fatally shot. The lack in this scene of "punch" and "drive" (additional Wallis complaints), it should be noted, is as crucial to Sam Spade's character in Dashiell Hammett's original novel as it is to Huston's and Bogart's interpretation of him.

Spade is a man who plays his cards close to his chest. He keeps his menace in reserve, the better to use it with force when he wants to. He is aware that everyone else is acting a role and that he is too. It helps his work to be, as Gutman (Sydney Greenstreet) says, "wild and unpredictable." He is a borderline figure, half within and half outside society's laws and conventions. Like a gunfighter or samurai, he rations his energy for moments of action.

Neither Bogart nor Huston changed his intentions in response to Wallis's remarks. Fortunately, as shooting went on, the other performers began to contribute more than sufficient "punch" and "drive": Astor (as Brigid O'Shaughnessy) her hyperventilating dissimulations; Lorre (as Joel Cairo) his coy expressions of outrage; Greenstreet his worldly avarice; Elisha Cook, Jr., (as Wilmer) his simmering resentment. Bogart himself at last burst through his reserve with stunning rage. No further complaints were heard.

If Wallis wanted—but did not get—the "old" Bogart as a performer, what he did get, as it turned out, was the "old" Bogart's *aura* as a factor in audience response to Sam Spade. He had been the villain and the killer so many times, his stereotyping had been so consistent (and increasingly a subject of reviewers' complaints), that spectators could not help but expect Spade to become another of the "old" Bogart's characters. He even returned to using some of the facial mannerisms—curling his upper lip and baring his teeth—that he had cut back on when working with director Raoul Walsh. When he acted angry and menacing, therefore, that behavior might have appeared the more "authentic" Spade, because more in tune with the old "Bogart type" than what Wallis had called his "leisurely suave form of delivery." Nevertheless, the film itself seems to record the opposite, as when Spade laughs to himself after an angry blowup with Gutman, suggesting that his outburst was an act.

The persona of the "old" Bogart was deeply ingrained in the ambiguous characterization of Sam Spade. Moviegoers in the fall of 1941 had little or no experience of Bogart as other than a bad guy—minor roles in *Dark Victory* and *They Drive by Night* had been the only exceptions in the previous four years. Part of the suspense of *The Maltese Falcon* lies in not knowing on which side Spade's choice will fall, within or outside the law.

It comes as something of a shock—given the demands of Hollywood's narrative conventions, as well as its moral codes—that he falls precisely on neither side. The climactic scene with Brigid O'Shaughnessy simultaneously fulfills and confounds audience expectations about the Spade character. He tells her he has known all along that she killed his partner, and now he is going to turn her over to the police—despite his love for her—because of his allegiance to professional codes. He acts coldly and viciously toward her, in the interests of conventional justice, but solely for his own private reasons. "You do such wild, unpredictable things," she echoes the Fat Man. "I won't play the sap for you," he replies.

The words are drawn directly from Hammett's novel, published a decade earlier. The movie completed what Hammett's fiction began: the enthronement of a cultural type in American (and worldwide) popular entertainment, with whom the name Bogart would eventually be synonymous. In his 1944 book *The Hollywood Hallucination* critic Parker Tyler called this figure "The Good Villain and the Bad Hero," inscribing the doubleness that had become the basic strategy of Bogart's performance style. In the postwar period, the cultural type came to be known more tersely (but also more broadly) as the antihero.

"A remake with Humphrey Bogart in it," the *New York Times* wrote of *The Maltese Falcon*, "could mean almost anything." Reviewers did not know how to approach a film with Bogart in it, because they were aware that Warner Bros. had little inkling of how to use the actor. Studio executives' treatment of him after *The Maltese*

Falcon continued and confirmed their inability to recognize the potential star in their employ. More precisely, they were hardly concerned with him at all: their concern was for George Raft. The studio wanted Raft to play the lead in *All Through the Night* (1942), a mixed genre concoction—part gangster comedy, part espionage thriller. He was ordered to report for a starting date in late July 1941; however, in a memo to an assistant marked "Confidential," Wallis wrote, "If Raft does not appear, we will go ahead with Humphrey Bogart."[12] Raft did not appear. Bogart was told to take over the part, and the film went into production two weeks after *The Maltese Falcon* finished. "He is unhappy about the idea of doing a role only because George Raft refused to do it," Bogart's agent wrote Steve Trilling on the day shooting started. "I think you should bring this matter to the attention of Jack Warner and point out to him that a story should be prepared for which they have Bogart in mind and no other actor because it seems that for the past year he's practically pinch-hitted for Raft and has been kicked around from pillar to post, and I am thinking mainly of the *Manpower* situation."[13]

Bogart's character in *All Through the Night* is a Broadway gambler out of the Damon Runyon school. He gets involved in capturing Nazi spies in Yorkville (Manhattan's Upper East Side neighborhood where German immigrants concentrated) after they kill the baker of his favorite cheesecake. Bogart played it more for comedy than for drama, and it helped that Jackie Gleason and Phil Silvers were members of his gang. Director Vincent Sherman was forced to begin shooting before the script was finished—an increasingly common occurrence in the turbulent period around the United States' entry into World War II—and the subsequent slowdowns merited one of Jack Warner's classic memos. "I saw Friday's dailies and they were over before I could get my cigar lighted," Warner complained in a memo to Wallis. "That great, no director can be."[14]

All Through the Night was released in January 1942, a few weeks after the Japanese attack on Pearl Harbor brought about the United States' declaration of war, and the *New York Herald-Tribune* liked it enough to write that it combined "entertainment with persuasive propaganda to become both a solace and a challenging reminder of the issues at stake in this portentous moment of history." The making of entertainment with persuasive propaganda, one might say, was something Hollywood attempted to do in peace as well as war; but its function became all the more firmly linked to state purpose in wartime.

It may have been that impending wartime conditions, with performers liable for military service, impelled Warner Bros. to analyze how it was using its contract roster, Bogart among them. Along with several others, he was not quite in the first rank of stars, had neither a top salary nor privileged contract provisions, and did not seem to fit into its plans for major productions. Underutilized, he caused trouble when assigned to minor films. The solution was to put him on the market.

Nevertheless, a request from Paramount for Bogart to play in *This Gun for Hire* (1942) was turned down (resembling both *The Maltese Falcon* and *All Through the Night*, the Paramount thriller made Alan Ladd a star). Shortly after, Columbia put in a request for his services. This time, how to respond became a topic of high-level discussion in the Burbank executive suites. "It has reached a time when you have to figure a rental price based upon the importance and demand of the talent rather than the contract salaries," the contract department head memoed Jack Warner.[15] On its own books, the studio figured that at his current rate they were paying Bogart $16,500 per picture. Based on the line of reasoning in his memo, the contract man proposed a price of $50,000 for a Bogart loan-out.

Negotiations began with Columbia. Loud squawks were soon heard from Gower Street. Testy letters flew back and forth between Columbia executive B. B. Kahane and Jack Warner. Kahane's complaint was that Warner Bros. was attempting an egregious overcharge, contrary to accepted movie industry practice on loan-outs; eventually he proposed that the company presidents, Harry Cohn on his side, Harry M. Warner on the other, adjudicate.

"It is a very peculiar thing," Jack Warner wrote indignantly to his brother, "when we do business with people we never go through these Eastside, pushcart methods, but whenever we do business with Columbia this always happens so I am not a bit annoyed by them." To Kahane he wrote, "I just wish I could get the same kind of deal, for you are getting important stars at one-half their value."[16] This is the first recorded instance when words like "important" and "star" were used by a Warner Bros. executive with reference to Bogart—for a specific purpose, of course, and not for the actor's eyes. The loan-out, by the way, was agreed upon, but did not actually occur until more than a year later, when Bogart worked for Columbia in *Sahara* (1943).

At last Bogart's status seemed to be rising in his studio's estimation. The terms of a new contract began to be discussed. It soon became clear that the actor who grew up on Manhattan's elite Upper West Side completely failed when it came to Lower East Side pushcart methods (whether it was his agent's responsibility or his own cannot be ascertained). Warner Bros. offered a seven-year deal starting at $2500 a week and rising in two-year increments to $3000 and $3500, with a final year at $4000. Bogart's counterproposal was a seven-year straight deal at $3000 per week, with no raises. Add up these figures, and it seems that Bogart's demand was *lower* than the studio's offer. Moreover, further negotiations "settled" the figure at $2750 per week, no raises, for the seven years. Over the life of the contract Bogart would get $110,000 *less* than the original Warner Bros. offer. What is more, the new contract contained not a word concerning the actor's screen billing—an essential element for most other performers, particularly those wanting to gain or preserve star status.

It seems quite possible that the delay in Bogart's stardom was due not entirely to the obtuseness of Warners executives, but also to his own deficiencies as a negotiator or in presenting himself as a performer deserving of special consideration. The first picture the studio put him in after signing the new contract—indeed rushed him into—was an old-fashioned gangster potboiler, *The Big Shot* (1942). Though Bogart gave his part some comic touches to leaven the standard 1930s plot (the film was structured as a long flashback to place its criminal events in the prewar past), it hardly qualified as "entertainment with persuasive propaganda." Archer Winston's response, in the *New York Post*, was that it was time for "movie gangsters [i.e., actors playing gangsters] to get wise to themselves. After ten or fifteen years in a 'crime does not pay' environment the toughest of them could not be blamed if he blew his brains out, joined a police department, or went over to the armed forces type of movie."

■ ■ ■ ■

At the end of his essay "The Good Villain and the Bad Hero," in *The Hollywood Hallucination*, Parker Tyler shifted suddenly from the subject of screen characters to a discussion of actors. Many actors, he provocatively asserted, were "racketeers of pantomime and voice": villainous, in his view, "to the extent that [they] do not rise above the level of hackwork in [their] profession." One typical figure was the actor who puts "virtuous acting equipment" to "villainously small use."[17] A prime example? John Garfield.

To grasp Garfield's situation at Warner Bros. at the beginning of the 1940s, take Humphrey Bogart's problems and multiply them manyfold. Garfield's basic choice was between B-picture assignments and suspensions. Any work he got in an A picture was because someone else turned the part down or, as with *Out of the Fog,* only after considerable infighting and intrigue. Besides *Out of the Fog*, Garfield's most substantial part was in *The Sea Wolf* (1941).

The studio had been trying for three or four years to put together an effective cast for an adaptation of the Jack London novel, with a script by Robert Rossen. Paul Muni had turned it down as early as 1937; Edward G. Robinson replaced him as the choice for the lead role of Wolf Larsen. After the success of *They Drive by Night* (released in July 1940), the project was revived with the idea of casting Ida Lupino and George Raft from that film as the romantic couple.

Raft balked. From New York, after reading the script, he telegraphed Wallis, "You told me in your office that it would be a fifty fifty part. I am sorry to say it is just the opposite. As I explained before I want to work but this is just a little better than a bit, I'm sorry to say. I don't blame this on you because you're a nice guy and I know you tried your best for me."[18] Bogart was lined up as Raft's replacement, but he was already occupied with another Raft turndown, *The Wagons Roll at Night*. Garfield was called up from the B-unit minor leagues.

Raft was right: it was entirely Robinson's picture. His portrait of the cruel, brutal, violent ship captain owed something to Jack London's mentors—Nietzsche, Darwin, Herbert Spencer—but perhaps more to scriptwriter Rossen's effort to create a metaphor for contemporary dictators. Though Garfield was back with his most sympathetic director, Michael Curtiz, in the context of Wolf Larsen's sadism his performance as a rebellious, sexy juvenile was largely eclipsed. As for the role of Goff in *Out of the Fog*—it would have been better for Garfield to have let Bogart take it. In this parable of resistance to fascism, he plays the fascist; his character, a small-time hood and extortionist who preys on the simple folk of Brooklyn's Sheepshead Bay, is an unredeemable louse. To comply with the Production Code, Goff's murder at the hands of "the gentle people" was changed into an accidental drowning; since the Brooklyn fisherfolk were fighting Nazis only symbolically, they could not be shown as getting away with murder. Remarked *Variety*, "John Garfield makes his satanic portrayal the very essence of symbolic villainy—so much so that audiences will resent his easy death in the drowning accident." The *Dallas Morning News* brushed off his performance as another of his "rapidly mounting string of heels."

These performances were accompanied by several suspensions for refusing parts. Missing documents in the Warner Bros. studio records make it difficult to know precisely what assignments he turned down, but they could not have been much more unsuitable than one he accepted, *Dangerously They Live* (1942). This was a B-unit production that got a sudden shot in the arm with the last-minute addi-tion of Raymond Massey; in distribution it was upgraded to an A picture, partly because of the putative timeliness of its story line in the spring of 1942. Massey plays a psychiatrist who is a Nazi agent plotting to capture a beautiful young woman working for British intelligence in New York. Garfield is a medical intern who gets involved when the kidnap vehicle crashes, leading the woman to feign amnesia. After sundry adventures in the locations favored by enemy agents in movies (a handsome country estate, a secret room behind a delicatessen), the Nazis are foiled; the film ends with Garfield and the woman in a clinch. The *New York World-Telegram* called it "clownish." Leo Mishkin's words in the *Morning-Telegraph* were "pathetic," "weak," and "silly." He concluded, "With the sick-ening news from Bataan [where Japanese forces had defeated Ameri-can and Filipino troops following the fall of Manila] spread all over the newspapers, *Dangerously They Live* seems even sillier than it would have ordinarily been. It's about time Hollywood got down to the realization that the people we are fighting are cruel, cunning, and ruthless, and not just the pack of dopes the screen seems bent on making them."

To be fair, it should be noted that the *New York Herald-Tribune*'s Howard Barnes (a not-undiscerning reviewer) praised both the film and Garfield's performance. He may have been influenced by nostal-gia after seeing Garfield's personal appearance, along with the pic-ture, on the Strand theater's stage. Garfield presented a dramatic scene from *Four Daughters*. One could look back to one of the most impressive motion picture debuts in memory, and screen out the fact that it had been followed by almost continuous decline in a dozen pictures over four years.

Garfield was on the list with Bogart of performers who were better off being traded than played. (On the set of *Dangerously They Live*, the assistant director reported that spirits picked up when Garfield was absent. "This company, as soon as Garfield isn't around, seems to take on an entirely different personality, and work is turned out much faster and everybody is considerably happier, and there are very few delays.")[19] In Garfield's case, the ploy of asking for more than double his salary on a loan-out worked without a hitch, perhaps because the borrower was wealthy MGM instead of Columbia. Though his current salary was $2000 per week, Metro agreed to pay Warner Bros. $5000 per week, for a minimum eight weeks, to use Garfield on *Tortilla Flat* (1942), their adaptation of John Steinbeck's novel. Garfield ultimately worked eleven weeks and one day, giving his studio a net profit from his absence of over $30,000. When war was declared on December 8, 1941, Garfield was playing a comic Hispanic named Danny in the unfamiliar precincts of Culver City. Half a century later it is difficult to apprehend the film's treatment of its subjects as other than condescending, if not racist; at the moment, however, it was completely to Garfield's benefit to get away from Burbank.

For one of the few times since *Four Daughters*—*Juarez* and *The Sea Wolf* are the lone exceptions—he was not burdened with the responsibility of carrying the picture as male lead. Spencer Tracy, the star, performed the role of Garfield's manipulative mentor in a confident, low-key manner that allowed the younger actor simply to play the romantic juvenile opposite Hedy Lamarr, his love interest. Karl Freund's MGM-style cinematography, moreover, gave Garfield more privileged close-ups than was usual at Warner Bros., with glamorous star-lighting to bring out his good looks. Though the picture was far from successful, either financially or critically, the Hollywood trade papers, for a change, gave Garfield some praise: "... definitely one of his better performances," said *Variety*. By 1942, however, it was far too late—and historically the wrong moment—to restore Garfield as the sex symbol he had briefly promised to become, less than four years previously.

■ ■ ■ ■

James Cagney took the opportunity of his unexpected trip to testify before Congressman Dies in August 1940 to confer with brother William about his next choice of assignment. Earlier in the year, William had been enthusiastic when the studio acquired rights to *One Sunday Afternoon*, a play with a turn-of-the-century setting that Paramount had made into a picture in 1933. "Last summer, out in Hollywood, the industry went in a big way for 'Nostalgia' as a cure for Movieland's ills, the answer to the cry for escape from the grimness of war," Lee Mortimer of the *New York Mirror* later wrote of this period. At the time, however, Cagney had other grimness he wished to escape—the joint legacies of his 1930s radicalism and his tough-guy screen persona. Of the two, the former was potentially more damaging to him, the latter quite clearly more vexing.

Just past forty, Cagney faced a different set of concerns from those of Bogart, nearly his age equal. Bogart was in a struggle to get parts commensurate with his ability, to improve his status, to move beyond stereotypes and construct a screen persona with enough uniqueness and complexity to make him a star. Cagney had his pick of parts, the status, and the star persona—only he did not like that persona anymore, had not, in fact, for years. Now he was in a position to do something about it. He was beyond pressing economic need. *Torrid Zone,* hardly among Cagney's classics, was doing brisk business in mid-summer 1940; eventually it would return more than $1.5 million in rentals to the studio, on a budget of around $700,000. *City for Conquest,* just in the can, would turn out to be even more profitable. Warner Bros. could bank on a distributor's share approaching $2 million just by putting Cagney's name on a picture.

The issue at heart was more personal. Cagney no longer wanted to be the Depression era's rebel hero. There was something about this persona that had disturbed him almost from the start, that he had tried to ameliorate—and not only because (as he told Congressman Dies) people picked fights with him in nightclubs. The issue was illuminated by John Mosher's comparison of Bogart and Cagney at the time of *High Sierra*: Cagney, Mosher wrote, was a figure of "pent-up tension and agonized neuroses."

Tension, yes of course, but neuroses? Was his screen image one of emotional disorder? Cagney's violent, babyish characterization of Tom Powers in *The Public Enemy* may have created this impression at the start of his career; yet nearly a decade had passed, and several dozen varied roles, to complicate it. In recent pictures, however, with the unjustly imprisoned reporter in *Each Dawn I Die* and the craven braggart of *The Fighting 69th*, he had once again portrayed extreme forms of aberrant behavior. Was there a continuity of neurotic psychic structure that underlay and unified his accumulated screen portrayals?

The question is directed as much to Warner Bros. as to Cagney. Beyond the actor's own contribution—his image and performance— lay treatments developed by the studio, and screenplays written by its writers. These texts contained narrative structures adapted, concocted, repeated, in scores of films, year after year. They contained the stuff of Hollywood romance comedy, comedy-drama, melodrama—but not all the stuff. What was missing in Cagney's case was the opportunity to play an adult male who had existing relationships with women.

As good villains and/or bad heroes, his screen figures had often been involved in rivalry over a woman. Sometimes the Cagney character won her affection and he gave her up; sometimes after winning he died for her own good; sometimes he won her at the fadeout; sometimes he lost her and died; once in a while he even lost her and lived. What he rarely did was experience a relationship during the narrative itself. Out of more than thirty Warner Bros. films up to this

point, the two exceptions to this pattern are not strong counterex-
amples: in *Taxi!* he was married though not very adult, and in *Each
Dawn I Die* his imprisonment separates him from his girlfriend
through nearly the entire film. In both his independent productions
Cagney seems to have made a point of giving his characters stable
relationships with women.

One Sunday Afternoon offered an opportunity to break with standard Warner Bros. stuff. The part of Biff Grimes in *The Strawberry
Blonde* (1941), as the work was renamed, provided Cagney with one
of his most striking, innovative characterizations (working with director Raoul Walsh, who had shown an ability to bring out unexpected performances from his actors, undoubtedly aided him). His
character is almost a nebbish. He is weak, coarse, none too bright—
yet, in Cagney's handling of the part, immensely likeable. (The role
of a sharpie with the old Cagney razzmatazz went to Jack Carson.)

In youth (a story told in flashback) Cagney's Biff and Carson's
Hugo Barnstead are rivals for the town beauty, played by Rita
Hayworth; Biff loses and marries a "plain" woman, portrayed by
Olivia de Havilland. The unscrupulous Hugo takes Biff into his construction business and maneuvers so that the uncomprehending
simpleton becomes legally responsible when the firm's use of infe-
rior building material is uncovered. Biff ends up spending five years
in prison. The story reaches the narrative present as Biff, plotting
revenge, awaits a meeting with his tormentor. But when he sees how
miserable Hugo and the beauty have become, he realizes that his
own simple happiness has already made him the victor. This not-so-
simple tale of a meek man's triumph was another box office success,
equal to *Torrid Zone* and *City for Conquest*, with rentals approaching $2 million.

If *The Strawberry Blonde* was a step forward—or at least away,
from old stereotypes—then *The Bride Came C.O.D.* (1941) marked
two steps back: an attempt at screwball comedy that (except for the
evidence of Cagney's expanding waistline) might have been gather-
ing dust on the shelf since 1934. He was once again the daredevil
womanizing pilot, resurrected from *Devil Dogs of the Air* and *Ceiling Zero*. The main difference from the earlier films was that his
love interest was also a figure of star status, Bette Davis, with whom,
coincidentally, he had not worked since 1934 (in *Jimmy the Gent*).

It seems likely that the studio had decided that Davis could use a
comic change of pace from her highly successful new screen persona
as a villainess in women's melodramas such as *All This and Heaven
Too* and *The Letter* (both nominees for Best Picture Oscars in 1940).
Instead of the mental or moral punishment her character was nor-

mally subjected to, however, *The Bride Came C.O.D.* substituted physical punishment. When pilot Cagney crash-lands his plane in the desert, passenger Davis falls rear-end first onto a cactus tree. Accompanied by comic music on the sound track, he pulls out the cactus thistles. Not once but twice more in the film she falls into a cactus, and on two other occasions Cagney shoots her in the behind with a slingshot.

The Epstein brothers took responsibility for the screenplay (William Keighley directed), and they knew what they were doing. The film's box office success outpaced all previous Cagney pictures; ultimately it earned over $2 million in rentals. With Hayworth and de Havilland in one picture and Davis in the next, Cagney had finally attained adult status for his screen persona, playing opposite female leads who were stars in their own right. *Photoplay* magazine marked the occasion with a caricature of the actor's face flanked by full-length likenesses of de Havilland and Davis in low-cut gowns, and a rhyming caption:

> The tough Jim Cagney's on a tear—
> Those dames are getting in his hair.
> We don't see why he's grouching so—
> Perhaps it's that he doesn't know
> It's Livvie and the Davis. Wow!
> We'd like to have them fan our brow![20]

In mid-1941, however, the studio had war rather than further romance in mind for Cagney. In its interventionist mode, Warner Bros. was preparing *Captains of the Clouds* (1942), a film extolling the Royal Canadian Air Force. Several writers had developed a screenplay about Canada's bush pilots—who fly small planes into remote northern villages and mining camps—assisting the war effort. Cagney was sent the script; brother William reported the actor's reaction to Hal Wallis: "He didn't like it and said that he wouldn't like it if he hadn't played it four times before."[21] For the record, he had only played the role three times before.

Wallis persisted, pressing what he called the "Patriotic angle."[22] He also argued that doing this picture would give the studio more time to do a thorough job preparing the George M. Cohan biopic that was the actor's more important intended vehicle. Cagney relented. By mid-July 1941 he was in Ottawa to take on the role (under Michael Curtiz's direction) of bush pilot Brian MacLean—his first screen appearance in Technicolor.

Cagney was right about the part and the story: both were straight out of his 1930s flying pictures. These were merely the pretext, however, for a propaganda film in support of the British cause (it contained a scene depicting Canadians listening to Prime Minister Winston Churchill's famous "We shall fight" speech, following the British evacuation of Dunkirk, France, under German fire); a lengthy appearance by Air Marshall W. A. "Billy" Bishop, Canada's World War I flying hero; and spectacular sequences on pilot training. Drummed out of the RCAF for bad boy behavior, Cagney's character (as in *Ceiling Zero*) redeems himself by sacrificing his own life for the group. By the time the picture was released the United States was in the war, and it earned $3.3 million in rentals for the studio, over $1 million more than *The Bride Came C.O.D.*

When Wallis saw the rushes of Cagney's death scene, he wrote a note to director Curtiz, sending a copy as well to the actor. "Cagney was very good in this," the executive wrote. "All these little added bits that Cagney has been putting in are fine. He certainly knows how to add color to a character."[23] This is a historic document: it marks the first time Hal Wallis had anything favorable to say (on the record) about his company's highest-paid star. He must have had an ulterior motive.

Indeed: he and Cagney were in a struggle over the development of *Yankee Doodle Dandy* (1942). Having acquired the rights to George M. Cohan's life, and expended seven months of labor on it—including research, consultations with the ill but still active Cohan, and three different script drafts—the studio had a problem. Its agreement with Cohan stipulated that Cagney portray him. Cagney had still not given his consent. Wallis was sending Cagney a signal that small embellishments and script alterations on the set for added "color" would, for a change, be all right with him. In addition, he assigned the Epstein brothers to add a little "color" of their own to the script. A few days following the memo, Cagney accepted the Cohan part, much to Wallis's relief.

Cagney's delay in accepting the Cohan role was caused not only by presumed "creative differences." There was also a business calculation linked to it. James and William Cagney had decided to invoke the rare clause Warner Bros. had permitted in the actor's contract allowing him to cancel at any time and set up as independent producers on their own. The question was when to let their plan be known. They never intended not to do *Yankee Doodle Dandy*: the success of that picture was crucial to their future as independents. They were taking a calculated risk in figuring that they could use James's contractual powers of refusal—the threat that he might walk out on Warner Bros. *before* making *Yankee Doodle Dandy*, effectively scuttling the project—to gain the control they wanted over the picture.

Ultimately—after the film became the biggest box office success in Warner Bros. history, and after Cagney won the actor Oscar for his performance—their strategy involved claiming that *Yankee Doodle Dandy* had been the Cagneys' idea from the start. In January 1943 William Cagney made what can only be considered a startling admission, as reported in the *New York Times*:

> *Yankee Doodle Dandy* was filmed because Burton Fitts, former Los Angeles District Attorney, called James Cagney a Communist during his campaign for re-election two and a half years ago. William Cagney then enlisted the aid of Congressman Martin Dies, who, not loathe to join the controversy, investigated James and pronounced him, unequivocally, a sound citizen.
>
> But even so, the Cagneys were tired of political labels. So William went to Warner Brothers and said to J. L. Warner, "There's one more thing to do. We should make a movie with him playing the damndest patriotic man in the country." Warner asked who. Cagney said: George M. Cohan.[24]

Why did the Cagneys volunteer this story to the press? Their candor might have been a sign of how strong they felt themselves after *Yankee Doodle Dandy*'s triumph. It might also have been a tactic to signal that James's radicalism was firmly relegated to the past. In the postwar purge of leftists and even liberals from the motion picture industry, Cagney—with his record of political activity—could not immunize himself from at least behind-the-scenes scrutiny. The role of George M. Cohan in *Yankee Doodle Dandy*, however, seemed almost to provide a shield against public questioning of his patriotism.

When the film was in preparation the question was not of patriotism, which Cohan possessed in abundance, but of humanity and humor—which Cohan may have had, but the script (in Cagney's view) lacked. The Epsteins were his solution: their forte was in delineating a particular male type, intense but not flamboyant, unaggressive but sexually attractive to women. This is the figure toward which their recent scripts had been moving the Cagney persona, and they achieved it fully for his portrait of Cohan.

The Cagneys' strategy went according to plan. In early October 1941 the actor accepted the role. In late November he served notice to Warner Bros. that he would be terminating his contract after completing *Yankee Doodle Dandy*. On December 3 the picture went into production. Even the United States' entry into World War II could not deter them: on Monday, December 8, the day after the Japanese attack on Pearl Harbor, Cagney feuded with dance director

Seymour Felix over a number they were rehearsing. Tuesday he refused to report; after a week's delay, Cagney's personal dance instructor, Johnny Boyle, temporarily replaced Felix (later Leroy Prinz took over as dance director). In the war's first week, these were the concerns of the actor preparing Hollywood's first important patriotic film.

For Cagney, getting the dance numbers right was too important for war to hinder or interrupt. *Yankee Doodle Dandy* was to be his reincarnation as a dancer—the song-and-dance man, as he put it, he had been at the start of his career. He had not danced on-screen since his own Grand National production, *Something to Sing About*. In recent films additional weight on his midsection had been noticeable. After committing himself to the Cohan role, he had trained and trimmed. His opening scenes in the film deliberately call attention to skills of performance—in the narrative, Cohan's; more significantly, his own.

Yankee Doodle Dandy opens with Cohan impersonating President Franklin D. Roosevelt in the Kaufman and Hart musical *I'd Rather Be Right*—the actual 1937 date is shifted forward to the film's wartime present. Cohan is summoned to the White House to accept, belatedly, a congressional award. As he and the president reminisce, the film shifts into a flashback and begins the Cohan biography. After some scenes of the boy George, played by a child actor, Cagney appears onstage in white hair and a flowing white beard. Afterward, in his dressing room, the provincial girl Mary (Joan Leslie) asks this wizened old trouper for advice about breaking into show business. When she presents some hackneyed routines, the doddering veteran suddenly breaks into an acrobatic dance. Gradually his makeup comes off and he is revealed as a man her own age— as Cagney is revealed reborn in youthful athletic vigor.

He displays his energy again and again in triumphant musical numbers—including the patriotic songs "Over There" and "You're a Grand Old Flag," for which Cohan was awarded the Congressional Medal. In between, in the "book" part of the musical film, Cagney presents a different figure, more like Biff Grimes in *The Strawberry Blonde*. The point of Cohan's egotism had been carefully made in early scenes with the child actor. Cagney's Cohan is comically brash as Cagney had often been in 1930s movies, but is also a gentle, diffident suitor; a devoted son and husband; a quiet family man—"an ordinary guy," as he says, "who knows what the ordinary guy wants to see."

It marked a new kind of doubleness for Cagney—not the contrasting violence and dependence of his early gangster films (nor the menace and comedy that Bogart had recently melded). It depicted an ordinary guy, but one capable of sudden dynamism in performance. This was as close to a self-portrait as Cagney was ever to achieve (much more than it was an accurate portrayal of George M. Cohan's life), and it gave a nation mobilizing for war an updated model, urban and ethnic, of the traditional American hero: benign in peacetime, ferocious when attacked.

Released at the end of May 1942, *Yankee Doodle Dandy* articulated, as few films do, its precise moment of national ideological formulation. It nearly doubled the earnings of *Captains of the Clouds*, bringing in more than $6 million in rentals to Warner Bros. In addition to his $150,000 salary on the picture, Cagney eventually gained nearly half a million dollars as his profit share. This would be useful seed money for his effort to produce films independently in an uncertain wartime world.

III

City Boys in War and Cold War

7

Heroes without Uniforms

With the exception of *Yankee Doodle Dandy*, little in the prewar careers of the city boy actors gave evidence that they were capable of playing exemplary roles—either on-screen or off—in a movie industry, and a nation, entering a global war. Much the same could have been said for most other Americans after Japan's attack on U.S. naval bases in Hawaii. Until that moment, public opinion had been deeply divided about how the government should respond to the European war (already more than two years old) and a Pacific war even older. The raid on Pearl Harbor shocked and unified the country. Its traumatic effects set in process an ideological transformation in which the city boys—ready or not—were enlisted as point men.

As the elements of transformation—the outrage and feelings of betrayal about the attack itself, the recognition that new ways of perceiving one's self and the world were necessary for survival—were worked out in the social realm, they were of course played out and replayed in popular narratives. Movie performers dramatized the transformation and demonstrated its effects on the fictive lives of their individual screen characters. This was regarded as an honorable, even an essential, part of the war effort. Who could be better at bringing to vivid realization the demands of war on consciousness and behavior than those who had represented social types in peacetime?

A number of motion picture personnel went into the armed forces; the skills of directors, writers, cinematographers, and technicians were put to work making training, documentary, and propaganda films. Though performers occasionally provided voice-over narrations on these films, their fame and visibility made them more effective in personal appearances and morale-building activities. Cagney and Bogart, who were well past conscription age, and Garfield, who was rejected for military service apparently because of heart irregularities detected during his medical examination, made trips to the war zones to entertain American troops. Garfield was one of the founders of the Hollywood Canteen, where motion picture personalities put on shows and mingled with service personnel. They continued their professional work throughout the war, as their screen personas were tailored to the needs of ideological transformation. They were called upon to repeat the drama of betrayal and self-recognition so often that the representation came almost to stand for the thing itself.

The motion picture industry, however, was not fully mobilized for war. For performers, the familiar conditions of Hollywood filmmaking remained in place—contracts and billing clauses, the system of suspensions, the detritus of ambition and struggle for place. Pearl Harbor did not affect Cagney's decision to go into independent production, despite the possible uncertainty of finding financing and materials in wartime. The onset of war did not prevent Warner Bros. from continuing to offer Bogart and Garfield as loan-outs to other studios, nor, when Bogart's loan-out was postponed, from slipping him into a potboiler like *The Big Shot*. The business side of moviemaking would determine, as much as anything else, the city boys' contribution to national ideological transformation.

■ ■ ■ ■

Purely by chance, Bogart was the one whom business circumstances favored first. At the time of Pearl Harbor—while Cagney was getting started in *Yankee Doodle Dandy* and Garfield continued on *Tortilla Flat* at MGM—Bogart was cooling his heels, awaiting word on when to take up his loan-out assignment at Columbia. Columbia was having difficulty putting all its elements together, however, and twice during December 1941 asked for delays; Bogart's work at Columbia would not begin until more than a year later, in January 1943. By that time many things had changed. It was the luck of a lifetime that Columbia could not use him, because Warner Bros. (*The Big Shot* notwithstanding) for one remarkable moment had figured out how.

When Bogart was freed up from his Columbia obligation, not one but two important projects in preproduction development at Warners wanted his services. One factor in his sudden rise in status may have been the continuing impact of *The Maltese Falcon* on the nation's reviewers. Following its initial release in October 1941, the picture was opening in a second tier of cities in December, and in such places as Baltimore and Dallas the praise for Bogart was more striking than ever. John Rosenfield in the *Dallas Morning News*, for example, called Bogart's Sam Spade "one of the more elegant performances of his eminent career." These words might have given Hal Wallis pause. Elegant? Eminent? Were they describing the actor Wallis had dropped to second billing on *High Sierra* because of his too-frequent appearance in B pictures? Each new batch of reviews confirmed what any open eye could see: Bogart's doubleness, his hardness and his humor; his ambiguity, leaving the spectator in doubt until the very end; his sudden, powerful bursts of temper. Impelled or not by the press notices, Wallis was finally changing his attitude toward Bogart. The qualities the reviewers noticed in the actor were qualities appropriate to representing a world of betrayal and transformation.

Wallis now wanted Bogart for two separate projects. The executive was relinquishing his post as Jack Warner's associate in charge of overall production, and taking on a new position as senior producer at the studio, acting as line producer on individual projects with first call on studio resources. In his old job, he assigned Bogart to *Across the Pacific* (1942); in his new role he selected Bogart to be the leading man in *Casablanca* (1943).

George Raft so assiduously cultivated the legend that he turned down the part of Rick Blaine in *Casablanca* that he seems to have convinced the one man above all who should have known better: in his ghostwritten autobiography, Wallis repeats the claim. Studio records make clear, however, that Wallis was committed to Bogart all the way. In April, Jack Warner sent the producer a memo asking, "What do you think of using Raft in *Casablanca*? He knows we are going to make this and is starting a campaign for it."[1] Wallis waited almost two weeks before making a written reply. He spoke of having thought the matter over carefully, but the dominant tone of his memo is resentment toward Raft for his many condescending turndowns (*The Sea Wolf, The Wagons Roll at Night, The Maltese Falcon,* and *All Through the Night* are just a few). Though he did not choose this occasion—or any other—to explain his new support for Bogart, Wallis's reply was as testy as he ever got with his boss. "Bogart is ideal for it, and it is being written for him," he wrote with finality.[2]

Across the Pacific had also been written for Bogart—as well as for Mary Astor and Sydney Greenstreet. It was intended less as a sequel to than as a reprise of *The Maltese Falcon* (John Huston once again would direct). It was an early probe at the themes of betrayal and transformation, but an imperfect one, since it looked back as much to the Black Bird story as to Pearl Harbor. The script by Richard Macaulay did, however, introduce some basic concepts: the shifting of narrative time back to specific dates in November and early December 1941, for example, so that the trauma of betrayal and the transformation process could be reexperienced directly by spectators.

The prime betrayal (understood by Americans as being committed by the Japanese) and the transformation to war are presaged in *Across the Pacific* by an apparent act of betrayal committed by Bogart's character. This act turns out retrospectively to be one of the signals of the transformation of Bogart's screen persona that takes place in the film. In a military court on Governor's Island in New York Harbor (where the date November 17, 1941, is prominently displayed), army captain Rick Leland (Bogart) is court-martialed and dismissed from the army. His insignia of rank are ostentatiously ripped from his jacket.

One might well think that this was one of the old Bogart's characters, caught infiltrating the army for the rackets—or else simply a career army officer with Bogart's familiar criminal traits of (screen) character. This impression would likely be confirmed when, after he tries to enlist and is rejected by the Canadian armed forces, he books passage on a Japanese freighter bound for the Panama Canal and drunkenly tells a fellow passenger that he'll sell his services to anyone who'll pay.

Of course, once they see that Bogart is talking to Sydney Greenstreet (claiming to be a sociology professor), spectators familiar with *The Maltese Falcon* might suspect that appearances are not what they seem. Mary Astor is also on board, as a vacationing Canadian from Medicine Hat (named Alberta, after her province). She and Bogart strike up a romance. The atmosphere of *The Maltese Falcon* is laid on so thick that Bogart even calls a young Nisei tough guy "a Jap gunsel"—an appellation Hal Wallis tried but failed to expunge from the earlier film when it was applied to Wilmer (Elisha Cook, Jr.).

There are times in *Across the Pacific* when the comedy tends to undermine the film's fictional rendering of critical historical events. Bogart in particular adopts a light, comic style of performance, for which the dialogue gives him ample opportunity. In a scene of violent struggle, as Bogart confronts an enemy with pistols drawn, he says, "Mine's bigger than yours." The casual, somewhat slapdash air of the production may have been abetted by the fact that Huston was notified to report for military assignment before he could finish the film.

Even so, the basic contemporary message comes through strongly. Bogart's character is revealed to be an intelligence agent, and his "disgrace," a pretext for going undercover. Greenstreet's sociology

professor turns out to be a Japanese spy, as does the Nisei "gunsel"—
a telling piece of ideological distortion that supported the U.S. government's action (taken several weeks before production started) to
relocate Japanese-American citizens away from the Pacific Coast
and into inland internment camps. The ship arrives at the Canal
Zone on December 6, 1941, the date marked by a prominent newspaper headline, "Hirohito Reply to Roosevelt Will Insure Peace—Say
Nomura, Kurusu" (Japanese officials in Washington at the time of
the attack on Pearl Harbor).

The film draws on the 1942 audience's outrage at what Americans
perceived as Japan's stab in the back: talking peace, planning a sneak
attack. The professor and the Nisei are to join up with a Japanese
imperial prince to bomb the Panama Canal simultaneously with the
raid on Hawaii. "You guys been lookin' for a war, haven't you?" Bogart confronts them, and the Japanese-American replies, "That's
right, Rick—that's why we're starting it." Bogart grabs a machine
gun and mows them down, preventing at least the raid on the Canal.
Warners promoted it as a "Jap-slapping story sensation."

The sense of international betrayal was clear enough in *Across the
Pacific*, as was the transformation of Bogart's screen persona, within
the narrative itself, from bad man to hero. What was missing was his
character's inner life: since he already was a military agent at his
mock court-martial, there was no crisis of conscience, no struggle
toward self-recognition and change. In terms of the ideological
framework of a betrayal-transformation narrative—which required
recognition of the collective social demand war made on millions of
individuals, involved one's understanding of a personal stake in the
greater good, and demanded a positive commitment to sacrifice and
possible loss—*Across the Pacific* was basically a nonstarter, no more
than a harmless diversion.

As the studio prepared *Casablanca* to go into production in late
May 1942, a team of writers was struggling to get a better handle on
these themes. The raw material was an unproduced play, *Everybody
Comes to Rick's*, by Murray Burnett and Joan Alison, purchased by
the studio within days after Pearl Harbor. It laid out the by now almost universally familiar story: Rick's Cafe, Ugarte and the "Letters
of Transit," Vichy France and the Germans, an embittered expatri-
ate American and his African-American sidekick, the reappearance
of Rick's former lover, her husband the Czech underground leader.
What the play principally lacked, however, was the same element
missing in *Across the Pacific*—the hero's inner consciousness con-
fronting the coming of war. The writers did take one concept from
the Panama Canal film, and made it even more condensed: they

shifted the time frame of *Casablanca* to early December 1941, so that America's impending entry into the war accompanied and reinforced character transformation.

Julius J. and Philip G. Epstein were given the assignment to turn a treatment by other hands into a full-fledged script. They had never before written a film in which Bogart had appeared, let alone one in which his screen character would be the dominant, and particularly socially significant, figure. Producer Wallis wanted them, however, for the same traits that Cagney had asked them to supply for his portrayal of George M. Cohan: their ability to create a distinctive male character who was intense but somewhat repressed, and whose strength initially was declared by the powerful reaction of others. This Epstein tropism would define Bogart's portrayal of Rick Blaine in *Casablanca*.

Like Huston, however, the Epsteins were committed to film work for the military. In the midst of preparing the *Casablanca* script, they were called to Washington: Frank Capra, the film director who had taken on the monumental task of producing the "Why We Fight" series explaining the nation's war aims to service personnel, assigned them to write the scripts. Though they continued to produce material for *Casablanca*—and, on a return trip to Hollywood, helped persuade producer David O. Selznick to loan Ingrid Bergman for the part of Rick's ex-lover—Wallis turned the script over to writer Howard Koch.

Politically radical, Koch was later subpoenaed as an "unfriendly" witness at the 1947 hearings of the House Un-American Activities Committee on alleged Communist infiltration of the motion picture industry (though he was not among those called to testify). It was he who changed Rick Blaine from the divorced ex-lawyer of the Burnett-Alison play into the former antifascist fighter in Ethiopia and Spain (this new characterization was a telling example of how swiftly the U.S. entry into the war revived the old liberal–left-wing popular front). Discerning political spectators would recognize the implication that Rick was a veteran of the Abraham Lincoln Brigade; this might explain one of the narrative's mysteries, why he had not been welcome back in the United States.

With the Epsteins continuing to supply material from near and far, and Koch trying to shape the screenplay toward a drama of "present-day significance," the script was no more than two-thirds written when shooting began on May 25.[3] Other films had gone into production with unfinished scripts, but the absence of an ending was particularly serious for *Casablanca*. It affected the performers' interpretation of their characters. Would the girl end up with the American or the Czech? The consistency of a performance required some sense of its totality—nuances of glance and gesture throughout a film could provide subtle signals of narrative direction and the characters' destiny. No one professed to have decided how it would turn out. The studio was even prepared to shoot two different endings.

This uncertainty turned out to have a crucial effect on the emotional aura of the finished film. Going into production, however, it was for Bogart only one among several uncertainties. His selection for the Rick Blaine part confirmed him as a star, yet the range of his roles had still been rather limited. Having been shepherded toward stardom by directors Walsh and Huston, on *Casablanca* he was working with director Michael Curtiz, with whom his past experience had not been promising. The last time Bogart had appeared in a Curtiz picture, it had been one of his periodic nadirs, the part of a Mexican outlaw in *Virginia City*. Earlier, in *Kid Galahad* and *Angels with Dirty Faces*, other Curtiz films, he had played craven bad guys. Like the Epsteins, however, Curtiz had been good for Garfield (in *Four Daughters* and *Daughters Courageous*) and Cagney (*Yankee Doodle Dandy*)—in fact, he had presided as director over perhaps their most memorable and successful roles. Would his rapport with them, and others, extend to a leading man whom he had previously known only as a minor bad man?

Beyond that was the question of Bogart's capacity to play a screen lover with the young and strikingly beautiful Ingrid Bergman. The romantic boy of Broadway and the early Fox films had played almost no part in Bogart's screen persona at Warners; the revival of his on-screen sexual attraction to women—with Ida Lupino in *High Sierra* and Mary Astor in *The Maltese Falcon*—had been, at least in terms of those narratives, ambiguous at best. His love scenes with Astor in *Across the Pacific* had been played more for laughs than for sighs. Would audiences, especially women, accept him as a fortyish lover of a woman in her twenties? The script helped by positioning her as an idealistic, impressionable young woman who had already made a commitment to the resistance hero Laszlo, an older man who was more a mentor in her eyes than a lover. Still, the Bogart-Bergman scenes would have to be convincing in their own right.

At least he would not have to carry the entire picture on his own shoulders. Huston had used him in nearly every scene of *The Maltese Falcon* and *Across the Pacific*; every other performance was clearly subordinate to his. In *Casablanca*, though Rick was the center of the narrative, Curtiz did not make him the visual center in quite the same way. A great many other actors were cast for the film who could carry a scene, with or without him.

Casablanca was a touchstone for how Warner Bros., too, was transforming itself in the early months of the war. Bogart was the only Warners contract player in the film who was a holdover from the 1930s. (Claude Rains, formerly on contract at the studio, had been let go and was hired as a freelance to play Renault, the French prefect of police.) He and Dooley Wilson, as Sam, were among the few American-born principals in the cast. Bergman, as Ilsa Lund, Paul Henreid as Laszlo, Conrad Veidt as Major Strasser, Greenstreet as Ferrari, Peter Lorre as Ugarte, S. Z. Sakall as Carl the waiter, had been important performers in England and Europe. Far down the credit list, as the croupier, was Marcel Dalio, the French actor who had played leading roles in two of Jean Renoir's prewar classics, *Grand Illusion* and *Rules of the Game*. Burbank had become as much a refugee center as the fictional Casablanca. Though the American audience may not have been fully aware of it, Curtiz had at his disposal an international cast of all-stars.

The director used their skills to shoot around Bogart as much as at him in the early part of the film. There were perhaps sound narrative reasons for this. Bogart at the beginning is called upon to be glum, sour, and cold: he is the Rick of "I stick my neck out for nobody." When Ilsa arrives, he grows even more morose and angry. The humor, the mystery—above all, the interest in and respect for this misanthrope—are supplied by the dialogue and behavior of other characters. Curtiz often places Bogart on the side of the frame, or even photographs his back in scenes with others.

Nowhere is this subtle displacement of Bogart from the visual center more clearly elevated to a principle than in his scenes with Bergman. Many of their scenes together are long-take two-shots, with Bogart in the left foreground of the frame, showing a shadowed right profile, and Bergman full-face in the middleground, given the full star-lighting treatment. As the center of attention—the focus of the spectator's vision—the actress carries these scenes. While Bogart is frequently passive or reactive, Bergman's performance makes their love affair believable. Her nervousness, her poignancy, her sadness, demonstrate Ilsa's vulnerability to him—heightened by Bergman's uncertainty as to which man her character would end up with.

We have known the answer for so long, of course, that it has become almost impossible to recover the feelings of audiences seeing the film in 1942 or 1943 for the first time. What did they think of the inscrutable, implacable Rick Blaine? Perhaps they read the clues in light of what they knew of Bogart's screen persona: Rick was like Sam Spade, looking out only for himself, somewhere on the edges of the law's boundaries; with a touch of Roy Earle, his sentimental streak; or even, if anyone could remember that far back, a bit like Grasselli in *It All Came True*, the nightclub owner who murdered someone and was on the lam with a price on his head. All of these traits became mixed, as well, with the strong political overtones that Howard Koch supplied for the script. Part of Koch's contribution was making Rick a surrogate for the United States in the months before Pearl Harbor: more specifically, for that substantial part of the American population that supported isolation from the European and Asian wars. The lines are blatant. "I stick my neck out for nobody," says Rick. "A wise foreign policy," responds Renault. Later, also from Renault: "Rick is completely neutral about everything."

As the Nazi major retorts, however, that was not always the case. Gradually we are filled in not only on the personal reasons for Rick's despair, but also on his political past—which did not end with the Loyalists' defeat in Spain. The dialogue makes clear that Rick had been continuing his political activities in Paris right up to the German occupation of the city; it is the Gestapo who have put a price on Rick's head.

What would an American who had fought with the Loyalists in Spain be doing politically in Paris in 1940? *Casablanca* does not require that we linger on the question; yet among the plausible readings of the film is a hypothesis that Rick is, or was, a Communist. This approach opens several lines of interpretation, for the Communists had been, during the period of the Nazi-Soviet pact, among the vociferous isolationists; then, after the Nazis invaded the Soviet Union in the spring of 1941, they switched back to interventionism. Rick recapitulates the Communist shift. Not only Ilsa's arrival in Casablanca shakes him, but also Laszlo's. When Rick is told that Laszlo is in Casablanca, Bogart draws back his upper lip in one of his familiar though by now rarely used mannerisms—the first strong sign of emotion he expresses. Though he continues to profess his neutrality, his obvious respect for Laszlo has also subtly recalled him to his own dormant ideals.

It has often been said about *Casablanca* that it takes public, political issues and resolves them on a personal, individual plane. As indisputable as this perspective is, it is possible to argue that the film also does the opposite: it takes personal issues and links them to the political. After Ilsa's reappearance in his life, when Rick sits drinking, alone with Sam in the closed cafe, he suddenly asks, "Sam, if it's December 1941 in Casablanca, what time is it in New York?" and adds, "I bet they're asleep in New York. I bet they're asleep all over America."

These lines do not refer to differences in time zones. Rick is projecting his own political torpor—now that he has recognized and begun to awaken from it—onto his own home city, his entire nation. Spectators in 1942 and 1943 could in turn project their own memories of December 1941, their own acknowledgment of the reality of war and the potential sacrifices it entailed, back onto the screen character.

There remained the question of exactly what sacrifice, if any, Rick would be called upon to make. Not until June 25, fully a month into shooting—and more than halfway through the production schedule—were the final script pages delivered. Though alternate endings had been considered (and would remain possible choices until the very end), the completed script opted for the same outcome as the original play. Rick would come to understand what had really happened on that day in Paris when Ilsa had apparently betrayed him—causing him to reject his past principles. Secure in her love for him, and his for her, he would regain his former idealism. Thus he would recognize how important it was for the Cause—for humankind—that Ilsa remain with Laszlo, as his support. The circle would be complete: the public events of the time, having been subsumed within the personal, would be returned to their paramount place.

Still, last-minute rewrites were coming in every day, providing the actors with unfamiliar lines to speak. Curtiz had established a shooting style that effectively represented the uncertainties of the narrative, though it frequently meant shifting Bogart to the periphery of the frame. It focused the camera's primary gaze on Bergman or even lesser members of the cast. Would the shift of Bogart's character toward moral certainty be accompanied by a similar movement of Bogart toward center screen? Bergman was giving a remarkable performance, as were many others; perhaps Curtiz's shooting style reflected his judgment about Bogart's capability as an actor.

Whatever the cause, conflict between the director and actor erupted on July 18, during shooting of the final airport sequence. Bogart and Curtiz got into repeated arguments. Producer Wallis was called in to adjudicate. Twice during the afternoon, for more than three hours total, the two men halted shooting for what the unit manager called "story conference."[4] Details of their discussions have never been divulged, though one later account claims the dispute was over whether Rick would shoot Major Strasser in the back. The specifics do not much matter. What was important was that Bogart was taking charge of his own screen persona—in all likelihood, for the first time. These were the most important scenes he had ever played. As his character becomes the dominant figure in the script pages, he was asserting his claim to become the dominant performer on the screen.

The airport scene in *Casablanca* became a classic moment for the Bogart screen persona. The hard man turns into a sentimentalist—and thereby grows stronger than ever. Bogart's face softens as his character's determination grows. Curtiz cuts back and forth between Bogart and Bergman as Rick tells Ilsa of his love for her, and his decision to stay behind while she goes on the plane with Laszlo. The eight-shot sequence ends with his words, "Here's looking at you, kid." Then two more shots: her face, then his, both silent.

The action continues. Laszlo and Ilsa leave. Rick shoots Strasser. Rick and Renault fade into the fog, heading for the Free French Garrison in Brazzaville. Rick has returned to the struggle. What began as wartime entertainment for ideological reinforcement had been transformed, by the skills its artists and craftspersons brought to the task, into an enduring work of popular mythology.

Casablanca won the Academy Award for Best Picture in 1943. Other Oscar winners were Curtiz for direction, and the Epsteins and Koch for screenplay. Wallis won his second Irving G. Thalberg award. Nominations went to Rains as supporting actor, Arthur Edeson for black-and-white cinematography, Owen Marks for editing, and Max Steiner for musical scoring. Bergman gained an actress nomination for a different performance, in *For Whom the Bell Tolls*. Among the nominees for the actor award was Humphrey Bogart—for his forty-sixth film, after thirteen years.

∎ ∎ ∎ ∎

John Garfield spent the spring of 1942 on the road, promoting war bond sales, the release of *Dangerously They Live*, and—with live performances from his role in *Four Daughters*—the memory of his own brief hopeful springtime as a movie actor. His situation at Warner Bros. remained bleak. In June he found work in Howard Hawks's *Air Force* (1943) by asking for a part (according to Hawks's later account), even if a small one. Though he was the only actor with star status in the cast, and was featured in the company's promotion, the main titles listed the performers by their rank as fictional crew members of the B-17 airplane, the *Mary Ann*. Garfield came ninth and next to last.

In its explicitness, *Air Force* is perhaps Hollywood's definitive ideological film project using the themes of betrayal and transformation to unite and fortify the American public's war will. A B-17 "Flying Fortress" takes off from San Francisco on an overnight training mission to Hawaii. The crew turns on the radio. After learning that Soviet ambassador Litvinov has arrived in Washington, they hear, "Mr. Kurusu and Admiral Nomura have assured the press that Japan's intentions are wholly peaceful." (Remember the headline in *Across the Pacific*.) The camera shows a crewman writing the date in the plane's log: December 6, 1941. Another shot, with the camera moving in even closer to the page, shows the next morning's date, December 7. They turn the radio on again, and hear Japanese voices and gunfire. "Who you got tuned in," someone yells, "Orson Welles?" It is not "War of the Worlds." It is the attack on Pearl Harbor.

The flight of the fictional *Mary Ann* becomes a symbolic recapitulation of the trauma of Japan's betrayal that, in American eyes, started the war. The plane lands at Maui, then flies to Hickam Field alongside Pearl Harbor, looking down on the burning and sunken American fleet (a scene created in miniature in the studio). "Take a good look at Pearl Harbor," the pilot tells the crew. "Maybe it's something you'll want to remember." From Hickam they fly to Wake Island—while they listen to a broadcast of President Roosevelt's Declaration of War—then to Clark Field in the Philippines, and eventually (after taking part in the Battle of the Coral Sea) to Australia.

Air Force gave special prominence to sabotage and outright warfare by Japanese-Americans on the Hawaiian islands. On Maui the B-17 is fired on by "local Japs—nice friendly fellas." At Hickam, the *Mary Ann*'s crew learns about vegetable trucks from Honolulu damaging fighter planes on the ground and a Japanese in a delivery truck firing a shotgun. At Wake Island, they hear of "a lot of fifth column work." Jack Warner's file on *Air Force* contains four letters protesting the film's implication (blatant assertion) that Japanese-Americans committed sabotage during the Pearl Harbor attack.

Military investigators after the raid in fact found no sabotage and no hostile acts against American armed forces by the islands' Japanese residents, four fifths of whom were American citizens.[5] Barely 1 percent of Japanese-Americans living in the Hawaiian islands were interned (they were taken to camps on the U.S. mainland), compared to the entire Japanese populations of the West Coast states. It was perhaps in service of this latter policy—carried out while *Air Force* was in production—that the film's falsehoods were directed.

Garfield's role is small, but central to the overall ideological project: his character experiences most sharply the trauma of betrayal and transformation. He plays Joe Winocki (not the crew's Jew—that's George Tobias, as Weinberg, the ex–Brooklyn cabbie); he is its "unmeltable" Eastern European ethnic. At the beginning he is a sour, angry, shunned outsider; having been demoted to gunner when he washed out of pilot training school, he plans to leave the service.

The feelings of betrayal by the Japanese strike him most acutely, perhaps because of his simmering resentment at everyone, including the American military, and himself.

He sets the stage for Roosevelt's war address by saying of the Japanese, "They send a couple of oily gents to Washington with an olive wreath for the President while the boys back home slam Uncle Sam over the head with a crowbar." His transformation is not so much moral or heroic, like Bogart's in *Casablanca*, though he does safely land the damaged plane after the pilot has been mortally wounded. Rather, he finds the Japanese a more appropriate object for his rage. At the end he is no more likeable than at the beginning—only a more effective and committed member of the war machine. The performance faded, as Hawks intended, into the coordinated group effort that the *Mary Ann* represented and to which personal transformation led.

While *Air Force* was nearing completion in October 1942, Warner Bros. embarked on its oddest, and most revealing, project of the war years—a musical "tribute" to itself called *Thank Your Lucky Stars* (1943). The title invited the audience to accept the idea that movie stars brought them (the spectators) good luck, and to be thankful for it. It also may have implied that luck (rather than, say, talent) accounted for stardom. For the stars—about a dozen of the studio's contract players, mostly performing as "themselves" in a frame story about a Hollywood benefit production—this putative denigration was accompanied by actual denigration on the screen, through self-parody, stereotyping, and mock humiliation. This curious film may perhaps be read as a symbolic punishment for (thus a diffusion of potential public resentment away from) movie stars who continued to enjoy their salaries and perquisites while others sacrificed in wartime.

Garfield put in four days' work on the film in November, early in its nearly seven months of intermittent production. His scene comes at the very beginning of the finished film. He appears as a guest on an Eddie Cantor–Dinah Shore radio program broadcast on the Warner Bros.–owned station, KFWB. Announcer Don Wilson asks Shore about Garfield: "Tell me, is he really that tough?" She replies, "Tough? John Garfield is the sweetest, mildest, gentlest boy you'd ever want to meet in the whole world."

Pan and dissolve offstage, where Garfield—lower lip pushed out menacingly—is holding Cantor by the lapels and says, "I'm warning you, Cantor, stop telling me what to do. We get out there and you cross me up, I'm gonna flatten you. Understand?" He shoves Cantor against a wall.

Wilson then introduces Garfield to the movie's radio studio audience as "that bad boy of Burbank." Onstage, Garfield performs and sings with a persona drawn from his 1930s crime and prison B pictures—similar to the death row inmate of *Castle on the Hudson* and the venal punk of *East of the River*. Some of the other stars, such as Bette Davis and Errol Flynn, were parodied in a good-natured way, in a manner enhancing to their star image; for Garfield, drawing on some of his weakest and least appealing past roles was like a blow below the belt. To top it off, the day after Garfield finished his brief appearance in *Thank Your Lucky Stars* he was suspended for refusing to accept a loan-out to Universal. For nearly two months he remained off the payroll, until early January, when Warners found another outside assignment he was willing to accept—and to swing the deal, the studio apparently offered to rent him at less than his contractual salary. RKO was the hiring studio with a mystery-espionage film called *The Fallen Sparrow* (1943).

Garfield was hardly RKO's first choice, either. After buying movie rights in March 1942 to Dorothy B. Hughes's thriller novel, that studio had spent half a year seeking a star for the lead part—an American veteran of the Spanish Civil War who gets involved with Nazi spies in New York. They offered the role to Cagney, unaware that Cagney wanted to put his past support for the Spanish Loyalists well behind him. Others who were considered or approached included Cary Grant, George Brent, and Randolph Scott. Garfield was a last-ditch choice as the project was ready to begin shooting.

Casting issues aside, it is surprising that *The Fallen Sparrow* made it to production at all. The Spanish Civil War was hardly a popular subject for Hollywood moviemakers. It is a comment on the liberal political climate at Warner Bros. (or the disorder of *Casablanca*'s script development) that no questions seem to have been raised about making Rick a Spanish Civil War veteran. That background, however, was not in the source play. In the case of *The Fallen Sparrow*, the hero's Spanish experience was the motivating force in the novel. Still, the perspective was more anti-Nazi than left-wing. The protagonist's enemies were Hitler and his minions, not Franco's Falangists. Had the book been any more specific about the ideological issues of the Spanish Civil War, it seems unlikely that RKO or any other studio would have gone near it.

Even so, the Spanish Civil War question was hotly debated at RKO. Only a week before shooting was to start, a production executive, William Gordon, informed the film's producer, Robert Fellows, that after "many conversations on this subject" a decision had been made to shift the location to "Nazi-invaded France of 1940, and not Civil War–torn Spain of 1938." (These were retrospective locations, since the film's events took place entirely in New York City.)

ILLUSTRATIONS

1. Boys playing cat stick, 1898.

2. Children's party, ca. 1900.

3. James Cagney as Mileaway and Lew Ayres as Louie, the Al Capone figure of *The Doorway to Hell* (1930).

4. Cagney as Tom Powers in *The Public Enemy* (1931). Those were real bullets, said Warner Bros., fired by an expert marksman.

5. The new metropolitan national hero. A publicity photo for *Taxi!* (1932).

6. Ruth Donnelly matches Cagney's hand gestures in *Hard to Handle* (1933).

7. Demonstrating a dance step in *Footlight Parade* (1933). Frank McHugh wears the tail.

8. Cagney contemplates the ass's head he will wear as Bottom the Weaver in *A Midsummer Night's Dream* (1935).

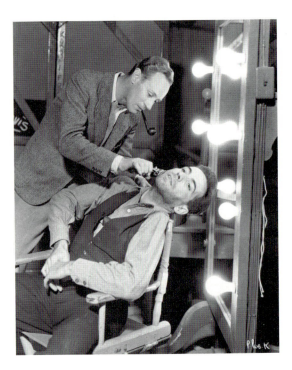

9. After helping Humphrey Bogart get his part, Leslie Howard performs another service on the set of *The Petrified Forest* (1936).

10. Bogart as a disgruntled factory worker in *Black Legion* (1937), with Dick Foran and Henry Brandon.

11. Bogart's makeup for *The Return of Dr. X* (1939). "Grewsome," Warner Bros. publicity called it.

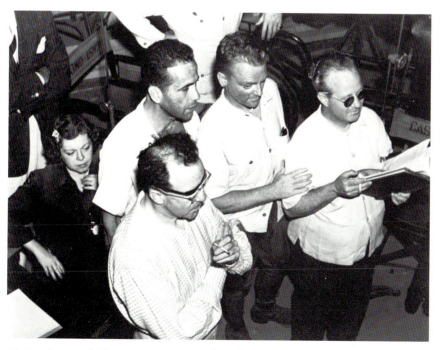

12. On the set of *The Roaring Twenties* (1939). *From left:* script clerk Virginia Moore, director Raoul Walsh, Bogart, Cagney, dialogue director Hugh Cummings.

13. John Garfield's first screen role as Mickey Borden in *Four Daughters* (1938). With Priscilla Lane and May Robson.

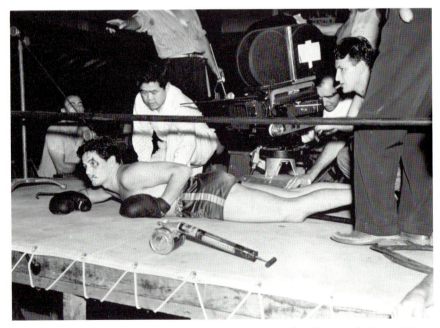

14. Cinematographer James Wong Howe sets up a shot for *They Made Me a Criminal* (1939).

15. Garfield publicity photo, 1941.
The caption called the shower cold.

15

16. Garfield publicity portrait.

16

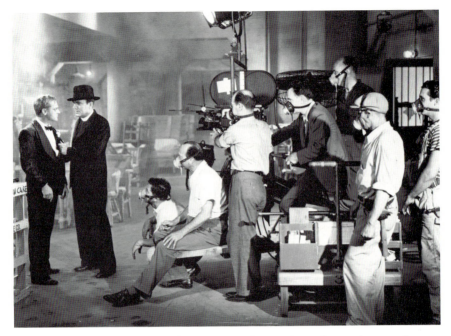

17. Crew and grips wear gas masks, Cagney and Pat O'Brien do not, for a smoke-filled shot from *Angels with Dirty Faces* (1938). Director Michael Curtiz sits in front of the camera.

18. Hugs from Olivia de Havilland and Rita Hayworth in this publicity shot for *The Strawberry Blonde* (1941).

19. Cagney's mother, Carolyn, and her children on the set of *Yankee Doodle Dandy. From left*: James, Edward, William, Jeanne.

20. Everyone's in costume but Cagney to rehearse the "You're a Grand Old Flag" number from *Yankee Doodle Dandy* (1942).

21. Bogart with Ida Lupino on the set of *High Sierra* (1941).

22. Peter Lorre, director John Huston, and Bogart prepare a shot for *The Maltese Falcon* (1941).

23. The romantic hero of *Casablanca* (1942), with Ingrid Bergman. "The part definitely establishes Bogart as a 'great lover,'" said the original caption.

24. The hero subjected to a dressing-down from S. K. Sakall in *Thank Your Lucky Stars* (1943).

25. Garfield poses with Sgt. Al Schmid, the World War II hero whose life he portrays in *Pride of the Marines* (1945).

26. Garfield and Lana Turner consider murder in *The Postman Always Rings Twice* (1946).

27. Lauren Bacall, a beatific Bogart, John Ridgely, and director Howard Hawks at a script meeting on *The Big Sleep* (1946).

28. Getting made up for *The Treasure of the Sierra Madre* (1948).

29. Garfield under examination in *Body and Soul* (1947).

30. Garfield under examination in *Force of Evil* (1948). This shot was part of a framing courtroom sequence that was eliminated from the final version of the film.

31. Garfield under examination before the House Committee on Un-American Activities, April 23, 1951.

32. Ward Bond points a finger at Broderick Crawford, bypassing Cagney, in *The Time of Your Life* (1948).

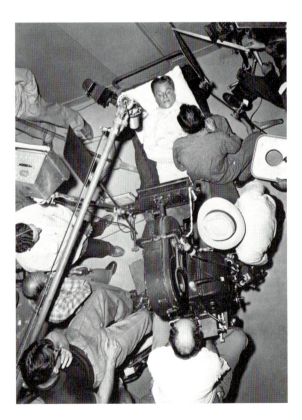

33. Back in the Warner Bros. straightjacket for *White Heat* (1949).

34. Garfield as a Cuban-American revolutionary in *We Were Strangers* (1949), with Wally Cassell and Jennifer Jones.

35. Garfield's final motion picture appearance, dying in the gutter at the end of *He Ran All the Way* (1951). Wallace Ford holds the gun, Shelley Winters is on the sidewalk.

36. Bogart as Dixon Steele, the screenwriter/suspect of *In a Lonely Place* (1950), imagines the way a murder may have been committed. With Frank Lovejoy and Jeff Donnell.

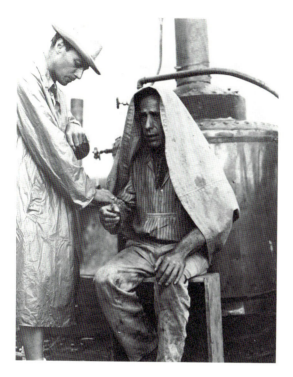

37. Checking Bogart's pulse on location for *The African Queen* (1952).

38. As Captain Queeg, Bogart looks Nixonian in a tense moment on the bridge in *The Caine Mutiny* (1954).

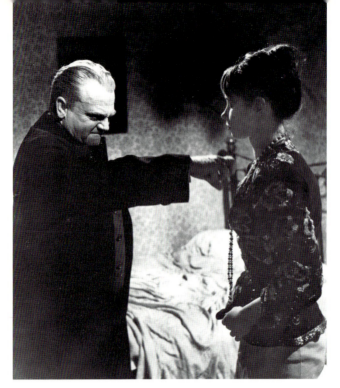

39. *Shake Hands with the Devil* (1959) made Cagney's Irish rebel a woman-hater, in this scene with Marianne Benet.

40. Cagney with Arlene Francis and director Billy Wilder on the set of *One, Two, Three* (1961).

Gordon listed three "dangers" in retaining the Spanish background: "1. Desire of State Dept. to maintain friendliest relations with present Spanish government. 2. Possibility of Spain as ally. 3. Offensive to most Latin Americans." Expanding on the last point, he suggested that nearly all Latin American countries recognized and traded with the Franco government and had sided with Franco's forces during the Civil War. Moreover, he added, those who opposed Franco had also disliked his foes, "because of their communism and anti-Catholicism."[6] This emphasis on the vital Latin American market was reinforced a few days later when a letter arrived from Joseph Breen of the Production Code Administration, saying, "we strongly urge that you consult your Foreign Department as to the advisability of the Spanish angle contained in this picture."[7] These pressures did not deter producer Fellows. He went ahead with the original plan, though on the day shooting began he received from Gordon a memo insisting that "protection takes" be made on the few scenes (six in all) in which Spain was mentioned.[8]

During production the debate continued. In early April the studio received a letter from a politically committed resident of Buffalo, New York, who wrote, "I see by the papers that you have in production a film, *Fallen Sparrow*, depicting the part played by the International Brigade in the Spanish Civil War, and that you are being afflicted with a case of Appeasement Jitters. I wish to register my vehement protest at your allowing the Spanish Ambassador to frighten you from making an honest anti-fascist picture."[9] William Gordon wrote in reply, "The tides of political or ideological pressure do not touch us."[10]

Someone elsewhere in the studio may have reviewed this exchange, for a memo to "Bill" (Gordon?), signed only "Q," takes issue with the very premise of the film's politics. The hero's "history in Spain is at no time made forthright and positive," the author wrote. "Large numbers do not have the faintest idea of the political and ideological problems back of the character. Before we ever can begin pulling for him with all our hearts we have got to know, *not* that he fought in Spain, but *why* he fought in Spain."[11]

Cogent as this note was—its criticism could be applied to the novel as well as the film—it came too late; production was already completed. The last word on the political and ideological front was left to Ulric Bell of the government's Office of War Information, who wrote to Gordon, "The film's presentation of the war in Spain speaks unusually well for American understanding of that early phase of the present worldwide struggle. . . . [It is] the first Hollywood film to correctly evaluate the war in Spain as an assault of the Axis and its sympathizers on democracy everywhere."[12]

It appears that the United States government and the movie industry's Production Code Administration were pursuing different foreign policies. On the other hand, the completed film makes no mention of either *Spanish* side in the Civil War; with *The Fallen Sparrow* as your source, you would think that only Americans and Nazis had fought in Spain.

Given the background of ideological disputation within the studio, one might not realize that the film is, if anything, more explicit politically than the novel. At least it uses a more effective signifier for its political background. In Hughes's book, the Nazis pursue the hero from Spain to New York because he had hidden a case of precious goblets they covet. Oddly, this "maguffin" does not detract from the psychological tension of the thriller; by its very implausibility it may even accentuate the taut atmosphere.

The movie, however, changes the precious artifact to the flag of the International Brigade. After the Brigade had killed one of Hitler's generals, according to the narrative, the Führer had sworn he would kill all its members and destroy its flag. Garfield's character, Kit McKitrick, had hidden the flag. The Nazis had captured and tortured him, keeping him alive until he would divulge its location; but he managed to escape before giving away his secret. (All of these background events occur prior to the film's beginning.)

Tenuous as its politics may have been—or even its narrative coherence—*The Fallen Sparrow* gave Garfield his richest opportunity to mold a character portrayal since his first film role of Mickey Borden in *Four Daughters*. As created by novelist Hughes, and further developed by screenwriter Warren Duff, Garfield's character Kit is New York Irish, with a knack for transcending class boundaries, moving easily from precinct house to penthouse. The film begins as he returns to New York from a period of recuperation in the West. Still vulnerable to memories of his ordeal, psychologically not fully stable, he nevertheless is impelled to return because his best friend has died mysteriously. Soon he finds himself in a nest of Nazi spies: he, and the flag whose whereabouts he still protects, are their targets.

In his performance Garfield created a physical correlative for the tortured veteran's mental weakness. His movements convey the impression of a powerful figure repressed or held back. There is a sense of forced immobility in his screen presence, an implosion that expresses itself in nervous eye movements, excessive perspiration, and ticlike gestures of his mouth and jaw.

The Nazis count on their tortures' effects to make him incapable of defending himself at the climactic showdown. They drug him to render him even more immobile, and prepare to inject him with a truth serum finally to gain the secret of the flag's hiding place. By force of will Kit breaks through his torpor and shoots his tormentor. At the end he is flying off to Lisbon, where the flag was kept. The Brigade is forming again.

The Fallen Sparrow does not rise above its implausibility as *Casablanca* does. Nevertheless, it certainly ranks among Garfield's most effective screen performances—in his review, the *New York Post's* Archer Winsten called it the best of his career up to then. Even Warner Bros. took notice. "John Garfield was excellent in *The Fallen Sparrow*," Steve Trilling, former head of casting, now Wallis's successor as production executive, wrote to Jack Warner, "and if at any time he is available, would also like to make a deal for him at whatever terms we set up."[13] Was Trilling not aware that Garfield belonged exclusively to Warner Bros. on a contract that had been signed more than four years previously and had three more annual options? The actor may have become a nonperson on the Warner lot, but the sparrow that fell at RKO was one that Warner Bros. noticed.

■ ■ ■ ■

With Bogart and Garfield playing veterans of the Abraham Lincoln Brigade during 1942–1943, it was clear that the war had restored the left to a position of acceptance—perhaps even prominence—in Hollywood. Bogart's next two films after *Casablanca* were both written by John Howard Lawson, one of the leading figures in the Communist party's Hollywood branch. In *Action in the North Atlantic* (1943) he plays a first mate on a cargo ship. In *Sahara* (1943), his loan-out at Columbia, finally accomplished, he plays a tank sergeant in North Africa. Howard Koch may have added some politics to *Casablanca*, but when ideologues like Lawson were creating his screen characters from scratch, there was no room for Rick Blaine's romantic individualism.

Action in the North Atlantic is a tribute to the "heroes without uniforms" (the film's working title) of the National Maritime Union who brave German U-boats and planes to deliver war materiel to America's Allies. It contains a sequence that would later become notorious: American seamen anxiously await approaching planes; then, when they see Soviet star markings, they shout, "They're ours, all right! Russian planes off the starboard quarter!" With Roosevelt's voice on the sound track, and actuality footage of ship construction and convoys at sea, the film's propaganda purpose had little need for character development or actors' performance. Letters from NMU and CIO members commended Warner Bros. for making a pro-labor film.

Sahara was credited as based upon an incident in a Soviet photoplay (perhaps Lawson's source), but it also strongly resembles John Ford's 1934 World War I desert action film *The Lost Patrol*. It has a United Nations cast—Americans, British, French, Australians and New Zealanders, a South African, a British Sudanese, and an Italian and a German as prisoners—fighting and struggling for survival in the Libyan desert. Bogart's sergeant compares his willingness to fight and persevere with the Russians taking a stand at Moscow. When asked what part of the United States he comes from, he answers, "No place, just the army." It was hardly more than a stereotyped role, but reviewers praised his toughness, his power, his authority.

In February 1943 Bogart took one day out from his work on *Sahara* to make his appearance in *Thank Your Lucky Stars*. The brief scene written for him—with its humiliation that seems more real than mock—unavoidably suggests an official Warner Bros. viewpoint on the actor's toughness, power, and authority.

Unshaven, wearing a hat, Bogart walks into the backstage area and encounters S. K. Sakall, the chubby, comic Middle European with the jiggling jowls who played the waiter, Carl, in *Casablanca*. "I'm talking to you, fatso," Bogart growls, but Sakall shouts him down, pushes him away, pulls his tie, calls him "chiseler." A guard queries, "Let the old man bulldoze you, eh?"

"Yes," replies Bogart, "that ain't like me. Gee, I hope none of my movie fans hear about this." As the sound track plays "Who's Afraid of the Big Bad Wolf?" Bogart pulls his collar up, scratches his ear, and exits.

Warner Bros. wanted a Bogart who could be bulldozed. When he returned from Columbia, the studio assigned him a part far removed in character from Rick Blaine and the hard-edged working-class and non-com heroes of the merchant marine and tank films. The picture was *Conflict* (made in 1943, but not released commercially until 1945); it concerns a man who murders his wife because he loves her younger sister. The machinations of a wily psychoanalyst drive him to reveal the crime. The story was far from resembling his recent triumphs. Instead, with its initial portrayal of a quarreling and disenchanted couple, it bore all too many similarities (except, of course, for the murder) to the actual state of Bogart's marriage to Mayo Methot.

It was well known at the time, not only by insiders but also by the general public, that the marriage was marked by bouts of drinking and violence. A 1944 *Life* magazine profile jauntily described an episode in which Mrs. Bogart hurled a highball glass and narrowly missed her husband, who calmly announced, "I live dangerously."[14] Beneath this media portrait of a contentious but improbably cozy couple, the movie community perceived a different reality.

Having given up her own acting career (as *Life* reported, to "concentrate" on his), Mayo Methot had become jealous of Bogart's recent successes, and the couple's drinking and violence were growing more severe. A psychoanalyst not half as wise as the one in *Conflict* might have noted the resemblance between the actor's marital difficulties and those depicted in the film; though without clinical evidence, one could hardly suggest whether Warner Bros. executives had assigned Bogart to the role unconsciously or deliberately.

Bogart did not complain about the picture's bearing on his marriage—at least for the record. He complained about its mediocrity. The first flare-up came early in April 1943 with telegrams between Burbank and Brawley, California, where the actor was finishing location work on *Sahara*. Jack Warner had heard from Trilling of Bogart's dissatisfaction and was wiring to set matters straight. He played his usual opening card, familiar from as far back as Cagney's arbitration hearing of 1932: "After all, Humphrey, it was our studio that made all this possible for you from the day I brought you from New York for *Petrified Forest*. . . . I am not fool enough to do the wrong thing with anyone coming along as grand as you are. You must give me credit for having intelligence to know what pictures to make with you."[15] Bogart replied with a conciliatory wire signed "Bogie," reserving his right to "make trouble" but agreeing to do the picture.[16] Warner's appreciative acknowledgment, to "Bogie" this time, seemed to close the matter. When starting time for *Conflict* came, however, Bogart refused to report. He was on his yacht off Newport Beach and not responding to the studio's telegrams. After a week without communication from him, the studio suspended him on May 3.

Three days later, Bogart came on shore to take a call from Burbank. He thought it was Steve Trilling, but Jack Warner himself was on the line, with a stenographer transcribing every word. They talked for half an hour, with bluster on both sides.

"I have heard the same talk from twenty people who talk just like you are doing, and I know one of them is now trying to get a job as just an extra," Warner threatened.

"You would never have offered this script to Flynn, Bette Davis, or anyone else, but you think I am a sucker, and because I signed that contract you are forcing me to do this," Bogart replied.

"This is a potent business, that is why people respect the motion picture industry, and I know you are making an awful error," Warner continued.

"What are you doing, frightening me?" Bogart responded. They rang off without either man giving in.[17]

Bogart had let slip to Warner that he had discussed his dilemma with Wallis and Curtiz, who were preparing *Passage to Marseille*, with Bogart to star. Immediately after the telephone conversation, the studio head covered that flank with a memo to Wallis saying, "This will not do. Inform Mike [Curtiz] that if Bogart should contact him, to let Bogart know I mean business and that he is not going to do any other picture until he does *Conflict*."[18]

The actor remained in Newport Beach throughout May. In early June, he capitulated. *Conflict* was made in the summer of 1943, though it did not see the light of a projector lamp in American theaters until two years later. In the interim, it was screened for American military personnel overseas. Perhaps it was a cautionary tale for those separated from their spouses. As the psychoanalyst in the film says, "People have impulses, compulsions, drives—towards escape. Escape from loneliness. They seek that escape. In the companionship of someone else. And lo, just when they think they've achieved it, they find they've put on their own handcuffs."

Perhaps it was a cautionary tale for Bogart. Was he contemplating altering his marital—or contractual—status? In the year of his first Academy Award nomination, of his new rank as an acknowledged star, he could still be pushed around facetiously by the likes of "Cuddles" Sakall, and for real by Jack L. Warner. The themes of betrayal and transformation were becoming appropriate to personal and professional, as well as national, life.

8

Ordinary Guys and
Private Eyes

In Hollywood's contributions to uniting the American people against treacherous enemies, where stood James Cagney, the Academy Award best actor of 1942? *Yankee Doodle Dandy*'s release in June 1942 kept him in the limelight, but Cagney did not work before the cameras for more than a year after the war's start. Behind the scenes he was waging his own private war. It held for him some of the same moral character as the World War itself—a struggle against betrayal and for the transformation of the motion picture industry.

Along with his brother William, Cagney was setting up an independent production company. At this point in Hollywood's history, independent production was not a novelty—a number of directors and producers had ventured in that direction before the war. Even Cagney had a taste of independence at Grand National in 1936–1937, though his legal entanglement with Warner Bros. had hampered that effort. Despite these past and present activities, the movie industry regarded Cagney's endeavor as something special. No successful independent production unit had been set up by a *performer* since the studio system consolidated in the 1920s; Charlie Chaplin's company was the only survivor of the many that existed before.

Chaplin had produced only three pictures between 1931 and 1941: he was not the Cagney brothers' model. There was more to their project than a desire to control James Cagney's screen image. They had in mind such independent producers as David O. Selznick and Samuel Goldwyn, whose organizations functioned as ministudios, with their own production facilities, contract talent, and a schedule of three or four pictures a year. When Cagney Productions, Inc., signed a distribution deal with United Artists—one day before production closed on *Yankee Doodle Dandy*—it called for the new company to deliver fifteen pictures over the next five years.

The Cagneys went into independent production not with the idea of forming a lean and purposeful unit to exploit James's audience appeal—now at its peak—but with the goal of developing screen projects; hiring writers, directors, and performers; perhaps even acquiring their own studio. Some of these activities were necessary to qualify as a business under internal revenue requirements, rather than a personal corporation designed to circumvent high wartime taxes on individuals. In the Cagneys' public pronouncements, however, was apparent a motive of even more emotional urgency—to demonstrate by independent achievement what a rotten job Jack Warner had done of managing James Cagney's career.

In their view, Cagney's success at Warner Bros. had occurred despite the studio rather than because of it. They would demonstrate how much better they could be at managing the actor's career than Warner had ever been. But getting back at Jack proved a tenuous foundation on which to build an independent production operation. Cagney Productions was able to complete only three pictures during a seven-year association with United Artists. The company's basic problem, according to one not-dispassionate observer, was William Cagney himself. "Bill was no filmmaker at all," director-cinematographer Byron Haskin said, years later. "Bill got a film together; it was a bomb. Time after time."

Haskin had started out as a silent film director, but he was working as a special effects cinematographer at Warner Bros. at the time the Cagneys went independent. He saw the Cagney operation as a chance to resume his career as director, but he turned down a Cagney offer, and lived to regret it. "All the Cagney outfit needed was a good journeyman guy who knew the score, and they would have made some top films," Haskin said. "I would have been the ingredient the Cagneys needed to make the thing work."[1]

In William Cagney's recollection, no journeyman guy would have made any difference—unless possibly he was a Justice Department antitrust lawyer. He claimed that Jack Warner scuttled the Cagney ship before it left the dock. In his version, Warner clout kept agents from offering the Cagneys property or talent and frightened off writers, directors, and performers who might have wanted to work with them. Remember Warner's telephone threat to Bogart: "This is a potent business, that is why people respect the motion picture industry." William even was convinced that Warner's muscle frightened the nation's movie reviewers into panning the Cagney brothers' films and calling (as indeed many did) for Jimmy to return to Burbank.

How realistic was it, however, to launch such ambitious plans in wartime? Fewer personnel were available, fewer films were being made. Hunt Stromberg, the big-time MGM producer who became an independent at the same time as the Cagneys, managed to complete two films during the war years; the independent Arnold Pressburger produced three; the great Selznick made none at all between 1940 and 1944. In this context, the Cagney record—one film, *Johnny Come Lately*, in 1943, another, *Blood on the Sun*, in 1945— hardly seems so meager. The first of these grossed $2.4 million in earnings paid to the distributor, the second $3.4 million. The latter figure tops all of Cagney's Warner Bros. films with the exception of *Yankee Doodle Dandy*. These numbers appear to indicate considerable success. In the world of independent movie production, however, numbers are not always what they seem. While a studio like Warner Bros. could amortize its overhead costs over three or four dozen pictures a year, the Cagneys had to finance their operating expenses out of actual or anticipated profits from only these two films.

With their expansive plans, and contractual obligations to United Artists, they had acquired by 1946 at least half a dozen literary properties, paying as much as a reported $250,000 for the rights to Adria Locke Langley's novel about a Southern demagogue, *A Lion Is In the Streets*. These acquisitions alone could have eaten up a fair share of the earnings from the two films. Most of these eventually were made into films under the aegis of Cagney Productions, but long after the primary purpose for setting up the company had been abandoned. That purpose, lest we forget, was to free James Cagney from the odious burden of his Warner Bros. screen persona. Making money was also a goal, but the question remained which would take precedence if the profit motive clashed with the desire completely to transform Cagney's screen character. From the United Artists viewpoint, exactly such a conflict arose just as soon as the camera started rolling on their first independent picture.

Even such an obvious choice as a war picture—as a follow-up to *Yankee Doodle Dandy*—was rejected by the Cagneys, partly because they wanted (as William told the *New York Times*) "no more cocky arrogance of the old Warners' formula kind."[2] One could not make a war picture if the star wanted to behave like the classic children's book hero Ferdinand the Bull, sniffing flowers in the meadow instead of fighting. The project they finally settled on for their first independent production, *Johnny Come Lately*, almost precisely fit the mood—so it seems at least in retrospect—of James Cagney's professional desires. Drawn from a Louis Bromfield novel, *McLeod's Folly*, it was a story set at the turn of the century, about a man running away from his past. Once a reporter, now a tramp, the hero pauses in a small town long enough to help an elderly woman newspaper publisher vanquish her nemesis, the town's corrupt mayor, and then moves on.

Warner's alleged interference did not prevent them from hiring as scriptwriter the playwright John Van Druten, who worked at Warner Bros. that same year adapting his play *Old Acquaintance* for the screen, and who was nominated for a screenplay Oscar in 1944 as cowriter of *Gaslight*. The director assignment was more problematic: it went to William K. Howard, a man Cagney's age who had been one of the more innovative directors of the early 1930s but whose career had been hobbled (reputedly by alcoholism) and was soon to end.

Johnny Come Lately went into production in early April 1943 and was released in September. The press response was of such a nature that only the idea of a conspiracy could make it explicable to William Cagney. "Jim Cagney and his brother evidently have much less respect for the Cagney acting talents than their old bosses, the Warner Brothers, had," wrote Alton Cook in the *New York World-Telegram*. "It is a backward start for William Cagney Productions," said John T. McManus in *PM*, "indicating, if anything, that Warner Bros., Cagney's old studio, knew lots better than William Cagney what was good for Brother Jimmy." Archer Winsten in the *New York Post* pleaded, "Please, Mr. Cagney, for the benefit of the public, yourself and Warner's, go back."

Let us pause to remind ourselves that critics are not infrequently disturbed by the new. The eternal problem for *Johnny Come Lately* is that it follows *Yankee Doodle Dandy*: any successor to Cagney's epiphany would seem a disappointment. It no doubt took considerable courage to strike out in an innovative way. There are those who praise the film's tone, and Cagney's performance, as Chaplinesque. Audience appetites were sufficiently whetted for a Cagney film, moreover, that it grossed $2.4 million for the distributors, despite the reviews, and earned Cagney Productions over $1 million in profits.

Still, there is no escaping that *Johnny Come Lately* is an anomaly. What is missing is the star himself. A Chaplin film never let you doubt that Chaplin was at its center, that *he* was what is was all about. *Johnny Come Lately* is about a lot of things and no one thing—certainly not about the screen character or the screen persona of James Cagney. Less, in this case, was not more; absence was not presence. It was more like disinterest. Even the setting is evanescent. Cagney's character seems to urge the narrative backward in time, to the mid-nineteenth-century youth of the elderly publisher, played by Broadway actress Grace George in her movie debut. (Miss George, who was married to William A. Brady, was the Bogart family's Upper West Side neighbor who aided Humphrey's start in the theater.)

The film was a pastiche. It was far from marking a decisive break with Warner Bros.; the avid Cagney fan with a longish memory might have recognized such familiar borrowing as the villain's use of defective construction materials from *The Strawberry Blonde*; the framed and unjustly imprisoned reporter from *Each Dawn I Die*; and the gambling hall/bordello and vigilante action from *Frisco Kid*. When Cagney is forced to use a gun—a concession to the distributor's wish for some "old Cagney" fireworks—he pumps his arm while shooting in the artificial manner he used in *Angels with Dirty Faces*. Non-Cagney homages in the film include Marjorie Main imitating Mae West and the town's police behaving like Mack Sennett's Keystone Kops.

One of *Johnny Come Lately*'s strong points—the work of the supporting cast—might even be said to resemble the way Michael Curtiz used his minor characters to play off and build up Rick in *Casablanca*. Here, however, the core that Rick's character provided to *Casablanca* is missing: Cagney is more of a passive onlooker—or maestro, if you will—while some of the old Warner Bros. stock company actors that he hired for the film, like Robert Barrat and Victor Kilian, have little set-piece scenes.

As for Cagney's tramp resembling Chaplin's tramp, the critical difference lies in Chaplin's poignant romanticism. While there are brief moments of sentimental feeling between Cagney's character and those played by Marjorie Main, Grace George, and Marjorie Lord as the publisher's niece (and pointed comic byplay with Hattie McDaniel as the publisher's cook), his primary emotion is directed toward a portrait of the publisher as a ravishing youth. The reporter turned tramp wants to escape his own past, into hers. There is a certain negative tone toward women in these sentimental gestures. As a tramp he seems to be running from women—they "pin a guy down," a fellow tramp agrees—and his interest in the publisher's youth, when she was a wife and not a newspaperwoman, seems predicated in part on his view that "running a newspaper is not a woman's job." Perhaps it was remarks such as this that led some 1940s newspapers with female publishers—like the *New York Post*—to pan the film.

Whatever Cagney thought aesthetically about his performance, he clearly recognized that economically and critically it would not do to repeat it. The next independent project would have to make him more active, more decisive, more integral to the narrative. Seventeen months passed, however, before Cagney went to work again on a motion picture set. During that period he served as president of the Screen Actors Guild and spent three months in England on a USO tour entertaining Allied troops, prior to the Normandy invasion of June 1944.

Blood on the Sun, the second Cagney Productions project, though also set in the past, was far more attuned to the present. It was a story about an American newspaperman working in Japan in the late 1920s who helps to expose the secret Tanaka Memorial—a document allegedly prepared by a Japanese prime minister, Baron Giichi Tanaka, detailing Japan's plans for expanding its Asian empire. Recent scholarship suggests that the Tanaka Memorial was not authentic (however, as Edwin O. Reischauer writes, "views such as it expressed were advanced by many officials at the time");[3] but that does not invalidate Cagney's film as an intervention in the political and military debates of the times. It was produced in November–December 1944 and released in June 1945, perfectly timed to have an impact as the nation celebrated victory in Europe and turned its full attention to the Pacific war.

After an original idea and a treatment by other writers, William Cagney hired Lester Cole to write the screenplay. If the Cagneys were tired of political labels, as William had told the *New York Times* in 1943—more specifically, worried about the possible consequences of James's radical past—what on earth was William thinking of? It was no secret in Hollywood that Cole was a Communist party activist.

A likely explanation derives from the fact that, as the war continued, the Communist party position seemed neatly to coincide with official American policy, and with Hollywood's representation of war issues. Communist writers like John Howard Lawson, Alvah Bessie, and Albert Maltz were getting important assignments from the studios, and their peers were honoring them with Oscar nominations. Before Cagney Productions hired him, Lester Cole had just finished working on a major Warner Bros. picture, *Objective, Burma!* (1945), starring Errol Flynn.

No doubt it seemed natural to utilize a rising writer like Lester Cole. The period of harmony, however, was coming to a sudden end. During 1945, the Communist party began once again to take an adversarial position toward American government policies, just as political rightists prepared to do battle against Communist influence and "infiltration." *Blood on the Sun* found itself caught up in this rising antagonism.

In the inaugural issue of *Hollywood Quarterly*, published four months after the film's release, screenwriter Cole attacked the Cagneys for substituting for his politically progressive ending a reactionary conclusion approved by William Randolph Hearst. His ending, as he described it, involves Cagney's character taking the secret Tanaka document to the League of Nations (precipitating Japanese withdrawal from the League) and predicting future American involvement in a Pacific war. In the actual ending, Cagney assists a Eurasian spy to escape with the document; wounded, he is rescued by an American diplomat. He refuses to shake hands with his Japanese antagonists, saying, "Sure. Forgive your enemies. But first get even."

It is the burden of Cole's argument—which he repeated and amplified in his 1981 autobiography *Hollywood Red*—that this ending coincided with Hearst's advocacy of a negotiated peace with Japan, rather than with the policy of unconditional surrender being followed by the American and Soviet governments. It may be that the decades have so cooled this controversy that it is impossible to imagine the heat of the moment; Cole's diatribe, however, seems on the face of it a touch preposterous—especially since it appeared in print after the Hiroshima and Nagasaki atomic bombs and Japan's actual unconditional surrender. What seems more likely is that Cole was using the changed ending as a pretext to raise other issues for ideological struggle: the rights of screenwriters and the abuses of Hollywood's capitalists.

Blood on the Sun, and its reception, were otherwise unremarkable. The film grossed $1 million more than *Johnny Come Lately*: audiences in summer 1945 surely got a *Rambo*-like thrill from seeing Jimmy Cagney win a fight to the death, judo-style, with a Japanese villain. Reviews were mixed. Howard Barnes raised a familiar refrain in the *New York Herald-Tribune*, writing, "Cagney and his brother William . . . should work a bit harder on material for one of the finest actors on the screen." *Time* magazine, in a positive review, took pains to label him "liberal Actor-Producer Cagney." Was this a soft-pedaling of the Cole script, which had Cagney proposing a toast to "the ten days that shook the world," or a tribute to the actor's humanitarian radicalism, which would soon be threatened again by the onset of the cold war? Lester Cole could not have been unaware that a published attack on Cagney Productions could have a much more deleterious effect than one against, say, Paramount Pictures. His article put a seal on Cagney's estrangement from the Hollywood left.

■ ■ ■ ■

There were open arms at Warner Bros. in mid-1943 for one actor who had been, not so long before, the studio's invisible man. No sooner had John Garfield passed through the gates on his return from RKO and *The Fallen Sparrow* than he was put to work, and steadily, except for several months in early 1944 when he traveled overseas to entertain Allied troops during the Italian campaign. It was as if, seeing Garfield play a street-smart New York Irish youth with leftist leanings, Warners executives realized once again that they had another Cagney in their midst—one who could be the "cocky, arrogant" screen persona the Cagneys deplored.

Imagining Garfield as a Cagney (as Warners had already done once before in the actor's career) effectively stripped him, to be sure, of the one truly remarkable aspect of his screen persona: his sexual magnetism. *The Fallen Sparrow* had restored a good part of the power that had unexpectedly surfaced in his debut film, *Four Daughters*, but Warner Bros. seemed to want resolutely to suppress it—or worse, channel it into a stereotyped male randiness.

In *Destination Tokyo* (1943), Garfield co-stars with Cary Grant in a story of a submarine mission into Tokyo Bay to obtain data for the first aerial bombing raids on Japan. Grant plays the captain; Garfield is a crew member named "Wolf" who provides comic relief through his obsession with women. Defusing an unexploded bomb after a Japanese air attack on the sub, Wolf says, "I once knew a dame who had a temperament just like a bomb." The script, for which Albert Maltz was credited as cowriter, contains the by now familiar left-wing touches: references to a Russian guerrilla and to "appeasers" who sold military materiel to Japan before the war. In his portrait of Wolf as a working-class enlisted man, however, Maltz did not do honor to the proletariat: "Strong arms, strong back, weak mind," Wolf says of himself as he volunteers for hazardous duty ashore in Japan. Garfield could do no more than connect the dots in portraying this utterly conventionalized caricature.

An even more dubious assignment was *Between Two Worlds* (1944); based on a 1923 play by Sutton Vane, it was also a remake of a 1930 Warner Bros. film, *Outward Bound*, starring Leslie Howard. The point was to update this philosophical drama about a hallucinatory voyage of the dead to a World War II setting—a time when, indeed, questions about the meaning of life and death, of an afterlife and of judgment, must have been occupying the thoughts of many. The task, however, seemed to be beyond director Edward A. Blatt, whose only other Warner Bros. credit is a similar updating of *The Petrified Forest* into the 1945 *Escape in the Desert* (with Duke Mantee and gang transformed into escaping Nazi prisoners of war); at least the challenge of drawing an adequate performance out of Garfield proved insurmountable. Wearing a trench coat, with a cigarette dangling from his lips and a curl over his forehead, Garfield caricatures a cynical newspaperman. Sara Hamilton in the *Los Angeles Examiner* judged his performance "frightfully distorted and overdrawn."

Heaven and hell, says Garfield's character in *Between Two Worlds*, "in a way they're really both the same place." It may have been heavenly to be a Warner Bros. movie star, but it could be hellish, too; getting away from poor roles and weak performances to entertain soldiers near the front may have been for Garfield a relief. He was still barely past thirty, and he seems to have identified strongly with servicemen. Along with Bette Davis, he had been a founder of the Hollywood Canteen, a counterpart of New York's Stage Door Canteen, where movie personalities waited tables as well as provided entertainment for military personnel.

Warner Bros. was planning a movie on the Hollywood Canteen, and months of delays—because of a dispute between the studio and the Screen Actors Guild over salaries for this picture—made it possible for Garfield to appear in it on his return. With its emphasis on the studio and its stars, *Hollywood Canteen* (1944) did not conceal its promotional purpose, but it was of a different order from *Thank Your Lucky Stars*. The performers' offscreen lives took precedence over their screen personas: they were "real people" who mingled with servicemen at the Canteen. In one scene, a soldier calls out to Garfield, "Hi, Johnny. I saw you last in Italy." Garfield replies, "Sure. South of Cassino. I remember."

This effort to inscribe Garfield's front-line visit in his films carried over into *Nobody Lives Forever*, one of those wartime productions, like Bogart's *Conflict*, held back from domestic release—in this case until fall 1946. A concoction of screenwriter W. R. Burnett, it featured a prototype of the bicoastal gangster, a bit like Jack Nicholson's character in John Huston's 1985 film *Prizzi's Honor*. Garfield plays New York racketeer Nick Blake, who, as the film opens, is medically discharged from service as a sergeant in the First Army. He returns home to find that his wife has betrayed him, financially as well as sexually. After getting his money back, he takes a Malibu beach house to recuperate. L.A. hoodlums get him involved in a scheme to bilk a wealthy young widow. He takes her to Mission San Juan Capistrano, where he tells her stories about his war experience on the Italian front, and they fall in love. He breaks with the L.A. bad guys and rescues her from their kidnapping.

Audiences would not have seen this inconsequential film until a full year after the film Garfield made after it, *Pride of the Marines* (1945), and likely would not have seen any connection between the two films. A link, however, there was: it lay in the changes Garfield was going through (perhaps because of his Italian experience), and in Warner Bros.' groping efforts to incorporate them into his screen persona—to include him centrally, if belatedly, in its wartime ideological representation of personal and social transformation. For Garfield, *Nobody Lives Forever* was like *Across the Pacific* in Bogart's career: an imperfect trying-out of themes and character traits that would emerge full-blown in a film capable of moving the actor into higher strata of confidence, mastery, popular appeal, and stardom. *Pride of the Marines* became Garfield's *Casablanca*.

The film was based on a *Life* magazine article of March 22, 1943, entitled, "Al Schmid: Hero." The *Life* article is narrated in a certain *faux* naive voice (perhaps to mimic the thoughts of its working-class subjects), and is filled with the usual wartime clichés. This is Al Schmid's story as told in a *Philadelphia Inquirer* editorial on the occasion of his death in 1982:

> After U.S. naval forces turned back the Japanese onslaught in the Pacific in the Battle of Midway in June 1942, two months later allied forces landed on a small island few people had ever heard of—Guadalcanal—commencing the long campaign to retake land the Japanese had captured. It was there that Pvt. Schmid, a 22-year-old Marine, fought his way into the pantheon of American military heroes.
>
> Assigned to man one of two heavy machine gun installations near Henderson Field, his orders were to protect the post with his life, if necessary, and in the great Marine tradition he carried out the order. During a fierce Japanese assault, Mr. Schmid's courage was pivotal. When the other machine gun post was overrun and knocked out, Mr. Schmid, though wounded and blinded, continued firing, following the directions of a partner.
>
> When the four-hour battle was over, of the 1,300 Japanese soldiers who stormed the airfield, two were captured, 18 were wounded and the rest were killed, with 200 of the Japanese dead sprawled around Mr. Schmid's position.[4]

President Roosevelt personally awarded Schmid the Navy Cross, and when he returned in January 1943, blinded from the battle, his hometown, Philadelphia, honored him with a parade and reception.

Warner Bros. was no stranger to movies made from headlines (such as Bogart's 1936 *Black Legion*), but those films had carefully constructed fictional characters. There were occasional films about the past exploits of still-living personalities, like *Yankee Doodle Dandy* or the 1941 film on a World War I hero *Sergeant York*. Nevertheless, it was rare then for movies to undertake what we now call docudrama, with actors in a kind of dramatized verisimilitude of living persons' recent experiences.

This the producer-director team of Jerry Wald and Delmer Daves (who had also made *Destination Tokyo*) set out to do. Al Schmid and his girl, Ruth Hartley; Al's friends and landlords, Jim and Ella Mae Merchant; Lee Diamond, the Brooklyn Jew who was the leader of Al's machine gun squad at Guadalcanal; Virginia Pfeiffer, Al's nurse in San Diego: all these actual people from Roger Butterfield's *Life* article would be represented on the screen. For Butterfield, however, what was important was the typicality of these individuals, this story. His myth (or truth) was that heroic deeds in wartime can grow from unprepossessing origins: they are born of necessity out of homely, average, daily life. This was the basic World War II American ideology which movies developed, propagated, and made their own: circumstances require people to transform themselves; acceptance of this fact by Rick in Casablanca, by Al in Philadelphia, produces heroic acts.

Al, however, was no mysterious, romantic Rick. He was a foundry worker who rented a room at the Merchants' working-class row house, and dated their friend Ruth. Where was the drama in Al Schmid's life? Wald put several writers to work on the Butterfield article. Marvin Borosky is credited with the adaptation, but Alvah Bessie and A. I. Bezzerides also worked on the synopsis. The screenplay was assigned to Albert Maltz.

Pride of the Marines was the ultimate challenge for a Hollywood Communist writer. There was little call to slip in references to Russian guerrillas or Soviet pilots or appeasers of fascism. The task was to create a dramatic motion picture narrative out of ordinary working-class lives—coping with war, transformation, courage in the face of the enemy, sacrifice, adjustment. Maltz rose to the occasion (and earned an Academy Award nomination for his effort). "Garfield is literally floating on air," Wald wrote to Daves after the actor had seen the script.[5] It was by far the best part in his career up until then.

Maltz's script and Garfield's performance—not to mention Butterfield's article and probably Al Schmid's actual life—portrayed a variation of the classic uncommitted American male. The variant was what mattered. Their Al was not a charismatic leader or globetrotting adventurer scarred by a lost love or an obscure wound. He was a guy in a blue-collar shirt with a lunch bucket who pulled down $40 a week welding at the foundry. His horizons were small. He had his pride: he held himself together; he paid his bills. He lacked, in a sense, vision of a larger life. "I like to live independent," says Garfield's Al. He was afraid of overburdening or eroding his hard-won modest place in life. This emotional constriction was not a metaphor for political isolationism, as in *Casablanca*. It was 1945, that battle had long ago been won; soon the war itself would be over. When Al in the movie learns of the great betrayal, on December 7, 1941, he says matter-of-factly, "The Japs just got through telling Roosevelt they love us," and in a few days he has enlisted in the marines.

Committing himself to his country, however, does help Al make a sudden, last-minute commitment to Ruth as he is about to depart for war from Philadelphia's 30th Street Station. It is this act that will test Al's pride and courage in the months to come. He is tested in battle only once. In the personal and emotional realms the test will be renewed. *Pride of the Marines* is less a film about war than one about reunion and reconstruction—about the effects of war on interrupted or postponed relationships.

This is not to say that a film written by Albert Maltz is not also political. *Pride of the Marines* endorses a postwar struggle for economic justice, so that *these* veterans will not have to sell apples on street corners and march to Washington like the Bonus Army. It condemns ethnic and religious prejudice. Maltz's approach to the color issue, however, went beyond Warner Bros.' ideological boundaries. Wald warned Daves about one script transgression: "In the recreation hall scene, please don't mix colored boys and whites around the piano. This stuff is usually cut out of pictures in the South."[6] The scene in the finished film has a white quartet performing "In the Evening by the Moonlight You Can Hear the Darkies Singing." These social theses are inserted only in the interstices of the personal story. No simple connection is drawn between Al Schmid's private struggle and the public sphere—only the suggestion that you, viewer, could be in my shoes. Al's blindness confronts him with the need to learn a new definition of pride. He has lost his sight and now figuratively must learn to see.

The filmmakers created for Al one of those psychoanalytically inspired 'dream sequences that were momentarily fashionable in mid-1940s films. With negative images, extreme low angle shots, and eerie electronic music, it moves Al through a reliving of his battlefield blinding to a projection of his reunion with Ruth. He is running along the 30th Street platform in his uniform. Ruth is there, she turns to him, they embrace. Suddenly a man with a cane, dark glasses, and a tin cup appears, then disappears. Then Al wears dark glasses, with lights flashing in them. He calls, "Ruth, Ruth," but she runs away down the platform.

The dream perhaps suggests that Al's vaunted pride is more a fear of rejection than an assertion of self. He cuts off communication with Ruth. Back in Philadelphia, however, unbeknownst to him, she serves as his chauffeur and drives him home. There, they argue over whether he will be a burden to her, or (more to the point) whether his helplessness will drain his self-respect. Assured of her love and need for him, Al finally seems ready to accept their relationship, his place in the postwar world. "I was just an ordinary guy," he says. "Now I'm less than ordinary." *Pride of the Marines* asks its spectators to accept the truth of that, yet also to believe in the transcendence of ordinariness through patriotism and the movie's muted upbeat ending.

Garfield's performance was perhaps the most notable of his career so far. His acting eschewed the histrionics of his newspaperman in *Between Two Worlds* and the artificiality of his randy submarine crewman of *Destination Tokyo*. He created Al Schmid for the screen with a kind of "naturalistic" restraint out of his own most effective screen persona, maybe out of himself. He was again a city boy: at home among the brick working-class houses of Lawndale with their identical porches, separated by white wooden railings, receding to infinity; prideful, truculent, secretly insecure. In his eighth year at Warner Bros., and with his contract drawing near its end, *Pride of the Marines* finally gave Garfield something he could himself take pride in—and perhaps build on.

■ ■ ■ ■

Having served his term in the purgatory decreed by Jack Warner, Bogart arrived on the set of *Passage to Marseille* immediately after finishing *Conflict* and a full three weeks after the Hal Wallis–Michael Curtiz picture had begun production. He was to play the role of . . . well, to tell the story the way the film narrates it, he is a crew member of a B-17 manned by Free French fliers in bombing raids from England over Berlin, who turns out to have been an escaped Devils Island prisoner, who turns out to have been an antifascist newspaper publisher railroaded to prison by rightists.

Besides its Chinese boxes series of flashbacks, the most remarkable aspect of *Passage to Marseille* is its representation of Hollywood's ideological consensus on the war. Its screenwriters were not—as was usual on this type of picture—Communist party members or sympathizers, but their political opposite. Casey Robinson was among the founders in early 1944 of the anti-Communist Motion Picture Alliance for the Preservation of American Ideals. John Charles Moffitt (credited as Jack on the picture) was one of the "friendly" witnesses at the House Un-American Activities Committee's notorious 1947 hearings on alleged Communist infiltration of the motion picture industry. Their script, however, can hardly be distinguished from the products of the Hollywood left, lacking only references to brave Russians. Particularly noticeable is its antifascist stance, especially its sustained attacks on Marshall Philippe Petain and the spirit of Vichy France.

Jean Matrac, the machine gunner–convict–publisher, is Bogart's grimmest role since *Black Legion*. "I've never seen a stronger face nor a stranger one," a British journalist says on encountering Bogart's stern visage as the Free French are about to take off on an air raid. Bogart looks older, his face more drawn; in at least one scene no effort is made to conceal his thinning hair. His character is tormented by the injustice done to him, by the wife he has been forced to leave, by the son whom he has never seen. In the escape sequence, it is clearly implied that he kills a fellow prisoner who might have impeded his group's departure; later, on board a ship that has rescued them, and after a battle against an attempted fascist takeover, he fires a machine gun at German airmen leaving their aircraft downed at sea. The ship's captain cries out, "You can't assassinate helpless men," and he replies, "Look around you, Captain, and see who are the assassins."

This scene caught the attention of several reviewers: the *New York Daily News* called it "wanton brutality" that should have been censored, and the *Brooklyn Eagle* noted that it was the first time an Allied fighter, as opposed to a Japanese or German one, had been so depicted in a war film. As for audience reaction, the reviewer wrote, they applauded. Bogart's character dies in the end, perhaps as the price for his transgressions according to Hollywood's code, although Jack Warner was arguing in favor of his living, even after production began.

It is tempting once again to draw a correlative link between Bogart's screen characterization and his personal state of mind. On one occasion during filming, Bogart was reported "suffering from a very bad hangover and being very unruly and hard to manage."[7] As soon as the film was finished, the "Battling Bogarts" took their squabbles overseas, where the actor entertained troops in North Africa and Italy from December 1943 to February 1944. Briefly, in the winter of 1943–1944, Bogart, Cagney, and Garfield were all in the war theater at the same time. Of the three, only Bogart had a project awaiting him on his return.

This was the Howard Hawks production *To Have and Have Not* (1945). Of the many legendary figures and tales surrounding this film—starting with the novelist Ernest Hemingway and including producer-director Hawks, William Faulkner in a screenwriting role, and the overriding actual love story that it launched—none has ever clarified how Bogart became associated with the project. It is not the purpose of legends, to be sure, to make things clear. *To Have and Have Not* was to be Hawks's second film for Warner Bros. on a five-year, five-picture contract signed in early 1942. The project began to come together in the fall of 1943. It seems natural that Hawks would want the man who played Sam Spade and Rick Blaine in the role of Hemingway's independent, violent, angry hero, Harry Morgan; but Bogart had been tied up for months, first in Jack Warner's clutches on *Conflict*, then with the Wallis-Curtiz team on *Passage to Marseille*, finally on the upcoming USO tour. Warners assigned Bogart to Hawks for a picture start in early 1944, after his return from Europe.

Hawks had previously worked with Cagney and Garfield, but his skills as an imaginative and innovative handler of performers (witness his role in the careers of Cary Grant, John Wayne, and Montgomery Clift, to name but three) had not accomplished much with them. In *The Crowd Roars* of 1932 he had helped Cagney play against the grain of his developing screen persona, to the studio's displeasure; the 1936 *Ceiling Zero* had been a romp under the shadow of Cagney's impending break with Warner Bros.; and Garfield had been relegated to a team-player role in the recent *Air Force*.

Perhaps Hawks was not fully comfortable with the city boy personality; his only previous film with much sense of urban life had been *Scarface* (1932), and the portrayal of the Al Capone figure in that film—as half-crazed, half-human—may have been actor Paul Muni's creation more than the director's. Bogart was not an actor associated with the outdoors, but he was a yachtsman in his private life: the part of a professional sailor fit him well enough.

There was an aspect of Hawks's plans for the film to which Bogart likely was privy from an early point, and he had not objected: Hawks had a protégée, a 19-year-old model he had named Lauren Bacall, whom he wanted for the female lead. She was under personal contract to him, and he had to convince Warner executives (who were still fussing about it on the day production started); without Bogart's acquiescence he would have been stymied. Bogart still had not experienced much in the way of significant love interests in his films as a star—in the most important one, Ingrid Bergman's performance had made their relationship believable. Hawks was promising Bogart the dominant role in relation to the Bacall character (the older man–younger woman pairing echoed *Casablanca*, as did many other aspects of *To Have and Have Not*). Meanwhile, the director was coaching Bacall to perform as Bogart's equal.

Hawks had many ways of capturing a performer's trust, or attention, but one unique method he had evolved (much to the consternation of various studios' executives) was to rewrite the script on the set in collaboration with the performers. Asking for guidance on what worked best, or might be fresh and different, Hawks could also give it. One can discount as among Hawks's innumerable fantasies his story of how he "grabbed [Bogart] by the lapels and pushed his head up against the wall, and said, 'Look, Bogey, I tell you how to get tough, but don't get tough with me.' "[8] Much more plausible is Hawks's account of seeing through Bogart's little fiction—the "bum lip" that prevented him from smiling—and telling the actor he better learn to smile.

Smile? He was the Cheshire Cat, or the man who swallowed the canary. He could not stop smiling. Within the first days of shooting he began to fall in love with Lauren Bacall. Hawks may not have grasped how serious Bogart was, but obviously he noticed the attraction and used it. In the history of movie kisses there are few more genuine than their second kiss, when his lips pursue hers as she pulls away, and she says, "It's even better when you help." The romance between "Slim" and "Steve" came almost to overshadow every other aspect of *To Have and Have Not*.

Though not quite all. There was the sudden, last-minute decision to shift the film's locale and time frame from Hemingway's Cuba in the 1930s to the French West Indian island of Martinique in 1940, after the fall of France. The change was forced by U.S. government apprehension that filming the Hemingway story would antagonize Cuban dictator Fulgencio Batista; it could not have been too unwelcome to Jack Warner, who was saved the costs of Cuban location shooting on a picture he already knew would go way over budget; nor to Hawks, for whom it served to legitimate his habit of rewriting scripts on the set.

Hawks's friend Faulkner (at that time a Warner Bros. contract writer) was brought in hurriedly to rework earlier script drafts by Jules Furthman. A finished script was nominally ready before production started, but Faulkner continued to rewrite until almost the end of shooting, and Hawks and his performers anyway only used the written words as takeoff points.

The shift in setting to an overseas department of wartime France placed the film even more firmly within the orbit of *Casablanca*. Here, with variations, were the uncommitted American antipathetic to fascism but unwilling to take a stand; the cafe with its piano player and political tensions; the resistance fighter husband and the potentially straying wife; and finally the American's surge of anger and involvement in the antifascist struggle. Following not only *Casablanca* but *Passage to Marseille*—and the film's release after the Normandy invasion and the liberation of Paris—it is understandable that contemporary reviewers might have grown a bit jaded with Humphrey Bogart's characters' figuring out what to do about Vichy France. *To Have and Have Not*, however, is not *Casablanca*, and the differences were critical, among other aspects, in the performance of the star.

Working with Hawks was, to begin with, a fundamentally different experience for Bogart from working with Curtiz. There are signs that the tensions between actor and director over the climactic scenes of *Casablanca* continued between them on *Passage to Marseille*. However Hawks and Bogart reached their understanding on the set of *To Have and Have Not*, the actor clearly felt empowered by the director, included as a crucial part of the creative process that Hawks conducted in his morning rewriting sessions.

Hawks's guiding hand is obvious, to be sure, in the character of Harry Morgan. For one thing, unlike Hemingway's Morgan (or Bogart's Rick or Spade or Roy Earle), he is a man without a past, one of Hawks's existential heroes, living only in the present, resembling most a figure like Cary Grant's Geoff Carter in Hawks's 1939 *Only Angels Have Wings*—or, looking forward, John Wayne's Sheriff Chance in the director's 1959 film *Rio Bravo*. (All three heroes are linked, indeed, by the women who love them, each of whom says a variant of the line, "I'm hard to get. All you have to do is ask me.")

Bogart rose to the challenge Hawks offered him. He was able to create a masterful figure without the mystery tacked onto his character by the narrative of *Casablanca*. He infused Morgan with a composed, laconic, self-sufficient calmness, a gentleness with power. Much of this aura may have emanated from his relationship with Bacall, so different from that with Bergman—beginning with the fact that he was the star, she the novice, and spilling over into their growing feelings for each other. Whatever the ideological thematics of the film, the joy of that relationship turned it away from the pathos of *Casablanca* into a romantic comedy.

One critical test of the tone of *To Have and Have Not* lies in its variation on Hawks's signature love triangle: the love of two men for each other, the impact of a woman's entry into the relationship. In its classic expression, *Only Angels Have Wings*, the relation between Geoff and the Kid (Thomas Mitchell) is altered by the arrival of Bonnie (Jean Arthur). The Kid's "nonsexual" love for Geoff ("all mustard and no hot dog") gives way to the woman's; the Kid dies, but Bonnie learns to dress and to love more like a man.

In *To Have and Have Not*, Bacall enters the relationship between Morgan and Eddie (played by Walter Brennan) by adopting Eddie's style and language—"Was you ever bit by a dead bee?"—so that Eddie complains, "I feel like I was talking to myself." Eddie does not die, Bacall does not dress or act like a man—becomes indeed even more sexual with her shimmying walk over to Harry at the film's conclusion. Bacall had already demonstrated what Hawks felt he could not get out of Jean Arthur: an insolent aggressiveness that could enable her to stand on equal footing with a tough man like Bogart. At the end of *To Have and Have Not* Morgan, Slim, and Eddie go off to the boat together.

Within days of completing *To Have and Have Not*, the studio assigned Bogart to *God Is My Co-pilot* (1945), a true story about an overage pilot who became a hero with the "Flying Tigers," a civilian American volunteer group that fought in China. Bogart refused the assignment. His decision may have been merely a symptom of a conflict of which money squabbles were the cause. In rejecting the picture, however, Bogart also proved more articulate than ever before about his abilities and preferences as an actor.

The part was not right for him, he argued in a telephone conversation with production executive Steve Trilling, not only because he was "a certain kind of character and personality"—different from the script's pilot hero—but also because it "was not an 'acting' role . . . other people were always doing things, played against his reaction." (Shades of the first part of *Casablanca*.) According to Trilling's notes, Bogart "didn't care if he did smaller pictures as long as the characters were playable," expressing a preference for playing next in a genre picture like *The Big Shot* rather than the high-budget A picture *God Is My Co-pilot*.[9]

Money, indeed, was in the background. The issue had surfaced near the end of production on *To Have and Have Not*. There occurred a dispute between director and star—one can only imagine that it may have had to do with Bacall—serious enough for Jack Warner personally to intervene. Once in Warner's office, Bogart seized the opportunity to state his desire for a new contract. Warner, it seems, sympathized with the request, but regretfully cited wartime restrictions on raises; he offered as consolation a concession on layoffs. Two days later, in Warner's absence, Bogart, his agent, and his business manager paid calls on other studio executives, proposing revisions of his January 1942 contract, including the right to do outside pictures and to make some pictures on a percentage basis.

When, a month later, *God Is My Co-pilot* was refused, Western Union was mobilized. Warner fired the first telegram. Other executives edited out the familiar refrain of how much the studio had done for Bogart since he was an unknown in *The Petrified Forest* days, so the gist of the final version asserted, among other things, that the actor was "putting the dollar above a man's right way of life."[10] Bogart replied with a wire twice the length of Warner's. He did not mince words about his contract—"at the time it was signed it was good. Now it is no good"—but he spoke more about his dignity and self-concept as an actor. "I am tired of the studio's attitude that I am a half-witted child. Don't like to be threatened and should like the same consideration as shown to Davis and to Flynn. You are not thinking of me when you put me in this picture." He alluded to his "very bad" part in *Passage to Marseille* as a case in which he trusted the studio to protect him and it did not. "You speak of my success as if you alone were responsible for it," he closed. "I feel that I have had something to do with that success."[11]

Bogart's reference to Davis and Flynn was likely based less on knowledge of their current deals with the studio than on Bogart's view that they were accorded more careful treatment. For his part, Flynn had signed a new contract in May 1942 on a three-year deal, plus options, specifying nine pictures in the first three years at $90,000 per picture (actually, he made only three): in addition, he secured the right to appear in occasional pictures produced by his own corporation for distribution by Warner Bros. Bogart, as previously noted, had only a couple of months before Flynn's deal signed on for seven more years at $2750 per week, less than the studio was willing to offer. Warner's response was to say that the actor was "bringing up issues . . . that are very confusing to me," so he could only enforce the legal provisions of the existing contract.[12] This meant that Bogart was suspended without pay for seven weeks while Dennis Morgan played the lead in *God Is My Co-pilot* (which turned out to be a rousing box office success).

Those seven weeks were consumed by his growing love for and obsession with Lauren Bacall. He spent much of the time in Newport Beach, writing to and calling her. *To Have and Have Not*, meanwhile, was beginning to preview, to ecstatic responses from studio personnel. Hawks was preparing another film for the two to play in together. What lay ahead was the Battling Bogarts' final confrontation—as soon as Bogart made the decision to seek a divorce from Mayo Methot and free himself to marry a woman more than twenty years younger than himself.

At least one of his desires was immediately gratified. Hawks's project, though not exactly small, would be a genre film: *The Big Sleep* (1946), based on the detective novel by Raymond Chandler. Hawks once again used Faulkner and Furthman in preparing the adaptation, along with Leigh Brackett, although as usual much of the actual dialogue would be written on the set.

The most famous of *The Big Sleep*'s legends concerns the impenetrability of the narrative. At one point, so the story goes, Hawks contacted Chandler to inquire, "Who killed Owen Taylor?" and Chandler's reply was, "Search me." As the film stands, it is almost impossible to tell who killed Shawn Regan, whose disappearance/ murder impels the entire narrative. Can't count the murders and can hardly explain them, goes the popular myth of *The Big Sleep*, though who cares when you've got Bogart's performance as private eye Philip Marlowe and the Bogart-Bacall magic.

The real mystery of *The Big Sleep* was that it got made at all. Bogart's personal turmoil dominated the production almost from its October 1944 start. On several days Bogart was late reporting for work; on others he came back late at midday after lunching with his agent at the nearby Lakeside Golf Club. One day in mid-December there was a delay when, according to studio production manager T. C. "Tenny" Wright, "It was necessary for Mr. Hawks to speak with Mr. Bogart for a half hour and straighten him out relative the 'Bacall' situation, which is affecting their performances in the picture." In fact, added Wright, who was investigating the situation at the behest of his superiors, "I understand there have been several instances when Hawks has had to take him to one side and talk with him at great length because he was dissatisfied with his performance, which was no doubt caused by his domestic troubles."[13] Hawks himself at the same time was telling Jack Warner he wanted out of his studio contract.

Things came to a head the day after Christmas—the sixty-second shooting day of a film originally scheduled for forty-two—when Bogart failed to appear at all. While the studio tried to track him down at the Beverly Wilshire Hotel, where he was staying, Mrs. Bogart called to say that he "had shown up at the house at 8:30 this morning very drunk," according to the unit manager's report. There converged at Bogart's home that morning several representatives of the studio production and security staffs, Bogart's agent and an assistant, the actor's secretary, and a doctor. Bogart awoke from sleep "and the atmosphere became extremely strained," with Bogart repeatedly asking, "Are we holding a wake?"

"I really do not feel that Bogart's condition can be straightened out over night," concluded the unit manager, "since he has been drinking for approximately three weeks and it is not only the liquor, but also the mental turmoil regarding his domestic life that is entering into this situation."[14]

Bogart nevertheless was able to work on and finish the picture about two weeks later. What sort of picture had he finished? Not one, apparently, that Warner Bros. was willing to release to the public. There are assertions that the film was shown to servicemen overseas during 1945, and that prints of this version continue to circulate, but the studio decided nearly a year after production ended to retake some scenes, cut some, and add others. Hawks was paid an additional $10,000, and eight performers from the film's cast were called back for six days of work in late January 1946.

By this time Bogart had gained his divorce from Mayo Methot and had been married, since May 21, 1945, to Lauren Bacall. The most important scene added in January 1946—the famous horse-and-rider sexual innuendo conversation between Marlowe and Vivian Sternwood in the restaurant—was perhaps legitimized by the wedded state of the performers. (The Production Code Administration questioned the line, "A lot depends on who's in the saddle," because of the "possibility of it being given a questionable interpretation in this particular context," but let it pass into film history.)[15]

Another scene was shot in the restaurant with Marlowe, Vivian, Eddie Mars (John Ridgely), and an actress not otherwise in the picture, but it was not used. Retakes included the film's early scene with Marlowe, Vivian, and Carmen Sternwood (Martha Vickers) in Vivian's sitting room and bedroom; the scene of Marlowe and Carmen in Marlowe's apartment; of Marlowe, Vivian, and Mrs. Eddie Mars (Peggy Knudsen) in the hideout; of Marlowe and Bernie Ohls (Regis Toomey) in the D.A.'s office; of Marlowe, Vivian, and Norris the butler (Charles D. Brown) in the Sternwood entrance hall.

The purpose of these retakes was clearly to strengthen the growing attraction between Marlowe and Vivian throughout the film. *The Big Sleep* no less than *To Have and Have Not* took a novel with a far different tone (in Chandler's case, about a private detective as knight-errant in a sexually and politically corrupt urban jungle) and turned it into a romantic comedy. When the film was finished in January 1945, however, it was not yet clear whether the outcome of the romance on which the film was based would be happiness or pathos. *To Have and Have Not* was in the theaters, Bacall and Bogart were in the gossip columns, and Mayo Methot had not yet agreed to go to Reno. A year later, life and the film were in harmony, and could be made more so. Though there were dissenting voices—the Warner Bros. files contain two letters from women, both saying that Bogart was "making a fool of himself" by marrying someone less than half his age—*The Big Sleep* became a celebration of the Bogart-Bacall romance.[16]

There are, to be sure, six violent deaths in the film (not to mention the disappearance which sets off the train of narrative events), and first-time viewers of *The Big Sleep* are to be excused if they focus on the who-killed-whom-and-why aspect of the story. A *New York Times* writer, for one, was disturbed enough by the film's "grim violent things" to condemn as well the "vicious" Marlowe and the "reckless" Vivian, who, the writer said, were "just as rough and hard-boiled" as the villains.

"It is this visual emphasis of toughness and malevolence on the screen [the *Times* writer went on] that seems to this anxious observer to be quite ominous and painful today. For plainly it isn't employed toward any constructive end; it is just used to give the audience vicarious and sadistic thrills. And, although some of our social thinkers say that such pictures tend to drain off in a thoroughly salubrious fashion the public's malevolent desires, we grimly recall that it was such films that predominated on the German screen between two wars."[17]

The passage of years, exposure to television's incessant depiction of actual and fictional violence, and (for its fans around the world) repeated viewings of the film make it difficult to regard the *Times* writer's concern as other than misguided—though it does speak more generally to the still-lively question of the links between the emerging film noir style and postwar American society. *The Big Sleep* is a noir film only by broadest definition; its ties to the dark vision of its source novel are equally tenuous. Some four decades after its creation it appears more a romance than a murder mystery; or, to put it from a spectator's perspective, after the mystery wears off its aspect as a romantic comedy emerges.

The images behind the opening credits give us our first clue: Bogart and Bacall in silhouette, he lighting her cigarette, then one cigarette placed in an ashtray, then another. This is a couple who have better things to do together than smoke, as moviegoers of 1946 already knew. Once the film starts, it is not Marlowe's toughness that catches your attention, it is his wit. He uses wit to protect and distance himself, to be sure, to maintain the professional demeanor of the private eye; but he uses it even more in verbal dueling, engagement and involvement through language, especially with Vivian. Through lengthy stretches of the film, where plot exposition often grows tedious or inexplicable, the repartee creates the tension and expectation that holds the spectator's interest.

That, and Marlowe's many sexual encounters. For an actor whose screen persona for nearly a decade had only occasionally included romantic entanglements, the homely mid-fortyish Bogart in Hawks's hands—and through his romance with Bacall—suddenly became, on-screen, catnip to every young lass he encounters. From the librarian to the Acme bookshop proprietress to the taxicab driver ("Tail job"; "I'm your girl, bub") to the hostess in Eddie Mars's Las Olindas club, women flirt with him, and more. This serves to establish Marlowe's attraction and also his discrimination. When he is drawn to Vivian Sternwood we know he has experience playing the field. We also see that Vivian is capable in the wit department of giving as good as she gets.

The film's narrative thrust then begins to shift toward the mystery of Vivian. Why is she mixed up with Brody and Agnes and Eddie Mars? Is she Marlowe's equal morally as well as verbally and (in potential) sexually? For, make no mistake, *New York Times* to the contrary, Marlowe in the film's terms is a moral man. Similar to the Hawks-Bogart conception of Harry Morgan in *To Have and Have Not*, Marlowe lacks the ambiguity of Sam Spade, the past mystery of Rick. He was what he was: a man who was in it for more than $25 a day plus expenses, a man who tested the world against his standards for it—first through language, ultimately through action. Finally, when Vivian unties him at Eddie Mars's hideout, and acts with daring in the showdown with the gunman Canino, he discovers that she is his equal in action, too.

"You looked good," Marlowe says to her in the car, after she has helped him kill Canino, "Awful good. I didn't know they made them like that anymore." Her reply is to say, "I guess I'm in love with you," and he repeats the words back to her. One may blanch, with the *New York Times*, because their love is sealed between his shooting of Canino and his shooting at Eddie Mars, forcing the villain out the door into a hail of bullets from his henchmen. One may wonder, as some critics have, about the prospects for their love in the violent, unstable world they inhabit, as they stand together, hearing the approaching police siren grow louder, in the film's final shot. As surely, however, as the dialogue's references to "red points" and the ration stickers on car windshields must have dated the film on its late summer 1946 release, *The Big Sleep* is a wartime film—in which the distinctions between good men and bad were meant to be clear, and with just cause violence was required to fight violence.

Perhaps the greatest wonder about *The Big Sleep*, given what we now know about its production circumstances, is Bogart's performance. Or perhaps it is no wonder at all. Loving Bacall on-screen and off, his character's and his own personal life enmeshed in uncertainty and travail, Bogart blended himself and Marlowe into one: the same laconic, caustic wit of his screen character produced the "Are we holding a wake?" line of his post-Christmas hangover. Where the drinking and the turmoil may have taken a toll was in his reversion to old mannerisms. It had been some years since he relied so heavily on gestures like linking his thumbs in his belt, putting his hands in his trouser pockets, pulling back his upper lip to reveal his teeth, and—almost a tic of the Marlowe character—tugging on his right earlobe.

Beyond these atavisms, it is difficult to see in the finished picture what Hawks may have been criticizing about Bogart's performance in the instances Tenny Wright's memo cited. With Hawks's ideas of manhood, and the spark of working with Bacall, Bogart in *The Big Sleep* fashioned his most complete screen persona to date: a man funny and tough, committed and vulnerable, sexy and loyal. It took a European like Jean-Luc Godard, in his 1959 *Breathless*, to make clear the tragic element missing from Bogart's developing screen persona; the moment that capped his wartime professional triumphs, linked with his personal happiness, was not one that encouraged the tragic sense. Complication would soon enough ensue.

9

American Dopes

Among Hollywood's talent elite, a prime professional yearning at the end of World War II was for a freedom which, in the broadest sense, the United States had fought the war to defend: freedom from totalitarian domination. In their desire for creative and entrepreneurial liberty it may come as no surprise that not a few directors, writers, and performers began to equate their employers with the dictators who had just been defeated by force of democratic arms. (This was the view anthropologist Hortense Powdermaker derived from her Hollywood informants in 1946–1947; she concluded that "Hollywood represents totalitarianism. . . . Its philosophy is similar to that of the totalitarian state.")[1] The path to independent production that Cagney and others had earlier laid down began to be followed by, among others, Garfield and Bogart.

In some sectors of America's political and business elites (with certain clear ties to the Hollywood community) was lodged a quite opposite desire for the postwar direction of the motion picture industry. These groups wished to drive left-wing viewpoints from American movies by purging the industry of those who held or expressed such views. Anticommunism was the simplest but not the sole reason behind this goal. Some of the intent was politically partisan: to link communism with the Democratic party. One ground for that attack lay in the wartime agreement among government, the movie industry, and the left about ideological representation of war aims—which could lead, for example, to blatant pro-Soviet films such as Warner Bros.' 1943 *Mission to Moscow* (the movie companies would have to wiggle out of the middle of that retrospectively embarrassing triad). Some was antilabor, or linked to union jurisdictional disputes. In the case of participating movie personnel the motives often were personal and emotional.

To the defenders of capitalist ideology, it mattered not that some of their targets were actively pursuing the ends of independent entrepreneurial capitalism. Garfield and Bogart were soon to discover, along with many others, that their professional goals and their political beliefs were intertwined, and, as the ideological winds changed, increasingly incompatible—and that one, voluntarily or by force of events, surely had to give way. When the drama of America's political Ice Age began, they would be among its most renowned players.

■ ■ ■ ■

In 1945, Garfield was waiting for the opportunity to bring his profession and his politics closer together. Almost from the time he completed *Pride of the Marines*, he made clear his determination to go into independent production as soon as his Warner Bros. contract terminated. His departure from the studio was settled when the California Court of Appeals affirmed the 1944 lower court decision in Olivia de Havilland's suit against Warner Bros., which declared that suspensions could not extend a contract beyond the legal limit of seven years. Since Garfield had been suspended more than a half-dozen times—totaling close to a year in lost work—he otherwise would have remained under Warner Bros. suzerainty into 1947, if not beyond. Now he knew that his time was definitely up in early February 1946.

After *Pride of the Marines* the studio aimed to put him in *Humoresque* (1946), a "city boy" tale about a violinist from the New York slums, from a Fannie Hurst short story previously filmed by Paramount in 1920. It was taking the writers longer than expected to turn it into a Warner Bros. star vehicle, however, and in the spring of 1945 the studio agreed to release Garfield to MGM as part of a two-picture loan-out that had been signed the previous year. Garfield would get his contractual salary, Warner Bros. would get nothing except relief from the obligation to pay him; it is not clear whether salary caps or other factors negated the customary four-plus-three or even more lucrative deals Warners had struck for its stars. The first (and, as it turned out, only) picture was *The Postman Always Rings Twice* (1946), MGM's belated effort to make a film from James M. Cain's 1934 novella about a drifter and a roadhouse proprietor's wife who rush into adultery and murder.

Banning *Postman* from the screen had been one of the early accomplishments of Joseph I. Breen when he became head of the Production Code Administration in 1934. MGM nevertheless bought the rights for $25,000 and waited for over a decade for the censorship climate to ease, while unauthorized versions were filmed in France in 1939 and in Italy by Lucino Visconti as *Ossessione* in 1942. Successful productions of two other Cain works—*Double Indemnity* in 1944 by Billy Wilder at Paramount and Warner Bros.' *Mildred Pierce* in 1945—may have led the PCA to relent on *Postman*. By 1945, however, the Production Code's ideology of retribution for transgression had become so firmly ingrained in studio procedures, at least at Metro, that the moral guardians had little to fear.

The Postman Always Rings Twice was still a controversial film for its time—some still questioned whether the story was fit for the screen at all—but it has not survived as an important one. The 1981 Jack Nicholson–Jessica Lange remake, and films in its spirit like *Body Heat* (also 1981), have so stamped the basic narrative situation with a late twentieth century sexual and moral (amoral?) aura that the Garfield–Lana Turner version has become even more an anachronism. With the district attorney and a motorcycle cop present in the opening moments (and on the scene of both the failed and the successful attempts at murder), the Law's omnipresence makes *Postman* a tale of retribution far more than transgression.

Contemporary reviewers did not exactly find the film chaste, but the *New York Times* captured the filmmakers' caution by calling it (in praise) "thoroughly inoffensive." Lana Turner is dressed so virginally in white from her high-heeled pumps to her turbans and platinum hair, her physical contact with Garfield so lacks sexual spark (in comparison to later versions), that a spectator might be surprised when she announces near the end that she is pregnant. The script by Harry Ruskin and Nevin Busch, and Tay Garnett's direction, do follow Cain's novella fairly closely; and Garfield's character, Frank Chambers, occasionally speaks by means of voice-over to echo the book's first-person narration. The film's fundamental gentility is made clear, however, by the change of the husband from Greek Nick Papadakis to Canadian Nick Smith, played by Cecil Kellaway with a provincial British accent.

MGM's *Postman* also shifted the time frame from Cain's early 1930s Depression setting to its own contemporary end of World War II—turning Cain's unemployed drifter into an ambiguous figure that 1946 audiences might have identified as an ex-GI at loose ends, on the road. This ties *Postman* to the postwar wave of noir films about dangerous females awaiting returning veterans on their perilous passage to the peacetime world. With so little passion permitted the adulterous lovers, however (and almost none of the sadomasochistic lure of their relationship allowed to remain from the book), what is left between them is a struggle for personal power—in which Turner's Cora, as the link to property, inevitably holds the upper hand. Frank lusts after Cora but knows he is subordinate to her, and his repeatedly expressed forebodings about the consequences of their deeds tend to emasculate him as much as they provide a further expression of the Law's omnipresent retributive presence. "This so-called man," Cora refers to him after the D.A. has coerced him into signing a complaint against her after they murder her husband (language famously echoed a few years later by Senator Joe McCarthy during the Army-McCarthy hearings).

Garfield's approach to his character's complexities was to tone down considerably his acting style from previous films. This may have been part of a conscious overall production strategy, in light of the potentially explosive material with which they were dealing, for there is little virtuoso work anywhere in the film, including in the camera work and lighting—special hallmarks of the period's more memorable noir films—with the exception of supporting performances. For Garfield, however, it marked the beginning of a strikingly different approach to performance that he was to carry over into later films. He is not only subdued, he is at times almost immobile, his hands loose at his sides, his mouth taut, moving only his eyes. He appears not emotionless but emotionally imploded, with the potential for violence that harshly erupts when he is confronted by the blackmailers.

To see him alongside Hume Cronyn (playing the defense attorney) is to see the supporting performer as a consummate actor, creating a memorable character through energetic use of gesture, movement, facial expression, and vocal intonation, while the star functions almost as an icon, a screen presence who needs little to be fully recognizable as the unique cultural type he had become. *Time* magazine's reviewer disliked Garfield in the part—"John Garfield is so familiar in the tough-man role that his mere presence threatens the audience's capacity for belief"—but, getting the familiarity right, missed the radical alteration of performance style.

This was neither the histrionic Garfield of *Between Two Worlds* nor the "naturalistic" performer of *Pride of the Marines*. Its sole antecedent in his picture career was perhaps the character he played in his last loan-out, *The Fallen Sparrow*, although his character's subdued emotions and physical immobility were there given both a psychological and a physiological explanation. In *The Postman Always Rings Twice* there was no explanation, nor was one needed. Garfield had finally and definitively become a star. Contrary to the *Time* reviewer's pronouncements, the audience did not need to believe he was a fictional character named Frank Chambers; it was sufficient that he was the screen persona Garfield, so much so that, in the conventional sense, he did not need to act.

His next picture was to confirm this transformation. What had held up *Humoresque*, however, was not the necessity of developing the story as a star vehicle for *him*, but for one of Warner Bros.' top women performers. An entirely new leading role and narrative line were added to the Hurst original by writers Clifford Odets and Zachary Gold for the Jerry Wald production. The part was offered to Bette Davis and eventually went to Joan Crawford, now triumphantly a Warner Bros. star after making her comeback as an "older woman" in *Mildred Pierce*. Crawford was to play a wealthy society woman, married, bored, and alcoholic, who falls in love with the young immigrant violinist played by Garfield and boosts his career, though her own life ends pathetically. In the intertextual world of Hollywood moviemaking, it seems plausible that the adulterous Crawford-Garfield relationship added to the Hurst story was inspired by the writers' (or producer's) knowledge that audiences would remember seeing, not so many months before, an adulterous Turner-Garfield relationship.

Humoresque was tinged with some of the old 1930s Warner Bros. city streets atmosphere, but it was principally a woman's melodrama. Garfield's character, though nominally the narrating voice, as in *Postman*, is not the central narrative interest. He opens the picture with a monologue shot in close-up, with *Postman*'s stern motionless expression, altered only by slight eye and lip movements. He identifies himself as a lost soul far from his roots, and the film shifts into flashback to begin the story among Lower East Side pushcarts. There, as if to validate his opening self-description, Garfield plays his character's youth with an open, smiling, expressive face. He is the ambitious, talented ghetto kid who finds his road to success through the patronage of a rich, selfish, possessive, thrice-married older woman. From the moment Crawford's character enters the film—one shot contemplates Garfield through the prism of her brandy glass—it is her picture, hers and the female audience for which it was intended.

One group of women spectators did not accept the film's outlook and ideology at all. The film ends like *A Star Is Born* (at that point, the original 1937 version), with Crawford's character recognizing that the noblest thing she can do with her "meaningless and absurd life" is end it. In a scene intercut with Garfield's concert, which he had accused her of trying to ruin, she walks into the sea. Surf crashes against the camera lens, which then descends completely under the water, observes bubbles rising, and then returns to the rolling surf, undisturbed by human presence. Some sixty-six women in a Milwaukee adult education class on "the Woman's Point of View" signed and sent to Warner Bros. a petition protesting this ending:

> We, the undersigned, wish to protest the hopeless attitude of defeat as revealed in the recent picture *Humoresque*. Despite its technical and musical perfection, and the splendid acting of the cast, we feel that suicide is a negative solution to the neurotic way of life and that because of Miss Crawford's tremendous influence on the lives of American women, this ill chosen ending will leave repercussions of doubt in solving personal problems in the lives of many.
>
> We feel that a splendid opportunity for improved adult behaviour was lost by not rehabilitating the main character somewhere in the middle of the picture . . . by having her adjust to her third husband's over-all personality . . . or adopting a child . . . or finding a new interest outside of herself.
>
> In this way a pattern for hope might have been instilled in the hearts of thousands of neurotic women lost in the side-show escapes of alcohol and promiscuity . . . who crowd our theaters and subconsciously pattern their lives after our film stories.[2]

Garfield's contract ran out with nearly two months still left to go on *Humoresque*'s production, but he continued until the end, saying, according to producer Wald, "Despite the fact that I'm doing a lot of yelling, you know I'll be only too happy to do anything I can to help sell the picture or make it better."[3] After *Humoresque* was released in late 1946 a Columbia Pictures executive wrote Wald, "Garfield should be very proud of his role and if he thinks he is going out to get something better than this—well, time will tell, but I have my doubts."[4]

Garfield, however, was not going out looking to get something: he was going out to create it for himself. His disagreement with the Columbia executive's viewpoint might be summed up in a line from *Humoresque*: at one of the rich lady's parties, a woman approaches the young violinist and naively asks, "Are you a prizefighter? You look just like a prizefighter." For Garfield, something better than a role as a violinist was one as a prizefighter.

In 1946 Garfield joined with his business representative, Bob Roberts, to form Roberts Productions; they began planning their first independent film based on the life of Barney Ross, a champion boxer and former marine who had conquered drug addiction. Roberts made an agreement with Enterprise Studios, a new company producing its own films and also acquiring others for distribution through United Artists. They secured a $1 million loan from the Bank of America and hired, as a writer for the Ross story, Abraham Polonsky, who soon shunted Ross aside in favor of his own tale of a boxer. Thus the production of *Body and Soul* (1947) took shape.

Body and Soul was to become, for some, a prime exhibit of the Red conspiracy in Hollywood. It was not the film's content that concerned the Red-hunters, it was the film's example of the way "Commies and pinks," as columnist Ed Sullivan put it in 1952, supported each other. "*Body and Soul* is the pattern that the Commies and their sympathizers in TV networks, agencies and theatrical unions would like to fasten on the newest medium," Sullivan wrote. "From the director on down, the Commies insert their members, freeze out those who are on the American side of the fence."[5]

One of the right-wing defenses of the Hollywood (and television) blacklists was that the left had practiced preferential hiring and boosted each other's careers in studio work before the tables turned after the 1947 HUAC hearings; and there may be a certain truth to this charge, which merits further exploration. That *Body and Soul* was the product of a private entrepreneurial company exercising its American capitalist freedom of choice, however, meant nothing at all to the purge mentality of the 1950s.

Body and Soul did come as close to a work of the left as any produced to that time in Hollywood. Scriptwriter Polonsky and the director, Robert Rossen (who, as a Warner Bros. writer, had written or cowritten the Garfield pictures *Dust Be My Destiny*, *The Sea Wolf*, and *Out of the Fog*, as well as *Marked Woman*, *Racket Busters*, and *The Roaring Twenties*), were then or had been Communist party members. Anne Revere, who played Garfield's mother, and Lloyd Goff (also spelled Gough), who played Roberts, the venal gambler-promoter, were party members or associates. Canada Lee, who played the black champion Ben Chaplin, was blacklisted after his name surfaced from FBI files during a spy trial, and died of complications from high blood pressure in 1952. Art Smith, a former Group Theatre performer who portrayed Garfield's father in a brief scene, was named by Elia Kazan in his 1952 HUAC testimony as a onetime party member. Bob Roberts was cited as a Communist by actor Martin Berkeley before the committee.

Where does that leave Garfield? Though surely a consistent supporter of liberal and left-wing causes, no one—despite much prompting by investigators—ever identified him as a Communist party member. One of the most serious bits of innuendo that later made up the mosaic of charges against him came in 1951 HUAC testimony from Roy Brewer, the right-wing leader of the International Alliance of Theatrical Stage Employees (IATSE), the motion picture union. In March 1945 the rival, left-wing Conference of Studio Unions (CSU) had begun a strike which even the Communists initially opposed. After months of stalemate—with neither the screen actors' nor screenwriters' guilds observing the picket lines—the CSU in early October decided to stage a mass picket at Warner Bros. and shut the studio down.

Warner Bros. responded with tear gas and fire hoses. By this time the Communists supported the strike, and several, like John Howard Lawson, appeared as moral witnesses of the Battle of Burbank. It was these events that so angered Jack Warner that he flew into HUAC's arms. It was also these events to which Brewer in his testimony linked Garfield—not exactly identifying him positively at the studio gates, side by side with Lawson and the pickets, but nonetheless leaving the distinct impression that he was there.

At that time Garfield was miles away in Culver City making *The Postman Always Rings Twice*. In reference to the second, 1946 CSU strike, Brewer testified about Garfield and the Communists: "He was not on their side and he was not on our side, but we had always considered him to be on their side."[6] For Brewer and the right, not to be with them was tantamount to being a Communist. Brewer's views, however, had not yet become national policy when *Body and Soul* went before the camera in winter 1947. That year was to be the last in Hollywood of the openness to progressive ideas that had been fostered by the wartime ideological unity of the left, the industry, and the federal government—even if its principal manifestation in 1947 was the relatively safe stance of opposition to anti-Semitism.

Gentleman's Agreement and its director, Elia Kazan, won Oscars in 1947, and *Crossfire*, RKO's slightly earlier film on the subject, and its director, Edward Dmytryk (soon to become one of the Hollywood Ten), were nominated. *Gentleman's Agreement* had three awards and four other nominations that year; *Crossfire* had five nominations; *Body and Soul* got one Oscar—to Francis Lyon and Robert Parrish for editing—and two nominations, Garfield for actor and Polonsky for original screenplay. Of the three films marking the last hurrah of the Hollywood era's progressivism, *Body and Soul* was by far the most radical: it was not about prejudice, it was about money.

Body and Soul bears some surprising surface likenesses to *Humoresque*, but their similarity only accentuates their difference. Both films narrate, through flashback, the careers of ambitious Lower East Side boys. Where the Warner Bros. city streets are picturesque and, in a sense, generic, *Body and Soul*'s are grim and temporally specific to the Great Depression years. In *Humoresque* the Jewish background of Garfield's character might be inferred by artifacts of set decoration like pushcarts; in *Body and Soul* it is clearly stated. The greatest contrast between the two films, however, lies in how they present the dilemmas of Garfield's characters: in *Humoresque*, he is a good man perhaps confused in values, led astray by a predatory woman whose elimination will put *his* life to right; in *Body and Soul* his problems derive from and must be resolved within his own value system, formed and dominated (but ultimately not conquered) by the values of the larger American society.

Garfield plays Charlie Davis, a boxing champion facing a title defense he is expected to throw; estranged from his mother and the woman he once loved, he lies on a table in his dressing room, saying to himself, recollecting his life, "All gone down the drain . . . all these years." A callow, belligerent street kid, he sees his only chance for advancement ("I don't want to end up like Pop") in his boxing skills. After Pop is killed by a bomb thrown at the speakeasy next to his candy store, Charlie revolts when his mother seeks charity to keep him in school. "I want money . . . money . . . money," he rants at his mother. "Better to buy a gun and shoot yourself," she says. "You need money to buy a gun," he replies.

Soon he is an up-and-coming challenger, with an apartment overlooking Central Park and a mink coat for his girl—and mired in the machinations of an icy gambler-promoter, Roberts. He wins the title from an injured black champion. "He's not just a kid who can fight, he's money," says his friend and onetime manager, Shorty, now being shunted aside; Shorty is killed by a car after being beaten by a Roberts thug.

Charlie remains mesmerized by the dollars that flow and fall like rain around him, while his girl leaves him, lamenting "the lost years of happiness, the promises broken, the lonely nights," saying, "It was all inevitable." Finally he is brought to reckoning by the courage of the black former champion, now his friend, who stands up to the money men, saying, "I don't scare no more" before his own death. Charlie wakes up from his sleep, actually and metaphorically, and wins the fight. He tells Roberts, "What are you going to do, kill me?" and, echoing one of Roberts's lines, "Everybody dies." He is reunited with his girl, saying, "I never felt better in my life," as the film ends.

Polonsky, for one, hoped that the film would be understood not as an exposé of prizefight corruption (about which a cycle of films developed in the late 1940s) but as an allegory of the actual and spiritual corruption of human values in the American capitalist system.

In that case, he made what seems a serious strategic error in winning a battle about the film's ending. Rossen, as Polonsky recalls it, wanted Charlie to be shot down for his defiance as he leaves the arena after the fight. Polonsky says that he prevailed on the ambiguous, but surely upbeat, ending. "Bob Rossen was fundamentally an anarchist by disposition," Polonsky later said. "He was also fundamentally mean, in many respects of the word. He also thought that death was truer than life, as an ending. But we who are radicals know the opposite is true."[7]

One's feelings about the two men may be colored by the fact that Rossen, in the anti-Red crucible, became an informer and continued his directing career, while Polonsky held firm to his principles and was blacklisted for years. To cast *Body and Soul* as a romance of individual redemption, however, as Polonsky wished, inevitably deflects the social analysis. Hundreds, if not thousands, of Hollywood movies depict society's problems being solved by individuals triumphing over evil men. Rossen was involved in his share of those, but one could argue that his screenwriting contributions to the downbeat endings of such films as *Marked Woman* and *The Roaring Twenties* made them both more memorable than *Body and Soul*, and "truer to life" in the sense that their protagonists caught in the nexus of capitalist forces find it less easy to escape them.

The film's ending may also be seen as stemming from capitalist calculation as well as from radical aesthetics. It was a box office and critical triumph, made money for Roberts Productions, Enterprise, and United Artists, and guaranteed another Bank of America loan for a succeeding picture. Who can say that a dead Charlie Davis, rather than one who says, "I never felt better in my life," would have achieved the same results?

Though acclaim for *Body and Soul* was generously spread by the press among many involved in its production, it is still surprising to discover (given the reviewing practices of the time) so much attention being given to the cinematography of James Wong Howe. He was singled out especially for the climactic fight sequences, filmed largely from a low-angled ringside position to create a newsreel-like air of realism. Other aspects of the cinematography are also remarkable: its combination of the grit and glitter, from poolroom to penthouse, of Warner Bros.' 1930s social dramas, with a new emphasis (influenced by *Citizen Kane*) on low-angle shots and depth of frame.

Howe was indeed a cinematographer of special importance to the city boys: as a Warner Bros. contract cameraman beginning in 1939, he shot Garfield in *They Made Me a Criminal, Daughters Courageous, Dust Be My Destiny, Saturday's Children, Out of the Fog,* and *Air Force*; Cagney in *The Oklahoma Kid, Torrid Zone, City for Conquest, The Strawberry Blonde,* and *Yankee Doodle Dandy*; Bogart in *The Oklahoma Kid* and *Passage to Marseille.* Since, in the case of Garfield and Cagney, Howe's credits include several of their most important and innovative films, his contribution to their images and careers deserves recognition.

Garfield's performance in *Body and Soul* earned his first Academy Award nomination since his debut in *Four Daughters,* and his only actor nomination. "It's a striking commentary on Hollywood and its waste of talents," Archer Winsten wrote in the *New York Post,* "that Garfield, an actor who was perfectly capable of doing this job nine years ago when he first left the New York stage, should have had to wait so long and impersonate so many variously repetitious types before he could realize his full capabilities."

It is a moot point whether Garfield could have created his portrait of Charlie Davis in 1938 or in the intervening years. His performance veers between the grim, tormented Charlie of the film's opening and closing sequences—akin to the style of *The Postman Always Rings Twice*—and the shallow, grinning, muscular "tiger" of the boxer's youth, a familiar presence from earlier days. His characterization of the young Charlie is tinged by a certain distance, however: a clear signal from the actor that the young man's pride, impatience, and temper are faults as much as strengths, signs of the structures of self and society that will plunge him into the money vortex. Someone (perhaps wardrobe designer Marion Herwood Keyes) had the brilliant idea of dressing Charlie frequently in expensive, broad-shouldered, tight-fitting overcoats, making him appear small and constrained within the commodities he craves.

Garfield deserved his press accolades and the honor of his peers' nomination; but his work was matched, if not exceeded, by the outstanding performance of Canada Lee as Ben Chaplin, the black champion. Lee gave this brief role such dignity and force, it may well be the most important African-American characterization up to that point in Hollywood movies. The Unity Awards Committee, a Los Angeles progressive group, cited Garfield and Lee among its honorees for their participation in what the *Los Angeles Daily News* called "a pro-Negro film." In the year of *Gentleman's Agreement* and *Crossfire,* Polonsky's allegory of capitalism seemed to have been perceived by some as another film against prejudice.

In the Oscar-winning *Gentleman's Agreement,* Garfield had the Canada Lee role—and received the same kind of raves Lee got for *Body and Soul.* His army captain David Goldman was the Jew, the victim of prejudice. The star part belonged to Gregory Peck (a gentile if there ever was one), who was merely passing for Jewish so he could write a magazine article exposing anti-Semitism. Garfield's was a brief role but was even more important to *Gentleman's Agreement* than Lee's was to *Body and Soul*, for it gave the solemn, self-important film some energy. The part called for a form of "naturalism," similar to that Garfield had utilized in shaping Al Schmid in *Pride of the Marines*. The movie's Jew had to be human—lively, likeable, vulnerable, open—to show that he was not a stereotype or a product of ethnic difference, that he was one who laughed and suffered like the rest of mankind. Garfield carries it off with a grace and subtlety that can be better appreciated as performance by comparison to the very different characterizations he had created just before it, in *Postman, Humoresque,* and *Body and Soul.*

After completing his work on *Gentleman's Agreement*, and while preparing for the release and promotion of *Body and Soul*, Garfield learned during September 1947 that his film's director, Robert Rossen, was among the nineteen "unfriendly" witnesses subpoenaed to testify before the House Un-American Activities Committee. In contrast to the several dozen witnesses friendly to the committee, the nineteen were clearly the targets of HUAC's hearing on "Communist infiltration of the motion picture industry" scheduled the following month. Garfield joined with other Hollywood liberals in a group formed to oppose the committee's inquiries. This was the Committee for the First Amendment, formed by directors John Huston and William Wyler, and writer Philip Dunne, to take an essentially civil libertarian stance—not specifically to support the nineteen but more generally to mobilize the industry and public opinion against HUAC's expected assault on movie content. (It was not until 1952 that the Supreme Court declared movies protected by the free speech provisions of the First Amendment.)

The First Amendment group's activities peaked on Sunday, October 26, following HUAC's first week of hearings dealing with friendly witnesses. On Monday morning, the 27th, Eric Johnston, head of the producers' association, was expected to testify. A liberal delegation, under the leadership of Huston and Dunne, flew on Sunday from Hollywood to Washington to back up Johnston's appearance. On Sunday evening the group sponsored a nationwide half-hour radio broadcast, "Hollywood Fights Back." More than forty individuals spoke from Hollywood, New York, and Washington against HUAC's threat to democratic rights. Four United States senators joined the many Hollywood figures. Garfield spoke from New York, where he was rehearsing for a return to Broadway theater:

This is John Garfield. There is no guarantee that the committee will stop with the movies. Already the American theater has been attacked. Already a witness friendly to the committee has assured us that 44 percent of the plays on Broadway in the last ten years have been subversive. That's news to Broadway and to the millions of playgoers who have seen these plays. Once they get the movies and Broadway throttled, how long will it be before the committee goes to work on the freedom of the air? How long will it be before we're told what we can and cannot say into a radio microphone? If you make a pitch on a nationwide network for the underdog, will they call you subversive? Will we have to think Mr. Rankin's way [Congressman John Rankin of Mississippi was a blatant racist and anti-Semite] to get into the elevator at Radio City? Are they gonna scare us into silence? If this committee gets a green light from the American people now, will it be possible to make a broadcast like this a year from today?[8]

Monday morning the first witness called was not Eric Johnston but John Howard Lawson, well known as a leader of the Hollywood Communists. Amid bullying by the committee chairman, Lawson belligerently refused on First Amendment grounds to answer the question whether he was then or had ever been a member of the Screen Writers Guild or the Communist party. Later, "unfriendly" witnesses repeated Lawson's stance more quietly. Ten men were cited for contempt of Congress for their refusal, eventually convicted, and sent to prison; an eleventh witness, Bertolt Brecht, escaped censure and soon left the country for East Germany; eight of the subpoenaed unfriendlies, including Rossen, were not called.

The liberals sat aghast as their First Amendment principles and they themselves became linked to the recalcitrant, when not truculent, behavior of the unfriendly witnesses. In the atmosphere of capitulation that swiftly followed—with the movie industry setting up a blacklist covering Communists and that wide and amorphous class known colloquially as pinkos or fellow travelers—liberals suddenly had to scramble to protect their careers and reputations. A glance at the credits of *Body and Soul* provided those who were inclined to probe a graphic example of a fellow traveling alongside certified Reds. At the height of his professional life (with an Oscar nomination for *Body and Soul* and acclaim for *Gentleman's Agreement* in his immediate future), Garfield had more reasons to fear for than to rejoice at his prospects.

■ ■ ■ ■

When the actor Sterling Hayden appeared before HUAC as an informer in spring 1951, he was asked by counsel Jerome Tavenner, "Who were those who spearheaded the Committee for the First Amendment, to your knowledge?" Hayden answered, "The first name that comes to mind is Humphrey Bogart, and his wife."[9]

The printed transcript does not record the sound of gasps or of reporters rushing to the telephones. For one thing, everyone knew that Hayden's knowledge was incomplete. While Bogart and Bacall had been perhaps the biggest star names among the liberal group, and had been prominently photographed and filmed during the excursion to Washington, they were spear-carriers rather than spearheads in the group Huston, Wyler, and Dunne had formed. For another, Bogart had long before 1951 taken the requisite protective steps to inure his career and reputation from the occasional slander or false memory uttered in congressional hearings. For a time, however, he seemed in jeopardy like many others.

After completing *The Big Sleep*, it seemed that he was placed in greatest jeopardy by his employer, Warner Bros. After the Hawks film was finished he was assigned to *The Two Mrs. Carrolls* (1947), an adaptation of a British play by Martin Vale. Only his impending fourth marriage could have distracted him from the meretricious nature of this project: in the middle of production he took a long weekend and flew with Lauren Bacall to Ohio, where they were married at novelist Louis Bromfield's farm. His personal joy permitted him to treat the picture as little more than a lark.

He plays an American artist in London with a penchant for charming women, marrying them, painting their portraits—with gruesome portent—and murdering them. The closest comparable role in his career was as the zombie killer in the 1939 B-picture howler *The Return of Dr. X*. In the climactic sequence, when he is trying unsuccessfully to kill wife Barbara Stanwyck, he strikes a pose, with his hands outstretched and fingers curled in a grotesque way, that looks for all the world like Nosferatu the vampire in F. W. Murnau's 1922 German silent classic.

One must wonder again—as with *Conflict*—whether the Warner Bros. unconscious was working overtime in casting Bogart as a wife-killer. One might guess this was a blatant attempt to capitalize on his divorce and remarriage, except that the picture was shelved for two years before its release in April 1947.

The studio permitted Bogart a six-month honeymoon before

he was called back in January 1946 for retakes on *The Big Sleep*. Thereupon it assigned him successively to parts in two westerns. He refused both, and went for a time on suspension. In the first, *Cheyenne* (1947), his role was taken by Dennis Morgan; in the second, *Stallion Rock* (also 1947), by Zachary Scott. It is difficult to guess at the strategy behind these assignments, since Bogart and the studio were in the midst of protracted negotiations over a new contract; but the refusals were sincere enough. Did Jack Warner and his clever executives have no worthy vehicle for the man who was now probably their number one star? Finally they took the opportunity of an outside offer and lent him to Columbia at $4766.66 per week, nearly double his salary. The studio—not the actor—pocketed the difference.

The Columbia project, *Dead Reckoning* (1947), paired Bogart with actress Lizabeth Scott, and it was promoted with the line, "Humphrey Bogart is out with a New Woman." It was not exactly a love-match. *Dead Reckoning* is a prime example of the postwar film noir fear and punishment of women. Bogart plays Ray Murdock, a former paratrooper searching a Southern city for a buddy who has mysteriously disappeared. The film opens with him eluding police, entering a church, and telling his story to a priest—the flashback narrative therefore is addressed to "Father." He gets involved with the femme fatale with whom his missing friend was also linked. For him, however, involvement and aggression are hard to tell apart. These are among Bogart's many misogynist lines: "All females are the same with their faces washed"; "I hated every part of her"; "I don't trust anybody, especially women"; and, "I heard of a girl once kissed a guy and stabbed him in the back at the same time." His character's view of women is summarized as follows:

Women ought to come capsule-size—about four inches high. When a man goes out for an evening he just puts her in his pocket and takes her along with him, and that way he knows exactly where she is. He gets to his favorite restaurant, he puts her on the table and lets her run around among the coffee cups while he swaps a few lies with his pals . . . without danger of interruption. And when it comes that time in the evening when he wants her full-size and beautiful, just waves his hand and there she is, full-size.

Still, Columbia was determined to exploit Bogart's new status as a masterful romancer. To this provocation, the woman replies, "What you're saying is, women are made to be loved."

It turns out he does not love her. When he learns that she was involved in his buddy's death, as well as others', he echoes Sam Spade: "A guy's pal is killed, he ought to do something about it," and tellingly adds, "And there's one other thing. I loved him more." She shoots him while he is driving. The car crashes; though he is only slightly hurt, she is mortally injured. On her deathbed she says, "I'm so scared. I wish you could put me in your pocket now." The old paratrooper says, "Geronimo." A shot of a parachute landing, and she dies.

Well, it was better than the picture assignments Warner Bros. had come up with—until the studio and the actor finally worked out the dollars. In late 1946 Bogart signed a new contract: it called for him to make one picture a year for the next fifteen years at $200,000 per picture. This figure nearly doubled his annual salary, and quadrupled his per picture fee. He was granted both script and director approval—the directors he approved in advance were Delmer Daves, Howard Hawks, John Cromwell (who did *Dead Reckoning* at Columbia), John Huston, and Michael Curtiz. In addition, he could also do one outside picture a year. He was set, so it seemed, for life. A separate contract clause paid him $200,000 for his work on a film already in progress, *Dark Passage* (1947), his first appearance before a Warner Bros. camera—save for retakes and new scenes for *The Big Sleep*—in well over a year.

Dark Passage began production in late October 1946 in San Francisco. It was to be almost completely a location shoot, a practice still unusual at the time; the motivation for leaving the studio may well have been another CSU strike that had erupted in September and embroiled the Warner Bros. lot once again in picketing and clashes between police and strikers. The Wald-Daves team (Daves wrote the script as well as directed) quite closely followed David Goodis's novel about a man unjustly convicted of murdering his wife, who escapes from San Quentin and has his face changed by a plastic surgeon to elude the police. Bogart plays the escapee and Bacall the mysterious woman who assists him and with whom he falls in love.

Wald and Daves hit upon a gimmick to solve the problem of the main character changing his face midway through the picture: in the early part the camera sometimes adopts his point of view, or shows his face in shadow, and we see a photograph of him that, if you stared at it, would be seen vaguely to resemble Bogart, with a mustache and much fuller cheeks. The suspense, however, is considerably diluted by our knowledge of Bogart's voice and the suspicion that, once the surgeon's bandages come off, it will be the familiar lined, craggy Bogart face: "I'll make you look older," the surgeon promises, "I'll make you look as if you've lived." To compound the problem, the withholding of Bogart's face deprives the picture's whole first section of scenes in which the star appears with others. Bacall and other players perform solo turns before the camera's/spectator's/main character's eye, and the film lacks the spark that performers working together can provide and that Bogart and Bacall so memorably generated in the Hawks pictures.

Dark Passage never quite recovers from this unsuitable (though perhaps necessary) strategy. The picture was not helped, either, by its variance from the film noir formula. Bacall is a totally good woman, and the evil woman, played by Agnes Moorehead, is far from a femme fatale; she kills, in fact, because the man she wants is not attracted to her. The texture of Goodis's novel—money troubles, dead-end white-collar jobs, and middle-class desperation—is missing also. *Dark Passage* is mostly a curiosity.

Bogart's first picture under his new contract, however, gave him everything he was looking for: a challenge, a change of pace, a memorable opportunity to innovate. It had all the texture one could ask for, and a perhaps welcome surcease from the Bogart screen persona's troubles with women. The part was as Fred C. Dobbs, "Dobbsie," in John Huston's *The Treasure of the Sierra Madre* (1948).

Treasure went before the camera in March 1947, nearly six years after preproduction had begun on the film, under the supervision of producer Henry Blanke. Huston had written a script in winter 1941–1942 that so excited one Warner Bros. executive that he predicted in a memo to Jack Warner that it "would probably go down as one of the greatest pictures of all time if properly directed and cast." This executive was especially enthusiastic because "any or all of your problem children could play it. There are important parts for three tough guys, and Raft, Robinson and Garfield could do it."[10] Robinson had been interested, and Blanke wanted Garfield to play Dobbs. The war took Huston away, however, and Blanke held up the project until his return. By that time the three problem children, Raft, Robinson, and Garfield, had left the Warner Bros. household, and the most dutiful, Bogart, had claimed the inheritance.

The part of Fred C. Dobbs was like nothing Bogart had done since the interminable string of villains he had played in the late 1930s. For a star who had risen to fourth place on an exhibitor's poll of money-making performers, with a firmly established screen persona along the Spade-Rick-Marlowe axis, to take the "Dobbsie" role was nothing less than a sign that he wanted to act rather than merely be a screen presence.

Bogart's Dobbs begins as a fast-talking, ebullient bum on the streets of Tampico, Mexico, and progresses—or descends—to the demented, obsessed, paranoid thief and would-be killer who betrays his prospecting comrades, Curtin (played by Tim Holt) and Howard (played by Walter Huston, the director's father). He begins as an unshaven man with longish hair and becomes a darkly bearded specter with thick, wild locks (triumphs of makeup: "[Bogart] has practically no hair left," producer Blanke noted).[11] He dies brutally under the machete blows of a Mexican bandit in a scene that mixes cruelty and levity in the "acid and comedy" manner Huston and Bogart employed so effectively in *The Maltese Falcon*.[12]

Bogart got a rich share of reviewers' praise for his portrayal of the unsavory Dobbs—several called it the best performance of his career—but the picture was regarded as an even greater triumph for Walter Huston, who won the supporting actor Oscar for his role as the irascible and philosophical old prospector (son John won both the director and screenplay awards; the film lost in the Best Picture competition to Laurence Olivier's *Hamlet*).

Despite its lack of "feminine" interest, which worried the trade papers, the film did exceptionally well at New York's Strand. One Los Angeles reviewer noted, however, that the audience she attended with found the picture "hilariously funny . . . and laughed indiscriminately at murder, fear, and the action's irony." It is unlikely that this particular experience was typical, but it does point up questions of tone, meaning, and interpretation: What exactly is *The Treasure of the Sierra Madre* about?

Clearly it is about greed, as many reviewers noted, and at least one pointed out its thematic resemblance to Erich von Stroheim's 1924 silent classic. Perhaps we should take a further clue, however, from the fact that this was the film liberals Huston and Bogart had completed shortly before taking their prominent roles in the Committee for the First Amendment. *Treasure* has many earmarks of a political text, and it offers itself to be interpreted allegorically no less than Polonsky's *Body and Soul*: it may be argued that prospecting for gold makes for a sharper analogy to the money nexus of modern capitalism than does the prizefight game.

"I know what gold does to men's souls," the old prospector says, and we can observe the process of transformation in Dobbs. When Howard and Curtin talk about the enterprises they could found with their money—Tim Holt is particularly eloquent describing the camaraderie of collective labor in a fruit orchard—Dobbs thinks only of creature comforts and excessive consumption. Later, arguing for a larger share of their diggings, Dobbs says, "In any civilized place, the biggest investor gets the biggest return, doesn't he?" Howard replies, "That's one thing in favor of the wilds." Dobbs continues to insist that his behavior is civilized. After learning that Dobbs has tried to kill Curtin, Howard refuses to condemn him: "He's not a real killer as killers go. I think he's honest as the next fella—or almost." He allows that under the same circumstances he would have been tempted, too.

This is different from the Social Darwinist message of Stroheim's *Greed*, where nature was brutal and civilization only a thin veneer. In *Treasure* nature's ultimate triumph is seen as comic and ironic, if not benign; civilization's battle for money and commodities is what is brutalizing. This seems clear enough in *The Treasure of the Sierra Madre* that even contemporary reviewers must have noticed it. Perhaps they did and forbore to mention it, because by the film's January 1948 release date the climate for political films had rapidly turned colder.

The HUAC hearings had occurred between the end of production on *The Treasure of the Sierra Madre* and the film's opening. Bogart had joined with Huston on the Committee for the First Amendment and had, like Garfield, spoken on the "Hollywood Fights Back" broadcast. Most of his remarks were taken from a *New York Herald-Tribune* editorial opposing the Hollywood hearing:

> This is Humphrey Bogart. Is democracy so feeble it can be subverted merely by a look or a line, an inflection, a gesture? There was an editorial in the *New York Herald-Tribune* which says it perfectly, and I quote: "If the moving pictures are undermining the American form of government and menacing it by their content, it might become the duty of Congress to ferret out the responsible persons. But clearly this is not the case. Not even the Committee's own witnesses are willing to make so fantastic a charge. And since no danger exists, the beliefs of men and women who write for the screen are, like the beliefs of any ordinary men and women, nobody's business but their own. As the Bill of Rights mentions. Neither Mr. Thomas nor the Congress in which he sits is empowered to dictate what Americans shall think."[13]

The *Herald-Tribune*, and Bogart, underestimated the committee's power. In the aftermath of the "unfriendly" witnesses' testimony, liberals found themselves on the defensive; Bogart's beliefs suddenly became the nation's business. Because of committee chairman J. Parnell Thomas's clever switch (replacing Eric Johnston with John Howard Lawson), it looked to all the world as if Bogart and his compatriots had flown to Washington to stand up for the Communists.

Bogart quickly sought to distance himself from the Hollywood

Ten. He implicitly accepted the committee's view that "freedom of speech, freedom of the screen, the protection of the Bill of Rights"—the principles he came to Washington to uphold—did not apply to Communists, real or alleged, or those who defend them. As the blacklists began, he had his own skin to protect. Even if Warner Bros. stood by him, it was unclear how the public would respond to "tainted" motion picture stars. He also had his own goals to consider: for the outside pictures permitted under his new Warner Bros. contract, Bogart planned to form an independent company to produce them. How would the banks feel about his fortuitous link with the Reds?

For a man with something to protect, however, Bogart had the unfortunate habit of putting his foot in his mouth. In New York after the hearings, he got together with an old friend, the show business columnist Ed Sullivan, who advised him that the situation was serious and that Bogart should disabuse the public of any notion that he supported the left. Bogart prepared a statement that began, "I'm as much in favor of Communism as J. Edgar Hoover." Sullivan printed it, and began receiving irate letters complaining that the actor had insulted the FBI director. Sullivan then called the FBI. "Sullivan stated he would like to know anything that we could tell him about Bogart," according to an internal FBI memo, "because he certainly is not going to let Bogart sell him a bill of goods, although he was frank to confess that he did not believe there was anything sinister about Bogart but that he had probably just been misled." On the bottom of this memo is a handwritten aphorism: "If a man sleeps with dogs with fleas he will get the fleas also!" It is signed, "H."[14]

Attached to the memo was a seven-page, single-spaced summary of the FBI's information on Humphrey DeForist (sic) Bogart. Its sources included *Who's Who in the Theater*, *Current Biography*, Warner Bros. press releases, and a security questionnaire Bogart filled out before his 1943 USO tour. Nearly two pages were devoted to the various times the *Daily Worker* mentioned Bogart's name, and there were references to numerous clippings pertaining to the Committee for the First Amendment. John L. Leech's accusations and Bogart's testimony before the Dies Committee are summarized, with the editorial conclusion that "his testimony is quite clear and very persuasive to the point that Bogart was innocent and as of 1940 had no connection with the Communist Party." Finally, there were three pages of data from agents, informants, and "highly confidential" sources listing every time Bogart's name came up within FBI earshot.[15]

The FBI was not about to make a case that Bogart was a Communist. He was, however, a man with fleas, and he continued to search for the antidote. After the flap over the Sullivan column he told the press, "I went to Washington because I thought fellow Americans were being deprived of their constitutional rights, and for that reason alone. That the trip was ill-advised, even foolish, I am very ready to admit. At that time it seemed the thing to do."[16] Right-wing columnist George E. Sokolsky took him to task for these remarks because of his continuing membership in, and support for, the Committee for the First Amendment: How could he remain in a group which took, in his view, such foolish, ill-advised action?

Bogart took his case to the public in *Photoplay* magazine with an article, under his own by-line, entitled "I'm No Communist." It was not a total capitulation. He tried to salvage some political space for liberals, and criticized HUAC for the "vaudeville show" atmosphere of its hearings. He associated himself with "Bob" Montgomery and Ronald Reagan in asserting that Hollywood did not deserve to be singled out for censure: it had few Communists and they were "under control." He also further denigrated the Committee for the First Amendment: "We may not have been very smart in the way we did things, may have been dopes in some people's eyes, but we were American dopes! Actors and actresses always go overboard about things."[17]

So that was it: he was merely a performer, not to be confused with someone who understood politics. Maybe, for that matter, he was sort of like Fred C. Dobbs: not a real Red as Reds go, as American as the next fella—or almost. He was tempted to be politically courageous, and, who knows, others in his shoes might have been tempted, too. He did not have to suffer Dobbsie's fate: he could repent and continue as a movie star.

■ ■ ■ ■

One name that did not appear in print or in public—among the Reds or the liberals—during the 1947 HUAC confrontation was that of James Cagney. In the political sphere it was as if he had fallen off the edge of the earth; and it was not much different in the motion picture sphere. Following *Blood on the Sun*, shot in late 1944 and released in 1945, Cagney did no screen work for seventeen months. Cagney Productions was continuing to acquire and develop properties, but nothing was close to shooting. In May 1946 he was offered a part in a Twentieth Century–Fox picture, *13 Rue Madeleine* (1946)—one which had previously been turned down by, of all dissimilar screen figures, Rex Harrison—and he took it.

The role was as Robert Emmet (Bob) Sharkey, "scholar and soldier of fortune, master of five languages and one of America's finest athletes." If it sounds like an unfamiliar Cagney persona, bear in mind that this was his first screen appearance—after fifteen years and forty-one pictures—in a film produced by someone other than Warner Bros. or under his own aegis. *13 Rue Madeleine* was notable chiefly as one of producer Louis de Rochemont's efforts to bring to feature films the "semi-documentary" style he pioneered with the *March of Time* newsreel series: a mix of actuality and fiction footage designed to simulate, as the film's opening titles claim, "the maximum of realism and authenticity." The film paid homage to secret military espionage work during World War II—forerunner of the CIA. Cagney's Sharkey is recruited to train and lead a group of agents into occupied France before the Normandy invasion. One of the group is known to be a German spy, and part of the job is to give him false information about where the Allied landing will take place. After various hair-raising scrapes behind enemy lines, Sharkey is captured and taken to Gestapo headquarters at 13 Rue Madeleine in Le Havre, where the German spy employs torture in an attempt to get the truth regarding the invasion site out of him. "He wasn't lucky," Sharkey's comrades say, "he's still alive." He holds out long enough for the air force to send bombers to blow him up and prevent the secret from escaping.

13 Rue Madeleine ends with its most memorable scene: Cagney/Sharkey in an interrogation room, tied to a chair, shirtless, with bruises covering his bare chest. As the bombs begin to fall, he bursts out in maniacal laughter that continues until the final explosion that obliterates him. It is both a stunning emotional moment in an otherwise conventional film—the joyous welcoming of death to stymie the enemy—and a sharp rupture with the sedate, avuncular screen persona Cagney seemed to prefer.

Cagney got one more chance to be the screen figure he wanted to be, in his own company's production of *The Time of Your Life* (1948). The Cagney brothers reportedly paid $150,000 for rights to William Saroyan's 1940 play, winner of New York Critics Circle and Pulitzer Prize awards; trade press accounts indicate they poured close to $2 million into the production. Principal shooting took place in summer 1947, and in the fall, while Garfield and Bogart were attempting to combat HUAC's assault on Hollywood, the Cagneys were struggling against their United Artists distribution deal.

United Artists had fallen into bleak financial straits and West Coast banks had cut off further production loans. Along with other independent producers, the Cagneys began looking for a lifeboat to avoid sinking with the UA ship—and where, of all places, would they find it but in Burbank, in the offices of Jack L. Warner. The plan was to have Warner Bros. distribute *The Time of Your Life*, and also to shift there other projects in development.

United Artists, which had received but two of the fifteen Cagney productions it had contracted for, fought to retain the third independent film, and managed by various inducements to do so. Both UA and Cagney Productions came out losers: the film grossed $1.5 million in box office rentals, less than half the proceeds of *Blood on the Sun* and well below those of *Johnny Come Lately*. Not even recouping their production costs, and with their continuing high overhead expenses, the Cagneys were looking at the collapse of their experiment as independent producers.

For experiment, if not fool's errand, is what in hindsight it seems—or perhaps a vanity operation spurred not by business or artistic motives but by James's rage at Warner Bros. The Saroyan project looks no less quixotic decades later than it did on its release. However much Saroyan's whimsy impressed late-Depression, prewar stage audiences and critics, its arch, static presentation of life's crossroads in a San Francisco saloon would be a hard sell to moviegoers. *Variety*'s reviewer went a remarkable distance out of his way to praise the Cagneys' "courage" in making such an offbeat film, while earnest Bosley Crowther of the *New York Times* was forced to admit that, however much in theory critics yearned for something different from conventional Hollywood fare, an effort like *The Time of Your Life* was not what he, at least, had in mind.

The Time of Your Life is especially disheartening for what it shows of the star himself. The lithe, supple, expressive body of the younger Cagney, and even the energetic figure of only a few years earlier in *Yankee Doodle Dandy*, are largely hidden from view in a performance of a man seen almost always only from the waist up, sitting behind a saloon table, wearing glasses, drinking champagne, smoking a pipe. His philosopher-philanthropist character presides over the doings in Nick's Pacific Street Saloon, Restaurant and Entertainment Palace. When he does finally stand up, he looks more stocky and round in the belly than ever before—though there is a scene (possibly added after disastrous sneak previews) in which he runs fast and punches out a villain. This image of a basically immobile Cagney is the most distressing aspect of *The Time of Your Life*: more so because it was clearly the actor's preference. Perhaps it should be seen as a metaphor, an objective correlative of this time in Cagney's life, when he was immobilized in his production efforts and in Hollywood's and the nation's politics.

The Time of Your Life is most interesting not for itself but for its portents: the actor Ward Bond, a member of the Motion Picture Alliance for the Preservation of American Ideals who was to become one of the key right-wing Hollywood administrators of the blacklist, plays a character named McCarthy (Senator Joe, elected in 1946, was not to emerge as a Red-hunter until 1950). The first time Cagney gets up from his chair in the film is to place a bet on a horse named McCarthy. He is too late, however. McCarthy wins, but Cagney does not. These names are only a coincidence, to be sure, but they do serve to cast a curious light on the static figure Cagney had become: poised motionless between his radical past and a future more closely in step with the reigning ethos of the McCarthy era.

I V

City Boys Grow Older

10

A Street Boy's Honor

By late 1947, John Garfield's post–World War II successes were like a brimming glass with a crack in it. Almost simultaneously with each new moment of acclaim—praise for his performance in *Gentleman's Agreement*, the Oscar nomination for *Body and Soul*—came a jarring blow to the vessel, emphasizing its fragility. In December 1947, within weeks of the HUAC Hollywood hearings, motion picture company heads instituted a blacklist of Communists and others alleged to advocate violent overthrow of the United States government. While Garfield might not have imagined himself vulnerable to exclusion, it would have been remiss not to be aware that the structure he had built for his motion picture life, Roberts Productions, with prominent leftist names like Rossen and Polonsky involved, had been rendered unsafe. A strategy for survival, as well as his publicly announced yearning for artistic fulfillment, lay behind his decision that fall to relocate in New York and devote some of his energies to theater.

Artistic fulfillment was in fact germane. Garfield was approaching his thirty-fifth birthday, not unknown as a time of disquiet in many men's lives. Cagney had been approximately the same age, more than a decade earlier, when he determined to break with the stereotyped screen character Warner Bros. had established for him; Bogart stood at a similar time of life when, by force of will and desperation, he discarded an old stage persona and forged a new one with his performance as Duke Mantee in *The Petrified Forest*, rescuing his career.

Garfield's situation was not exactly comparable. He was driven neither by dissatisfaction nor need. HUAC and the impending repression aside, he was artistically in as strong a position as he had ever been. Still, a desire for greater accomplishment and respect than he had yet attained as a movie performer fueled his ambitions—and, solidly launched in a successful independent production venture, he had a luxury of choice that neither Cagney nor Bogart had in their quests for transformation. Freedom, however, can sometimes pose a greater risk than necessity.

The immediate test was Garfield's opportunity to play the role of Stanley Kowalski in Tennessee Williams's *A Streetcar Named Desire*. Elia Kazan, who had been persuaded by Williams to direct the play, had offered the part to Garfield before or during production on *Gentleman's Agreement* in the summer of 1947. The play's producer, Irene Mayer Selznick, daughter of one movie mogul and at that time the estranged wife of another, thought him "a natural for Stanley." She negotiated for months with Garfield's agent, until talks broke down, she recalled, over Garfield's "demand to be guaranteed the movie role, along with his refusal to play more than a few months."[1] The part went to the young and little-known Marlon Brando.

Garfield soon found himself having to explain why he had turned down the role of a career, in what was immediately recognized as one of the greatest American plays ever staged. In public, he took his stand on grounds of financial disagreements with the producer. It was also said that he had viewed the play as belonging basically to the Blanche character, and did not want to return to Broadway in a secondary role. The issue of time constraint was, as well, a real one—he was obliged to return to Hollywood soon for his company's new production. Perhaps he also doubted whether his skills were equal to the part: he was a star and a type, while Brando, as Selznick later wrote, was "more dimensional."[2] Perhaps the offer had come just a little too soon, before the HUAC hearings gave his Broadway move a certain thrust of urgency. His status empowered him to avoid the risk, and miss a classic opportunity.

The vehicle he chose held none of the perceived ambiguities of *Streetcar*. He would unequivocally be the star; it was a noncommercial production for which his low salary could be publicized as a contribution to the art of theater; and it was planned as a limited run. The play was *Skipper Next to God*, by the Dutch author Jan de Hartog, staged under the auspices of the Experimental Theatre project of the American National Theatre and Academy, with old Group Theatre hands Lee Strasberg as director and Cheryl Crawford as producer. Originally it was scheduled for six performances only, but interest in the play—or in Garfield—caused it to be continued on a more commercial basis, and eventually it ran for ninety-four performances, closing when Garfield left for his movie commitment.

Garfield's role was as captain of a Dutch ship carrying European Jews to refuge across the Atlantic. Refused landing in South America and again in several United States ports, the captain—after extended intellectual and theological anguish—scuttles his ship off Long Island and goes down with it, after sending his passengers off in lifeboats. Garfield's presence on a New York stage for the first time in nearly a decade prompted the theatrical reviewers to greater depth in discussing performance than was their wont. Perhaps on no other occasion—save for the flurry engendered by his striking movie debut in *Four Daughters*—was his acting style so closely scrutinized in print.

Garfield was strong wine for the theatrical press. They found him "fiery," "forceful," "vigorous," "robust." "He is about the best physical actor we have," Robert Sylvester wrote in the *New York Daily News*, summarizing a critical consensus that was largely positive. Others welcomed him "back in the medium in which he belongs," or conceded that he "remains an actor after all his years in the cinema." There was an undertone of criticism, however, counterpointing his physical performance with his ability to convey the captain's inner conflicts.

Brooks Atkinson of the *New York Times* addressed the problem with gentle circumlocution by writing, "He can also translate emotion into something egregious by portraying it too deliberately, as in the studied and elaborate scene when the captain is disillusioned about his father. This is a fault in the right direction." Richard Watts, Jr., in the *New York Post* put it more succinctly: "He is not always successful in suggesting the effect of the emotional struggle upon the young skipper." Others described this aspect of his performance as "staccato," "mannered," or "muddled." It is impossible to know for certain what relation these opinions bear to Garfield's actual performance—at least with films we have the screen image on which to form our own impression. There does emerge, however, from more than a dozen commentaries in then-newspaper-rich New York, a general consensus on Garfield as an actor: confident, compelling, and attractive, though perhaps a bit too stylized, too shaped, capable more of energy than of nuance.

Questions of performance were at issue in Garfield's career during winter and spring 1948. The Actors Studio had been formed the previous year, and Brando's performance in *Streetcar* was one of the first to give prominence to "The Method"—the Actors Studio's adaptation of Stanislavski acting principles. Kazan had been one of the Studio's founders; Brando's interpretation of Stanley was widely recognized not only as a personal triumph, but also as fundamentally a triumph of collaboration between director/teacher and performer. In turning down *Streetcar* Garfield had missed that chance at collaboration and at immersion in the very thing the reviewers of *Skipper Next to God* suggested he lacked: The Method's insistence on a strong emotional inner core to performance.

Garfield had worked with Strasberg on *Skipper*, to be sure, and Strasberg was to join the Actors Studio that same year and soon become its leading figure. Strasberg and Kazan were far from alike, however, in their interpretation of The Method: Strasberg in particular equated the Stanislavski approach with the familiar movie notion of screen personalities as "natural" actors. "The simplest examples of Stanislavski's ideas are actors such as Gary Cooper, John Wayne, and Spencer Tracy," Strasberg said. "They try not to act but to be themselves, to respond or react. They refuse to do or say anything they feel not to be consonant with their own characters."[3] The problem with this concept is that movie performers almost never are just "themselves": their screen personas are constructs of generic and studio types, codes, and mannerisms, which come to seem "natural" only through repetition and promotion. Still, Garfield's performance in *Skipper* seems consonant with Strasberg's views—in that Garfield, from the evidence of the reviews, seemed to be performing very much like his familiar screen persona.

Garfield had already begun in his movie work, however, to alter that familiar persona. In *Postman* and in parts of *Humoresque* and *Body and Soul*, he had discarded the ebullient, energetic, boyish figure he had played in most of his screen career, for a more grim, imploded, and immobile acting style. Returning to Hollywood in spring 1948, he was in a position as never before to impose his own ideas on his forthcoming screen performance in *Force of Evil* (1948).

This new Garfield-Roberts production had been placed in the hands of Abraham Polonsky, who had won the battles with Robert Rossen over *Body and Soul*'s ending and emerged as an officer of the company and its main creative figure. Polonsky was to choose the property, supervise the script (eventually he wrote it), and direct the film. It was his first directing assignment; and though he had many strong ideas about shaping the project, it is not clear that any of them had to do with performance.

Polonsky worked on a script in early 1948 along with Ira Wolfert, adapting Wolfert's novel about big-city corruption and the numbers racket, *Tucker's People*. The economic climate for Garfield's independent company, meanwhile, began to grow frostier, and not just because of HUAC. United Artists was in financial trouble, and the banks were balking at additional production loans to independents who had distribution deals with UA. Enterprise, the Cagneys, and

Howard Hawks all tried, unsuccessfully, to withdraw pictures committed to UA. With the old-line studios beginning to open their doors to independent producers, Enterprise shifted its future films to MGM, signing a four-picture financing and distribution agreement.

In these unsettled circumstances Roberts Productions tried to strike a deal with Columbia Pictures for the new Garfield film. The Breen Office so tartly rejected the Polonsky-Wolfert screenplay, however, that Columbia backed out, and Roberts returned to Enterprise as part of the MGM arrangement. Polonsky spent April and May revising the script to overcome PCA objections, and *Force of Evil* began shooting in June, finishing early in August. The production coincided with Enterprise's collapse—the independent company was crushed by the box office disaster of its expensive and highly touted big film of 1948, *Arch of Triumph*. In September, Enterprise suspended operations, leaving Garfield and *Force of Evil* to the tender mercies of MGM, the most ideologically conservative studio in town.

MGM did not burn the *Force of Evil* negative. It carried the film safely through postproduction (there were last-minute retakes in late November, probably at Breen Office insistence), and released it as a crime drama between Christmas and the New Year, not an unpropitious time to launch a film. If *Force of Evil* suffered a fate akin to that of *Arch of Triumph*, studio malice or failure to promote do not appear to be obvious causes—although MGM may have alienated audiences by promising in its promotion something quite different from their actual experience of the film.

What complicates an assessment of *Force of Evil* is the film's special status in postwar movie history. It was Abraham Polonsky's only opportunity to direct before he was blacklisted. It was not the last movie made by figures on the Hollywood left before their repression and exile, but Polonsky's articulate and intellectual commentary in later years may have made it seem so: if not the last one, then the only important one. Respect for Polonsky's talent, and rage at its suppression, fueled what may be called a certain excess of praise for his single film. In 1968, as Polonsky was preparing to direct his second film, more than twenty years after the first, critic Andrew Sarris wrote that "*Force of Evil* stands up under repeated viewings as one of the great films of the modern American cinema."[4]

Force of Evil is a film about corruption—corruption that pervades the lives of all its characters, invades and shapes their social formation, beguiles the innocent and as yet uncorrupt. From the opening high-angle shot from a Wall Street tower overlooking Trinity

Church in lower Manhattan, it does not take long to recognize that the numbers racket is a stand-in for American capitalism, for power, control, and corruption in the nation at large. No wonder the Breen Office was stern in rejecting the original script, and Columbia dropped it like a hot stone. No wonder critics of the early and mid-1960s, rediscovering the film in the final years of the Production Code's suzerainty, found it so striking and rare a Hollywood product.

Several decades of post-Code freedom have blunted the impact of *Force of Evil*. Corruption in American life became, for a time in the Watergate era, a not-infrequent movie theme, and Francis Ford Coppola, for one, in *The Godfather, Part II* (1974) carried the link between social and private corruption toward deeper and more baroque dimensions than Polonsky was permitted to attain. For the Production Code Administration's tactic was only rarely to prevent a film from being made or released; rather, it used the threats of those possibilities to force the changes required to bring it within the bounds of approved ideology. In *Force of Evil*'s case, that meant conveying the message that however extensive corruption's reach, it is not total, and it will be defeated. *Force of Evil* is indelibly marked by the proscription.

To gain Production Code approval for his script, for example, Polonsky wrote—and at least partly shot—a courtroom scene that was to frame and relate in flashback the film's main narrative action. Surviving production stills from this sequence show Garfield in the witness chair. This image of testimony, however, in the wake of the HUAC hearings and the first wave of blacklisting, was perhaps too prescient for comfort, and Polonsky dropped it. Garfield supplied the required Code ideology in a voice-over commentary, a medium with greater possibility for ambiguity and multiple meanings.

Garfield's character, Joe Morse, once a street kid, has climbed the heights to a Wall Street law partnership through his ties to Tucker, the numbers boss. At Tucker's behest, Morse is planning what the film insists is a normal business move, a takeover of smaller competitors—by criminal means in an illegal business, but *Force of Evil* does not make a fine point of the difference. On July 4, Independence Day, the sentimental "suckers" who bet the numbers are known to favor seven-seven-six. Tucker and Morse will arrange things so that seven-seven-six wins, bankrupting the neighborhood numbers banks and leaving them vulnerable to Tucker's monopoly control.

The scenario is complicated for Morse, however, because his older brother Leo happens to run a small-time numbers shop. Leo had sacrificed his ambitions to help put Joe through law school, and disdains the criminal foundation of Joe's success. Joe, in turn, desperately wants his brother's approval. When the brothers meet we see animation and expression in Garfield's face for the first time. Joe's ill-fated attempt to protect Leo sets in train the events that lead to the older brother's death. Even more explicit than the link between American capitalism and the numbers racket is the analogy of these two brothers with the fratricidal biblical pair Cain and Abel.

As much as any other controversial aspect of the film, the Breen Office was concerned with the possibility that audiences might sympathize with the small, independent, picked-upon Leo. In the Code's terms, he is a lawbreaker no less than the big Tucker syndicate. Could the ideological gatekeeper have been just a tad sensitive to the question of monopoly just then? In the year of *Force of Evil*'s production the Supreme Court decided the *Paramount* case, the Justice Department's suit against the major motion picture companies as violators of the Sherman Antitrust Act. The Court ruled against the movie companies and ordered that their monopoly be broken up by divestment of theater ownership. As an exposé of monopoly practices, was Polonsky's script suggesting the big Hollywood studios were forces of evil? The question was not necessarily resolved when some dialogue was added to show that Leo was no saint, but a long-time petty grafter.

Garfield's Joe uncomfortably straddles the high-rise world of Tucker and Wall Street and the neighborhood world of Leo and his origins. He wears three-piece suits with a watch fob, yet on his desk and elsewhere in his office are statuettes of football running backs and passers. These signifiers of athletic skill serve as references to Garfield's previous starring role in *Body and Soul* and to the power bottled up inside him by the role he has chosen to play as Tucker's man. Where the boxing champion walked out on the fight game's corruption, Joe Morse has been formed by a society seemingly without alternatives to corruption, whether of Tucker's big-time or his brother's penny-ante variety.

Garfield acts this self-imprisonment by carrying almost to an extreme his new imploded, constrained performance style: a kind of body tension as of strength repressed, withheld. Until that first meeting with Leo, when he smiles and enlivens his face, he maintains an immobile expression, hardly moving any part of his face other than his mouth to speak. This was an effective aspect of his new style, but it needed, on the evidence of *Force of Evil*, some energy from other actors to play off against his repression of energy: Lana Turner's sexiness, or Joan Crawford's neurosis, or the superb ensemble playing of Canada Lee, Anne Revere, and others in *Body and Soul*.

This *Force of Evil* lacked. "The people emerged except where I agreed to wrong casting," Polonsky once remarked, but on the whole the major supporting parts—Thomas Gomez as Leo, Roy Roberts as Tucker, the newcomer Beatrice Pearson as Garfield's love interest—do little to complement him or play against his suppressed style.[5] The result is that performance plays a relatively small part in the film's impact. Perhaps Polonsky, hoping to create a truly Marxist film (as opposed to the vaguely ameliorative progressive films he criticized fellow Hollywood leftists for making), had studied too long in the school of Sergei Eisenstein. *Force of Evil* is notable for the literary language of its dialogue, its striking vertical camera work—its visual theme is of movement down, down, down—and occasional *Potemkin*-like montages. Its actors are mostly types: in their company Garfield's performance style lacks force, even if it aptly communicates his character's sense of strength constrained.

It would have been interesting to see those courtroom scenes. Joe Morse's bursting of his bonds is conveyed mostly through voice-over, as Garfield, primarily in long shots, descends the steps to the rocky river's edge beneath the George Washington Bridge to find his brother's body. "I turned back to give myself up to [the district attorney]," are his last voice-over words, "because if a man's life could be lived so long and come out this way—like rubbish—then something was horrible, and had to be ended one way or another, and I decided to help."

The final say is the Production Code's, as Polonsky freely admitted. It insisted that the Law remain outside the film's circles of corruption. "One informs not only to escape punishment and regain acceptance but to share once again in the authority of the state," the director said in 1962. "It is a hard life outside the pale."[6] In 1948 neither Garfield nor Polonsky had yet faced the decision that the fictional Joe Morse, by the authority of the Breen Office, had been forced to make.

■ ■ ■ ■

While *Force of Evil* was still in postproduction, Garfield went before the camera again in director John Huston's first independent film, *We Were Strangers* (1949). This, too, was a political film, and its subject matter made it a great deal more daring for the times than *Force of Evil*, which could be, and was, passed off as a genre work.

We Were Strangers was a film about revolutionary violence to throw off the yoke of political tyranny. The trade paper *Hollywood*

Reporter called it "a shameful handbook of Marxian dialectics" and "the heaviest dose of Red theory ever served to an audience outside the Soviet."[7] Virginia E. Williams of the California Federation of Women's Clubs attacked it as "cleverly disguised propaganda to advance the Communist Party Line."[8] Garfield himself was not the target of this invective, but in those days it was dangerous to be found in the wrong company.

One would not have thought that John Huston in 1948 was anything other than right company. *The Treasure of the Sierra Madre*, released earlier in the year, would win him Academy Awards as director and screenwriter. The Breen Office handled the project with a kind of respect and protection notably lacking in its treatment of *Force of Evil*. There were elements of the political right wing in Hollywood, however, who condemned Huston for his leadership of the Committee for the First Amendment. Huston disparaged *We Were Strangers* and had subsequently little to say about it, but in choosing such an inflammatory subject at that politically inhospitable moment, he was telling his detractors what they could do with their Red-baiting.

The film was drawn from a novel by *New York Daily Mirror* writer Robert Sylvester. That source may well have had something to do with the glowing review of the film in that notoriously reactionary newspaper, as well as the strongly positive line taken by Louella O. Parsons in the Hearst press. When the Communist party newspaper, the *Daily Worker*, weighed in with an attack on the film, it was comparatively easy to line up right-wing praise and left-wing condemnation—as did an officer of the distributing company, Columbia—and answer Virginia Williams's charge.

These were politically confusing times—and *We Were Strangers* was a politically confusing, if not also confused, film. Its subject was the overthrow of Cuban dictator Gerardo Machado y Morales in 1933. To establish the extent of Machado's tyranny, the movie opens with scenes of a supine legislature unanimously declaring public assemblies acts of treason, mounted police clubbing people in the streets, and secret police assassinating a university student. The slain student's sister, China (pronounced "Cheena") Valdez, played by Jennifer Jones, joins a clandestine opposition cell. Its leader turns out to be Garfield's character, Tony Fenner, visiting Cuba from the United States, ostensibly as a talent scout for music acts.

Under Fenner's direction, the group concocts an audacious revolutionary scheme. Near China's house is a cemetery where dignitaries are interred. They identify the family plot of a leading politician. They will dig a tunnel from China's house to the burial ground, plant bombs beneath the family grave site. Confederates will assassinate the politician, and when the president and his cohorts gather for the funeral, blam! The entire regime will be wiped out.

The tunnel digging occupies much of the film. The plotters debate the morality of killing innocent people to achieve their political aims. A young intellectual falters and breaks away, only to be run over and killed by a truck. "Sure the people may rise up and do the job themselves—tomorrow—or next year," Fenner exhorts the others. "We can't depend on that—we can't pull out now." Meanwhile China, maintaining her job as a bank clerk, is oppressed by a brutal secret agent, played with villainous zest by Pedro Armindarez.

When the tunnel is finished and bombs planted, the politician is killed by others as planned. Then, in a shocking reversal for the conspirators, his survivors decide to bury him outside the city. The police close in. With machine guns and dynamite the revolutionaries fight back, and Fenner is fatally wounded. Almost simultaneously "the people" rise up, arm themselves, and topple the regime. Fenner dies minutes before the revolution is achieved.

Jose Yglesias, writing in the *Daily Worker*, objected "to using a putschist bombing as characteristic of the fight for national independence." The Germanic rhetoric seems a little outdated by several generations of national liberation struggles and by films like Gillo Pontecorvo's *The Battle of Algiers* (1966), where bombings of innocent people are depicted as tragic but inevitable aspects of "the fight for national independence." Even *Variety*, on purely dramatic terms, complained that the "Machado overthrow occur[red] without relationship to the film's plot development (and without explanation)." Unlike the revolutionaries in *The Battle of Algiers*, these had no visible links to mass organizations or support; indeed, Fenner's leadership seemed to be directed from abroad. Another of Yglesias's objections was more telling: for its happy ending, *"We Were Strangers* contends that freedom returned to Cuba with Machado's ouster. That was not the case; Wall Street simply commanded with another figurehead." Historical accounts of Cuba's 1933 upheaval support this view. When President Franklin D. Roosevelt took office that year he sent Sumner Welles as his special ambassador to Cuba. Welles's assignment was to protect American investment on the island from the economic programs of Machado's radical opposition; to accomplish that, he had to prevent a seizure of power by "the people" such as the film's ending depicts.

It was Welles who engineered Machado's ouster, according to historians. The United States refused to recognize a revolutionary government and maneuvered into power more "moderate" leadership.

Pontecorvo tried to present precisely the principles of such an intervention in his 1968 film *Quimada!* (also known as *Burn!*), which required another era and another political culture for its making.

As the mysterious American Fenner (it turns out later in the narrative that he is a native Cuban who went with his family to the United States as a child), Garfield in Huston's treatment was almost as shadowy as his character. In scene after scene the actor is barely lighted, with his face in half- and sometimes full shadow. Grime covers his face and clothes from the interminable tunnel-digging. A late-blooming romance with Jennifer Jones's China, and the final shoot-out, do not basically alter a solemn and reserved performance, that is literally as well as figuratively cast into the background by Almindarez's bravura bad guy. *We Were Strangers* marks only a minor note in Garfield's career (and perhaps also in its director's), but it deserves to be better known than it is—if for nothing more than its early place in Hollywood's expanding subgenre of films about Americans in Third World revolutions.

Neither *Force of Evil* nor *We Were Strangers*, as it happened, gave Garfield much opportunity to develop his perspective on the performance issues that were engaging the New York theater world. It was not necessarily that movies were an unsuitable medium for the strongly psychological basis of the Method acting style: Montgomery Clift, who along with Brando had been one of the original students at the Actors Studio, had given a controlled, subtle, and sexually ambiguous performance as John Wayne's adopted son in the 1948 Howard Hawks film *Red River*—and had made a memorable film debut earlier in 1948 in *The Search*, for which he received an Oscar nomination in the actor category (going one better than Garfield, who was nominated as supporting actor for his first film).

Garfield could act with the same kind of restraint as the new breed of Method actor like Clift or Brando, but his performances seemed to lack the psychological dimension—the sense that what was being communicated through repression was a complex inner life. What Garfield signaled through suppression was his energy and power, smoldering under wraps, ready to burst forth.

The possibility that something more complex may have been contained in his performance as Joe Morse in *Force of Evil* was unintentionally undercut by Polonsky's decision to add the voice-over: rather than gesture, or facial expression, or dialogue intonation, offscreen words defined the character. Talk—loud, fast talk—had always been the hallmark of Garfield's performance style. He could not compete with the young Method performers in conveying the state of a psyche in quieter, less demonstrable ways.

Still, his desire to develop as an actor was one of the reasons he returned to New York after *We Were Strangers* and accepted the leading role in Clifford Odets's new play *The Big Knife*. There were also a number of other reasons: It was Odets's first theater production in more than seven years; like Garfield, both his style and status were being challenged by younger men, in his case the playwrights Arthur Miller and Tennessee Williams. It was a play about a Hollywood actor, and while it may not necessarily have been written either *about* Garfield or with him in mind for the lead, under the circumstances it was inevitable that that would be suggested (though most reviewers saw the protagonist more as a stand-in for Odets himself). It was a chance for Garfield to work with an old friend on a project that could not but be more satisfying than their last theatrical experience together, *Golden Boy*, when Garfield was denied the leading part Odets had written specifically for him.

With all these inescapable reasons for leaping with gusto into the role of Charlie Castle in *The Big Knife*, from a tactical viewpoint it was among the worst decisions Garfield could have made in the prevailing political climate. Whatever the political problems with *Force of Evil* and *We Were Strangers*, they were Hollywood establishment products—major studios, the Breen Office, and, for the latter at least, influential figures in the press stood behind them. *The Big Knife* could not be understood other than as a full-scale attack on Hollywood. One could be sure that the Hollywood establishment would not take kindly to it. Odets was grimly burning his bridges to the movie community; Garfield could not afford to turn it against him—for the sake of Roberts Productions (for which he was then the only asset) or for whatever support it might tender him against the encroaching Thought Police.

Few who wrote about the play on either coast were inclined to accept Odets's castigation of the motion picture industry without qualm. Most of them criticized the playwright, but one important voice put the blame on Garfield: Hedda Hopper, the *Los Angeles Times* syndicated Hollywood columnist, whose right-wing views placed her in an increasingly powerful position during the era of repression. Odets had written into the play a prying gossip columnist who clearly resembled Hopper. She got even by attacking not the repatriated writer but someone her words could still palpably damage: "*The Big Knife*, Clifford Odets' play which pokes fun at Hollywood, with John Garfield starred, didn't get cheers when it opened out of town," she wrote. "Serves Garfield right. This town was very good to him, and since this is the way he shows his gratitude, perhaps he deserves a failure."[9] Hopper's readers could sense a more ominous resonance in these words than might be apparent several decades later.

The Big Knife got few cheers but was not exactly a failure either. Opening at the National Theater on February 24, 1949, with Lee Strasberg as director, it ran 108 performances until it closed after Garfield decided to leave the cast in May. It was a melodrama about a movie actor who had to decide between a fourteen-year, multimillion-dollar studio contract—and saving his soul. The extratextual problem lay in the premise: contracts for more than seven years were illegal in California (as Olivia de Havilland's suit against Warner Bros. had definitively proved), and in 1949 the studios anyway were facing far too much economic uncertainty to be making long-term commitments. Perhaps the contract was not meant to be taken literally: it was just a metaphor for selling out.

The textual problem was that there was not really a decision to make—nor a soul to lose. The studio knew it had Charlie over a barrel because he had drunkenly run over a child and let his publicity man take the rap and go to jail. Charlie signs the contract early, then agonizes while the studio bosses plot to murder the floozie who was in the car and could tell the truth about their long-term property. At his moral nadir, Charlie slits his wrists in the bathtub. It makes one feel like the Milwaukee women's group who wrote to protest Joan Crawford's suicide in *Humoresque* (another script in which Odets had a hand), suggesting there must be some more constructive solution. Charlie could have started an Actors Studio in San Quentin.

There does not seem to be much of Garfield in Charlie Castle, other than that both men changed their last names. Garfield refused to renew his Warner Bros. contract, set up his own independent company, made room in his career for the stage and developing his craft. If Garfield sold his soul, it was in going to Hollywood in the first place—indeed, this might be Odets's point, not only about the actor but also about himself and all the other Group Theatre members who went west. That would make it harder, however, for Hollywood to stand in (as Odets sometimes suggested) for Anytown, U.S.A., where all bosses are scheming and all men sell out their dreams. Sharing the Broadway stage that year with Willy Loman in Arthur Miller's *Death of a Salesman*, Charlie Castle was the one who did not enter the American vernacular.

With a new Odets play to whet their critical appetites, reviewers found little space to comment on Garfield's acting. "John Garfield gives an interestingly moody performance that can be tremendously powerful at the crucial moment," Brooks Atkinson wrote in the *New York Times*. "John Garfield plays the actor with his characteristic forthrightness, candor, and attractive earnestness," said Richard Watts, Jr., in the *New York Post*. These were as descriptive as any of the reviewers got. Was this a new Garfield, coming closer to The Method under Strasberg's direction, or the outgoing, talkative, transparent familiar one? Whichever, Howard Barnes in the *New York Herald-Tribune* gave the opinion that "the actor has never been finer as the ill-fated screen idol of the work."

Garfield left the play with two separate movie deals in the works. One was at Twentieth Century–Fox, the other at Warner Bros., where Bob Roberts was trying to negotiate a multipicture contract. Both projects, curiously, involved adaptations from Ernest Hemingway—at Fox it was a script based on the short story "My Old Man," at Warners it was the novel *To Have and Have Not*, which had lent little more than its title to Howard Hawks's 1945 Bogart-Bacall film. Fox had its script ready first, and *Under My Skin* (1950) went into production in late summer 1949. Warners spent the rest of the year kicking names around for the Harry Morgan part—Burt Lancaster, John Wayne, Kirk Douglas, and even Cagney were suggested—but ultimately waited for Garfield (and a revised script) and shot *The Breaking Point* (1950) the following spring.

During June 1949—when Garfield was probably already on a European holiday—his name appeared on front pages across the country in connection with a Soviet espionage case. A former Justice Department employee, Judith Coplon, was being tried for giving secret United States documents to the Russians: one of several 1949 events, along with the Alger Hiss perjury trial and revelation of the Soviet atomic bomb, that fueled American hysteria over internal subversion and shaped social and political life at mid-century. One of the documents referred to in the case was an FBI memorandum concerning communism in Hollywood, and the defense read it into the record over government objections.

The document named more than a dozen prominent Hollywood figures who had been identified as Communists or supportive of Communist causes by the Bureau's movie industry informants (among whom, though not necessarily in this instance, was Ronald Reagan). Several were from the Hollywood Ten group who had testified before HUAC in 1947 and were soon to go to prison for contempt of Congress for refusing on First Amendment grounds to answer questions about their political affiliations. Some of the names, like that of actor Fredric March, had come up as early as the 1940 Dies Committee hearings, when Cagney and Bogart had also been involved. By 1949, however, Cagney and Bogart had made their separate peace with the right.

Garfield's name was listed along with performers Edward G. Robinson, Sylvia Sidney, Paul Muni, and Melvyn Douglas, and writers Dorothy Parker, Donald Ogden Stewart, and Ruth McKinney. Although nothing untoward happened to Garfield because of this specific incident—both film assignments eventually went forward—it put him and the others on notice. The Bureau was not yet satisfied that the contempt citations, and the blacklist that followed, had brought about the ideological purge of Hollywood it desired.

Under My Skin began shooting in September 1949. Two other former Warner Bros. colleagues were prominently involved: producer and screenwriter Casey Robinson and director Jean Negulesco, who had also worked with Garfield on *Nobody Lives Forever* and *Humoresque*. The film basically followed the Hemingway story line, with the significant addition of a love interest, and the elimination of the boy's first-person narration. Garfield plays an American steeplechase jockey who rides the Italian and French tracks—a hero to his son, though a bum in the world's eyes—who is paid to throw races and then rides to win. Beaten up by the crooks he doublecrosses, he is fatally injured in a racetrack accident, leaving the son in the presumably more capable hands of the girlfriend. The movie was a desultory effort—the short story was also not among Hemingway's best—marked by a reversion on Garfield's part to some Burbank B-picture habits. He sneers a lot, looks cynical, and continually juts out his lower lip. "In a portrayal that is all mannerism and no meat," *Time* magazine wrote, not unfairly, "actor Garfield summons up neither the appeal of a hero nor the fascination of a heel."

The Breaking Point promised to be a different matter. Garfield had a friend and supporter in producer Jerry Wald, and director Michael Curtiz had launched him in *Four Daughters* and drawn distinctive performances from him in *Daughters Courageous* and *The Sea Wolf*. Warner Bros. paid him $175,000 for the role, indicating the value the studio placed on the film and his participation. Curtiz involved the actor in early discussions about script development and characterization, prompting a three-page letter in which Garfield detailed his ideas.

The project emerged as a realistic treatment of Hemingway's novel, updated to the postwar period and relocated to the West Coast. Different from Hawks's romantic version, Harry is a married man and a father; though pursued by other women, he is still faithful to and in love with his wife. He has a black man for a sidekick. An ex-GI with a failed fishing business in Newport Beach, he gets in trouble taking on shady jobs trying to make ends meet. It is as if someone (perhaps Wald, in collaboration with screenwriter Ronald

MacDougall) wanted to assert that it was still possible in the Hollywood of 1950—despite the repression—to make something that approximated a serious, socially relevant film.

The movie draws on the major Harry Morgan episodes of the novel: the sport fisherman who stiffs him; smuggling the Chinese, and Harry's shooting the smuggler; transporting the bank robbers, when the black mate is killed. When the navy impounds his boat after the smuggling incident, Harry's wife (played by Phyllis Thaxter) berates him: "Don't give me that Purple Heart routine. You've got a wife and two kids to think about—keeping us together, getting us enough to eat, clothes for our backs. That's the biggest war there is and you'd better realize it."

Hemingway himself was rarely quite so socially relevant. Hawks, who admired the novelist but not the novel, may have been more practical when he gutted the work and turned it into romantic comedy—though he at least had an actual war for melodramatic background. *The Breaking Point* was a sincere effort that seemed to have no spark. Unlike the novel, the film ends with Harry surviving, going to the hospital to have his left arm amputated; the black man's son is left alone on the dock, pathetically looking for his dead father. Garfield plays Harry as desperate and angry, and what *Time* said about his performance in *Under My Skin* might serve for *The Breaking Point* as well. There were some respectful reviews, but the film made little impact.

Less than a month after *The Breaking Point* finished shooting, the Korean War broke out. The United States, under United Nations auspices, went to war against a Communist country for the first time in the cold war era. In an atmosphere of ever-more-fervid anti-communism, the Hollywood right, collaborating with the FBI, saw an opportunity to expand the purge of leftists and liberals begun in 1947. At the first HUAC hearings nineteen "unfriendly" witnesses had been subpoenaed, and only eleven called to testify. Some right-wing groups had drawn up lists of alleged Hollywood Reds and sympathizers with more than two hundred names.

Several people from these lists voluntarily approached the FBI or HUAC to recant and cooperate, or seek official clearance so their careers would not be jeopardized by innuendo. By the end of 1950 it had become clear that the HUAC hearings would resume, if nothing else as a court of contrition, where those condemned by the forces of history could expiate fifteen years of political activism and perhaps deflect the tide. Garfield could well predict, as one of the most prominent names on the lists, that he would be among the first to be called. After completing *The Breaking Point*, he reactivated Roberts

Productions—while it was uncertain that a studio would hire him, United Artists (whose eagerness for product perhaps overcame its fears) still put money behind him. Roberts purchased rights to a 1947 novel, *He Ran All the Way*, by Sam Ross, and—no party to the blacklist—hired the well-known leftist writers Hugo Butler and Guy Endore to prepare the screenplay. Another radical, John Berry, was selected to direct.

Production of *He Ran All the Way* (1951) took place in fall 1950, but release was delayed until the following June—according to *Life* magazine, because exhibitors refused to consider it until after Garfield's HUAC testimony. As it was, Berry's and Butler's names had to be removed from the promotional and advertising material because, along with seven others, they had defied HUAC, refused to honor their subpoenas, and gone "underground"—Butler eventually to exile in Mexico, Berry to France.

Life praised *He Ran All the Way* by calling it "a simple, old-fashioned tale of violence told in the simple old way." The magazine ridiculed the boycotters by suggesting, "It is about as subversive as a Roy Rogers western." That is praise to be taken circumspectly. Where nearly all of Garfield's recent projects had represented some facet of postwar progressivism or liberalism (*Under My Skin* was the only one without apparent social perspective), *He Ran All the Way* was a film in retreat, a work that voiced the emerging ideology of the conservative 1950s.

Garfield plays a troubled young punk with an alcoholic, abusive mother. He participates in a payroll holdup and fatally shoots a policeman. On the lam, he meets a young woman at a public swimming pool, escorts her home, and is attracted to her working-class family as a refuge both emotional and tactical. He holds them hostage, and the film's theme becomes the question of patriarchal authority in defense of the family. The girl's father (played by William Ford), a press operator, is first shown at work wearing an apron. Is he man enough to protect his family from lawless violence? The daughter, portrayed by Shelley Winters, is attracted to the punk. He gives her money to buy a getaway car, but in the final scene, when the car has not shown up, he turns on her, and she shoots him. The car belatedly arrives as he dies in the gutter: the camera pulls back to show father hugging daughter. Only the difference in the family's social class separates this film from mid-1950s suburban melodramas like *Rebel without a Cause* and *The Desperate Hours* (both 1955). In comparison to 1930s crime films, *He Ran All the Way* lacks a sense of social context. Perhaps Garfield and his embattled colleagues saw that their only chance of getting into theaters was to take on the coloration of the emerging ethos. The best part of the film is James Wong Howe's cinematography—a dazzling array of moving camera shots, low angles, and tight close-ups.

What else was available to Garfield was the kind of *pro bono* stage work he had done previously for the American National Theatre and Academy. At the end of 1950 he began rehearsing the title role in an ANTA production of Paul Green's American version of Ibsen's *Peer Gynt*, with Lee Strasberg again as director. The production opened at the ANTA Theatre on January 28, 1951, and ran for thirty-two performances. While there were some positive reviews, enough criticism came from those who usually praised him to suggest that he was unsuited for Ibsen's buoyant amoralist. "Mr. Garfield is an admirable and likeable realistic actor," Brooks Atkinson put it magnanimously in the *New York Times*. "He has a magnetic personality and a warm voice; and he is winningly sincere. But he never gets *Peer Gynt* off the ground. His performance is literal and casual, and is completely lacking in poetic animation."

His spirits were likely too heavy to get anything off the ground. His subpoena arrived March 6, 1951, just after *Peer Gynt* closed. By that time he had already engaged the famous New York attorney Louis Nizer, whose firm also represented Paramount Pictures. Their strategy was to research thoroughly the actor's prior political affiliations—to prepare to be forthcoming but to admit no wrongdoing. He issued a statement to the press: "I have always hated communism. It is a tyranny which threatens our country and the peace of the world. Of course then, I have never been a member of the Communist party or a sympathizer with any of its doctrines. I will be pleased to cooperate with the committee."[10] This approach pleased neither left nor right. The *People's Daily World* attacked him; so did right-wing columnist Victor Riesel, at a rally of the Motion Picture Alliance for the Preservation of American Ideals. It seemed clear that it would fare little better with HUAC. What the committee sought became apparent on March 21, when actor Larry Parks admitted that he had been a member of the Communist party—the first Hollywood witness before it to do so.

Parks was then invited to partake of the ritual that would be required of all who had condemned themselves: condemning others. Parks's wan protests were taken as a sign of his incomplete repentance. Finally he named seven performers as members of his party cell. Then he was asked about his knowledge of the Communist activities of several dozen other people—Garfield, Cagney, and Bogart among them. He denied any knowledge. It is interesting that Congressman Francis C. Walter then assured the witness that all the individuals mentioned had already been issued subpoenas. If this was the case, neither Cagney nor Bogart was among the nearly one hundred witnesses called during the following year.

Garfield's testimony was scheduled for April 23: the eighth day of hearings, the eighteenth witness to be heard. (He had been interviewed earlier by two committee investigators.) Press photographs of the actor, without makeup at the witness table, show a tired, puffy face with circles under the eyes, looking older than his thirty-eight years. Committee counsel Frank S. Tavenner, Jr., questioned him about his press statement, and he reiterated all three parts: that he abhorred communism; that he had never been a party member; that he was willing to answer any question about his experiences and affiliations. Then their duel began.

The committee's strategy was to break down Garfield's opening position by methodically going over his participation in what they considered Communist or Communist-front organizations: a lengthy record of involvement would render meaningless his disavowal, would make his political history appear identical to that of a Communist, whatever the technicality of party membership. Garfield's counterstrategy was to deny when he could, to fail to remember when he could not deny, and to take the offensive in asserting his own liberal Democratic viewpoint.

Communists, Garfield avowed, "never did trust me. I was a liberal, and I don't think the Communists like liberals, and I was quite outspoken about my liberalism."[11] He brought minutes of Screen Actors Guild meetings, from his tenure on its executive board, to demonstrate his opposition to the postwar movie industry strikes (which the committee and the Hollywood right believed were led by Communists) and told a little anecdote about running into Ronald Reagan at a meeting of actors against the strike. He called for the outlawing of the Communist party so people would not be confused by seeing it on election ballots.

Garfield's tactic was a novel approach to the problem of testifying before HUAC. Previous witnesses had been abjectly compliant—or, one might say, abjectly defiant, availing themselves of the Fifth Amendment privilege against self-incrimination and refusing to answer questions concerning their political affiliations. Abjection had been the committee's aim, and had one way or another been obtained. (It was more than a year later when Lillian Hellman issued her famous declaration, "I will not cut my conscience to fit this year's fashion"—but that had come in a letter to the committee, and in her public testimony she was forced to take the Fifth.)[12]

Garfield tried to be neither compliant nor defiant, and above all he was not abject. He was disingenuous, to be sure, and one might say gutless or soulless in his eagerness to turn Communists into criminals—even if you take into consideration the era and the number of distinguished people who propagated the same view. His goal was to avoid the blacklist and continue his movie career without suffering the ritual of informing on others (assuming he had names to name). He impressed several committee members and outraged others.

Republican Donald L. Jackson of California, whose western Los Angeles district embraced parts of the movie colony, was particularly incensed. He expressed skepticism about the accuracy and cooperativeness of Garfield's testimony, and incredulity at the actor's claim that he did not personally know anyone in New York or Hollywood who was a member of the Communist party. When Garfield volunteered the information that the *Daily Worker* had panned his performance in *Skipper Next To God,* Jackson cuttingly remarked that the committee shared its opinion.

It was inevitable that Jackson's view would carry the day. At the moment of its greatest power, HUAC was not about to allow its purposes to be stymied by the most clever of lawyers or witnesses. The committee announced that it was sending Garfield's testimony to the FBI to check against its own voluminous documentation on the actor to see if there were grounds for charging him with perjury. This information, when it appeared in *Variety*, put him in a kind of limbo with other liberal movie workers, less publicized than he was, who were finding it difficult to get work because they were on right-wing lists of participants in Communist-front activities.

In late May the committee's request—via the Justice Department's Criminal Division—arrived at the Bureau. The FBI already knew that Garfield was not a Communist; there is evidence in the Bureau's files (obtained through the Freedom of Information Act) to suggest that if a solid case could have been built against him, Garfield would have been subpoenaed as an "unfriendly" witness at the 1947 hearings. (A chilling document from that era, dated February 8, 1952, discusses "the Security Index File of individuals to be apprehended and detained in connection with the Detention of Communists Program"—bureaucratically known as DETCOM; Garfield is listed in a special section of "Prominent Individuals" who were "not [to] be apprehended immediately upon placing the DETCOM Program in effect.")[13]

Still, the possibility of putting Garfield behind bars for perjury seemed a worthwhile consolation for not being able to prove him a Communist. The FBI—enlisting the aid of intelligence branches of the army and navy—began an "intense investigation" to substantiate that Garfield had lied to the committee when he had denied having taken part in certain activities about which he was questioned.[14]

In the meanwhile, Garfield tried to behave as if he had a career to conduct. He had bought the rights to Nelson Algren's novel *The Man with the Golden Arm*, and announced his intention to make it as a Robert Productions film—a singularly impractical choice, for even if a bank were willing to finance Garfield, none would put up money for a film about heroin addiction that would surely be denied Production Code approval. (When Otto Preminger made the film in 1955 he had already, with *The Moon Is Blue* [1953], broken the taboo against releasing a film without a Production Code seal, and learned that notoriety generates box office success.) Meanwhile, in late 1951 the Bank of America took possession of an estimated $25 million worth of Enterprise releases, including *Body and Soul* and *Force of Evil*, because of loan defaults.

Then there was the possibility of devoting himself to the theater, even if that meant a diminution of his lifestyle. ANTA proposed a revival of Odets's *Golden Boy*, with Garfield playing Joe Bonaparte, the role that Harold Clurman had denied him in the original 1937 Group Theatre production. (That the hurt never left him was poignantly made clear when he tried to tell HUAC about it; Counsel Tavenner cut him off, saying he was not interested in a "personal story.")[15]

Golden Boy, directed by the playwright, opened at the ANTA Theatre on March 12, 1952. Clurman continued to maintain that "[Garfield] wasn't really a tragic actor . . . he didn't have the inner torment for Joe Bonaparte," but whatever was the case for the 24-year-old in 1937 could no longer be said of the tormented man of 1952.[16] "This strikes me as one of the finest performances that I have ever seen Mr. Garfield give," Richard Watts, Jr., wrote in the *New York Post*, "and it serves to remind us once more that, provided with the proper sort of role, he is one of the most brilliant and satisfying of American actors."

Golden Boy played fifty-five performances—its original limited run was extended from four weeks to seven—but the production's success was overshadowed by torment, both outer and inner. Elia Kazan had appeared before HUAC in executive session in January 1952 and detailed his own Communist party membership in the 1930s, but he had refused to name others (testimony the committee never made public); on April 10 he returned to submit to the ritual, again in executive session, but this time released to the press. He named the other members of his party unit at the Group Theatre, including Art Smith and Tony Kraber, who were performing in the *Golden Boy* revival, and the playwright Odets.

Odets himself appeared in executive session on April 24 and on

May 19 and 20 at HUAC public sessions. He named some of the
same names, but when asked by Tavenner if he ever knew Garfield
to be a member of the Communist party, he answered, "No, sir."[17]
This was an unkind cut by Counsel Tavenner. So many names had
been named by that point that if Garfield had been lying about Communist party membership it would have come out already. Tavenner
also surely knew something else: Garfield had indicated his readi-
ness to repent his previous testimony. Perhaps the counsel was
merely signaling to the actor the committee's implacable enmity to
anyone who dared think he could outsmart it.

By late winter 1952 Garfield no longer thought he could outsmart
anyone. It would soon be revealed—or at least asserted—that the
actor had taken a number of steps to put himself right with the right.
He was said to have visited the FBI several times and was preparing
to appear again before HUAC. He was said to have contacted Arnold
Forster of the B'nai B'rith Anti-Defamation League, who had served
as a "clearance" liaison for Jewish individuals on the right-wing
lists, and with Forster's help had drafted a *mea culpa* to be published
in *Look* magazine, entitled, "I Was a Sucker for a Left Hook." He was
said to have called Victor Riesel, the columnist who had reviled him
at a Hollywood right-wing rally, and confessed how he and "other
emotional and sentimental actors who sought to become crusaders"
had been captured by the Communists.[18]

All these revelations were delivered secondhand, because the
actor was no longer able to speak in his own "warm voice." On the
night of May 20–21, 1952—the very night after Tavenner again
raised the issue of his possible Communist party affiliation—
Garfield died of a heart attack in the apartment of a woman friend at
3 Gramercy Park in New York. He was nine weeks past his thirty-
ninth birthday. The inevitable rumors circulated as to the circumstances of his death. Officially, he had fallen ill after dining at Lu-
chow's and had lain down in his underwear on the friend's bed,
where she found him dead the following morning.

The right, as noted above, made an immediate effort to claim him,
as it were, as a deathbed convert. The left added him to its list of
repression's victims: Canada Lee, from *Body and Soul*; J. Arthur
Bromberg, from the old Group Theatre and the cast of *The Big Knife*;
and Mady Christians, all dead prematurely from diseases of the
heart. At his funeral at Riverside Chapel more than ten thousand
people jammed the streets, most of them adult women who were
paying homage, along with all else, to the Mickey Borden of *Four
Daughters* with whom the Depression generation of urban adolescent girls had fallen in love.

Garfield's last image on film, in *He Ran All the Way*, was as an outlaw dying in the gutter. "He defended his streetboy's honor and they killed him for it," Polonsky later said: of the man, not the film character.[19] The circumstances of his death and the aura of his screen persona combined to fix an impression of Garfield for history: the man-child from the teeming streets, the "natural" who put his soul on the screen and gave his heart to ideology, and ultimately to the inquisition. It is true that he played roles younger than his age: his screen characters were almost invariably in their twenties, and in the one movie where necessarily he was a more mature man, *Force of Evil*, he appears youthful in part because he plays a younger brother. Callow as he may have appeared on the screen, however, or to his intellectual colleagues, Garfield was not simply a waif amid the forces.

He was first of all an actor. Whatever his limitations—and the costs of having given his best years to Hollywood as younger men like Brando and Clift surpassed him in the postwar years—he sought continually to improve himself and rise above the system. A Hollywood career, however the industry romanticized it then or we do now, required skills in planning and management as much as any other. The roster of those who did not manage (or were not managed) well would be a long one, and Garfield was on that list for a long time. He took the risk of doing something about it: Roberts Productions was one of the few independent companies in the 1940s built around a performer, and the accomplishment of producing *Body and Soul* and *Force of Evil* should not be minimized. Those films gathered together some of the most important talent from the Hollywood left, and stand among the more significant efforts in Hollywood history to put liberal and progressive perspectives on the screen.

That achievement suggests another way of looking at Garfield's screen persona: it was not that of a waif, but of a political person. His young men, at their best, yearned for a society commensurate with, and open to, their own aspirations. They were not always equal to the task, and the ideological framework of his films often deflected or absorbed the political import of his characterizations; but he struggled to create the conditions in which his views would be unfettered, and he has a greater claim than most Hollywood performers to have succeeded.

The limitations of his screen persona, however, also applied to his role as a political person, in and outside Hollywood. His brief success as a Hollywood independent could not be translated into a stance in the wider world, where neither the government nor the

Communist party tolerated anyone who accepted no allegiance. If he had actually joined the Communist party, both the government and his allies would have offered him formulas within which many played out the political dramas of the cold war years; but screen formulas had undermined a career of striking promise, and Garfield was determined to live and die without them, even if he did not know what might take their place.

11

He Didn't Stand Still

Unlike John Garfield, Humphrey Bogart got rid of the Communist fleas "H." of the FBI had found on him. That might not have been so simple a task as, from a later vantage point, one might imagine. Bogart had belonged to some of the same committees as Garfield, including the Committee for the First Amendment that had criticized HUAC. His name was also linked to progressive organizations retrospectively condemned as Communist fronts. During the war he had appeared in films written by members of the Hollywood Ten—even his legendary screen character, Rick Blaine of Casablanca's Cafe Americain, when his past is sufficiently scrutinized, turns out a Communist. The circumstantial evidence in Bogart's case was ample enough for HUAC to have destroyed his career, had it chosen to, as effectively as it did Garfield's and many others'.

Bogart's survival is simple to explain: he put on the flea collar early, when it was still easy to obtain and relatively painless. All it took was an FBI clearance and a disavowal of communism in *Photoplay* magazine. Whatever abasement it entailed involved only himself—not, as it soon after would become, the fingering of others. One could say he was a coward for the actions he took to protect himself, but he was surely no coward for the actions he took that put him in jeopardy: when he and Lauren Bacall joined the First Amendment group's protest flight to Washington they were not so naive as to be unaware that every camera would be focused on them, leading no doubt many others besides Sterling Hayden to imagine them as prime instigators.

The 1947 hearings and the trip to Washington came at precisely the moment when Bogart was fulfilling his primary goal following his new Warner Bros. contract, signed the previous December: setting up his own independent company to produce the annual outside picture the contract permitted. It is easy to imagine (and rumors circulated about the situation) that the financing of this project was held in abeyance until Bogart's political views were certified as satis-factory. His company had in fact acquired its first story property in September 1947, just before the hearings, but at least two distribu-tion deals fell through before it got off the ground nearly a year later—after the *Photoplay* article had appeared.

There was a further complication in Bogart's professional life that did not stem from politics, but clearly had—in the broader sense of the term—ideological implications. This was the issue of age. Bo-gart, like many of the experienced stage actors who entered film work after sound came in, was in his late forties. How much longer would audiences tolerate his screen persona as a romantic hero? It was a question to which the sociology of American filmmaking and moviegoing had not yet provided an answer.

Warner Bros. had recently allowed Edward G. Robinson's contract to lapse when the actor was around fifty years of age. Robinson had staged another of his comebacks by starring in two independent Fritz Lang films, *The Woman in the Window* (1944) and *Scarlet Street* (1945), as older men whose desires for younger women precipitate tragedy. In *Double Indemnity* (1944) and *The Stranger* (1946) Robin-son had played avuncular older men in struggle with younger roman-tic villains, respectively, Fred MacMurray and Orson Welles. It was not clear, however, that Jack Warner had committed himself to the tune of $200,000 a picture for the man who played Spade, Marlowe, or Rick to become a paternal figure or a tragic one.

The Treasure of the Sierra Madre, the first picture under the new contract, had produced a surprise aberrant performance by Bogart as the demented Fred C. Dobbs, but that deviance had been well recom-pensed by the film's critical triumph and box office success. There was little chance the studio would resurrect Dobbsie and turn him into a formula. It had more than enough formulas for Bogart already at its disposal, and most of them went into *Key Largo* (1948). In this film, Bogart plays a returning World War II veteran who stops off at a hotel in the Florida Keys and encounters romance and the neces-sity to fight evil. The romance was once again with offscreen wife Bacall. The evil was provided by the aforementioned Robinson; while Bogart plays the younger man, unlike MacMurray and Welles, he is not the villain.

The film was drawn from Maxwell Anderson's prewar play about a disillusioned Spanish Civil War veteran learning once again of the need to fight; the liberal filmmakers (producer Jerry Wald and direc-tor John Huston, with a script by Huston and newcomer Richard Brooks) tried to update the play's message, even though after Octo-ber 1947 Bogart was unlikely ever again to play a veteran of the Abra-ham Lincoln Brigade. Robinson's Johnny Rocco is a Prohibition-era gangster who had been deported ("Like I was a dirty Red or something") but has returned with counterfeit money and great hopes of getting the mobs together again. What has to be fought is the possibility that post–World War II America will repeat the mistakes of the post–World War I period and allow crime and corruption to thrive; what has to be kindled is the civic spirit of the drifting war veteran, who echoes the initial pose of *Casablanca's* Rick, saying, "I fight nobody's battles but my own."

Of course he does fight the good fight—"Your head said one way, your whole life said another," the woman tells him after his first brave deed. He kills Rocco and his four henchmen aboard a boat, in a scene reminiscent of Hemingway's *To Have and Have Not*, if not Hawks's. However imitative of his Rick Blaine and his Harry Morgan, when the film was finished Bogart's character still seemed a shadow of these former selves. Jack Warner called for additional material "to strengthen Bogart's characterization in the film and give a better understanding to his ways of thinking."[1]

Three more shooting days were given over to added scenes and retakes to build up Bogart's part, but in the end we still do not quite know why he initially holds back—probably from neither cowardice nor conviction, but from a sense of tactics. Bogart's performance is rather subdued, and he appears in far fewer shots than had been the case in most of his starring vehicles. He seems unable to give much personality to a poorly conceived character—although Huston once told a reporter that a key scene motivating the veteran's "non-resistance credo" had been cut by the studio.[2]

Huston just as likely found it difficult to bring to life a character who lacked elements of evil. Bogart's earlier performances for the director—as Spade, as the army undercover man in *Across the Pacific*, and as Dobbsie—had possessed in different degrees the combination of "acid and comedy" that had made the actor a star. His *Key Largo* character had neither. The film belonged to Robinson for his tour-de-force gangster, memorably introduced in his bath with a cigar and a drink, and made larger than life by cinematographer Karl Freund with low angles and tight close-ups. Claire Trevor won the supporting actress Academy Award for her performance as Rocco's "faded, hard-drinking gunmoll."

■ ■ ■ ■

Though the moment had arrived for Bogart to take a decisive role in shaping his own screen characterization, his efforts to set up a production company continued to suffer temporary setbacks. The threat to the company's financial backing engendered by his political activism had been overcome by his series of ideological autocritiques. Then in December 1947 occurred the sudden death of Mark Hellinger, the former Warner Bros. writer and producer who was Bogart's principal business partner. Within several months the legal problems connected with Hellinger's holdings were resolved, and Bogart's company, Santana Productions, was ready to go forward with Bogart's business manager, A. Morgan Maree, and another former Warner Bros. producer, Robert Lord, in the front office roles.

Their first project was based on the property Hellinger had acquired in September 1947, Willard Motley's controversial novel about juvenile crime, *Knock on Any Door*. The Production Code Administration had found the novel offensive to Code principles and tried to discourage companies from going forward with it. The combination of Bogart's political entanglement and Breen Office disapproval scared David O. Selznick and Samuel Goldwyn away from involvement with Santana, but Harry Cohn of Columbia Pictures took it on, and the film began shooting in August 1948, with Lord producing and Nicholas Ray as director.

Knock on Any Door (1949) was a curious choice for Bogart's first independent project. The novel's notoriety certainly guaranteed the film initial box office interest, but the focus inevitably was on the juvenile—the young tough who wants to "live fast, die young, and have a good-looking corpse," played by John Derek in his film debut. The choice of Hollywood newcomer Nicholas Ray to direct only heightened this emphasis. When Santana signed him, Ray's first two films for RKO had not yet been released, though *They Live by Night* (1948) had been screened for the trades and had made an impression for its sensitive treatment of Farley Granger and Cathy O'Donnell as the doomed young outlaw lovers. Given the PCA's concern, Bogart and Lord may have sought a director who could handle young performers, figuring the star could take care of himself.

Knock on Any Door turned out much that way. In terms of narrative and screen time, Bogart's part dominated, and contained considerably more breadth than his *Key Largo* role. He plays an attorney who rose from the slums to work for a leading law firm, but defies the firm and loses a partnership when he takes on the defense of "Pretty Boy" Nick Romano, accused of a holdup murder. The film alternates between scenes of Nick's trial and flashbacks showing both the lawyer's struggle to escape the urban jungle and the circumstances that trap his client in a cycle of poverty and crime. In his summation the lawyer asserts that society is guilty for the young hood's crimes; but the jury finds him guilty, and the film ends with a shot of Nick combing his hair as he enters the death chamber.

Knock on Any Door marks a return to the environmentalist view-point favored by late 1930s social problem films like *Dead End*; similarly, Bogart's performance style also reverts to atavistic man-nerisms. He rubs his thumb under his lower lip, bares his upper teeth, pulls his jacket back, and places his hands on his belt. The characterization was not without possibility—a mature man of sub-stance, capable of physical action reminiscent of his own street boy days—but somehow neither the actor nor the director was capable of raising it above conventionality. *Knock on Any Door* aroused con-temporary interest as a message picture, but when its notoriety faded there was little in it to hold posterity's attention, least of all the star's first performance for himself.

With his own company launched, further properties in the pipe-line, and a contractual commitment to Warner Bros. of great length but indeterminate intensity, Bogart found himself working more steadily than he had over the previous half-dozen years. The ques-tion was, besides making money, to what end? When Cagney fought with Warner Bros. and formed his own company, he had a specific quarrel with the studio's conception of his screen persona and a defi-nite idea of how he wanted to transform it. When Garfield refused Warner Bros.' renewal offer and set out on his own, he sought control over his screen characterizations. Bogart's halfway position on the issue of autonomy seemed consistent with his incapacity clearly to conceive the direction in which he should go.

Nevertheless, in 1949 he made three pictures, his most in any year since 1943. The reviews of the first of these, *Tokyo Joe*, a Santana production shot in January and February, laid out his problem bluntly. "The picture is not saved," said *Time*'s critic, "by the pres-ence in the Bogart role of a tired, beat-up looking actor who no longer seems to project the hard combustibility that he made famous." Bo-gart, wrote *Cue*'s reviewer, "is getting to be a bit mature for these impetuous Lothario roles, and maybe even a little weather-beaten."

Here was a mangy lion without teeth. Something was beating on him, and it was probably the ravages of age. Half a century may seem the bird of youth to late twentieth century eyes, but at mid-century it spelled o-l-d. What it meant for an actor to be that age, and to attempt to appear other than soft, cautious, and ready for the rocking chair, had not yet been determined. Bogart was a pioneer of movie star maturation, and it was not a comfortable position to be in.

Nor was *Tokyo Joe* exactly the perfect vehicle in which to cross the aging threshold. Written by a number of hands, and directed by Stuart Heisler, its "Bogart role" is an American who ran a gambling den in Tokyo before the war, left before Pearl Harbor to fight on the U.S. side, then returns after the war to pick up the pieces. From this farfetched premise even more absurd doings ensue; yet one can read signs of effort by the writers to construct a new Bogart persona, or at least modify the old one.

There was, for example, the issue of guilt, for which expiation is required. Previous Bogart heroes had possessed flaws necessitating correction or transformation, but, as with *Casablanca*'s Rick Blaine, these were based not on his own misdeeds but on his misapprehension of the acts of others. In *Tokyo Joe* he had left behind a White Russian wife who was pregnant (unbeknownst to him) with his child. To atone, he gets involved with some Japanese militarists who would otherwise reveal to U.S. occupation authorities that the wife (now ex-wife) broadcast propaganda during the war in order to protect her (his) child.

That there is also a political dimension to the issue of guilt becomes clear when an American officer tells him he is "up to [his] neck in this Communist-inspired, Communist-directed plan." Well, it sure looked like his co-conspirators were simple old-fashioned right-wingers like the ones who had started the war in the first place; perhaps the filmmakers added the line to keep up with the times and U.S. occupation policy in Japan, which had switched its postwar enemy from the right to the left. In any case, the Bogart role foils the plot and appears to be fatally wounded in the process—though the film ends before we know for sure whether he dies.

Curiously, the American reviewers were so interested in commenting on the star's moth-eaten, storm-battered appearance that they neglected the political angle entirely. However, a British periodical, *News Review*, led off its review by calling *Tokyo Joe* "Humphrey Bogart's personal war against Communism," raising at least implicitly the question of whether the actor was also using the film to expiate further what had been declared the guilt of his own past political behavior.

For his annual Warner Bros. effort, the actor agreed to a script called "Jet Pilot," and it was filmed in summer 1949 as *Chain Lightning* (1950). Stuart Heisler was again the director, but it was probably only coincidence that the film builds on a theme similar to that of *Tokyo Joe*: a woman left behind in the war, the hero's failure of responsibility. In the studio's version, however, there was to be only a happy ending—a supporting player could die, but not the star. *Chain Lightning* was a film about testing supersonic jet aircraft. It was likely based on some of Chuck Yeager's feats as a test pilot, and even refers to him in the dialogue. Its costumes and action also had the look of a 1930s Saturday afternoon matinee Buck Rogers serial, and indeed the fictional space hero is also evoked in the dialogue.

Time—which seemed to have it in for Bogart—did not even bother this time to mention how ancient and incongruous the actor looked as a test pilot. It merely commented: "Tough-guy Bogart still conveys emotion by baring his teeth in a grimace that gentler folks reserve for the moment after biting into a wormy apple." As an antidote, Philip K. Scheuer of the *Los Angeles Times*, the all-time industry cheerleader among daily reviewers, gave the actor a much-needed piece of puffery: "He is back to being the Hemingway kind of hero—cynical, saturnine, belligerently male."

The controversy over *Chain Lightning*, however, did not concern Bogart's performance. It erupted over a report in Walter Winchell's nationally syndicated column suggesting that the name J. Redmon Prior, given a story credit on the film, was actually the *nom de plume* of Lester Cole, one of the blacklisted Hollywood Ten. Winchell was correct; and though Bogart had nothing to do with Cole's involvement in the project, few things were as likely to turn the actor more saturnine than the threats which inevitably ensued of picketing and boycotting his pictures.

■ ■ ■ ■

In the fall of 1949 Santana put into production the company's third picture, *In a Lonely Place* (1950). Producer Lord chose as the source a 1947 thriller novel (with the same title) by Dorothy B. Hughes, author of quirky psychological mysteries—one of which, *The Fallen Sparrow*, had given Garfield an unexpected opportunity for a memorable performance in the 1943 RKO film.

Hughes's *In a Lonely Place*, however, was quirky to a special degree: it told the story of a serial killer through the murderer's consciousness. It made the daring and delicate effort to balance the reader's revulsion toward the narrator/killer with sympathy for his terrible flaws, and drove the narration forward through the battle of wits between the killer, trying to disguise his criminality, and his pursuers, seen through his eyes, closing in on him.

In another decade, even during the waning years of the Production Code Administration, a film like Alfred Hitchcock's *Psycho* (1960) could tell a story much like this one, even if not from the killer's viewpoint. In 1949, however, the Breen Office was likely to permit only a shadow of it to pass through its protective sieve. Robert Lord's original submission to the PCA included a copy of the novel and a note saying, "We intend to have the protagonist kill only one person within the framework of the story. He has killed another person before the story begins."[3]

Further negotiations followed. At one point Lord, sorely tried, wrote to Joseph I. Breen, "I wish Mr. Bogart were Shirley Temple so that we could do tales of sweetness and light with him. But since he is not, we will have to push the steam roller uphill to make pictures of this type with him."[4]

During the first week of production in October the distribution company, Columbia, released a synopsis of the film-in-progress indicating that Bogart's character, Dixon Steele, kills his love interest in the film, Laurel Gray (played by Gloria Grahame)—a murder that does not occur in the book. By the time the film was released this had become an "almost" murder, and the Bogart role ends up killing no one at all. The one murder of which he is suspected is finally attributed to a minor character who just happens to have the same name as the film's associate producer.

In a Lonely Place thus became a film about a man with rage enough to kill, but who does not. In the context of this production history, however, the difference becomes almost a technicality. Some of the film, if not most of it, clearly was shot from the perspective that the Bogart character would turn out a killer. There is a shot—well known to students of film noir lighting—of Dix Steele narrating a reenactment of a murder to his friends, police detective Brub Nicolai (Frank Lovejoy), and Brub's wife (Jeff Donnell). "It's wonderful to feel her throat crushing under his arm," Dix says, and the lighting on Bogart's face shifts to harsh direct key light that accentuates his cruel, almost demented, appearance. Later in the film, a similar lighting and look are repeated just before he begins to choke Laurel. Whether it was aesthetic or moral reasons that inserted a telephone ring at this point and stopped the deed, neither characters nor spectators are in any further doubt that Dixon Steele has murder in his heart.

Literary origins and production development, helpful as they are in analyzing the undertones of *In a Lonely Place*, only partially hint at the movie's diverse qualities and impact. Screenwriter Andrew Solt and director Nicholas Ray shaped a far different work, in most respects, from the Hughes thriller. They added strong strands of comedy and romance (Columbia promoted it with a song, "I Hadn't Anyone 'Till You," and, in one city, a contest on love at first sight). They developed offbeat minor characters—Martha the masseuse (Ruth Gillette), Effie the housekeeper (Ruth Warren), Waterman the thespian (Robert Warwick)—that were a feature of Ray's early films; there was, in addition, a superb performance as Steele's agent by Art

Smith, the former Group Theatre actor, who was about to be black-listed. They made Steele a screenwriter in the film (Hughes's killer only pretended to be a writer) and gave a sharp, only partly satirical critique of the movie trade.

What they did not do is attempt to explain Dix Steele's murderous tendencies. We learn that he has not had a screenwriting success since before the war; that he was an officer in the war; that he hates what he considers prostituting his talents. Still, the film refuses to credit professional failure, a veteran's maladjustment, or Hollywood as specific causes of his anger and violence. Some attention is paid to a possible relationship between creativity and homicide—Dix's imagination, his "genius," making him an abnormal man—yet the writer himself professes that he can do his killing vicariously, in the movies that he writes. Dix's suggestion to police is that the murderer they are hunting is a man like himself—"only without my artistic temperament."

One of the most powerful scenes in *In a Lonely Place* occurs when Laurel casually mentions to Dix that Martha the masseuse "beats [her] black and blue." Her words abruptly impel him to ask a question eliciting her feelings for him. He stands over her and puts his hands on her throat. Then he bends and kisses her. The moment disturbingly links violence and eroticism, and casts a shadow over the scenes of romantic happiness between them that immediately follow.

In a Lonely Place has almost invariably been treated as a work by Nicholas Ray, imbued with the director's pervasive concerns about male characters in his films of the 1950s: issues of maturity, solitude, violence, rebellion, and responsibility. It has hardly been recognized as a Bogart film—not only produced by the actor's company, but concerned more specifically with his screen persona, and marked by a deliberate approach to performance style. Bogart's portrayal of Dix Steele can be linked to his classic Warner Bros. roles and to his screen persona as Sam Spade and Rick Blaine and Philip Marlowe, not as a continuation but as a critique.

Looking at Dix, one can see that Bogart's performances in his classic roles had the same breadth of characterization—not only the mix of "acid and comedy" that Robert Lord had long before noted, but also a link between romance and violence. In *The Maltese Falcon*, *Casablanca*, and *The Big Sleep*, the most romantic moments are frequently also the most violent, as when Marlowe and Vivian Sternwood's growing love accompanies the shootings of Canino and Eddie Mars, or Rick and Ilse's passionate final scenes occur when he shoots Strasser at the airport and commits himself to war.

Cagney needed to reduce the violent side of his screen persona before he could add romance to it; Bogart did not rid himself of violence, but transformed it into socially acceptable forms—as a private eye or man at war—as his romantic image developed. What *In a Lonely Place* does is strip the professional veneer from the character's violence. What is left is not a hero but a sadist: a man whose victims are not criminals or Nazis but innocent people, particularly women. Bogart's performance as Dix Steele shares most of the characteristics of his classic performances except that the tie between the killer and the lover is laid bare, without the romanticism, the genre conventions, or the political ideology which underlay it in previous films.

Bogart does not use a gun in *In a Lonely Place*. There are no moments for audiences to cheer as he pumps lead into a noxious villain—surely not when he extols the wonderful feeling of crushing a throat, or with his hands around one. *In a Lonely Place* is a radical demystification of the classic Bogart hero. The role of Dix Steele is among the most interesting examples of a performer's critical reevaluation of his screen persona, and surely belongs on the list of Bogart's great performances.

■ ■ ■ ■

When *In a Lonely Place* began production, Robert Lord gave an interview indicating that the picture might be Santana's last. Perhaps his exasperated note to Joe Breen indicated that he (and by implication the company's part-owner and major asset) was tired of pushing the steamroller uphill, looking for suitable parts for the star. Shirley Temple, for that matter, was having difficulties, for she too was growing older. In any event, Santana's principals put their backs to the wheel yet another time, a year after *In a Lonely Place* (and following another Bogart effort for Warner Bros.), for *Sirocco* (1951).

Drawn from a novel by Joseph Kessel, and directed by Curtis Bernhardt (reunited with Bogart after their previous work together in the much-lamented *Conflict*), *Sirocco* is a film of considerably more interest for its tropes than for itself. The setting is Damascus 1925, with the French controlling Syria under a League of Nations mandate, and Syrian freedom fighters trying to win their country's independence. Bogart is Smith, an American who owns a gambling den and runs guns to the rebels on the side. *Sirocco* is *Casablanca* in the wrong place at the wrong time—not so much Syria in the 1920s as America in the 1950s.

Among the political issues raised in the film is the question of informing: it is difficult to believe this is merely a coincidence in a film made in late 1950 with additional scenes shot in March 1951, at the time of the renewed HUAC hearings. Zero Mostel plays the informer, obliquely trying to warn Smith of his having named names with the line, "The things people do to people." Later Bogart's character acknowledges, "He was trying to tell me he fingered us." Among the personal and professional issues raised is the question of Bogart's attractiveness to women. A French colonel's girlfriend flirts with him. "What a man," she says. "You're so ugly. Yes you are. How can a man so ugly be so handsome?"

Ultimately the plot closely recapitulates *Tokyo Joe*. Bogart plays a man who has behaved badly and must sacrifice himself to gain redemption. He joins the French side and aids the liberal colonel (played by Lee J. Cobb) in seeking a truce with the rebels. In the process Smith is shot and fatally wounded; then the shooting stops. The additional scenes made in March apparently were intended to provide the film with a more upbeat ending, but the Breen Office disapproved. *Sirocco* invites interpretation as yet another parable of Bogart's own postwar political entanglements: a man gets involved with rebels against the dominant authority, and his belated effort to assist the constituted power only assures that his former allies will destroy him.

Well, the parable was not exact. Bogart's former allies did not have the power to destroy him—not even when Sterling Hayden named him before HUAC as leader of the Committee for the First Amendment—and the constituted authorities, which did have that power, chose not to use it. Though his deaths on film were only metaphorical, however, that does not mean his career in films was in the pink of health. Santana claimed to be earning money, but, with the exception of *In a Lonely Place*, was making little or no contribution to Bogart's screen image. Meanwhile, his relationship with Warner Bros. was rapidly deteriorating.

Beyond all the specific disagreements, not all petty in themselves, the basic problem lay in the changing economic structure of the motion picture industry. The major studios were beginning the slow process of divesting their theater holdings after the federal antitrust case had been decided against them. Motion picture attendance started to drop in the late 1940s, even before the first big impact of television. Stars, directors, producers, and agents were growing increasingly interested in the financial and creative opportunities of independent production rather than the old studio factory system.

The former monopoly companies were losing dominance at either end of the filmmaking process—production and exhibition—and were beginning to concentrate on financing, distribution, and real estate. Under these circumstances, from the Warner Bros. viewpoint, a decade-plus commitment to a performer, no matter how prominent, made no more sense than Charlie Castle's fourteen-year deal in Odets's *The Big Knife*.

Then there were the specific disagreements. One concerned Lauren Bacall's unhappiness with her status as a contract player at the studio. Another was Bogart's dissatisfaction with the quality of scripts offered to him. On the studio's side, there was pique at Bogart's occasional drunkenness and his propensity on those occasions to bad-mouth the studio and his own films.

Bacall had given birth to the Bogarts' first child in January 1949 and begun working again soon after. She made two pictures during the following year but then refused an assignment and in May 1950 was put on suspension. Jack Warner used the occasion to work up a plan offering her contract as hostage in a deal that would lead to modification or cancellation of Bogart's. In his notes for a possible negotiation with Bogart's business people, Warner stressed the economic possibilities of reuniting the Bogart-Bacall team on-screen. "They can make big money together," he pointed out. "Am sure if Bacall was in *In a Lonely Place* instead of Gloria Grahame they would have had a bigger box office. That combination is well-accepted by the public."[5]

Warner's talking points raise several intriguing issues. For one, why did Warner Bros. not exploit the couple's box office potential again after *Key Largo*? The answer probably was that the studio found it difficult to come up with scripts that could exploit their special on-screen chemistry. The "love interest" part in *Chain Lightning* was played by Eleanor Parker with a constant look of distress, and *The Enforcer* (1951), Bogart's subsequent Warner Bros. assignment, had no major female roles at all.

Another question concerns Bogart's status as a romantic screen figure. What else besides his pictures with Bacall—more specifically, Howard Hawks's direction of the couple in *To Have and Have Not* and *The Big Sleep*—gave him any claim to a reputation as a screen lover? *Casablanca*, of course, but one could argue that romance works there through a brilliant script and inspired handling of composition by director Michael Curtiz, as well as by Ingrid Bergman's carrying the primary performance responsibility. Certainly Bogart's own company, with Florence Marly in *Tokyo Joe* and Marta Toren in *Sirocco*, had produced neither memorable casting nor story construction to support the romantic claims made for Bogart's characters in the scripts.

This may be one of the reasons why, of the three projects submitted to Bogart for his 1950 Warner Bros. commitment, he chose one that required no exertions of a romantic nature. An independent production of United States Pictures, financed and distributed by Warner Bros., *The Enforcer* (called *Murder, Inc.* in Great Britain) was a minor confection featuring Bogart as an assistant district attorney tracking down a gang of contract killers. It was structured with flashbacks within flashbacks, and it is not clear whether that infinitely receding narrative was exacerbated or alleviated by five days of retakes and added scenes shot by Raoul Walsh in relief of the original director, Bretagne Windust.

Several weeks after the additional work was done, Bogart was overheard at New York's "21" Restaurant, according to a telegram from the studio's East Coast office to Jack L. Warner, "announcing in a loud voice to everyone within earshot what lousy picture *Enforcer* is. Ridiculous to try and arrange press interviews. He is only looking for trouble."[6] This incident, one of several the studio had been noting over the previous year, only accelerated the efforts of Warner Bros. executives to change the Bogart contract, which had been discussed internally for some months.

Finally, in November 1950, an agreement was reached to modify and amend the contract. Warners did not obtain its immediate cancellation or earlier termination, as had been wished, but it reduced the money part to $160,000 for the next picture and $150,000 for all others remaining, with a penalty to Bogart if he refused future scripts. In addition, the actor gave up the right of director approval, and both parties agreed to cancel the fifth year of their agreement—that is, 1951.

As the New Year dawned in 1951, Bogart was hardly at the height of his professional achievements. *The Enforcer* and *Sirocco* were in the can and their release in 1951 would do little else but tarnish his luster. He and Warner Bros. had agreed to take the year off, and Santana was contemplating closing up shop. There was, however, one project in development, ready to go forward if financing could be worked out. It was a film based on C. S. Forester's 1935 novel *The African Queen*.

A 1953 divorce case involving producer Sam Spiegel (who used the name S. P. Eagle as his picture credit) revealed some of the ways *The African Queen* (1952) was financed, and yielded insight into how independent pictures were produced in Hollywood at that time—or perhaps into Spiegel's manner of doing business. Bogart was to get $35,000 up front, $125,000 in deferred payments, and 25 percent of the film's profits; later, he permitted Spiegel to pass up the upfront money and raise the actor's profit share to 30 percent. Katharine Hepburn, the co-star, was to receive $65,000 up front, $65,000 deferred, and 10 percent of the profits. Director John Huston, who already owned 50 percent of Horizon, the production company, with Spiegel, was to be paid $87,000 for his work on the film.

Warner Bros. owned screen rights to the book, and writer John Collier had done a screenplay for the studio; Warners wanted $50,000 for the rights but accepted a lien on the film in lieu of cash, and Collier got 6 percent of the profits for his interest. Another 5 percent was given to a man who mortgaged Spiegel's home for $25,000. A British company, Romulus, put up the production costs in Africa and England in return for 100 percent of Eastern Hemisphere returns until its costs were repaid, thereafter 75 percent of profits in that area and 25 percent of Western Hemisphere profits. Several American companies made loans to cover domestic expenses.

However you add these figures up, it seems that something in excess of 75 percent of the picture's potential profits were committed in advance in order to acquire the resources to produce it. Later, when the picture had become enormously successful, various other claimants emerged, such as creditors on outstanding loans to Horizon on earlier, less successful pictures. Who ever realized any returns on his or her points is one of film history's minor mysteries. Some commentators have exclaimed over *The African Queen*'s record budget for its era, but as every industry insider knows, inflating costs is the common way to keep profit participants empty-handed.

Huston claimed he never got any money from the film, including salary contractually owed to him. On the advice of Bogart's business manager, A. Morgan Maree, who was looking into possible discrepancies in Horizon's bookkeeping, Huston sold his half-ownership back to Spiegel. Bogart was apparently satisfied enough with his income from the film that he chose not to take Spiegel to court.

This financial fallout lay in the future. With money in hand, *The African Queen* began three months of location shooting in April 1951 in what was then the Belgian Congo (now Zaire). Accounts of the filmmaking have been given by Huston; by Hepburn; by Bacall, who accompanied her husband; and even in an article in the Sunday supplement *American Weekly*, "African Adventure," attributed to Bogart, who, according to the others, preferred nothing more adventurous than sitting in his tent with a drink.

When *The African Queen* opened in February 1952, it won almost universal acclaim, with the notable exception of such highbrows as the *New York Times*'s Bosley Crowther and Gilbert Seldes of *Saturday Review*, both of whom compared its low-comedy tone unfavorably to director Huston's serious earlier work like *The Treasure of the Sierra Madre*. They are right. One might add, though, as the reviewers did not, that the political high tragedy of the intervening years had made it nearly impossible to make a film such as *Treasure*, and low comedy was an understandable response.

Bogart had shrewdly seen the possibilities for himself in the part of Charlie Allnutt, the dissolute but ultimately heroic Cockney skipper of a boat called *The African Queen*—changed to a Canadian in the film, perhaps in deference to the actor's accent. What was brilliant, not least from Bogart's viewpoint, was the choice of Hepburn to play Rose Sayer, the missionary's spinster sister. Rose in Forester's novel is thirty-three; any number of actresses could have fit her description. Hepburn was forty-three when the film was made, while Bogart was fifty-one. No effort was made to reduce or disguise their years in the film, and the romantic comedy of Allnutt and Rosie's relationship (which has contrasts of breeding rather than of class) marks one of those rare moments in Hollywood movies (until very recently) depicting sexual attraction between a middle-aged woman and man.

The construction of Bogart's screen character in *The African Queen* confirmed what many had noted at previous times in his career, that comedy was an essential complement both to his tough and his romantic side; indeed, without the comic leavening the romantic Bogart had been less than convincing. The last time all those elements had worked together was in *The Big Sleep* (Dobbsie in *Treasure* and Dix Steele in *In a Lonely Place* had been powerful performances of a different kind).

This is not to compare Charlie Allnutt with Philip Marlowe. Bogart built his Allnutt characterization broadly along comic lines— though given such scenes as his stomach gurgling at dinner early in the film, he had little choice. The giveaway lay in how he composed his features. In the past, baring his upper front teeth had been one of his stock mannerisms—the biting-into-a-wormy-apple look *Time* magazine derided. For *The African Queen*, he appears in virtually every scene with his mouth open and his upper front teeth visible— not in the old tough-guy grimace, but in an exaggerated expression meant to signify Allnutt's basically simple nature, amply fulfilled in the scene in which he happily imitates a hippo and a monkey.

What was significant at the time, however, was not the lack of complexity in Bogart's portrayal, but the comedy itself. He had played so many dour and doomed characters over the previous three or four years that they could have stolen a promotional line from Greta Garbo: "Bogart laughs!" He demonstrated his versatility to those who had forgotten or never known he had it. More important, he showed his resilience: it was as if a cloud had been lifted from his brow, the cloud formed by the Committee for the First Amendment, which had led him to all those guilt-ridden and expiatory roles. All this he had done working as an equal with one of Hollywood's most distinguished female performers, as he rarely had the opportunity to do.

The African Queen's low comedy warmed the hearts of a movie industry looking for signs of hope in a difficult era. Among its Academy Award nominations were Best Picture, director, actress, and actor. Bogart's competitors included the two young exemplars of "The Method" whose performance style had engaged Garfield's concern, Marlon Brando and Montgomery Clift, as well as the veterans Fredric March and Arthur Kennedy.

The selection of Bogart for the actor Oscar for *The African Queen* was a vote not strictly for a performance, and not precisely for a career. It was a recognition of a phenomenon, of a sea-change: of an event that had the force of lifting an actor above mere criticism and establishing him beyond the conventional, in the realm of those who have found freedom to do as they please on the screen.

■ ■ ■ ■

Since he was not bound in 1951 to the Warner Bros. contract limitation of one outside picture, Bogart used his new freedom to help out a friend, writer-director Richard Brooks, whom the actor had met when Brooks co-authored the *Key Largo* screenplay. He agreed at the last minute to step in and take the lead role in a project that Brooks had developed from his own original story and sold to Twentieth Century–Fox, *Deadline U.S.A.* (1952). The following year, 1952, Bogart's only screen work was in another film written and directed by Brooks, *Battle Circus*, for Metro-Goldwyn-Mayer.

These two Bogart-Brooks collaborations may be seen as premature pilots for two popular 1970s television series—"Lou Grant" and "M⋆A⋆S⋆H," respectively—or as proof of the basic continuity of popular entertainment. In *Deadline U.S.A.*, Bogart plays the editor of a New York newspaper who fights the rackets and teams with a dowager publisher (portrayed by Ethel Barrymore) to keep the paper from being sold to a yellow tabloid. In *Battle Circus* he is a surgeon with a mobile army surgical hospital in Korea. Neither of these acts of friendship provides much in image or word to remember it by.

The only remaining limitation on Bogart's freedom, it turned out, was his Warner Bros. contract. The studio apparently prevented him from appearing in Hal Wallis's Paramount production of *Come Back, Little Sheba* (1952); Burt Lancaster got the male lead opposite Shirley Booth's award-winning performance. Warners offered him something called "Alma Mater" instead, but he turned that down in favor of *Battle Circus* at MGM (and $200,000 instead of $160,000). He also expressed his pique at Warner Bros. by telling columnist Hedda Hopper, "In five years when I have no hair or teeth, Warners will have to keep putting me in pictures."[7]

These remarks infuriated Jack L. Warner—as intended. The studio head appealed to his law firm for a way to cancel the Bogart contract; he was informed it was impossible. "The contract is simply a bad contract from the point of view of the studio at the present time," an attorney concluded.[8] Indeed, there were not just five years but a decade more to go in which the studio was obliged annually to offer him the opportunity to make a picture on the actor's option to accept or reject. Warner had to content himself with a sharply worded letter, signed by an underling, calling the actor, as usual, an ingrate.

Bogart liked the restrictions imposed by the Warner Bros. deal no better than did Jack Warner. The actor turned down two more Warners proposals in 1952 and 1953 and planned his work schedule as if the one outside picture per year provision did not exist. Finally, in September 1953, both parties agreed to termination. *The Enforcer*, it turned out, was Bogart's muted last hurrah in Burbank. Warners—which had labored for two decades with too narrow a conception of Bogart's range—had only stood in the way of Bogart's plan for 1953: to show off his versatility once and for all, his capacity to take risks, his ability to surprise. This was to be the year of, in order of their making (and their release in 1954), *Beat the Devil*, *The Caine Mutiny*, and *Sabrina*.

Beat the Devil reunited Bogart with John Huston under the banner of the actor's Santana company. Lacking a divorce case, it is not easy to know who paid for this film (the British company Romulus was involved, as well as Italian backers, and others) and who hoped to take money out of it—though there was little chance of any profits to parcel out. *Beat the Devil* was a pleasurable fiasco. Bogart had bought the rights to Claude Cockburn's novel (published under the name James Helvick) on Huston's recommendation, but the production was ready to start before a satisfactory script was in hand. As shooting was set to begin at Ravello, Italy, a hill town above the Amalfi coast south of Naples, Huston ran into the writer Truman Capote in Rome and enlisted him to come down and help write scenes just ahead of camera work.

It was hardly the first time in American film history that scenes were written one jump ahead of their production (*Casablanca* is a famous example, among many others), but it was most unlikely that new lines were messengered back to the Breen Office for approval, as was the requirement in Hollywood. When Production Code officials saw the finished film there were some marked differences from the preliminary script, long since discarded, that they had approved. *Beat the Devil* was found to be unacceptable on the grounds of its violation of Code provisions concerning the treatment of adultery and exposure of the female breast. Some two months later a Code certificate was issued for the film, though it was not clear what had been cut or changed to make it acceptable: the swap of spouses is still quite apparent, as are shots of Gina Lollobrigida's ample cleavage.

The uncertainty and delay seemed to affect the enthusiasm of the film's American distributor, United Artists. It released the film in a "saturation" booking, a simultaneous opening in many theaters throughout the country; in the days before nationwide television advertising of movies, this meant a swift demise for a film whose prospects were considered too bleak for a careful, city-by-city "platform" release.

Beat the Devil has survived in late-night television and university cinema societies as the sport it is—a film worth watching mainly for the obvious enjoyment its performers are taking in its absurdities. There is also the poignant reminder of the immortal Sam Spade and Joel Cairo in the reunion of their all-too-mortal, clearly aging portrayers, Bogart and Peter Lorre.

Bogart returned to Hollywood after completing *Beat the Devil* and stepped into the greatly different role of Lt. Cmdr. Philip Francis Queeg, captain of the navy minesweeper *Caine*, in Stanley Kramer's production based on the best-selling Herman Wouk novel *The Caine Mutiny*. "His performance is a high point in the history of screen acting," the *Hollywood Reporter* wrote in its review. If it is difficult to assent to that rare encomium, it may be because there is little in Wouk's original narrative, nor in director Edward Dmytryk's respectful and portentous handling of it, that later generations have found as compelling as did 1950s readers and audiences.

The ideological issues of the film concern loyalty to authority and the failure of the intellectual—two subjects in which Hollywood in the early 1950s, like the rest of the country, felt deeply implicated. Bogart's performance as the mentally unbalanced captain with the steel balls clicking in his hand was almost inevitably overdetermined; his fears and rages provided precisely the ultimate test of loyalty, not to authority at its best but at its weakest, that the intellectual mutineers failed. Overdetermined as well were the film's pop-psychoanalytic explanations—"inferiority feelings arising from an unfavorable childhood and aggravated by adult experiences," a psychiatric expert intones at the court-martial—and no doubt also the *Hollywood Reporter's* hyperbolic praise.

The excruciatingly lengthy, tight close-up of the actor as he portrays the captain exhibiting his symptoms in the court-martial witness chair was the kind of scene to which the *Reporter* was responding. For a characterization of a weak, paranoid, devious man, one might prefer Bogart's Fred C. Dobbs in *The Treasure of the Sierra Madre*—certainly it is embedded in a more imaginatively complex film.

From Queeg it was back to comedy. In fall 1953 Bogart went into *Sabrina*, Billy Wilder's adaptation of the romantic Broadway comedy by Samuel Taylor *Sabrina Fair.* He plays Linus Larrabee, the stuffy financier who fakes an infatuation with the chauffeur's daughter in order to prevent her from making off with his dissolute younger brother—and, of course, falls in love with her himself. Audrey Hepburn portrayed the girl and William Holden the brother, a romantic lead role that Wilder shaped into an homage to Bogart's days as a Broadway juvenile, complete with the line, "Tennis, anyone?"

Sabrina was a good deal more conventional a work than *Beat the Devil*, and perhaps for that reason Wilder was able more effectively to exploit its absurdities. The director and his cinematographer, Charles Lang, Jr., added some depth to the comedy by shooting it in dark tones, almost as a film noir. This was linked to the broader humor of playing off Bogart's effete character against reminders of the actor's tough-guy past. In one scene, the financier takes out a gun and fires it—to test a sheet of plastic. Bogart plays the straight man with a kind of earnest zest that exaggerates the film's incongruities without turning them into farce. "Humphrey Bogart's delightful performance of an industrial hermit who turns unintentional beau," wrote Bosley Crowther in the *New York Times*, "is one of the most surprising and affecting that he has ever done"—a critical accolade with which one can agree.

Lauren Bacall quotes Cary Grant as saying to Bogart around this time, "You get all the good parts now, Bogie—how do you get so many of them?" Linus Larrabee in *Sabrina* was certainly a role well suited to Grant, who played many quite like it in his career; and maybe Wilder preferred Bogart for the elements of surprise and cognitive dissonance he brought to the film. "Because I keep working," Bogart was reported as replying.[9] By adding availability and visibility to his newly demonstrated versatility and resilience, Bogart was able to survive and thrive, during the 1950s transformation of the American film industry, as well as any performer of his generation.

The judgment of time, however, has not so far given much pride of place to Bogart's "good parts" and steady work of the 1950s—notwithstanding high praise from such disparate contemporary sources as the *Hollywood Reporter* and the *New York Times*. Of the even dozen films Bogart worked in following his final Warner Bros. effort, *The Enforcer* (1951)—and this arbitrary dividing line leaves out earlier postwar clinkers like *Chain Lightning* and *Tokyo Joe*—only *The African Queen* comes close to sustaining a reputation similar to his Warner Bros. classics of the 1940s. The decline of interest in these 1950s films may be based on the vagaries of popular (or academic) taste, and could be subject to change. It may rest on factors concerning Bogart's age, his acting skills, or the very versatility that frequently put him into parts, as in *Sabrina*, far removed from his iconic image as Spade or Rick or Marlowe. Oddly, it may also have as much to do with Bogart's ability, admired by Cary Grant, to keep himself actively involved at the center of 1950s Hollywood filmmaking.

From *Sabrina* on, Bogart found parts in prestige films by some of Hollywood's most important directors—first Wilder, then Joseph Mankiewicz, Michael Curtiz, and William Wyler. There lies the rub. The 1950s movie industry's notion of a "prestige" picture—a concept especially important at that time as Hollywood sought to turn movies into cultural events to stem the tide of audience defection to television—has not worn well.

These frequently tended to be costume epics set in biblical times; but when "prestige" movies dealt with contemporary life they were often comedy confections, like *Sabrina*, or portentous theme films, like *The Caine Mutiny*. Ironically, one of Lauren Bacall's films from the period, *Written on the Wind* (1956), which she brushed off as "soap opera," has gained in interest over the years, and is regarded more highly a generation later than any of Bogart's "prestige" pictures from the period; "soap opera" or not, it addresses questions of wealth, power, family, and sexuality in a form that continues to evoke a lively response from later generations.[10]

"Because I keep working": 1954 was as active a year for Bogart as 1953, with three "prestige" projects—with Mankiewicz, *The Barefoot Contessa* (1954); with Curtiz, *We're No Angels* (1955); with Wyler, *The Desperate Hours* (also 1955).

Both the symptoms of the movie industry's problems and, to some extent, an exploration of them were present in *The Barefoot Contessa* (1954), an independent production that Mankiewicz both wrote and directed. This film was the subject of two separate plagiarism suits (both ultimately dismissed), so its story of an unknown young woman becoming a movie star and marrying a foreign aristocrat was not exactly novel. It also had the misfortune to appear in the same year as a more widely acclaimed version of the star myth, the Judy Garland–James Mason *A Star Is Born*. For Bogart, one of its attractions was likely the opportunity for three months' work in Italy, at Cinecittà in Rome and on location in San Remo and Portofino. He plays Harry Dawes, a "washed-up ex-drunk" director rescued by a rich-as-Croesus neophyte producer so he can turn a Spanish dancer into a star. The girl, played by Ava Gardner, turns out to be a cineaste who immediately recognizes the name Dawes—"Did you not direct Harlow and Lombard," she asks him in Hemingway-style from-the-Spanish English—and links him with her other favorite directors, Lubitsch, Van Dyke, Fleming, and La Cava. No wonder *The Barefoot Contessa* became a European cult film, with its direct intervention in the period's *politique des auteurs*.

This is an aphorism-by-the-minute movie with much serious talk about the relation between movies and life. What is missing from it (as in most Hollywood-on-Hollywood movies) is any real insight into professional issues. "Would you help me to become a really good actress?" the Spanish dancer asks Dawes the director, but we never actually see the character do movie work—we have to take the film's word that her screen test is a smash, because it only shows us the viewers in the screening room; we do not even get to see her stage performance. The most concrete statement about performance in the film is a line Bogart delivers: "The single most difficult thing in the world is getting an actor to stand still."

In *The Barefoot Contessa*, the single most difficult thing appears to have been getting the actors to be animate. Bogart's scenes with Gardner have a particularly awkward feel; among other things, she continues throughout the film to speak in a stilted style of translated English. Moreover, the possibility of a sexual spark between them is vigorously extinguished. Bogart's character is faithful to a young blonde script girl, while the amorous life of Gardner's character takes place offscreen.

John O'Hara wrote in *Collier's* that she is "made out to be a cold fish and there are even some hints that she doesn't like fellows at all." When she does fall head-over-heels for a fellow he turns out to have suffered a war wound O'Hara "thought Ernest Hemingway had a copyright on." Worse yet, when she tries to please him by producing an heir with somebody else, he shoots her dead. *The Barefoot Contessa* suggests that the next incarnation of the 1950s Hollywood "prestige" picture would be the twelve-hour television mini-series—minus the sexual evasions.

We're No Angels, a Paramount production, reunited Bogart with the director of *Casablanca*. Curtiz was now freelancing after making more than eighty pictures in nearly thirty years at Burbank, and having played, as we have seen, a major role in the careers of all three city boys. The actor and the director had last worked together in *Passage to Marseille*, and anyone who remembered the harsh Devil's Island scenes from that movie might have had trouble accommodating the lugubrious slapstick manner in which the opening sequences of *We're No Angels* presents the French penal colony. The film rewards the spectator's patience, however, and offers one of the most unusual performances of Bogart's career.

Bogart, Peter Ustinov, and Aldo Ray, prison escapees, make up the unlikely trio of non-angels who take over a shopkeeper's household with robbery and mayhem in mind—only to bring unexpected Christmas good cheer to the family. Ustinov's droll performance is the film's highlight, but Bogart's is easy to underestimate. He gives a deliberately stagey performance: parodying other characters (as when, hand to chin, back straight, and body swaying, he mimics a young woman) and parodying his own screen image (as when he roars in his best guttural, "Beat their heads in, gouge their eyes out, cut their throats"). Bogart's broad, comic acting style in *We're No Angels* is probably the closest he came on-screen to the way he must have appeared as a romantic boy back on Broadway in the 1920s in genteel farces like *The Cradle Snatchers*.

From a historical and ideological perspective, *The Desperate Hours* was perhaps the most important of all of Bogart's 1950s films. Playwright Joseph Hayes wrote the screenplay from his own highly successful first novel and subsequent theatrical dramatization, and William Wyler produced and directed the film for Paramount. The fact that John Garfield had, only three years earlier, appeared in a very similar story in *He Ran All the Way* counted for nothing, precisely because *The Desperate Hours* was set not in an urban working-class environment, as the earlier film, but in middle-class suburbia.

The Desperate Hours was one of the key markers identifying the renewed hegemony of bourgeois values in American popular entertainment, after several decades of Depression and war-generated cultural production. Its situation—challenging the father to defend family and property from criminals who invade his home—harked back as far as D. W. Griffith's early one-reeler on the same theme, *The Lonely Villa* (1909).

Bogart's escaped convict Glenn Griffin is probably the most brutal role of his career. There had been some unsavory characters back in his Warner Bros. B-picture days, but none so central to the narrative, nor any whose terrorism was directed so exclusively at innocent women and children. Moreover, unlike the 1930s Warner crime films, there is little effort to situate Griffin's criminality in a social context—he is an antisocial deviant whose resentment of the bourgeois father is a sign only of his personal weakness and envy, not of any failures of the social order. To the actor's aging face was added a scar on his left cheek and a beard stubble that accentuated his middle-aged jowls—and in performance there was none of the irony that sometimes leavened the villains of his Burbank servitude.

The opposite figure in the film is, to be sure, the bourgeois father, played by Fredric March. One theme that has the potential to move the work beyond black-and-white dichotomies is a comparison of the two men as educators and authority figures—the father to his wife and children, the criminal to his confederates, one of whom is his younger brother. Another is the question of what it takes for the bourgeois father to triumph (in *He Ran All the Way*, the girl, not the father, shot the Garfield character). "I got it in me," the father tells Griffin, "You put it there." He orders Griffin out of the house and shoves him down a stairway, whence the criminal is machine-gunned by the law. As the family is reunited at the end, this is likely to mean that "it"—whether backbone, or courage, or a tinge of evil—will make him a stronger bourgeois patriarch than heretofore.

Bogart kept working. Early in 1955 he was a late addition to *The Left Hand of God* (1955) at Twentieth Century–Fox, and almost certainly the key to getting a difficult subject before the camera. William E. Barrett's novel about an adventurer who is forced to masquerade as a priest in civil war–torn China had ended up at Fox after unsuccessful attempts to develop a script at Warner Bros., by the author himself, and by Howard Hawks in collaboration with William Faulkner. At Fox, Bogart's participation brought the work into focus after further months of script preparation.

For Darryl Zanuck, Fox's head of production, the solution to the script problems was simple: make over the protagonist in the image of the actor who had been signed to play him. The character, Jim Carmody, "is wonderful," Zanuck wrote in a memo on a script draft, "but I believe that we should take more advantage of the Humphrey Bogart type. Carmody in his dialogue is written a trifle too much like a straight leading man. He should be more cynical, hard-boiled and a trifle more bitter. The great value of the story is that you take a cynical, hard-bitten, tough guy and compel him to impersonate a priest."[11] You can take the man out of Warner Bros., but you cannot take Warner Bros. out of the man: it was true for Zanuck and he made it come true one more time for Bogart. The actor got to play the Humphrey Bogart type under Edward Dmytryk's direction. The only consolation was that no other performer could do it better.

In the last two months of 1955 Bogart took a role in a muckraking film about the prizefight world, *The Harder They Fall* (1956), directed by Mark Robson, based on a novel by Budd Schulberg. Bogart plays a former sports columnist whose paper had folded and who gets drawn into the fight racket for the money. "Man passes forty," he says, "he shouldn't have to run anymore"—articulating the general narrative tactic of the period to position fiftyish actors ten to fifteen years younger. He participates in a prolonged fix (more than two dozen fights' worth) to build up a South American fighter for a title shot. At the end he has a sudden change of heart, gives away his ill-gotten gains, and begins to write an article, saying, "Boxing should be outlawed in the United States."

Of Humphrey Bogart's more than seventy film appearances in a career spanning a quarter-century, *The Harder They Fall* was among his least distinguished—both in characterization and performance. If any actor ever looked like he was going through the motions, it was Bogart in this film. He was bothered more than usual by a persistent cough (during production on *The Barefoot Contessa*, stories circulated that there was difficulty achieving successful takes not ruined by Bogart's coughing). In fact he was mortally ill. Early in 1956, within a few weeks of completing *The Harder They Fall*, Bogart went for a series of medical tests that led to an operation for throat cancer. He was not to work in motion pictures again. On January 14, 1957, at the age of fifty-seven, he died of cancer.

Reviewing *The Left Hand of God* in 1955, the *New Yorker*'s film critic wrote of Bogart that he was "an actor who had maintained over the years a singularly decent professional standard in his work for Hollywood." This is perhaps backhanded praise and it makes for a rather muted epitaph, but it speaks a basic truth about the performer, or at least the beginning of one. Bogart *was* a professional, before (and after) he was a type, or an icon. He never rested content with the formulas of his popular triumphs, even when Jack Warner or, belatedly, Darryl Zanuck forced them on him. He subjected them to a fundamental critique, as in *In a Lonely Place*. He parodied them; he avoided them. Name an actor who, in two calendar years of work, varied his screen persona as much as Bogart did in 1953–1954: comic con man (*Beat the Devil*), neurotic naval officer (*The Caine Mutiny*), stuffy executive (*Sabrina*), avuncular film director (*The Barefoot Contessa*), comic convict (*We're No Angels*), brutal criminal (*The Desperate Hours*). When he possessed the greatest power over his own destiny, versatility mattered to him most.

No one, however, mistook him for Olivier. A singularly decent professional standard is not the stuff of legend; whatever the merits of those half-dozen films made in 1953–1954, few would rank them among the actor's most important works, or his most memorable. At his death, Bogart's significance and his legacy remained unclear.

Then came the Brattle Street Theatre revival. At examination time the small movie house near Harvard Square began to program Bogart films—particular Bogart films—and the college boys would chant his lines and take courage for their ordeal from the characters Zanuck described as cynical, hard-boiled, hard-bitten, and bitter: Spade and Rick and Marlowe. The lover-killer reemerged as icon for the romantic, violent 1960s, regardless of ideologies. "Bogie" and "Casablanca" became names outside text and context, the one standing for the myth of the tough guy, the other for the myths of transformation and commitment to a social goal greater than the self.

There they remain, little altered by new views of men and women that have emerged in recent decades, less challenged by modern (or postmodern) views on gender than by his own largely ignored auto-critique of *In a Lonely Place*. (The minor chord, that here was a man who turned tail from his politics in 1947–1948, whose will to survive was greater than his courage, is whispered but heard hardly at all.) Bogie the celluloid monument hides a more interesting and complex figure, Humphrey Bogart, the man and the actor.

12

Top of the World

How vulnerable was James Cagney because of his radical past in the era of postwar repression? The actor's FBI file contains a report on an item in a November 1947 *People's Voice* suggesting that the left still counted Cagney among its numbers: the newspaper listed him as one of "Hollywood's Progressives who are under smear attack" and among those "whom the Thomas Committee would like to drive out of employment in the movie industry."[1]

This reference appears on page 150 of a 158-page summary of the Bureau's headquarters' files on Cagney compiled in December 1950—on the eve of the second round of HUAC Hollywood hearings. A further thirty-page document was put together by the Los Angeles office in April 1951. The answer is that he was no less vulnerable than any of the prominent figures for whom no direct testimony of Communist party membership was elicited—like Garfield or Edward G. Robinson—who were nevertheless subpoenaed to testify and subsequently blacklisted.

The more important question therefore is, Why was Cagney neither subpoenaed nor blacklisted? On currently available evidence, there is no clear answer. The most suggestive circumstantial clue is the presence of Ward Bond in two Cagney Productions films, *The Time of Your Life* (1948) and *Kiss Tomorrow Goodbye* (1950). As a leader of the Hollywood right wing, Bond was not likely to have associated himself with one of Hollywood's progressives who had not taken the necessary steps to purge himself of prior radicalism. This cleansing, however, almost invariably required public recantation, as in Bogart's "I'm No Communist" *Photoplay* article or Garfield's purported "I Was a Sucker for a Left Hook." Cagney's rehabilitation left no public record—but it was successful enough to protect him from a HUAC subpoena, and preserve his career.

Incomplete as the political record is in these critical years, it does provide an illuminating context for important developments in Cagney's work life for which professional explanations appear reasonable, but not entirely sufficient. One was his nearly two-year hiatus—from summer 1947 to May 1949—when he did no movie work at all. Perhaps this had to do with financial difficulties of Cagney Productions or morale problems over the state of his career, with the unorthodox *The Time of Your Life* so egregious a flop. Twenty-two months without work, however, at least raises the question, Was he now, more than ever, too hot to handle?

Another development was his May 1949 contract with Warner Bros. This may have come as no surprise to industry insiders who were aware of the Cagney brothers' unsuccessful efforts in late 1947 to shift distribution of *The Time of Your Life* to Warners from United Artists; the public, however, knew only of Cagney's rage and bitterness toward Jack L. Warner. The conviction that they knew how to make money together led both sides to put aside past resentments. Though the Cagneys had a reputation as tenacious negotiators, they could hardly have regarded the Warner deal as anything other than a rescue from a very unpropitious place. In addition to a contract for the actor's service, the agreement called for Warners to finance and distribute Cagney Productions films. Cagney signed to do three Warner Bros. pictures over three years at $250,000 per picture ($50,000 more than Bogart was making at the time). Over the subsequent five years the company also handled four Cagney company productions—two with the actor, two without.

On the day the contract was signed, shooting began on the first Warner Bros. picture, *White Heat* (1949). Perhaps the most startling development of all was Cagney's willingness to appear in a gangster role—the kind of part that had nurtured his resentment against the studio in the first place. "I'm glad to be playing this sort of role again," Cagney told a reporter for the *New York Times* on the set. "Some audiences who never saw me as a hoodlum on the screen think of me as a song and dance fellow."[2] If not an admission of defeat, being a gangster on-screen was for Cagney a way of effacing his long-sought freedom and separateness—a return to a zone of convention and security that was political as well as artistic and financial.

White Heat was not exactly a conventional gangster picture. The genre had changed several times over since Cagney had burst forth a star as Tom Powers in *The Public Enemy*. The strong social, environmental, and ethnic themes of the Depression-era classics had been eroded by Production Code pressures and returning prosperity. War films tamed social deviance and turned it into heroic hatred of the enemy. The postwar cycle of crime films, later to be known as film noir, was absorbed with psychologically and sexually motivated personal transgression. The old-fashioned underworld had fallen (temporarily) out of cinematic favor, except as an atavistic threat to a better postwar social order, as in *Key Largo*.

White Heat was conceived in cognizance of these trends—but just as much in homage to the prodigal son whose return to the Burbank fold the film celebrated. It was as if the filmmakers had gone back to the archives to study not only *The Public Enemy* but also Cagney's earliest work at the studio in *Sinner's Holiday, The Doorway to Hell*, and *Other Men's Women*. The shot of Cagney's character, the gangster Cody Jarrett, jumping from a bridge onto a railroad car in *White Heat*'s opening sequence, for example, is a tribute to a similar leap in *Other Men's Women*—except that the thirty-year-old actor did it himself, and in *White Heat* the feat is performed in long shot by a stuntman.

Even more important to *White Heat* was a character trait central to his first Warner Bros. role in *Sinner's Holiday* (and also exploited to a lesser degree in *The Public Enemy* and in studio publicity about Cagney in the early 1930s)—a son's excessive dependency on his mother. In *White Heat* the mother-son relationship was buttressed by an elaborate psychological explanation: insanity ran in the family, and the child used fake headaches to gain the mother's attention. A major innovation compared to the 1930s treatment of the theme, however, came in the characterization of the mother. *White Heat*'s Margaret Wycherley gives a richly perverse performance as an ambitious, jealous, and doting mother pushing her son to ever-higher goals in crime. "Top of the world, son," is her motto, and it receives its apocalyptic fulfillment.

It was also in salute to earlier times that the studio assigned Raoul Walsh to direct the script by Ivan Goff and Ben Roberts, from an original screen story by Virginia Kellogg. Walsh had worked with Cagney on *The Roaring Twenties* and *The Strawberry Blonde*, films in which the actor had crafted relaxed, sympathetic, and unconventional characterizations. Walsh had a more sophisticated sense of performance than standard Hollywood history gives him credit for (to which his crucial work with Bogart on *They Drive by Night* and *High Sierra* also attests). He helped Cagney make the brutal, cruel, and murderous Cody Jarrett more human and understandable, pitiable if not likeable.

The director's most formidable challenge on *White Heat* was dealing with the actor's physical condition. Nearly two years without movie work had done nothing but exacerbate Cagney's overweight, immobile appearance in *The Time of Your Life*, in which the actor had performed almost every scene seated. Walsh responded to this problem by shooting Cagney primarily in close-up and medium close-up. In *White Heat* the actor is more a face than a body. Much of his acting consists of head, eye, and mouth movement: blinking, raising his eyebrows, knitting his forehead, biting his lip—sometimes inscribed in the narrative as communication, at other times as evidence of psychological disorder.

One further aspect of *White Heat*'s postwar adaptation of the gangster genre is the prominent role the film gives to law enforcement procedures—to an insistence that authority possesses both methodology and intellect superior to those of the criminal class. The myth of the gangster is confronted not merely with superior firepower (as in the climaxes of such films as Howard Hawks's 1932 *Scarface* or *Angels with Dirty Faces*) but with a new science of the law, both in psychology and surveillance.

Ma says, "You're the smartest there is, Cody," but *White Heat* insists that she is wrong: the United States Treasury Department is smarter. Cody knows the story of the Trojan Horse (told to him by Ma) and puts his gunmen inside an empty petroleum truck for the big refinery holdup. The Feds, however, know a new technique of radio-directed pursuit (elaborately explained in the film) that can follow the criminals and help them foil the crime.

When Cody returns to prison, the Feds assign an agent (played by Edmond O'Brien) into the pen with him to befriend him, encourage his dependency, take on the role of a surrogate Ma—and help break up his gang. In the midst of the refinery holdup, when Cody discovers his buddy is a cop, his maniacal laughter indicates that he has gone over to insanity. The music swells when the agent makes it over safely to the police side, but audience sympathies may not be so easily swayed.

Cody climbs to the top of an oil tank, where the agent shoots him. Cody's gun accidentally fires into the tank. "Made it, Ma. Top of the world," Cody shouts amid the flames, and then the tank explodes. The final moments recall Cagney's earlier scene of maniacal laughter in *13 Rue Madeleine* as a World War II secret agent who laughs as Allied bombers blow him up and save him from further Gestapo torture. For spectators, the pleasures of myth, performance, and that recollected intertextual link can provoke more thrills and empathy than an earnest contemplation of the law's superiority.

"Pick up the pieces folks, Jimmy's in action again!" Warner Bros. touted Cagney's return. *White Heat* became a box office triumph, earning $3 million in domestic and foreign rentals for the studio; it ranked as the third most popular Cagney Warner Bros. film, behind only the wartime hits *Yankee Doodle Dandy* and *Captains of the Clouds*. Reviewers brushed aside both the old gangster genre staples and the new psychological and scientific gimmicks, but admired the verve and energy with which Walsh, Cagney, and the supporting cast made something lively and memorable out of such unpromising material.

It was a little like *The Public Enemy* all over again—even a paunchy Cagney who had lost his footwork could make crime and violence more attractive than a lawful life, though a fiery death was the price. Bosley Crowther devoted a *New York Times* column to this theme, noting (quite like reviewers of *The Public Enemy* nearly two decades earlier) how a youth in the Strand audience greeted one of Cagney's "vicious capers with a rhapsodic 'Bee-you-tee-ful!' The echo rang grim and horrendous in that youngster-packed theater."

Such dire warnings about the deleterious effects of gangster pictures on America's youth had no more influence on Cagney in his latest phase than it did on Warner Bros. executives in the early Depression years. In spring 1950 he began shooting *Kiss Tomorrow Goodbye* (1950), the first Cagney Productions picture under the Warners deal; it turned out to be a gangster film both more violent and more amoral than *White Heat*—with a good deal less of the style and quirkiness that made the Walsh film a perverse treat.

In response to *Kiss Tomorrow Goodbye*, the state film censor in Ohio took the almost unprecedented step—for the Production Code era—of completely banning its showing. The grounds were that it was "sordid, sadistic" and told how to commit a crime.[3] This cost the studio almost $100,000 of revenue, according to a Warner Bros. executive, or an additional 7.5 percent on top of its $1.3 million in domestic rentals.

With its early chain gang scenes, *Kiss Tomorrow Goodbye* evoked the 1932 Depression-era Warner Bros. classic *I Am a Fugitive from a Chain Gang*—but any resemblance between the two films ends when, during a successful escape, the convict played by Cagney shoots his escapee partner in the head. Based on a 1948 novel by Horace McCoy, *Kiss Tomorrow Goodbye* opens at a trial at which almost the entire supporting cast (including a prison guard, policemen, and a lawyer) stand accused of participating in the multifarious crimes of the now-deceased Cagney character. The film proceeds in flashbacks from trial testimony.

Counting the number of people Cagney's character shoots, slugs, slaps, beats, knees, and stomps proves to be nearly as difficult as keeping track of the murders in *The Big Sleep*. Lacking a scientific explanation for his character's behavior (as was offered in *White Heat*), Cagney simply performs as if demented, with a variety of facial tics reminiscent of Bogart in his B-movie phase: pursed lips, gritted teeth, jutted jaw, and the like. Gordon Douglas directed from a script by Harry Brown, a reminder once again of the inability of Cagney Productions to obtain top-level directors for its independent efforts. Unlike *Johnny Come Lately*, this problem could not be blamed on a boycott instigated by Warner Bros. That it was a problem, however, was reflected in Cagney's performance.

Jimmy the recidivist gangster was already too much of a good thing. Cagney made an about-face for his second Warners picture, going into a musical set at the United States Military Academy, *The West Point Story* (1950). Otherwise, some audiences who never saw him as a song-and-dance fellow on the screen might have thought of him only as a hoodlum. *The West Point Story* also harked back to Warner Bros. 1930s films—in this instance, an earlier West Point musical, *Flirtation Walk* (1934), and Cagney's own military adventure films, *Here Comes the Navy* and *Devil Dogs of the Air*. Of all coincidences, the producer of all three Depression-era movies, Louis F. Edelman, also produced *The West Point Story*. To make the déjà vu all the more intense, the studio dug up from out of the past one of its former war-horse directors, Roy Del Ruth—with whom Cagney had made four films in 1931–1933.

As an exercise in nostalgia—it also drew elements from *Footlight Parade* and *Yankee Doodle Dandy*—*The West Point Story* was notable chiefly for Cagney's getting himself in shape to be a song-and-dance fellow. About six months older than Bogart, he was facing similar problems of maintaining a screen persona for an actor passing fifty years of age—even though he had moved his birth five years forward, so the press reported him to be still in his mid-forties. It is interesting that in *Kiss Tomorrow Goodbye* his character's age is given as thirty-seven, and he is addressed on one occasion as "young man." Where Bogart remained thin and showed his age in the face, Cagney's aging seemed to occur in the body, in his tendency to overweight. That was something he had overcome for *Yankee Doodle Dandy*, and he showed in *The West Point Story*, if little else, that he was capable of doing it again.

For the final picture on its 1949 contract, Warners found something else for him to play besides hoodlum or hoofer. Adapted by Goff and Roberts (of *White Heat*) from a Harlan Ware novel, with Gordon Douglas again directing, *Come Fill the Cup* (1951) features

Cagney as an alcoholic newsman who hits bottom, then climbs back. What starts as a social problem film, however, ends as crime drama, as if unable to resist the notion that, unless Cagney is dancing, audiences love him best when he is punching and shooting. The violence overrides an otherwise subtle Cagney performance that utilizes the actor's coy humor and rich gestural repertoire to portray a chastened, diffident, but candid figure (also lost when the plot turns violent is a brilliantly comic, ironic performance by Gig Young as another, but unredeemed, lush).

There was apparently no interest on either side in extending Cagney's Warner Bros. performance contract; the second and third pictures after *White Heat* had not been particularly successful, and, on the business front, they were squabbling about financial terms on Cagney Productions releases. With no independent projects ready to get off the ground, the actor was at loose ends. His interest in freelance work seemed also not to be very strong (it was not until mid-1954 that he began to pursue freelance assignments). After six idle months, however, he responded positively to an offer from Darryl F. Zanuck at Twentieth Century–Fox to play the part of Captain Flagg in *What Price Glory* (1952), a remake of Fox's famous 1926 silent film about World War I—based, in turn, on a Broadway play by Maxwell Anderson and Lawrence Stallings.

Zanuck, as it turned out, no less than Jack Warner, still had his memory's eye fixed firmly on a trim prewar actor. "Cagney was sensational in *Yankee Doodle Dandy*," the Fox executive harked back a decade as he proposed for the Flagg role the man who had played George M. Cohan.[4] (As a gauge of Zanuck's thinking, the other actor he considered for the part was John Wayne.) When Cagney arrived on the set, however, in his Falstaffian girth he might have been mistaken for Orson Welles.

Corpulent became the reviewers' adjective of choice. Beefy and plump were common synonyms; even the ever-upbeat *Los Angeles Times* noticed a "trace of paunch." Old and small were secondary terms in the more expansive critical texts. These observations were not, however, necessarily negative. Cagney the actor had made his name on Broadway about the same time that the play's characters, Captain Flagg and his sidekick Sergeant Quirt, began their careers as fictional folk heroes. It was as if the reviewers were commenting equally not only on the actor but on how the character had weathered the years. The living figure as well as the fictional had, as the *New Yorker* put it, "become, in a unique sense, a cliché himself. . . ."

If anybody had something negative to say about *What Price Glory,* it was that the remake desecrated a popular classic (though numerous sequels produced by Fox in the early 1930s had already accomplished that). Directed in an extremely broad manner by John Ford, the 1952 version was notable chiefly for its reshaping the World War I story through a post–World War II viewpoint on American-European cultural relations.

The film begins with a voice-over placing the action in France, 1918. The American protagonists are identified as U.S. Marines, "veterans who had seen service all over the world. China. Cuba. Santo Domingo. Mexico, and the Philippine Islands." In this context, France, 1918, turns into one more episode in American imperial expansion.

Indeed, the French in *What Price Glory* play the role of comic natives much as do, in other films, the darker-skinned denizens of those earlier way stations in the advance of gunboat diplomacy. French women fall in love with American men; they learn to speak the Americans' language. Like *An American in Paris* (1951), *Roman Holiday* (1953), and innumerable other films of the period, *What Price Glory* used the romantic conquest of European women by American men as a trope for American assertion of postwar cultural supremacy over the Old World.

Zanuck planted one arcane intertextual note in the film. When a German officer is taken prisoner, Cagney's Captain Flagg speaks Yiddish to him, and is understood. Cagney fans with long memories would have recalled that Jimmy spoke Yiddish in the 1932 *Taxi!*, a film Zanuck supervised as associate executive at Warner Bros. To be the occasion of serendipitous delight for the inevitably dwindling corps of *Taxi!* devotees, however, was hardly consolation for being described in a dozen ways as a man about to bust his britches—and, in the *New Yorker*'s sense, as a performer playing out a stereotype of a successful screen persona.

What had become of his desire to take control of his own screen image? The creation of Cagney Productions had been the result of that wish, and the company's distribution deal with Warner Bros. continued. After *Kiss Tomorrow Goodbye*, in fact, it had produced two additional pictures, *Only the Valiant* (1951) and *Bugles in the Afternoon* (1952), neither of which, however, employed the company's namesake star. After *What Price Glory*, Cagney returned to his own independent base to make *A Lion Is In the Streets* (1953), a film that might enable him to be perceived again as an actor—rather than as a man too fat, old, and short for his job, and perhaps insufficiently aware of the slightly ridiculous figure he had, in some eyes, become.

▪ ▪ ▪ ▪

The project had been in mind since early 1945, when Cagney Productions claimed to have paid a quarter of a million dollars for Adria Locke Langley's fictional account (with the same title as the film) of the rise and fall of a Huey Long–style Southern governor. Within a year, however, *All the King's Men*, Robert Penn Warren's classic, had eclipsed the Langley novel. Then the 1949 Columbia Pictures adaptation of Warren's book won the Oscar for Best Picture, and Broderick Crawford gained the actor Oscar for his portrayal of a charismatic, corrupt politician. There did not seem much reason for Cagney to do a version of a similar figure, other than to avoid the total loss of a quarter-million when the book's option expired.

In the months after the Columbia film came out, however, a new phenomenon had emerged in American politics: the rise to prominence of Senator Joseph McCarthy of Wisconsin as focus and catalyst of the anti-Communist movement in American society. Cagney's film was in preproduction development during the critical presidential election campaign of 1952, when McCarthy's demagoguery almost challenged his party's candidate (and eventual two-term president), Dwight D. Eisenhower, for dominance.

To make a political film in the vortex of 1952 was an inevitably different and more difficult act than even in the increasingly roiled waters of 1949, when a project like Huston's *We Were Strangers* could still be supported. One might imagine that, for an actor who had managed mysteriously to suppress his radical past and miraculously escape HUAC and McCarthyite scrutiny, it could have been a daring or dangerous thing to do.

From this perspective, the almost complete disappearance of *A Lion Is In the Streets* from historical or critical memory is somewhat surprising. The reason may lie in the film's fundamental contradictions. They began to emerge even before shooting started when the story was changed so that the demagogue's political rise was curtailed—he became not a governor but an unsuccessful aspirant for the office, as if in 1952 it was courting subversiveness to suggest that an unprincipled man could gain high office in the United States. The contradictions became apparent when it was decided to shoot the film in Technicolor, and more blatant still when Franz Waxman— recent Oscar winner for musical scoring on *Sunset Boulevard* (1950) and *A Place in the Sun* (1951)—prepared a lusty, folkloric score. With Raoul Walsh directing, the Cagneys could have no complaint of Warner Bros. preventing talent from joining the project; indeed, in terms of production values there were signs of too much Warners involvement. The film was too pretty, too lush, too folksy: to be serious about demagoguery perhaps demanded the aesthetics of black and white.

The narrative only added to the movie's problems. Basically, *A Lion Is In the Streets* was a Warner Bros. Depression-era Southern social problem film—like *Cabin in the Cotton* (1932) or *They Won't Forget* (1937)—passed through the ideological meat grinder of the 1950s, which scrambled whatever toughness or cynicism had leavened the prewar films' compromises. Cagney's Hank Martin is a man who turns from peddler to politician when he deduces that sharecroppers remain poor because the cotton gin gives them short weight, and observes that their children are sick and uneducated because the state government fails to provide sufficient health or educational services. He leads a group of armed sharecroppers in confrontation with armed deputies at the cotton gin—as powerful a scene of old-fashioned class struggle as any in Depression-era movies, especially remarkable in the context of 1952.

However, these elements of radicalism are depicted in the film not to enlist audience sympathy (or political analysis), but to be demonstrated as errors. *A Lion Is In the Streets* insists at copious length that Hank Martin is wrong to accuse the propertied classes of malfeasance (the short-weighing was done not at the instigation of the gin's owner but by venal employees). It neglects, however, to address its own initial critique of government, opting instead for the tried-and-true method of condemning the man who holds the ideas, ergo the ideas are presumed to fail with him.

Martin is adulterous and ambitious: he cheats on his wife and his supporters, and she and they expose him. He is assassinated by the widow of a martyr to his cause. "You sold out," she condemns him. His dying words are, "Never knew folks could be so all-fired smart." The visual motif behind the opening and closing credits is of a lion, trying and failing to assault the Lincoln Memorial's seated Lincoln figure. The final words are Lincoln's—about not fooling all the people all the time. It is presumably to be understood that calling for more government support for health and education is wrong.

Cagney's performance undercuts the film even more—just because he is vintage Cagney. Vibrant, bursting with manic energy, walking with his cocky bounce and his whole body tilted forward, he shapes a characterization that works against the narrative's insistence on his evil. Walsh's direction once again surely played a role, in his fourth collaboration with the actor.

A Lion Is In the Streets, however, lacks the solid generic structure of a film like *White Heat*, where performance can play against narrative necessity: the audience can like a bad man who it knows is doomed. In the political film, the audience constantly is being told it should find dangerous and disreputable a character for which Cagney's performance fulfills other expectations; there is no way out of the contradiction. The film's lack of impact or resonance—despite the efforts of Cagney and Walsh—is not so surprising after all.

This was the last Cagney Productions film (save for *The Gallant Hours* in 1960, for which a new joint production entity was created). Some sixteen months were to pass before the actor worked in a film again. This was in sharp contrast to Bogart: these were the months when *Beat the Devil*, *The Caine Mutiny*, and *Sabrina* were made. Bogart had a strong screen persona but was able to play with it, work against it, intensify and complicate it. In contrast, even with his versatility, Cagney seemed stuck much more in stereotype.

Perhaps it was the different trajectories of their careers. Cagney had been a star since the early 1930s; when people remembered his greatest moments they harked back fifteen or twenty years. He was a historic figure—a young, thin, sprightly, tough icon of the Depression years. In Bogart's case, few people were likely to remember much of him before *The Maltese Falcon*. With the aid of makeup and a hairpiece, he retained much the same appearance of his early stardom, an indeterminate "middle age."

At the time of *Come Fill the Cup*, a British reviewer wrote of Cagney: "I don't think there's another actor—or actress—who has so often made second-rate films tolerable for me. Swagger, charm, privateering, and a touch of hysteria enable him to carry off almost any beastliness or sentimentality." This somewhat backhanded compliment turned out also to be backward-looking. In his mid-fifties, what had worked in the past was not necessarily a formula for the future.

■ ■ ■ ■

Beginning in mid-1954 Cagney suddenly began working steadily; for the next year and a half he worked more intensively than at any time since the prewar years, completing six films in a burst of renewed professional energy (or was it renewed professional opportunity, a clearance linked to the end of HUAC's Hollywood investigations in 1953?). Four of these films were released close together in the spring and early summer of 1955—probably by happenstance, since they were from three different distribution companies—but they gave the clear impression of a comeback. There was even an Academy Award nomination—his third—for his performance as Martin (The Gimp) Snyder in *Love Me or Leave Me* (1955).

This surge of activity won the attention of the popular press. "Cagney's Year," Louella O. Parsons titled her June 1955 column in *Cosmopolitan*—significant recognition from a barometer of right-wing opinion in Hollywood. In the fall there were feature pieces about the actor in *Look, Collier's,* and *Coronet,* now-defunct but once-influential magazines. The Cagney revival culminated journalistically in January 1956 with a three-part, first-person ("as told to") *Saturday Evening Post* feature, "How I Got This Way."

In all the accounts, "this way" turned out to be a new Cagney. Publicity about the actor's personal life had always depicted him as a quiet, private man; now he was a quiet, private country gentleman. Photographs accompanying the articles showed Cagney farming on Martha's Vineyard with his two teenaged adopted children. He was a benign patriarch, whose contributions to soil conservation appeared bemusingly to share precedence with his status as a revived movie star. He had come a long way from his East Side upbringing, further still from what, already in the 1950s, was emerging as the classic Cagney screen image—a hoodlum squeezing half a grapefruit into Mae Clarke's profile.

Taken as a group, Cagney's four 1955 pictures indicate that attention was paid to the problem of his screen persona. The films embrace and exploit the actor's past—not so much through repetition of performance style, however, as from deliberate evocation through memory, symbol, and contrast. Performance itself, if not quite subordinated, is subsumed within the structure of strongly written characterizations. The roles were intended not simply as "Cagney parts," to be carried off by swagger, charm, and hysterics, but as sharply delineated, idiosyncratic figures in themselves. In order of appearance (not necessarily of production) the films were *Run for Cover,* a Paramount western directed by Nicholas Ray; *Love Me or Leave Me,* an MGM wide-screen biopic based on the career of singer Ruth Etting; *Mister Roberts,* an independent production adapted from the popular novel and Broadway play, distributed by Warner Bros.; and *The Seven Little Foys,* another biopic, this time starring Bob Hope, with Cagney doing a brief reprise of his George M. Cohan role in *Yankee Doodle Dandy.*

Run for Cover was a curious vehicle to inaugurate a comeback. Cagney's only previous acquaintance with the western genre had come in *The Oklahoma Kid,* a film he had treated as a comic romp. Westerns had taken a more serious turn in the postwar period, particularly after the HUAC hearings and the McCarthyite repression left many filmmakers reluctant to make old-style social problem films: they put their social commentary covertly, or in coded form, in genre films. Nicholas Ray's recent western, *Johnny Guitar* (1954), had been, to some, an outrageous example, with its treatment of gender, sexuality, social change, mob violence, and, quite possibly, Hollywood's community behavior during the blacklist. A performer could be certain a Ray film would be neither staid nor conventional.

Run for Cover was not particularly a triumph for either director or actor, but it holds interest for the continuity it demonstrates with Ray's major work of the period. Like *Johnny Guitar*, it deals with questions of guilt and innocence, mob behavior, community leadership; like *Rebel without a Cause* (1955), it concerns relations between generations, and the formation of character. The narrative revolves around the ties between Cagney's character, called Matthew, and a young man, Davey, played by John Derek. Meeting as strangers on horseback, by a string of misperceptions and hasty judgments the two men are accused of robbing a train and are hunted down by a posse of townspeople, who severely wound the boy before their mistake is discovered. Recalling a dead son, the older man nurses the younger back to health. The boy is embittered because he must walk with a limp from an improperly healed leg wound.

The older man becomes sheriff of the lawless town and makes the boy a deputy. After a series of crimes, the two find themselves chasing bandits in the desert, where the boy suddenly shoots and wounds the older man, admitting he was an accomplice of the criminals. The generational drama plays itself out as the boy, in a final act of self-redemption, kills a confederate to save the older man's life—and then the older man kills the boy.

One is tempted to regard this convoluted work (with a screenplay credited to Winston Miller from a story by Harriet Frank, Jr., and Irving Ravetch) as yet another allegory of Hollywood under the blacklist—where false accusations, moblike posses, lynch law, betrayals, and the slaying of the young by their patriarchal elders represent a community in chaos. Cagney gives a subdued and what seems consciously a mature performance, with little of swagger and less of hysteria until the end, when, in shooting the boy, he takes on the demented look (head down, mouth open, eyes rolled up) he utilized when firing a gun as far back as *Angels with Dirty Faces*. In context, it is a culmination of the wild disorder that permeates the setting.

Love Me or Leave Me was a different kind of project entirely: a sentimental, scandal-tinged melodrama, a prestige CinemaScope Metro-Goldwyn-Mayer musical biography, with Doris Day's name appearing before Cagney's in the credits—the first time he relinquished top billing since the early 1930s. She was the star and his was the "character" role in a story based on the lives of singer Ruth Etting and her manager-husband Martin (The Gimp) Snyder, who gained notoriety in the 1930s by shooting her accompanist-lover. (MGM later paid Etting and Snyder $12,500 each to settle lawsuits alleging defamatory depiction.)

The Snyder role added grit to what might otherwise have been just another 1950s Eastmancolor bittersweet success story with songs. Cagney's characterization marked a return to the social environment from which his early stardom grew—Chicago gangland of the 1920s. This time, however, he was not a brash, pretty, sexually passive Irish boy like Tom Powers; he was a lame, plain, crude, brutal Jewish hustler. In his Snyder there was recognizably the Warner Bros. 1930s ethnic hero, but with crucial defects: the loss of youth, grace, and humor. Here was swagger without charm, and hysteria not as performance technique—to fill in a script's rough sketch—but as personality core. His pugnacious, screaming anger was part of his character's tawdry but (at least as the film presents it) not wholly unredeemable obsession.

After all of Snyder's storms, Cagney abruptly shifts pace in a closing scene. Snyder has shot the lover; in jail, subdued, defeated, resigned, he greets Etting on a visit. The actor puts all his character's deep emotions in the top half of his face: he conveys Snyder's feelings with his eyes, a shift of his eyebrows in opposite directions, the movement of his forehead. It was a signature moment for an actor who had made his supple body an instrument, showing that neither his own age nor his character's disability could diminish subtlety, only concentrate it. In the Academy Award balloting, he lost out to Ernest Borgnine, who won the actor Oscar for *Marty*.

Cagney worked back into shape to make a brief return as a dancer in Paramount's *The Seven Little Foys*, where he appears in a cameo as George M. Cohan at a Friars' dinner honoring the film's subject, Eddie Foy, played by Bob Hope. He and Hope trade banter about ego and age, then Cagney gets up on a table and performs a short routine from *Yankee Doodle Dandy*. The two performers then dance a duet to the song "Mary."

He may have appeared trim, but he could well have been corseted beneath his black-tie attire, judging from appearances in *Mister Roberts*, a film whose production overlapped with that of *The Seven Little Foys*. Cagney's part was not much more extensive than in the biopic, and no less limited in conception. Henry Fonda gets top billing as Roberts in the adaptation (directed by John Ford, and, after Ford's illness, Mervyn LeRoy) of the best-selling novel and hit Broadway play. The young Jack Lemmon as Ensign Pulver walked off with the film—and the supporting actor Oscar. Cagney's role as captain of the navy ship *Reluctant* is signaled by the comic music accompanying his first appearance, in a bathrobe, obsessively watering a potted palm tree. He plays the part as if he were Tom Powers grown old (and law-abiding), who became a merchant marine steward instead of a beer runner, and ended up as martinet of a navy cargo ship.

Back in circulation, Cagney no longer squawked at unpromising roles as he had when he was indentured at Warner Bros.—in 1950s Hollywood, complaining was a luxury a freelancer could not afford. As part of a two-picture deal with MGM (probably the second picture was a reward for accepting the first one), he rescued the studio from a jam, at whatever cost to himself a bad film might extract. MGM's trouble was caused by Spencer Tracy. Still under contract to the studio, the actor had been assigned to a western, *Tribute to a Bad Man* (1956). He had just made *Bad Day at Black Rock* (for which he too received a 1955 Oscar nomination) and was determined not to follow a good role with a clinker. Though the new picture was all set to begin shooting at a remote location, Tracy caused several weeks' delay, doing all he could to get himself canned from the film. MGM finally obliged him, also canceling his contract. With location costs mounting, the studio was obviously grateful that Cagney was willing to step in.

Tracy may have behaved badly, but his reasoning was sound. Despite a prestige director, Robert Wise, and picturesque CinemaScope cinematography by Robert Surtees, *Tribute to a Bad Man* turned out, arguably, as the most mediocre film of Cagney's career so far. John Wayne might have made something of the role that Tracy spurned: he had played its definitive prototype as Dunson in Howard Hawks's *Red River* (1948). The part Cagney took up was of yet another crusty, ruthless, frontier patriarch, building the West to serve post–Civil War America. This one corrals and tames wild horses so they can pull wagons in the cities—and the irony of his impending obsolescence by the internal combustion engine is heavily underlined. He has rescued a damsel from iniquity; she happens to be a tall, dark, cigar-smoking Greek immigrant, played by Irene Papas in her American film debut. Her name is Jocasta (Jo, for short), so when a young cowhand falls for her it is hard not to see OEDIPAL TRIANGLE subliminally written on the screen in bold capitals. The ending is Freudian rather than as with Sophocles: she opts to stay with the old man, who gives the boy his favorite horse as consolation.

Even while the western was in production, Cagney was proposing changes on his second MGM picture—his reward film—then in de-

ɣ
velopment, *These Wilder Years* (1956). Though it got little if any
more respect than *Tribute to a Bad Man* (1950s reviewers were often
more kind to bad westerns than to family melodramas), there are
aspects of the film worthy of interest. For one, after seven pictures
over the previous half-decade, it was Cagney's first film with a contemporary setting since 1951. The long hiatus pointed up a significant shift in the actor's career: in the 1930s at Warner Bros. he had
seemed to embody the style and tempo of the era. As he aged and
culture changed, however, he had been unable to sustain a contemporary persona—as had performers such as Cary Grant and, in his
own way, Bogart, whose screen image was never exactly *au courant*
even though most of his films were set in the present time of their
making.

These Wilder Years addressed this issue in Cagney's career (here
the actor's input at the script development stage may have been crucial) by reformulating what had been only implicit in several earlier
films, particularly the westerns *Run for Cover* and *Tribute to a Bad
Man*: the position of his screen characters as surrogate or symbolic
fathers. In *These Wilder Years*, his role is in fact a man searching for
his place as a father. His character, a successful industrialist, sets
out to right a wrong by trying to find a boy born out of wedlock
twenty years earlier, whom he had fathered (though Cagney was in
his mid-fifties, the fictional character was in his early forties).

His quest takes him to an agency for unwed mothers in his old
college town, where he becomes involved with the problems of a
pregnant sixteen-year-old (played by Betty Ann Keim). Determined
to force the agency to release information, he is confronted with his
own youthful irresponsibility—his denial of fatherhood twenty
years earlier, with the remark that "it could have been any one of
sixteen other guys." Older and wiser, he adopts the girl, and gains a
daughter—and soon after, a grandson—in one swoop. It *was* a tear-
jerker, but as rich in human feeling (alongside *Love Me or Leave Me*)
as anything he had done in years. Roy Rowland directed, and Barbara
Stanwyck co-starred as head of the agency; Cagney looked a little
bulbous, but the subdued nature of his performance seemed paradoxically to radiate more of his old energy than his red-faced ranting in
Mister Roberts or *Tribute to a Bad Man*.

Man of a Thousand Faces (1957), produced at Universal, also appeared to develop out of the concerns of *These Wilder Years*, even
though the subject was the biography of a famous performer. Universal made the film to honor (and exploit) its silent star, Lon Chaney, who had died in 1930. Its box office appeal may have centered
on the film's effort to duplicate Chaney's secret makeup tech-

niques—and Cagney's re-creation of the actor's performances in the silent classics *Hunchback of Notre Dame* (1923) and *Phantom of the Opera* (1925)—but the narrative revolved around issues of family and fatherhood.

One obvious source for this symmetry between two otherwise disparate films, made at two different studios, was that writer Ralph Wheelwright was credited as story source for both. (Cagney's contract gave him the right of both script and director approval. Ivan Goff and Ben Roberts of *White Heat* and *Come Fill the Cup* were called in to assist R. Wright Campbell with the screenplay—the trio and Wheelwright won Academy nomination for a writing award; Universal genre director Joseph Pevney, a former actor, was chosen to direct.)

Man of a Thousand Faces recalls the silent era less in its spectacular reconstructions than in its somber treatment of family pathos and conflict. Cagney's Chaney as both son and father is marked by the circumstance that his parents are deaf-mutes. The deterioration of Chaney's first marriage, occupying fully half the film, is presented as caused by his wife's fearing that their child will be similarly disabled (Dorothy Malone plays the wife). Chaney's entire film career is shown as primarily a means by which his life can become secure enough for him to gain custody of the child.

Chaney's success also seems to derive from a lifelong experience with disability and abnormality. Much of this theme is centered on speech: the parents' muteness, the first wife's ruining her singing voice by swallowing acid in a suicide attempt, Chaney's loss of speech at the end from throat cancer. One of the most emotionally evocative scenes is a lengthy take of Cagney/Chaney performing as a cripple in *The Miracle Man* (1919); then, after the camera stops, he gets up and dances a jig. (The Universal film carefully elides the fact that the picture was a Paramount production, and that Chaney's character only masqueraded as a cripple.) This was perhaps more a Cagney than a Chaney touch—a bit of insouciance that was one of the few bursts of Cagney energy in a performance otherwise subordinated to the quieter manner of his character.

Some commentators have found Cagney's Chaney a high point of his career, one calling it his best performance since *Yankee Doodle Dandy*. Part of this praise, one suspects, derives from the tour-de-force nature of the makeup scenes: Chaney as the hunchback Quasimodo angrily spotting his ex-wife on the set is a physical objective correlative for the character's distorted anguish at seeing her. Ultimately, however, the Chaney role falls more in the category of "song-and-dance fellow" than "hoodlum" in Cagney's split screen persona. To favor it over Cody Jarrett in *White Heat* or even Martin (The Gimp) Snyder in *Love Me or Leave Me* is perhaps to miss the enduring Cagney: the man who, in his own right, and without makeup, could with humor, rage, and pathos construct emphatic portraits of twentieth-century urban American sociopaths.

▪ ▪ ▪ ▪

With Humphrey Bogart's death a few weeks after *Man of a Thousand Faces* finished production, Cagney was left as the last of the city boys. How much more he wished (or would be able) to maintain that screen persona was an open question. He was about to take on responsibility for directing a picture, *Short Cut to Hell* (1957); in it he also makes a brief screen appearance, sitting in a director's chair and speaking into the camera before the opening credits. He introduces the film's two young leads and remarks, "As time wears on, we keep having to introduce new ones wherever they can be found."

A remake of *This Gun for Hire* (1942), the film is of interest chiefly for whatever evidence it may give of director Cagney's conception of the acting of others. Robert Ivers as the punk has a James Dean look but plays his tough guy coldly and one-dimensionally. Georgiann Johnson as the girl is a bit more stylish, with a kind of comic vivaciousness reminiscent of Ann Sheridan in her Warners days. This B picture did not launch these two young performers into the "great future" Cagney's prologue predicted for them.

Short Cut to Hell demonstrated that he had no problem directing urban sociopath characters—even though he could not assist a less-skilled performer to give the role depth or redemptive personality traits (or perhaps by now he saw little to redeem in the type). Still, there remained before him a commitment (made with Universal at the time *Man of a Thousand Faces* was in production) to attempt a version of the figure once more. As time wore on, maybe it was still possible to recycle old performers in old roles one more time.

Not, however, in *Never Steal Anything Small* (1958), a film that could make *Tribute to a Bad Man* look like a classic. Producer Aaron Rosenberg and director Charles Lederer (who also wrote the screen story and screenplay based on an unproduced play by Maxwell Anderson and Rouben Mamoulian) seem to have had the idea—there is no getting around it—of making a musical comedy about corruption in the longshoremen's unions. It was as if they had taken Elia Kazan's *On the Waterfront* (1954) and turned the vicious, corrupt union boss Johnny Friendly into a song-and-dance man.

Its problems were signaled by the months of sneak previews and reediting it went through before being released early in 1959. Somewhere along the way the idea came up to add an exculpatory epigraph: "This picture is sympathetically dedicated to Labor and its problems in coping with a new and merry type of public enemy . . . the charming well-dressed gentleman who cons his way to a union throne, and never needs to blow a safe again." Merry as a word to describe Cagney's larcenous, ambitious dockworker (and song-and-dance man) is an extreme case of wishful thinking.

By the late 1950s the energy generated by Cagney's 1955 comeback seemed to have completely dissipated. The ghost of Cagney's radical past also resurfaced—though only behind the closed doors of the FBI. A new associate, A. C. Lyles, who had produced *Short Cut to Hell*, proposed to the Bureau a television series based on J. Edgar Hoover's book *Persons in Hiding*. Lyles mentioned that Cagney was interested in the project; he may not have been aware that this reference was a kiss of death. According to an internal FBI memo, made available under the Freedom of Information Act, the Bureau consulted its files and concluded (all that remains visible among extensive material blacked out for "security" reasons) that Cagney was linked to numerous Communist front organizations. "Certainly with this background we don't want to have anything to do with Cagney," the memo recommends.[5]

Cagney worked overseas for the first time (other than location work in the Pacific for *Mister Roberts*) on *Shake Hands with the Devil* (1959), a film shot at Ardmore Studios in Bray, Ireland, south of Dublin. It was, however, a British film rather than Irish—with a British producer-director, Michael Anderson, and such performers as Glynnis Johns, Michael Redgrave, and Sybil Thorndike—and one can only wonder how thoroughly Cagney knew the ideological waters he was dipping into. Based on, but significantly altered from, a 1934 novel by Reardon Conner, the film is set in 1921, "the year of the Black and Tan"—the British military units who waged war against Irish Republican forces before the Anglo-Irish treaty was signed at year's end. The film is careful to condemn violence and extremism on both sides, but its main narrative thrust is against the uncompromising stance of the Irish Republican Army for unification of all Ireland under one flag; in effect, it was making a clear expression of support for the continuation of British control of Northern Ireland.

Cagney's character is central to that ideological project. He plays Sean Lenihan, a surgeon and lecturer at a Dublin medical college, who is secretly a commandant in the Republican forces. The other main character, played by Don Murray, is an American World War I veteran studying medicine at Dublin who gets caught up in the struggle when the Black and Tan fatally shoot his friend. The British forces arrest an elderly aristocratic patriot (played by Dame Sybil) for harboring a fugitive, and the Irish under Lenihan's leadership retaliate by taking hostage a British woman. They will execute her if the ailing aristocrat should die in prison.

The denouement is heavily dependent on the portrait of the revolutionary leader the film draws. Cagney's character is depicted as repressed sexually to such an extent that violence is the only outlet for his feelings—perhaps, by extension, a "theory" for the cause of political rebellion in Ireland. He voyeuristically spies on Kitty, a provocative barmaid, as she swims in the nude (and spectators are offered a limited share of his view); when she invites him to act on his desire, he strikes her. The next day, when she inadvertently comes into an area where an armed action is about to begin, he shoots her—without justification—as a suspected traitor.

This act sets the stage for the climax. The sickly patriot dies in prison. Lenihan orders the execution of the British hostage. The young American, meanwhile, has fallen in love with her. When he sees that none of the revolutionaries wants to assist Lenihan in the woman's assassination, the American shoots the crazed Irishman to prevent him from committing the murder. He throws his gun away, and the film ends. (In the original novel, the execution is carried out, and violence rages on.)

The Gallant Hours (1960) was the product of a joint venture with Robert Montgomery, for which the two actors set up a onetime production entity, Cagney-Montgomery Productions. Montgomery produced and directed, and Cagney performed as Fleet Admiral William F. Halsey, in this docudrama about the navy's Pacific commander battling the Japanese in the early months of World War II. Halsey's age was sixty-two at the time of the film's events; Cagney celebrated his sixtieth birthday a few weeks after the production ended. It was the first time ever—other than in perhaps a few scenes in *Yankee Doodle Dandy*, twenty years before—that one of his screen characters was older than the actor's chronological age.

▪ ▪ ▪ ▪

The Gallant Hours marked thirty years for Cagney in the movies. Only a handful of performers equaled his record of longevity, only a very few males had maintained the consistency of a top-billed name star: from his own age group, Gary Cooper, Clark Gable, Spencer Tracy, and, among those slightly younger, Cary Grant, John Wayne, and James Stewart. Certain of these figures might be called actors, others, personalities—this latter term in the sense in which Lee Strasberg conceived of it, that their performances were "natural" emanations of their inner selves.

Cagney was not this latter sort of "natural" screen personality. There were too many screen Cagneys, for one thing. There was the sexually immature and violent figure who stemmed from Tom Powers in *The Public Enemy*, was memorably reconstituted as the psychopathic mama's boy of *White Heat*, and lately was resurrected for *Shake Hands with the Devil*. He was also the song-and-dance man, who shaded over into the biopic interpreter of stage and screen stars, from Cohan in *Yankee Doodle Dandy* to Chaney in *Man of a Thousand Faces*. There were efforts to represent the "real" Cagney—at least the actor's self-image as a gentle, considerate, philosophical soul, in his own independent productions like *Great Guy* and *The Time of Your Life*. Finally, there was the comic, lady-killer, fast-talking con man, the figure who predominated in Cagney's Depression-era Warner Bros. movies far more than the psychopathic criminal.

An ambiguous and complex portrait can be drawn from all these types—the city boy. He is mercurial and funny, quick to anger, needful of women and resentful of that need, a performer at heart, clever with words, operating at the edge and beyond the law, melancholy but resilient. If one were to choose a single film that best exemplified these traits in the Cagney screen persona—that encapsulated the many Cagneys—the sentimental choice here would be the film the actor made in the fall of 1932, after ending his lengthy one-man strike against Warner Bros.: the aptly named *Hard to Handle*.

It is quite impossible to imagine that Billy Wilder had *Hard to Handle* in mind when he and collaborator I.A.L. Diamond adapted a Ferenc Molnar play into *One, Two, Three* (1961); but the serendipitous fact is that the character they wrote—and Cagney's performance in the role—uncannily revives the quintessential Cagney persona from that picture made nearly thirty years earlier.

Even the differences derive from similarity. Cagney's character in the 1933 film was named "Lefty" as an obvious intertextual poke in the ribs to audiences who knew, if not yet of his involvement in left-wing causes, at least that the studio regarded as subversive his independent frame of mind. In *One, Two, Three* he might as well have been called "Righty" for his character's intransigent ridicule of communism—a nickname that would also have reflected his 1960s political stance.

At the time and in the circumstances of *One, Two, Three*, to be sure, few Americans would have been likely to dissent from the cold war attitudes Cagney's character and the film, in part, represent. While the movie was shooting in Berlin during the summer of 1961, the East German regime erected the Berlin Wall between the Eastern and Western sectors of the divided city, precipitating a brief international crisis. The problem of being overtaken by events was solved in the film by an opening Cagney voice-over that refers to the sealing off of the border and places the film's action a few months earlier—since the narrative requires passage between the two zones. Wilder and Diamond's script is so filled with topical references, however, that spectators from a later generation may need a historical glossary, or encyclopedic Trivial Pursuit knowledge, to follow it.

If any motion picture homage was intended, it would not have been to an obscure and none-too-successful early-Depression Warner Bros. programmer like *Hard to Handle*, but to MGM's classic 1939 comedy spoof of communism, *Ninotchka*, written by Wilder, directed by Ernst Lubitsch, and starring Greta Garbo. *Ninotchka* was a more one-sided film than *One, Two, Three*. Set in Paris, it made clear that the choice between communism as gray ideology and capitalism as glamorous romance was no contest.

One, Two, Three, however, was set in Germany, and Wilder had some scores to settle with others besides Reds: brownshirts, for one, and rednecks, for another. No target in the film is quite so lambasted as communism, but the sweep of its slashing satire takes on German authoritarianism and class pretensions as well as nazism, and American philistinism and commercial imperialism on top of those. As in *Hard to Handle*, nothing is sacred except self-interest.

Making Cagney's character Berlin branch manager for Coca-Cola laid a none-too-subtle satiric foundation for the complications that followed. He is called upon to host his boss's ditzy Southern belle daughter, who promptly marries in secret a handsome but flamingly ideological East German youth. Cagney's character first schemes to get rid of the Red husband, then has to scheme doubly hard to rescue him. The young man proves at the end, to the Coke man's chagrin, that he can learn capitalism's values quickly, and all too well.

Wilder and Diamond wrote one of the period's wittiest scripts. Besides all the blatant political jokes, they manage to make a running risque laugh line out of the word "umlaut"—how could the censors deal with that one?—and include such priceless touches as East German police torturing the young man by playing a record of "Yellow Polka Dot Bikini." Art director Alexander Trauner's set of the ballroom in an East Berlin hotel (the Grand Hotel Potemkin, formerly the Goering, before that the Bismarck) is a masterpiece of drab decadence, and Wilder tops it by having the bandleader sing "Yes, We Have No Bananas"—in German. The director perhaps resisted utilizing Cagney's knowledge of Yiddish, though there is one moment in a hectic scene where a salesman enters and utters the word "schmuck." Cagney turns sharply with "What did you say?" and then the man explains that he is selling jewelry (the German word for jewelry is the same as the Yiddish word for jerk).

Comments Cagney made to a reporter in Munich during the film's production indicate that he was giving thought to his own career longevity, and his early days in the movies. Wilder may well have intended his casting of Cagney as a kind of homage—to the actor and, more broadly, to his generic identity. At one moment, while talking to an American military policeman, the Cagney character makes a sudden hand gesture, and the MP goes into the classic stand-up comic's mimicry of Cagney: elbows in, as if hitching up his pants. The broader touch comes in a moment of crisis when Cagney says, "Mother of Mercy, is this the end of little Rico?"—a slight variant on lines spoken by Edward G. Robinson in *Little Caesar* (1931), which might be interpreted as suggesting a kind of generic melding together or confusion among actors, movies, and unforgettable (though not necessarily correctly quoted) lines.

Whatever the multiple sources for recollection—or whether there was any specific memory of "Lefty" Merrill in *Hard to Handle* at all—Cagney's C. R. McNamara came as close to reviving that figure as a body thirty years older (the source of additional jokes—"arrogant, fat, and bloated," the hothead Red calls him) could do. Arrogance at least united the two. Some commentators have criticized Cagney for bellowing through his part, but that was his con-man persona to perfection: loudmouthed, vain, peremptory, but with a supreme self-confidence beyond egotism, permitting insults both to define him and leave him unfazed.

"Mein Führer," his wife (played by Arlene Francis) sarcastically addresses him, and if one can accept the charm and harmlessness paradoxically indicated by that phrase, then both *One, Two, Three* and Cagney's performance rank as unmitigated triumphs. After the Wilder film, Cagney retired from acting, and there could have been few more suitable ways to go: a performance that recalled why he was a Depression-era star, and even promised comic redemption for America's cold war mentality, and, as the ditzy belle puts it, "Coca-Cola colonialism."

■ ■ ■ ■

In the 1960s and 1970s Cagney pursued his agricultural interests, centered at a farm he had purchased in Millbrook, New York. Temptations to return to acting work—sure to come his way, as homage to its now-glorious past became more and more a condition of Hollywood's existence, and nostalgia a prevailing American cultural sentiment—he steadfastly resisted. In 1974 he did accept the American Film Institute's second annual award for life achievement at the movies; Cagney was the first performer so honored, following the inaugural award to director John Ford.

Two years later he published an autobiography, *Cagney by Cagney*. As an example of its genre, the book was more candid and interesting than most. For the first time publicly in years, Cagney adverted to his past politics. He conceded, as the press reported at the time, that one motive for making *Yankee Doodle Dandy* was "to remove the taint that apparently still attached itself to my reputation," even though he retrospectively characterized himself as a Roosevelt liberal.[6] In this and other ways he linked himself ideologically with (at that time) California's Republican governor Ronald Reagan. They had been together at Warner Bros. and as Screen Actors Guild officers. They had both been used by the left, Cagney suggested, and once they discovered this, they put their liberal connections behind them and grew increasingly conservative.

In 1977 Cagney suffered a stroke, and his life at Millbrook came more and more under the care and supervision of a neighbor, Marge Zimmerman, who became the manager of his professional affairs. It was she—according to a lengthy and controversial *Life* magazine article in 1984—who prompted Cagney, past the age of eighty, to make a surprise return to the screen in Milos Forman's 1981 film adaptation of the E. L. Doctorow novel *Ragtime*.

Though both homage and nostalgia played a part in his casting, and he received first screen credit as of old, Cagney's role as New York City police chief Rhinelander Waldo was basically a gimmick—on a par with having novelist Norman Mailer portray the architect Stanford White (and in contrast to a vivid, vigorous brief performance by Pat O'Brien as a lawyer). Marge Zimmerman was billed on the screen as "assistant to Mr. Cagney."

Cagney appears in all of his scenes, except the first, wearing a black homburg and sporting an orange-colored mustache ostentatiously curled up at the ends (though in at least one sequence the mustache lacks curls; continuity was napping). Most of the time he was photographed from the chest up, occasionally from the neck up. There are one or two shots of him standing, one of him seated showing his legs, another seated where he looks quite round in the paunch. He rarely moves his body, and then very slowly. His voice occasionally barks with energy like the old Cagney, at other times sounds disconcertingly like the cartoon character Mr. Magoo. Nostalgia may have been served by his appearance, but hardly his image: it was a misconceived idea to place him in a film that was misconceived in most other ways as well.

There was yet another, even more problematic appearance in a 1984 television movie, *Terrible Joe Moran*. Cagney's health was rapidly failing, and on Easter Sunday, March 30, 1986, at age eighty-six, he died. It was front-page, banner-headline news in the next day's New York tabloids, attesting to his status as a cultural icon. He had not died, as had Garfield, in youth and travail; or, as Bogart, in productive, revitalized middle years. His life had run a full course; a quarter-century had passed since his active professional career had ended, and an enduring public image, commensurate with the ever-more-exalted status accorded former movie players during the Reagan years, had formed.

The keys to Cagney were his versatility and energy. He was feisty, vital, cocky, intense, explosive. He embodied extremes of American society, antisocial outlaw and patriotic entertainer. He was hoodlum and hoofer, Tom Powers and George M. Cohan. Ronald Reagan, president at the time of Cagney's death, may or may not have been essaying a synthesis when he called Cagney a "classic American success story."[7] The president's emphasis, understandably, was broad and national. It was a sign that Cagney had succeeded in overcoming his origins, or in lifting what had begun as specific and parochial into the broader national arena. Both possibilities were true.

Here and there at least there were references to the actor's social formation: New York's East Side city streets. Decades of movies and popular myth, however, had transformed this setting with generic coloration: it had been distilled into gangsters and tough guys. These figures, in the American fashion, had in turn become displaced and mobile, as likely to be found out on the road and in little hick burgs as strolling down Broadway.

If there was still a trace of ethnicity in this image (the spunky red-haired Irishness could never completely be effaced), what was missing entirely was social class. What Lincoln Kirstein saw in Cagney's first movie performances—the wrath, the humor, the quick, sharp tongue—were class traits, in which, as he put it, ordinary lower-middle-class Americans could recognize themselves. Ordinary lower-middle-class Americans had not been eliminated, to be sure, in the half-century from *The Public Enemy* to *Ragtime*, but the specificity of a social milieu had been lost to memory and representation.

This perhaps was the deepest meaning of Cagney's "classic American success story." He had taken the spirit of city streets and made it national. The city boy had become a fundamental marker of American culture in the middle decades of the twentieth century. By the 1980s, however, while the city streets remained, with new elements of class and ethnic character, their place in American society and ideology had fundamentally altered.

If the little kids jumping around in the water spray on a steaming city street, in a dim newsreel at the opening of *Ragtime*, did not make it to the suburbs in their lifetime, their children did. For the descendants of the white ethnic lower-middle-class Americans who had teemed in city streets at the beginning of the century, the city boy was not even a memory, but a character encountered—like the cowboy—solely in the popular arts. As the twentieth century neared its close, his successor as the central iconographic male figure in American culture had not yet been identified.

Acknowledgments

Let's begin with the films. In researching 164 films of Cagney, Bogart, and Garfield, some ubiquitous, some rare (before the Turner Entertainment Company released several of those rarities on videocassette or cable channel TNT), I was generously aided by many individuals and institutions. My colleague William K. Everson made available prints from his own collection, as well as his encyclopedic knowledge of American film history. Ann Harris, Ed Simmons, Cathy Holter, and their staffs at the George Amberg Film Study Center, Department of Cinema Studies, Tisch School of the Arts, New York University, supported my work in many ways.

At film archives and collections, I was assisted by Maxine Fleckner, Wisconsin Center for Film and Television Research; Donald Crafton, Yale University Film Study Center; Jeff Scheftel, UCLA Film Archives; and the staff at the Motion Picture, Broadcasting and Recorded Sound Division, Library of Congress. Others who helped me gain access to prints were Kit Parker, Kit Parker Films; Randy Paul and Stuart Linder, Films Incorporated; Ken Kamins and Sal Laudicina, Metro-Goldwyn-Mayer/United Artists; Joe Seechack and Paul Nobel, WNYN, Secaucus, New Jersey; and Beth Dinice and Nancy Barnes. With their aid, I was able to screen all but four of the 164 films; I'm still looking for *Body and Soul* (1931), *Bad Sister*, *Women of All Nations*, and *Starlift*.

Leith Adams and Bob Knudson guided me through the resources of the Warner Bros. Archives, University of Southern California; quotations from documents in the archives are used with the kind permission of Jeremy N. Williams, vice-president and general counsel, Warner Bros. Inc., which retains ownership of all quotations. John Hall and David Chierichetti aided my research in the RKO Radio Pictures/RKO Pictures, Inc. Corporate Archives, and Herbert S. Nusbaum made available materials at Metro-Goldwyn-Mayer. For assistance in my work at their collections I also thank Linda Mehr, Sam Gill, Howard Prouty, and Barbara Hall, Margaret Herrick Library, Academy of Motion Picture Arts and Sciences; Audree Malkin, Theater Arts Library, University of California, Los Angeles; Mary Ann Jensen, Theatre Collection, Princeton University; Ray Holland and

Ned Comstock, Department of Special Collections, Doheny Library, University of Southern California; and the staffs of the State Historical Society of Wisconsin and the Billy Rose Theatre Collection, New York Public Library at Lincoln Center. Research on illustrations was aided by Jan-Christopher Horak, Robin Blair Bolger, and Paolo Cherchi Usai, International Museum of Photography, George Eastman House; and Mary Corliss and Terry Geesken, The Museum of Modern Art/Film Stills Archive, New York.

For giving me access to their knowledge and experience in interviews, I am grateful to John Bright, Marie Dyches, Rose Hobart, Irving Rapper, William Schaefer, Vincent Sherman, and Blanche Sweet. Also assisting me in conversation or correspondence were Hume Cronyn, John and Ann Del Valle, Philip Dunne, Elaine Gethard, Bill Hendricks, Robert Parrish, and Malvin Wald. Elise Morris transcribed substantial portions of the manuscript as well as interviews and notes. Others who have provided aid, criticism, and support include Adriano Aprà, Lino Miccichè, and Vito Zagarrio of the Mostra Internazionale del Nuovo Cinema; Ellen Alderman, Lorenzo Codelli, Daniel Czitrom, Julia Erhardt, Howard Feinstein, Julie Fischer, Jeff Gerecke, Park Goist, Roy Grundmann, Miriam Hansen, Vance Kepley, Jr., Marian Lipschutz, James Livingston, Russell Merritt, Valerie Molof, Charles Musser, James Naremore, Dana Polan, Jeanine St. Germain, Louise Spence, and Robert Tunick.

The late John Cushman helped to instigate and encourage this project, and Joanna Hitchcock and Annette Theuring of Princeton University Press helped to bring it to completion. Lilyn Sklar, George and Norah Harris, and my children, Leonard Sklar, Susan Sklar Friedman, Kate Tentler, and Justin Tentler, have provided inspiration. My greatest debt is to Adrienne Harris, to whom this book is dedicated.

Abbreviations Used in
Notes and Sources

BRTC   Billy Rose Theatre Collection, New York Public Library at Lincoln Center

MPAA   Motion Picture Association of America, Production Code Administration files, Academy of Motion Picture Arts and Sciences, Beverly Hills, California

WBA   Warner Bros. Archives, University of Southern California School of Cinema-Television, Los Angeles

Notes

1. A Society of Ragamuffins

1. E. L. Doctorow, *Ragtime* (New York: Random House, 1975), pp. 269–70.
2. Theodore Dreiser, *The Color of a Great City* (New York: Boni and Liveright, 1923), p. vi.
3. James Cagney, *Cagney by Cagney* (Garden City, N.Y.: Doubleday, 1976), p. 194.
4. Harvey Warren Zorbaugh, *The Gold Coast and the Slum: A Sociological Study of Chicago's Near North Side* (Chicago: Univ. of Chicago Press, 1929), pp. 154–55.
5. Herbert Asbury, *The Gangs of New York: An Informal History of the Underworld* (New York: Knopf, 1928), Introduction, n.p.

2. Roughneck Sissy and Charming Boy

1. Lincoln Kirstein, "James Cagney and the American Hero," *Hound & Horn* 5 (April–June 1932): 466–67.
2. Maxwell Anderson, "Outside Looking In," typescript, BRTC, Act II, pp. 16–17.
3. George Abbott, *"Mister Abbott"* (New York: Random House, 1963), p. 118.
4. George Kelly, "Maggie the Magnificent," typescript, BRTC, Act I, p. 19.
5. Barry Connors, "Hell's Bells: A Comedy in Three Acts," typescript, BRTC, p. 2.
6. Clive Hirschhorn, *The Universal Story* (New York: Crown, 1983), p. 74.
7. Cast list, miscellaneous folder, *The Doorway to Hell* file, WBA.
8. Dr. Carleton Simon to Will H. Hays, letter, November 15, 1930, *The Doorway to Hell* file, MPAA.

3. The Private Enemy

1. Warner quoting himself in a 1932 negotiation with James Cagney, from a deposition taken in 1936 in connection with Cagney's suit against the studio. Deposition of Jack Warner, February 15, 1936, *James Cagney v. Warner Bros. Pictures Inc.*, Cagney legal file, WBA.
2. Henry Cohen, "Introduction: An Ordinary Thug," in *The Public Enemy*, ed. Henry Cohen (Madison: Univ. of Wisconsin Press, 1981), p. 28.
3. Darryl F. Zanuck to Col. Jason S. Joy, January 6, 1931, *The Public Enemy* file, MPAA.

4. Cohen, *The Public Enemy*, p. 111.
5. Zanuck to Dorothea Hill, memorandum, September 4, 1931, Cagney legal file, WBA. The new contract, dated October 14, 1931, was retroactive to September 16, the date *Taxi!* began production.
6. Lincoln Steffens, *The Autobiography of Lincoln Steffens* (New York: Harcourt, Brace, 1931), p. 799. Steffens was quoting his own comment in a conversation with Bernard Baruch.
7. Alfred Kazin, *On Native Grounds: An Interpretation of Modern American Prose Literature* (Garden City, N.Y.: Doubleday, 1942, 1956), Anchor edition, p. 201.
8. Joseph Wood Krutch, *The Modern Temper: A Study and a Confession* (New York: Harcourt, Brace, 1929), Harvest edition, pp. 14, 160–61.
9. "Huzzah for Mr. Cagney," *New York Times*, July 29, 1934, sec. 9, p. 3.
10. R. J. Obringer to Herbert Freston, memorandum, January 3, 1934, Cagney legal file, WBA.
11. *The Letters of Lincoln Steffens*, ed. Ella Winter and Granville Hicks (New York: Harcourt, Brace, 1938), 2:935.
12. Conference notes, "The Finger Man," March 23, 1933, *Lady Killer* file, WBA.
13. Roy Del Ruth to Hal Wallis, memorandum, n.d., *Lady Killer* file, WBA.
14. Wallis to Michael Curtiz, memorandum, December 1, 1933, *Jimmy the Gent* file, WBA.
15. Wallis to Ray Enright, memorandum, July 19, 1934, *The St. Louis Kid* file, WBA.
16. Wallis to Enright, memorandum, July 21, 1934, *The St. Louis Kid* file, WBA.
17. *New York Times*, August 18, 1934; *New York Evening Post*, January 23, 1935.
18. Wallis to William Keighley, memorandum, March 7, 1935, *G Men* file, WBA.
19. Forrest Clark, "James Cagney," *New Theatre* 2 (December 1935): 15, 34.
20. R. Lewis to Obringer, memorandum, September 21, 1934, Cagney legal file, WBA.
21. Obringer to Lewis, memorandum, April 16, 1935, Cagney legal file, WBA.
22. Lewis to Obringer, memorandum, n.d. [1935], Cagney legal file, WBA.
23. Wallis to Harry Joe Brown, October 9, 1935, *Ceiling Zero* file, WBA.
24. *Cagney by Cagney*, p. 69. A wildly inaccurate version of events is told in Doug Warren with James Cagney, *James Cagney: The Authorized Biography* (New York: St. Martin's, 1983), pp. 113–14.
25. *James Cagney v. Warner Bros. Pictures Inc.*, Los Angeles County Superior Court, Hall of Records, Los Angeles. Complaint to Cancel Contract, February 6, 1936, p. 2.
26. *James Cagney v. Warner Bros. Pictures Inc.*, Los Angeles County Superior Court, Hall of Records, Los Angeles. Findings of Fact and Conclusions of Law, April 2, 1936, p. 9.

4. BABY FACE

1. Interview with Rose Hobart, December 13, 1984, Woodland Hills, California.
2. John Mason Brown, *The World of Robert E. Sherwood: Mirror to His Times 1896–1939* (New York: Harper & Row, 1965), p. 319.
3. Leslie Howard to Warner Bros., cablegram, September 9, 1935. This document ended up in the Edward G. Robinson legal file, WBA.
4. Louise Brooks, *Lulu in Hollywood* (New York: Knopf, 1982), p. 62.
5. Robert Lord to Wallis, memorandum, July 16, 1936, *Black Legion* file, WBA.
6. Wallis to Warner, memorandum, July 31, 1936, *Black Legion* file, WBA.
7. Wallis to Lloyd Bacon, memorandum, January 12, 1937, *Marked Woman* file, WBA.
8. Obringer to Reeves Espy, Samuel Goldwyn Inc., December 1, 1937, Bogart legal file, WBA.
9. Interview with Irving Rapper, January 23, 1985, Los Angeles.

5. THE STUDIO LABYRINTH

1. Wallis to Bacon, memorandum, March 15, 1938, *Boy Meets Girl* file, WBA.
2. Wallis to Sam Bischoff, memorandum, March 31, 1938, *Racket Busters* file, WBA.
3. "Lady Doctor" final script, March 16, 1938, *King of the Underworld* file, WBA.
4. Brooks, *Lulu in Hollywood*, p. 62.
5. Frank Mattison to T. C. Wright, memorandum, September 30, 1938, *They Made Me a Criminal* file, WBA.
6. Lee Hugunin to Wright, memorandum, January 5, 1940, *Saturday's Children* file, WBA.
7. Eric Stacey to Wright, memorandum, August 6, 1940, *East of the River* file, WBA.
8. Obringer to Morris Ebenstein, letter, July 20, 1939, Cagney legal file, WBA.
9. Bill Cagney to Wallis, memorandum, December 13, 1939, *Torrid Zone* file, WBA.
10. Charles Einfeld to Wallis, memorandum, April 16, 1940, *City for Conquest* file, WBA.
11. Louis Bromfield to Wallis, February 12, 1940, *It All Came True* file, WBA.
12. Steve Trilling to Wallis, memorandum, March 5, 1940, Bogart legal file, WBA.
13. Contract, October 2, 1937, Paul Muni legal file, WBA.
14. Bogart to Wallis, telegram, May 4, 1940, *High Sierra* file, WBA.

6. PUSHCARTS AND PATRIOTISM

1. House of Representatives, Seventy-sixth Congress, Hearings before a Special Committee on Un-American Activities, *Investigation of Un-American Propaganda Activities in the United States* (1940), Vol. 3, Executive Hearings. Bogart's testimony appears on pp. 1375–78, Leech's on pp. 1381–91.
2. "Humphrey Bogart," August 30, 1940, FBI Bogart file.
3. House of Representatives, *Investigation*, p. 1123.
4. Ibid., pp. 1485, 1487–88. Cagney's testimony appears on pp. 1481–89.
5. Wallis to Warner, memorandum, September 18, 1940, *High Sierra* file, WBA.
6. Bogart to Wallis, telegram, September 27, 1940, *High Sierra* file, WBA.
7. Bogart to Warner, telegram, January 16, 1941, *Out of the Fog* file, WBA.
8. Warner to Wallis, memorandum, January 16, 1941, *Out of the Fog* file, WBA.
9. Bogart to Wallis, telegram, March 6, 1941, Bogart legal file, WBA.
10. Bogart to Trilling, memorandum, n.d. [March 17, 1941], Bogart legal file, WBA.
11. Wallis to Henry Blanke, memorandum, June 12, 1941, *The Maltese Falcon* file, WBA.
12. Wallis to Wright, memorandum, July 5, 1941, *All Through the Night* file, WBA.
13. Sam Jaffe to Trilling, letter, August 4, 1941, Bogart legal file, WBA.
14. Warner to Wallis, memorandum, September 13, 1941, *All Through the Night* file, WBA.
15. Obringer to Warner, memorandum, October 10, 1941, Bogart legal file, WBA.
16. Warner to Harry M. Warner, November 8, 1941; Warner to B. B. Kahane, November 8, 1941, Bogart legal file, WBA.
17. Parker Tyler, *The Hollywood Hallucination* (New York: Creative Age, 1944), p. 136.
18. George Raft to Wallis, telegram, October 23, 1940, *The Sea Wolf* file, WBA.
19. Stacey to Wright, memorandum, September 25, 1941, *Dangerously They Live* file, WBA.
20. *Photoplay*, August 1941, p. 69.
21. Bill Cagney to Wallis, memorandum, April 4, 1941, *Captains of the Clouds* file, WBA.
22. Wallis to Einfeld, memorandum, June 18, 1941, *Captains of the Clouds* file, WBA.
23. Wallis to Curtiz, memorandum, September 25, 1941, *Captains of the Clouds* file, WBA.
24. Thomas F. Brady, "Facts behind 'Yankee Doodle Dandy,'" *New York Times*, January 10, 1943.

7. Heroes without Uniforms

1. Warner to Wallis, memorandum, April 2, 1942, *Casablanca* file, WBA.
2. Wallis to Warner, memorandum, April 13, 1942, *Casablanca* file, WBA.
3. Howard Koch to Wallis, memorandum, May 11, 1942, *Casablanca* file, WBA.
4. Al Alleborn to Wright, memorandum, July 18, 1942, *Casablanca* file, WBA.
5. The behavior of Japanese-Americans in Hawaii during the Pearl Harbor attack is discussed in Roger Daniels, *The Decision to Relocate the Japanese Americans* (Philadelphia: Lippincott, 1975), pp. 26–28. Daniels writes, "careful investigation had disclosed that there had been no sabotage during or after the Pearl Harbor attack and that, with the exception of one Nisei on the tiny island of Niihau who collaborated with a downed Japanese pilot and then committed suicide, no act of hostility against the United States had been committed by a resident Japanese of either generation" (p. 27).
6. William Gordon to Robert Fellows, memorandum, January 12, 1943, *The Fallen Sparrow* file, RKO Radio Pictures archive, Los Angeles.
7. Joseph I. Breen to Gordon, letter, January 15, 1943, *The Fallen Sparrow* file, RKO.
8. Gordon to Fellows, memorandum, January 19, 1943, *The Fallen Sparrow* file, RKO.
9. Charles J. Stupich to RKO, letter, March 30, 1943, *The Fallen Sparrow* file, RKO.
10. Gordon to Stupich, letter, April 8, 1943, *The Fallen Sparrow* file, RKO.
11. "Q" to "Bill," memorandum, April 20, 1943, *The Fallen Sparrow* file, RKO.
12. Ulric Bell to Gordon, letter, n.d., *The Fallen Sparrow* file, RKO.
13. Trilling to Warner, memorandum, June 30, 1943, Garfield legal file, WBA.
14. George Frazier, "Humphrey Bogart: He Has a Hard, Unhappy Face and a Hard but Happy Life," *Life* 16 (June 12, 1944), p. 55.
15. Warner to Bogart, telegram, April 6, 1943, Bogart legal file, WBA.
16. Bogart to Warner, telegram, April 6, 1943, Bogart legal file, WBA.
17. Transcription of Warner-Bogart telephone conversation, May 6, 1943, Bogart legal file, WBA.
18. Warner to Wallis, memorandum, May 6, 1943, Bogart legal file, WBA.

8. Ordinary Guys and Private Eyes

1. Byron Haskin, *Byron Haskin*, interviewed by Joe Adamson (Metuchen, N.J.: Scarecrow, 1984), pp. 140–41.
2. Theodore Strauss, "The Firm of Cagney Brothers, Inc., Producers," *New York Times*, September 5, 1943, sec. 10, p. 3.

3. Edwin O. Reischauer, *Japan: Past and Present*, 3d. ed. rev. (New York: Knopf, 1964), p. 170.
4. "The Pride of the Marines," *Philadelphia Inquirer*, December 7, 1982, p. 10-A.
5. Jerry Wald to Delmer Daves, memorandum, November 7, 1944, *Pride of the Marines* file, WBA.
6. Wald to Daves, memorandum, January 11, 1945, *Pride of the Marines* file, WBA.
7. Stacey to Wright, memorandum, September 22, 1943, *Passage to Marseille* file, WBA.
8. Joseph McBride, *Hawks on Hawks* (Berkeley and Los Angeles: Univ. of California Press, 1982), p. 102.
9. Bogart's telephone conversation with Trilling quoted in Trilling to Obringer, memorandum, May 27, 1944, Bogart legal file, WBA.
10. Warner to Bogart, telegram, May 25, 1944, Bogart legal file, WBA.
11. Bogart to Warner, telegram, May 26, 1944, Bogart legal file, WBA.
12. Warner to Bogart, telegram, May 29, 1944, Bogart legal file, WBA.
13. Wright to Obringer, memorandum, December 26, 1944, Bogart legal file, WBA.
14. Stacey to Wright, memorandum, December 26, 1944, Bogart legal file, WBA.
15. Breen to Warner, January 25, 1946, *The Big Sleep* file, WBA.
16. Victoria Ward to Warner Bros., February 8, 1945, Bogart legal file, WBA.
17. Bosley Crowther, "Violence Erupts Again," *New York Times*, September 1, 1946, sec. 2, p. 1.

9. AMERICAN DOPES

1. Hortense Powdermaker, *Hollywood, the Dream Factory* (Boston: Little, Brown, 1950), p. 327. For Powdermaker's self-critique of her work in Hollywood see her *Stranger and Friend: The Way of an Anthropologist* (New York: Norton, 1966), pp. 209-31.
2. Gretchen Colnik to Warner Bros., May 1, 1947, *Humoresque* file, WBA. Ellipses in original.
3. Wald to Trilling, memorandum, April 4, 1946, *Humoresque* file, WBA.
4. William H. Graf to Wald, letter, January 30, 1947, *Humoresque* file, WBA.
5. Quoted in Stefan Kanfer, *A Journal of the Plague Years* (New York: Atheneum, 1973), p. 178.
6. House of Representatives, Eighty-second Congress, Committee on Un-American Activities, *Communist Infiltration of Hollywood Motion Picture Industry* (1951), pt. 2, p. 516.
7. Barbara Zheutlin and David Talbot, *Creative Differences: Profiles of Hollywood Dissidents* (Boston: South End, 1978), p. 76.
8. From the recorded broadcast of "Hollywood Strikes Back," October 26, 1947.

9. House of Representatives, *Communist Infiltration*, pt. 1, p. 145.
10. Paul Nathan to Warner, memorandum, April 11, 1942, *The Treasure of the Sierra Madre* file, WBA.
11. Blanke to Don Page, memorandum, February 4, 1947, *The Treasure of the Sierra Madre* file, WBA.
12. Producer Robert Lord coined this perceptive term discussing Bogart's role in *The Maltese Falcon;* Lord to Wallis, memorandum, December 22, 1941, *Across the Pacific* file, WBA.
13. "Hollywood Strikes Back" broadcast.
14. L. B. Nichols to [Clyde] Tolson, memorandum, November 24, 1947, FBI Bogart file.
15. M. A. Jones to Nichols, "Humphrey DeForist Bogart, Summary Memorandum," November 24, 1947, FBI Bogart file.
16. Quoted in a letter from Congressman Chet Holifield to Bogart, December 10, 1947, cited in Philip Dunne, *Take Two: A Life in Movies and Politics* (New York: McGraw-Hill, 1980), p. 202.
17. Humphrey Bogart, "I'm No Communist," *Photoplay*, March 1948, p. 87.

10. A Street Boy's Honor

1. Irene Mayer Selznick, *A Private View* (New York: Knopf, 1983), pp. 300–302.
2. Ibid., p. 303.
3. Quoted in Richard A. Blum, *American Film Acting: The Stanislavski Heritage* (Ann Arbor, Mich.: UMI Research Press, 1984), p. 52.
4. Andrew Sarris, *The American Cinema: Directors and Directions 1929–1968* (New York: Dutton, 1968), p. 220.
5. Quoted in William Pechter, "Abraham Polonsky and *Force of Evil*," *Film Quarterly* 15, no. 3 (Spring 1962): 51.
6. Ibid., p. 53.
7. *Hollywood Reporter*, April 22, 1949.
8. Virginia E. Williams, California Federation of Women's Clubs, Los Angeles District, to Harry Cohn, letter, May 9, 1949, *We Were Strangers* file, MPAA.
9. Quoted in Gerald Weales, *Odets the Playwright* (London and New York: Methuen, 1985), p. 160.
10. "Garfield Denies Red Ties," *New York Times*, March 8, 1951, p. 13.
11. House of Representatives, *Communist Infiltration*, pt. 2, p. 335.
12. Eric Bentley, ed., *Thirty Years of Treason: Excerpts from Hearings before the House Committee on Un-American Activities, 1938–1968* (New York: Viking, 1971), p. 537.
13. H. H. Clegg to Tolson, memorandum, February 8, 1952, FBI Garfield file.
14. FBI New York office to Director, FBI, memorandum, August 1, 1951, FBI Garfield file.

15. House of Representatives, *Communist Infiltration*, pt. 2, p. 332.
16. Fred Fehl, *On Broadway: Performance Photos by Fred Fehl* (Austin: Univ. of Texas Press, 1978), p. 209.
17. Reprinted in Bentley, *Thirty Years of Treason*, p. 523.
18. Victor Riesel, "Garfield Bared Traps by Reds," *New York Daily Mirror*, May 22, 1952.
19. Pechter, "Abraham Polonsky and *Force of Evil*," p. 53.

11. HE DIDN'T STAND STILL

1. Warner to Trilling, memorandum, March 13, 1948, *Key Largo* file, WBA.
2. Frank Eng column, *Los Angeles Daily News*, June 23, 1948, p. 36.
3. Lord to Breen, letter, March 21, 1949, *In a Lonely Place* file, MPAA.
4. Lord to Breen, letter, June 8, 1949, *In a Lonely Place* file, MPAA.
5. Warner, "Notes for Talk with Morgan Maree," n.d., Bogart legal file, WBA.
6. Mort Blumenstock to Warner, telegram, October 16, 1950, Bogart legal file, WBA.
7. Hedda Hopper, "Bogart Clears Way for Battle Circus," *Los Angeles Times*, May 19, 1952, p. 10.
8. Ralph E. Lewis to Obringer, June 11, 1952, Bogart legal file, WBA.
9. Lauren Bacall, *By Myself* (New York: Knopf, 1979), p. 219.
10. Ibid., p. 247.
11. Darryl Zanuck, "Memorandum on First Draft Continuity of February 2, 1955," February 7, 1955, *The Left Hand of God* file, Twentieth Century–Fox Archives, Theater Arts Library, University of California, Los Angeles.

12. TOP OF THE WORLD

1. "Background and Main File Summary" [December 20, 1950], p. 150, FBI Cagney file.
2. Ezra Goodman, "Back at the Old Stand," *New York Times*, June 12, 1949.
3. *New York Herald-Tribune*, September 27, 1950.
4. Zanuck to Sol Siegel, "Letter on First Draft Continuity of August 15, 1951," August 22–23, 1951, *What Price Glory* file, University of California, Los Angeles.
5. Jones to [Gordon A.] Nease, memorandum, February 26, 1958, FBI Cagney file.
6. *Cagney by Cagney*, p. 104.
7. *New York Newsday*, March 31, 1986, p. 3.

Sources

PRIMARY DOCUMENTS

In addition to the films themselves, the foundation of this study lies in the archival records of the American film industry and, for its political dimensions, Federal Bureau of Investigation files obtained through the Freedom of Information Act. Warner Bros., which produced or distributed nearly two thirds of the Cagney, Bogart, and Garfield pictures, has also made available for research more of its records than any other motion picture company. Warner Bros. production, legal, and other documents are held in the Archives of Performing Arts, University of Southern California Library, Los Angeles; The State Historical Society of Wisconsin, Madison; and the Theatre Collection, Princeton University Library, Princeton, New Jersey.

Other motion picture company records consulted include the RKO Radio Pictures/RKO Pictures, Inc. Corporate Archives, Los Angeles; archives of Metro-Goldwyn-Mayer Studios, Culver City, California; story and script documents of Fox Film Corporation and Twentieth Century–Fox in the Theater Arts Library, University of California, Los Angeles; and records of Universal Pictures in the Archives of Performing Arts, University of Southern California Library. Additional collections of primary materials utilized include the MPAA Production Code Administration case files and the John Huston Papers in the Margaret Herrick Library, Academy of Motion Picture Arts and Sciences, Beverly Hills, California. The extensive clippings files on individuals, productions, and special topics at the Margaret Herrick Library also were used, as well as clippings files at the Billy Rose Theatre Collection, New York Public Library at Lincoln Center, and the files of the Film Study Center, The Museum of Modern Art, New York.

The Federal Bureau of Investigation released edited versions of its Cagney, Bogart, and Garfield files in response to Freedom of Information Act requests. Documents relating to Garfield were also provided by other divisions of the United States Department of Justice; the United States Army Intelligence and Security Command, Department of the Army; and the Federal Communications Commission. The Central Intelligence Agency withheld classified documents pertaining to Garfield in its files.

What follows is a selected list of additional sources and a bibliographic guide to writings on the subjects of this book.

GENERAL STUDIES

While thousands of books have been published on individual movie stars, only a handful of works have treated film performance or the star system.

Prominent among these are James Naremore, *Acting in the Cinema* (Berkeley and Los Angeles: Univ. of California Press, 1988) and, by Richard Dyer, *Stars* (London: British Film Institute, 1979) and *Heavenly Bodies: Film Stars and Society* (New York: St. Martin's, 1986). Other valuable studies include Charles Affron, *Star Acting: Gish, Garbo, Davis* (New York: Dutton, 1977); Richard A. Blum, *American Film Acting: The Stanislavski Heritage* (Ann Arbor, Mich.: UMI Research Press, 1984); and Virginia Wright Wexman, ed., *Cinema Journal* 20, no. 1 (Fall 1980), Special Issue on Film Acting. Scholarly articles have been collected in Christine Gledhill, *Stardom* (New York: Routledge, 1990), and Carole Zucker, *Making Visible the Invisible: An Anthology of Original Essays on Film Acting* (Metuchen, N.J.: Scarecrow, 1990).

Richard deCordova has written the first extended study on the early history of film stars, *Picture Personalities: The Emergence of the Star System in America* (Urbana: Univ. of Illinois Press, 1990). Important works on the American film industry which help to place the star system in the context of the Hollywood studio system include David Bordwell, Janet Staiger, and Kristin Thompson, *The Classical Hollywood Cinema: Film Style & Mode of Production to 1960* (New York: Columbia Univ. Press, 1985); Douglas Gomery, *The Hollywood Studio System* (New York: St. Martin's, 1986); and Thomas Schatz, *The Genius of the System: Hollywood Filmmaking in the Studio Era* (New York: Pantheon, 1988). Robert Sklar, *Movie-Made America: A Cultural History of the American Movies* (New York: Random House, 1975), and Garth Jowett, *Film: The Democratic Art* (Boston: Little, Brown, 1976), lay the foundation for cultural and social analyses of motion pictures in American society.

WORKS ON CAGNEY, BOGART, AND GARFIELD

The basic filmographies, with credits and cast lists, appear in the series published by Citadel Press, Secaucus, New Jersey: Homer Dickens, *The Films of James Cagney* (1972); Clifford McCarty, *Bogey: The Films of Humphrey Bogart* (1965); and Howard Gelman, *The Films of John Garfield* (1975).

Among the best books on an individual star is Patrick McGilligan, *Cagney: The Actor as Auteur* (San Diego: A. S. Barnes, 1975, 1982); note the major revisions and shifts of approach between the first and second editions. Cagney authored *Cagney by Cagney* (Garden City, N.Y.: Doubleday, 1976), and participated in Douglas Warren with James Cagney, *James Cagney: The Authorized Biography* (New York: St. Martin's, 1983). Other works include Ron Offen, *Cagney* (Chicago: Regnery, 1972); Andrew Bergman, *James Cagney* (New York: Pyramid, 1973); Michael Freedland, *Cagney: A Biography* (New York: Stein & Day, 1975); and Richard Schickel, *Cagney: A Celebration* (Boston: Little, Brown, 1985).

The most useful works on Bogart so far are memoirs, and portraits by friends: Nathaniel Benchley, *Humphrey Bogart* (Boston: Little, Brown, 1975); Lauren Bacall, *By Myself* (New York: Knopf, 1978); Louise Brooks, "Humphrey and Bogey," in *Lulu in Hollywood* (New York: Knopf, 1982), pp.

57–69; Alistair Cooke, "Humphrey Bogart: Epitaph for a Tough Guy," in *Six Men* (London: The Bodley Head, 1977), Penguin edition, pp. 125–46; and Verita Thompson with Donald Shepherd, *Bogie and Me: A Love Story* (New York: St. Martin's, 1982). Popular works proliferate; a sampling includes Paul Michael, *Humphrey Bogart: The Man and His Films* (Indianapolis: Bobbs-Merrill, 1965); Joe Hyams, *Bogie: The Biography of Humphrey Bogart* (New York: New American Library, 1966); Alan G. Barbour, *Humphrey Bogart* (New York: Pyramid, 1973); and Allen Eyles, *Humphrey Bogart* (New York: Doubleday, 1975; revised and expanded, London: Sphere, 1990). There are numerous writings in languages other than English.

Garfield remains the least studied of the city boys. In addition to a biography, Larry Swindell, *Body and Soul: The Story of John Garfield* (New York: Morrow, 1975), there are George Morris, *John Garfield* (New York: Jove, 1977), and James N. Beaver, Jr., *John Garfield* (South Brunswick, N.J.: A. S. Barnes, 1978).

1. A SOCIETY OF RAGAMUFFINS

A wider selection of Byron's photographs may be found in Joseph Byron, *Photographs of New York Interiors at the Turn of the Century: From the Byron Collection of the Museum of the City of New York* (New York: Dover, 1976), and Byron, *New York Life at the Turn of the Century in Photographs: From the Byron Collection of the Museum of the City of New York* (New York: Dover, 1985).

My views on American culture in the 1920s derive from perspectives presented in Robert Sklar, "Introduction," in *The Plastic Age (1917–1930)*, ed. Robert Sklar (New York: George Braziller, 1970), pp. 1–24. Erving Goffman, *The Presentation of Self in Everyday Life* (Garden City, N.Y.: Doubleday, 1959) provides insight into the performative aspects of daily life.

The most extensive treatment of the gangster genre in the silent era is Gerald M. Peary's dissertation, "The Rise of the American Gangster Film, 1913–1930," University of Wisconsin–Madison, 1977. John Raeburn gives a valuable concise overview in "The Gangster Film," in *Handbook of American Film Genres*, ed. Wes D. Gehring (New York: Greenwood, 1988), pp. 47–63. Pre-1930 films are also discussed in Carlos Clarens, *Crime Movies: From Griffith to the Godfather and Beyond* (New York: Norton, 1980) and Eugene Rosow, *Born to Lose: The Gangster Film in America* (New York: Oxford Univ. Press, 1978).

2. ROUGHNECK SISSY AND CHARMING BOY

My treatment of dependency and the city boy figure draws on Dorothy Dinnerstein, *The Mermaid and the Minotaur: Sexual Arrangements and Human Malaise* (New York: Harper & Row, 1976), and Jessica Benjamin, *The Bonds of Love: Psychoanalysis, Feminism, and the Problem of Domination* (New York: Pantheon, 1988). Dependency in Japanese culture is treated in Takeo Doi, *The Anatomy of Dependence*, trans. John Bester (Tokyo: Kodansha, 1973). Michael Paul Rogin takes on "momism" in relation to a later period of American cinema in "*Kiss Me Deadly*: Communism, Motherhood, and Cold War Movies," in "*Ronald Reagan*," *the Movie: and Other Episodes in Political Demonology* (Berkeley and Los Angeles: Univ. of California Press, 1987).

The "tough guy" is broadly covered in Rupert Wilkinson, *American Tough: The Tough-Guy Tradition and American Character* (Westport, Conn.: Greenwood, 1984). The figure of the genteel romantic hero is analyzed in Robert Sklar, *F. Scott Fitzgerald: The Last Laocoon* (New York: Oxford Univ. Press, 1967).

Performers' contract and salary information is drawn from the Richard Barthelmess legal file, Princeton University, and the Bette Davis, Olivia de Havilland, Errol Flynn, and other legal files and production records, WBA. Leo C. Rosten discusses star salaries at the end of the 1930s in the chapter on actors in *Hollywood: The Movie Colony, the Movie Makers* (New York: Harcourt, Brace, 1941). "Most New Faces on Screen Came from Legit Stage within Past Two Seasons—Names of Many," *Variety*, October 1, 1930, p. 2, lists scores of Broadway performers on Hollywood studio rosters. On *The Doorway to Hell* see Gerald Peary, "*Doorway to Hell*," *The Velvet Light Trap* 16 (Fall 1976): 1–4.

3. THE PRIVATE ENEMY

William Schaefer, Jack Warner's private secretary beginning in 1933, provided important information about his boss and the studio in an interview with the author, July 12, 1984, Sherman Oaks, California. Nick Roddick, *A New Deal in Entertainment: Warner Brothers in the 1930s* (London: British Film Institute, 1983), is a study of the studio's films and mode of production. Rudy Behlmer, ed., *Inside Warner Bros. (1935–1951)* (New York: Viking, 1985), reprints documents from WBA. Clive Hirschhorn, *The Warner Bros. Story* (New York: Crown, 1979) is a useful record of the studio's production. Executive autobiographies such as Jack Warner (with Dean Jennings), *My First Hundred Years in Hollywood* (New York: Random House, 1964), and Hal Wallis and Charles Higham, *Starmaker: The Autobiography of Hal Wallis* (New York: Macmillan, 1980), say little; more illuminating is the mailroom memoir by Stuart Jerome, *Those Crazy Wonderful Years When We Ran Warner Bros.* (Secaucus, N.J.: Lyle Stuart, 1983).

John Bright discussed his work as screenwriter on Cagney's early 1930s pictures in an interview with the author, January 22, 1983, West Hollywood, California. An excerpt from his autobiography was published as John Bright, "Naming Names: Sam Ornitz, James Cagney, The Hollywood Reds, and Me," *Film Comment* 23 (November–December 1987): 48–51. In addition to the published screenplay (see Notes), *The Public Enemy* is treated in Jack Shadoian, *Dreams and Dead Ends: The American Gangster/Crime Film* (Cambridge, Mass.: MIT Press, 1977), pp. 43–58, and Stephen Louis Karpf,

The Gangster Film: Emergence, Variation and Decay of a Genre, 1930–1940 (New York: Arno, 1973), pp. 61–86.

Other early 1930s Cagney films receiving scholarly attention are *Footlight Parade* in Mark Roth, "Some Warners Musicals and the Spirit of the New Deal," *The Velvet Light Trap* 17 (Winter 1977): 1–7; *A Midsummer Night's Dream* in Robert F. Willson, Jr., "Ill Met by Moonlight: Reinhardt's *A Midsummer Night's Dream* and Musical Screwball Comedy," *Journal of Popular Film* 5 (1976): 185–97; and *G Men* in Richard Gid Powers, *G-Men: Hoover's FBI in American Popular Culture* (Carbondale: Southern Illinois Univ. Press, 1983), pp. 52–64.

4. BABY FACE

Rose Hobart discussed working with Bogart on Broadway in the early 1930s in an interview with the author, December 13, 1984, Woodland Hills, California; Blanche Sweet described the stage production of *The Petrified Forest* in an interview with the author, February 12, 1985, New York. Vincent Sherman provided information about his work as a Warner Bros. writer and director in an interview with the author, December 11, 1984, Malibu, California, and Irving Rapper about his work as dialogue director and director in an interview with the author, January 23, 1985, Westwood, California.

Peter Roffman and Jim Purdy, *The Hollywood Social Problem Film: Madness, Despair, and Politics from the Depression to the Fifties* (Bloomington: Indiana Univ. Press, 1981), covers another important Warner Bros. genre in which the city boys often appeared. *Marked Woman* is treated in Charles W. Eckert, "The Anatomy of a Proletarian Film: Warner's *Marked Woman*," *Film Quarterly* 17 (Winter 1973–1974): 10–24, and Karyn Kay, "Sisters of the Night," *The Velvet Light Trap* 17 (Winter 1977): 48–52. See also Brian Neve, "The Screenwriter and the Social Problem Film, 1936–38: The Case of Robert Rossen at Warner Brothers," *Film & History* 14 (February 1984): 2–13.

5. THE STUDIO LABYRINTH

In addition to interviews noted earlier, Marie Dyches provided valuable insight into Warner Bros., from her perspective as a studio publicist, in an interview with the author, December 12, 1984, Beverly Hills, California.

An extensive analysis of Cagney's performance in *Angels with Dirty Faces* is in Naremore, *Acting in the Cinema*, pp. 157–73. The *Dark Victory* screenplay is published in Bernard F. Dick, ed., *Dark Victory* (Madison: Univ. of Wisconsin Press, 1981); see also "Casey Robinson on *Dark Victory*," *Australian Journal of Screen Theory* 4 (1978): 5–10.

6. PUSHCARTS AND PATRIOTISM

While most works on the Hollywood left focus on the postwar period, the most thorough study, Larry Ceplair and Steven Englund, *The Inquisition in*

Hollywood: Politics in the Film Community, 1930–1960 (Garden City, N.Y.: Doubleday, 1980), also extensively treats both the 1930s and the war years.

The *High Sierra* screenplay is published in Douglas Gomery, ed., *High Sierra* (Madison: Univ. of Wisconsin Press, 1979); see also Shadoian, *Dreams and Dead Ends*, pp. 67–82, and Kenneth D. Alley, *"High Sierra—*Swan Song for an Era," *Journal of Popular Film* 5 (1976): 248–62. Virginia Wright Wexman studies Bogart's performance in *The Maltese Falcon* in "Kinesics and Film Acting: Humphrey Bogart in *The Maltese Falcon* and *The Big Sleep,*" *Journal of Popular Film and Television* 7 (Winter 1979): 42–55; other works on the film include James Naremore, "John Huston and *The Maltese Falcon,*" *Literature/Film Quarterly* 1 (1973): 239–49; Virginia Wright Wexman, *"The Maltese Falcon* from Fiction to Film," *Library Quarterly* 45 (January 1975): 46–55; Leslie H. Abramson, "Two Birds of a Feather: Hammett's and Huston's *The Maltese Falcon,*" *Literature/Film Quarterly* 16 (1988): 112–18; and William Luhr, "Tracking *The Maltese Falcon*: Classical Hollywood Narration and Sam Spade," in *Close Viewings: An Anthology of New Film Criticism,* ed. Peter Lehman (Tallahassee: Florida State Univ. Press, 1990), pp. 7–22.

The *Yankee Doodle Dandy* screenplay is published in Patrick McGilligan, ed., *Yankee Doodle Dandy* (Madison: Univ. of Wisconsin Press, 1981); see also Robert Milton Miller, *Star Myths: Show-Business Biographies on Film* (Metuchen, N.J.: Scarecrow, 1983), pp. 83–94.

7. HEROES WITHOUT UNIFORMS

Studies on Hollywood during World War II include Colin Schindler, *Hollywood Goes to War: Films and American Society 1939–1952* (London: Routledge & Kegan Paul, 1979); Bernard F. Dick, *The Star-Spangled Screen: The American World War II Film* (Lexington: Univ. Press of Kentucky, 1985); and Clayton R. Koppes and Gregory D. Black, *Hollywood Goes to War: How Politics, Profits, and Propaganda Shaped World War II Movies* (New York: Free Press, 1987).

The *Casablanca* screenplay is published in Howard Koch, *Casablanca: Script and Legend* (Woodstock, N.Y.: Overlook, 1973); see also Ronald Haver, "Finally the Truth about *Casablanca,*" *American Film* 1 (June 1976): 10–16; Charles Francisco, *You Must Remember This . . . : The Filming of Casablanca* (Englewood Cliffs, N.J.: Prentice-Hall, 1980); Robert Ray, *A Certain Tendency of the Hollywood Cinema, 1930–1980* (Princeton, N.J.: Princeton Univ. Press, 1985), pp. 89–112; Gary Green, " 'The Happiest of Happy Accidents'?: A Reevaluation of *Casablanca,*" *Smithsonian Studies in American Art* 1 (Fall 1987): 2–13; Robert F. Willson, Jr., "Romantic Propaganda: A Note on *Casablanca*'s Prefigured Ending," *Film & History* 19 (December 1989): 87–91; and Richard Raskin, *"Casablanca* and United States Foreign Policy," *Film History* 4 (1990): 153–64.

The *Air Force* screenplay is published in Lawrence Howard Suid, ed., *Air Force* (Madison: Univ. of Wisconsin Press, 1983).

8. Ordinary Guys and Private Eyes

Cagney's move to independent production is studied in Kevin Hagopian, "Declarations of Independence: A History of Cagney Productions," *The Velvet Light Trap* 22 (1986): 16–32. The broader context is treated in Tino Balio, *United Artists: The Company Built by the Stars* (Madison: Univ. of Wisconsin Press, 1976), and Janet Staiger, "Individualism versus Collectivism," *Screen* 24 (July–October 1983): 68–79. Lester Cole expressed his views on *Blood on the Sun* in "Unhappy Ending," *Hollywood Quarterly* 1 (October 1945): 80–84, and *Hollywood Red: The Autobiography of Lester Cole* (Palo Alto, Calif.: Ramparts Press, 1981). For changes in Communist policies that affected the Hollywood left, see Maurice Isserman, *Which Side Were You On?: The American Communist Party during the Second World War* (Middleton, Conn.: Wesleyan Univ. Press, 1982).

Works that treat both *To Have and Have Not* and *The Big Sleep* include Robin Wood, *Howard Hawks* (London: British Film Institute, 1968, 1981); Bruce F. Kawin, *Faulkner and Film* (New York: Ungar, 1977); Gerald Mast, *Howard Hawks, Storyteller* (New York: Oxford Univ. Press, 1982); and McBride, *Hawks on Hawks*. The *To Have and Have Not* screenplay is published in Bruce F. Kawin, *To Have and Have Not* (Madison: Univ. of Wisconsin Press, 1980); studies include Robin Wood, "To Have (Written) and Have Not (Directed): Reflections on Authorship," *Film Comment* 9 (May–June 1973): 30–35, and William Rothman, "To Have and Have Not Adapted a Novel," in *The Modern American Novel and the Movies*, ed. Gerald Peary and Roger Shatzkin (New York: Ungar, 1978), pp. 70–79.

Writings on *The Big Sleep* include John Blades, "*The Big Sleep*," *Film Heritage* 5 (Summer 1970): 7–15; Raymond Bellour, "The Obvious and the Code," *Screen* 15 (Winter 1974–1975): 7–17; James Monaco, "Notes on *The Big Sleep*/Thirty Years After," *Sight and Sound* 44 (Winter 1974–1975): 34–38; Wexman, "Kinesics and Film Acting" (cited above); Roger Shatzkin, "Who Cares Who Killed Owen Taylor?" in *The Modern American Novel and the Movies*, ed. Peary and Shatzkin, pp. 80–94; Gill Davies, "Teaching about Narrative," *Screen Education* 29 (Winter 1978–1979): 56–76; David Thomson, "At the Acme Bookshop," *Sight and Sound* 50 (Spring 1981): 122–25; William Luhr, *Raymond Chandler and Film* (New York: Ungar, 1982); and Annette Kuhn, "*The Big Sleep*: Censorship, Film Text and Sexuality," in *The Power of the Image: Essays on Representation and Sexuality* (New York: Methuen, 1986).

9. American Dopes

Richard Dyer writes about *The Postman Always Rings Twice* in "Lana: Four Films of Lana Turner," *Movie* 25 (Winter 1977–1978): 30–52. Russell Campbell discusses *Gentleman's Agreement* in "The Ideology of the Social Consciousness Movie: Three Films of Darryl F. Zanuck," *Quarterly Review of Film Studies* 3 (Winter 1978): 49–71. The screenplay of *The Treasure of the Sierra Madre* is published in James Naremore, ed., *The Treasure of the*

Sierra Madre (Madison: Univ. of Wisconsin Press, 1979); see also Stuart M. Kaminsky, "Gold Hat, Gold Fever, Silver Screen," in *The Modern American Novel and the Movies*, ed. Peary and Shatzkin, pp. 53–62.

10. A STREET BOY'S HONOR

To the vast literature on HUAC and the Hollywood blacklist published before 1980 and cited in the bibliography of *Inquisition in Hollywood*, the principal addition has been Victor Navasky, *Naming Names* (New York: Viking, 1980). Elia Kazan gives his views on Garfield and the casting of *A Streetcar Named Desire* in *A Life* (New York: Knopf, 1988).

On *Force of Evil*, see Christine Noll Brinckmann, "The Politics of *Force of Evil*: An Analysis of Abraham Polonsky's Preblacklist Film," *Prospects* 6 (1981): 357–86, and Shadoian, *Dreams and Dead Ends*, pp. 134–48. *The Breaking Point* is studied in Tom Flinn and John Davis, "*The Breaking Point*," *The Velvet Light Trap* 14 (Winter 1975): 17–20.

11. HE DIDN'T STAND STILL

Bogart's work and personal life, and his final illness, can be followed in Bacall, *By Myself*; Bogart's coughing on the set of *The Barefoot Contessa* is recounted in Kenneth L. Geist, *Pictures Will Talk: The Life and Films of Joseph L. Mankiewicz* (New York: Scribner's, 1978), p. 251.

On *In a Lonely Place* see David Thomson, "*In a Lonely Place*," *Sight and Sound* 48 (Autumn 1979): 215–20. Katharine Hepburn's account of *The African Queen* is *The Making of* The African Queen: *How I Went to Africa with Bogart, Bacall and Huston and Almost Lost My Mind* (New York: Knopf, 1987). *The Desperate Hours* is discussed in Martin Dworkin, "*The Desperate Hours* and the Violent Screen," *Shenandoah* 11 (1960): 39–48.

12. TOP OF THE WORLD

Cagney's last years are recounted in Anthony Cook, "Cagney's Curious Comeback," *Life* 7 (March 1984): 58–70. The *White Heat* screenplay is published in Patrick McGilligan, ed., *White Heat* (Madison: Univ. of Wisconsin Press, 1984); see also Shadoian, *Dreams and Dead Ends*, pp. 191–208. For a discussion of *Shake Hands with the Devil*, see Kevin Rockett, Luke Gibbons, and John Hill, *Cinema and Ireland* (Syracuse, N.Y.: Syracuse Univ. Press, 1988), pp. 164–67.

Index